AUG 1 8 1995

FEELING AND EMOTION

A HISTORY OF THEORIES

By

H. M. GARDINER
Late Professor of Philosophy
Smith College

RUTH CLARK METCALF
Formerly Assistant Professor of Philosophy and Psychology
Smith College

and

JOHN G. BEEBE–CENTER
Lecturer in Psychology
Harvard University

GREENWOOD PRESS, PUBLISHERS
WESTPORT, CONNECTICUT

Originally published in 1937 by American Book Company

First Greenwood Reprinting 1970

Library of Congress Catalogue Card Number 74-98223

SBN 8371-3683-0

Printed in United States of America

INTRODUCTORY NOTE

There is a type of professor, of comparatively narrow reputation abroad, who is yet an impressive personality in his own college, wielding great influence on his colleagues and in the shaping of the institution, and putting his stamp on successive generations of students. He is usually a man who does his own thinking; he has often marked and sometimes picturesque peculiarities of temperament; and he finds his fulfillment less in the discovery of new truth than in the upholding of principles he believes to be fundamental, and in the inculcating of these principles in the minds of those with whom he comes into immediate contact.

It was to this type that Professor Gardiner belonged. An Englishman by birth, he kept to the end the purity of his accent, a certain blunt honesty, and the manners and code of an English gentleman. Though his higher education was obtained in America and Germany, he never became either American or cosmopolitan. He broadened and mellowed, but his foundations remained unmoved. His temper was conservative, and innovations in academic practice or in philosophic method he met with suspicion. He believed in the value of testing by time and experience.

With such a temperament it was natural that his scholarly studies were historical and critical rather than speculative and constructive. A philosopher by training, grounded at a time when psychology was not yet recognized as an independent science, he followed the development of modern psychology with detachment, and discussed its problems with the vocabulary and from the

v

point of view of a philosopher. His main interest for most of his professional life was in the theory of the emotions, and his critiques on contributions to such theory, published in philosophical and psychological reviews over many years, were highly valued by his colleagues. When he retired after forty years of teaching at Smith College, he devoted a large part of his leisure to the completion of a book which would give a compendious account of the treatment of the affections from the time of the Greeks. He succeeded in carrying the history to the end of the eighteenth century, finishing eight of the chapters of the present volume and part of the ninth. These eight chapters have been revised and the ninth completed by his pupil and former colleague, Dr. Ruth Clark Metcalf, who has accomplished her task with skill and devotion. The writing of two chapters dealing with the nineteenth century has been undertaken by Dr. Beebe-Center of Harvard University.

To these two scholars is due the gratitude of the College which Professor Gardiner served so long, and of the many students whom he influenced and inspired. They will welcome the publication of this volume as a permanent record of the thought and interests of their friend and master.

W. A. Neilson

Smith College
Northampton, Mass.

EDITOR'S NOTE

The first three chapters of this book were published separately by Professor Gardiner before his death. Chapter I appeared under the title " The Psychology of the Affections in Plato and Aristotle; I, Plato" in the *Philosophical Review* for September, 1918; XXVII, 469–488. Chapter II, which continued this study, was entitled " Part II, Aristotle," appearing in the same magazine for January, 1919; XXVIII, 1–26. The third chapter was published in the *Psychological Review* for May, 1919; XXVII, 204–229. It was entitled " Affective Psychology in Ancient Writers after Aristotle." We are indebted to the editors of these journals for their permission to reprint this material.

A complete bibliography of all references made in this volume is appended.

TABLE OF CONTENTS

CHAPTER I

CHAPTER II

CHAPTER III

CHAPTER VI

CHAPTER VII

CHAPTER VIII

CHAPTER I

The Beginnings of a Doctrine of the Affections: from Heraclitus to Plato

The earliest Greek thinkers show comparatively little interest in the inner life of man. Their speculations are characteristically cosmological, not psychological. Human nature is not altogether ignored; human life, in the large sense, is contemplated and criticized; a beginning is made of the unending philosophical task of distinguishing a realm of spirit and of relating it to the order of the physical world. But there is at first no clear recognition of conscious phenomena worthy of study on their own account. Such subordinate attention as is given to the scientific study of man is largely confined to his bodily constitution, his physical generation, and his elementary processes of cognition. His pleasures, pains, and passions, so far as they are considered at all, are treated for the most part from the practical point of view of ethics or in their relation to health and disease. The free psychological discussion of the affections is an achievement of modern times, but the roots of all modern doctrines strike deep in the speculations of the Greeks.

The first considerable attempt at an affective psychology was made by Plato. But Plato drew largely on his predecessors and his work in this field, with all its originality, marks rather the end of a period than the beginning of a new one. His point of departure is the discussion concerning the relation of pleasure to good in contemporary ethics,

1

but his views concerning the nature of pleasure and the affective life generally are greatly influenced by earlier opinion, which in its main trend was biological or physiological.

The scanty record of extant fragments bears out Aristotle's statement that the early Greek thinkers recognized only material causes.[1] They explained affective phenomena, as they explained other phenomena, by relations of such principles as dry and wet, hot and cold, notably by the maintenance or disturbance of their normal mixture in the body.[2] Thus Heraclitus (*ca.* 500 B.C.) tells us that a dry soul is the wisest and best, but that it is "pleasure or death" to become moist, a state exemplified by the soul of the drunken man; and, in general, the gratification of desire is connected by him with the exchange of dry soulfire with moisture.[3] He notes the pleasurable effects of contrast — health with sickness, abundance with hunger, etc. — and speaks of the difficulty of contending with passionate anger.[4] Empedocles (born *ca.* 490 B.C.) teaches that men think and also feel pleasure and pain by means of the corporeal elements; connecting these feelings, apparently, with the existence or disturbance of their harmony in the body, particularly in the blood about the heart, which he regarded as the seat and substance of the whole mental life.[5] Anaxagoras (born *ca.* 500 B.C.) is said to have

---

[1] Aristotle, *Metaphysica*, A, 3, 984 b 7.

[2] Cf. G. L. Duprat, "La psycho-physiologie des passions dans la philosophie ancienne," *Arch. f. Gesch. d. Phil.*, XVIII (1905), 395–412.

[3] *Fragmente*, 77, 117, 118 (H. Diels, *Die Fragmente der Vorsokratiker*, 73, 78). Cf. J. Burnett, *Early Greek Philosophy*, 36, 140.

[4] Aristotle, *Ethica Nicomachea*, II, 3, 10, 1105 a 8 quotes Heraclitus as saying: "It is harder to fight with pleasure than with wrath," but the Fragment says only, θυμῷ μάχεσθαι χαλεπόν (it is difficult to fight with pleasure), which Aristotle also quotes: *Politica*, V, 11, 1315 a 30; cf. *Ethica Eudemia*, II, 7, 1223 b 23.

[5] H. Ritter and L. Preller, *Historia Philosophiae Graeco-Romanae*, I, sec. 139. The reference by Hippocrates, *The Sacred Disease* (*Works*, II,

shared with Empedocles the view, afterwards held by Plato,[6] that plants experience pleasure and pain as well as animals.[7] From his doctrine that the sense organ is stimulated by " the unlike," he seems to have drawn the inference that sensation is always accompanied with pain, which, if not at first perceptible, becomes so whenever the sensation is unduly prolonged or intense.[8] To Diogenes of Apollonia (*ca.* 460 B.C.), a contemporary and opponent of Anaxagoras, is assigned a more positive doctrine. He made pleasure and pain depend on the aeration of the blood; pleasure arising when the properly aerated blood permeates the body freely, pain arising under the contrary conditions. A similar explanation is given of courage and health and their opposites. The organ most sensitive to pleasure and hence most readily showing the symptoms of disease, he held to be the tongue.[9] Democritus (born *ca.* 460 B.C.), who identified happiness with tranquillity, represented this state as attained by discrimination and moderation in respect to pleasure, excess and deficiency being both liable to cause disturbance in the soul. Philosophy frees the soul from passions as medicine heals the body.[10] That Democritus considered the desired equilibrium physical as well as mental, follows from his whole atomic theory;

---

856), to those who held the heart to be the organ of thought and emotion, a reference unintelligible to the translator, is probably to Empedocles.

[6] *Timaeus,* 77 B (B. Jowett, *The Dialogues of Plato,* III, 499).

[7] Pseudo-Aristotle, *De plantis,* 815 a 15 ff.

[8] Cf. Theophrastus, *De sensu,* 29 (*Opera,* I, 658), where the doctrine is sharply criticized. A similar view, in which, however, the pain is more distinctly limited to the initial disturbance of equilibrium, is attributed by F. Dieterici, *Die Philosophie der Araber,* VII, 37 to the Arabian philosophers of the tenth century A.D. The exact opposite of this ancient doctrine appears in a modern writer, H. R. Marshall, *Consciousness,* 373, 379 : every presentation, on its first appearance, is normally pleasant.

[9] Theophrastus, *De sensu,* 43 (*Opera,* I, 664).

[10] *Fragmenta ethica,* I ff. (F. W. Mullach, *Fragmenta Philosophorum Graecorum,* I, 340 ff.).

thought, i.e., the life of mind, is a mixture or blending of corporeal elements, and its function is seriously impaired if the mixture is unduly hot or cold.[11] It is probable that he held the different mental functions to be more or less definitely localized.[12]

A notable advance in the biological theory, one destined to exert great influence on subsequent thinking even down to modern times, appears in the writings of Hippocrates (born *ca.* 460 B.C.) and his school. In addition to the principles of hot and cold, dry and wet, and the vague general conceptions of harmony and discord employed hitherto, new principles of explanation are introduced, such as coction, evaporation, exhalation, the nature and combination of the several humors, and the free flow of the πνεῦμα, or vital spirit. Hippocrates is the first writer definitely to connect the whole conscious life, including the emotions, with the brain. When the brain is overheated, terrors and fears arise; when it is unduly cold, grief and anxiety. Evidence that fear is due to excess of heat is found in the flushed face and red eyes of the subject of a horrible dream. The heating of the brain is attributed to the flow of bile, its cooling to the flow of phlegm. When the bile returns to the veins and trunk, the fear is allayed. When black bile passes too freely to the brain, melancholy is engendered, a state of persistent fear. In general, the explanation of morbid states reduces to a disturbed balance of

[11] Theophrastus, *De sensu,* 58 (*Opera,* I, 670).
[12] The tradition varies. Aetius and Plutarch, drawing on Epicurean sources, say that Democritus placed the rational faculty in the chest, but distributed the irrational over the whole body (H. Diels, *Doxographi graeci,* 390; *Die Fragmente der Vorsokratiker,*· 387, 405). Theodoret (cited by H. Diels, *Doxographi graeci,* 391) makes him place the governing faculty in the head. In a spurious letter of Democritus to Hippocrates, which H. Diels, *Vorsokratiker,* 468 ff., assigns to the time of the Empire, but which E. Zeller, *Die Philosophie der Griechen,* I, 809 quotes as genuine, thought is localized in the brain, the impulse of resentment in the heart, and the appetite in the liver: the view which is substantially Plato's.

aridity, moisture, and temperature in the brain, which is abnormally hot or cold or dry or wet. Madness — we are reminded of the doctrine of Heraclitus — is a consequence of its humidity.[13]

The underlying cause of all mental and bodily affections is the mixture of the corporeal elements. If the mixture is balanced, each element being duly tempered by its opposite and blended with the other constituents of the organism, the bodily condition is at its best; but if the balance is destroyed, if one of the elements through coction, through thickening or attenuation of the fluids and the formation of humors, or from any other cause, becomes " separated out," there is disease and pain.[14] This doctrine, the foundation of which is to be found in Empedocles, may be taken as the first definite formulation of a biological theory of pain. Hippocrates is not so clear on the subject of pleasure. In the treatise on *Regimen* we have a doctrine of " temperaments," in which the primary consideration is the combination of hot-dry and cold-moist, of fire and water. The perfect temperament results from the equilibrium of these elements. Where fire abounds in the constitution, the subject is easily excited and unless careful in his use of meat, liable to outbursts of furious rage.[15]

Besides the mixture of the elements and the related quality and distribution of the humors, Hippocrates reckons as a distinct and fundamental cause of emotional dispositions the character of the passages for the pneuma, according as they hinder or facilitate its movements, and according as its deficiency or excess in any part, by affect-

---

[13] *The Sacred Disease* (*Works*, II, 855 f.). The doctrine of the humors is most fully developed in the work *De natura hominis* (*Opera omnia*, I, 348–371).

[14] *Ancient Medicine* (*Works*, I, 171–174).

[15] *Regimen* (*Opera*, I, 616 ff.; esp. 654, 666). The classical doctrine of the four temperaments was developed later by Galen.

ing the supply of blood, introduces disorder.[16] The introduction of this conception of the pneuma, which, as distinct from the external air, Hippocrates also calls φῦσα
(breath),[17] is of the most wide-reaching significance in
the history of physiological psychology. We meet with
it again and again in various stages of development: in
Plato and Aristotle, in the Stoics, throughout the whole
of the Middle Ages, in the period of the Renaissance, in
Descartes and Hobbes, and even down to comparatively
recent times, when its function as an explanatory principle becomes gradually supplanted by that of nervous
energy. The doctrine connects itself with the primitive
conception of the soul as breath, a conception derived
from the phenomena of breathing and of death. It is also
connected, probably, with observation of the foamlike
character of fresh-flowing blood and of animal seed. Diogenes of Apollonia, opposing the dualism of Anaxagoras,
had made " air " the very living, self-transforming matter
of the universe, as Anaximander had done before him; and
early Pythagoreans taught that the world " breathed."
The affinities of the doctrine are, therefore, of wide range.
The conception of the pneuma itself underwent many
transformations. Most commonly it was regarded as intimately connected with the blood, often as its finest exhalation or distillation. To it were ascribed the animal
heat and the animating functions of the body. It was the
immediate material substratum of the soul, perhaps even
the soul itself. After Praxagoras in the time of Alexander
had discovered the distinction between the arteries and the
veins, and the arteries were found in the dead body to

---

[16] *De salubris victus ratione* (*Opera,* I, 665 f.). Cf. F. Poschenrieder, *Die platonischen Dialoge in ihrem Verhältnisse zu den hippokratischen Schriften,* 48.
[17] *De flatibus,* VI, 3 (*Opera,* I, 569 ff.)

be empty, it was readily assumed that these were the passages through which the pneuma was transmitted. In this sense a generation later Eristratus taught that the vital spirit, inhaled from the air, rushes through the arteries to the centers, especially the brain and the heart, and there occasions thought and movement and exercises general control over all the organic functions.[18]

Hippocrates not only puts forth a theory of mental and bodily perturbations, but carefully notes many of their symptoms. The most sensitive organs in this regard are the diaphragm and the heart. The diaphragm throbs and palpitates in unexpected joy or grief, being easily moved " on account of its thinness." The heart is still more sensitive, since " veins," i.e., blood vessels, run to it from all parts of the body, and it has valves. In the shock of surprise or in a fit of passion it contracts, in good humor it dilates. The lungs also are affected in outbursts of anger, and there is a rush of heat and humors to the head. In joy and grief the whole body is perturbed.[19] These observations do not, to be sure, carry us very far, but they mark a beginning in the scientific study of the organic changes and external expressions of emotions, the analysis and interpretation of which are now regarded as among the central problems of a psychology of the affections.

The incidental consideration of pleasure, pain, and emotion noted so far is connected mainly with physical speculation and medical theory and practice. In the fifth century B.C. it is stimulated and accentuated by the new interest in the moral life. Here the influence of Socrates and the Sophists was great, but indirect. A Prodicus can admirably portray the wretchedness of a life devoted to

[18] Cf. R. D. Hicks, *Encyclopædia Britannica*, 9th ed., article " Stoics."
[19] *The Sacred Disease* (*Works*, II, 856 f.).

sensual pleasure, while Callicles and Thrasymachus defend it as good;[20] but on neither side, apparently, is any effort made to elucidate the nature and conditions of pleasure. Thrasymachus is reported to have developed rules for acting upon the feelings of an audience; but, as Plato remarks, neither he, nor any other Sophist, deems it necessary to lay a deeper foundation for the art in logic and psychology.[21] Socrates (born *ca.* 470 B.C.), in the traditional view of his teaching, seems not to have gone much farther. He too has no definite theory of pleasure. If he had carried out his ethical doctrine and determined more precisely the relations of pleasure, utility, and good, the three chief ingredients in his conception of happiness, he would no doubt have been led to a more constructive theory of pleasure. The defect in his psychology is thus intimately connected with the undeveloped character of his ethics. The psychological interest which attaches to many of his sayings about pleasure and the feelings incident to the manner and temper of one's life, he himself seems not to have noticed.[22] The decisive step was taken when his disciples, Antisthenes and Aristippus, developed into a sharp antithesis of theory the elements in the moral ideal which he had managed practically to combine. With the denial, on the one hand, that pleasure was good at all, but rather an evil,[23] and the affirmation, on the other, that it was the sole ultimate good, it became necessary to consider and define with greater accuracy than heretofore the

---

[20] Xenophon, *Memorabilia of Socrates*, II, 1, 21 ff.; Plato, *Republic* (*Dialogues*, III, 1–338) ; *Gorgias* (*Dialogues*, II, 325–421).

[21] *Phaedrus*, 267 C (*Dialogues*, I, 475).

[22] Cf. Xenophon, *Memorabilia*, II, 1, 18 ff.; IV, 5, 9–11.

[23] Diogenes Laertius, *Works*, IX, 101. According to Diogenes Laertius, *ibid.*, VI, 3, Antisthenes went so far as to say that he would rather be mad than pleased, but later Cynics admitted that some pleasure might be good, namely, ἡδονὴ ἀμεταμέλητος (a pleasure not to be regretted).

nature, conditions, and effects of pleasure and pain: an inquiry which the controversy over hedonism has kept alive ever since.

The Cynics regarded pleasure as negative, the negation or cessation of pain; they adopted and universalized the idea suggested by Anaxagoras, and soon to be taken up in a qualified form by Plato, that the pleasures of sense involve antecedent pains. Some even denied the reality of pleasure and characterized it as an illusory appearance.[24] This negative conception the Cyrenaics emphatically repudiated. The absence or removal of pain, they said, is not itself pleasure, nor is the absence of pleasure pain, but both states are positive. These states are not, indeed, to be regarded as fixed, stable, and immutable realities; they consist essentially in a process or movement. Pleasure is a smooth or gentle movement; pain is a movement harsh or rough. The intermediate state, in which there is neither pain nor pleasure, is one of rest, or of motion too slight to be perceived.[25] Even pleasure, to be felt, requires a certain degree of intensity. Accordingly, the younger Aristippus, grandson of the founder of the school, compared the state in which we feel pain to a storm at sea; that in which we feel pleasure to a gentle undulation, pleasure being also likened to a favoring breeze; and that in which we feel neither pleasure nor pain to a calm. This threefold division, expressed in similar metaphors, is ascribed to all the school.[26] Pleasure, moreover, they regarded as an

---

[24] Plato, *Philebus*, 44 B; 51 A (*Dialogues*, IV, 616, 625), the reference being probably to the Cynic School. Cf. E. Zeller, *Die Philosophie der Griechen*, II, i, 4, 308.

[25] *Philebus*, 42 E, 53 C, 54 D (*Dialogues*, IV, 613 ff.); Aristotle, *Ethica Nicomachea*, VII, 12, 1152 b 12 — 1153 a 13; Diogenes Laertius, *op. cit.*, II, 85–90. Cf. E. Zeller, *op. cit.*, 353 n.

[26] Eusebius, *Praeparatio evangelica*, XIV, 18; Sextus Empiricus, *Adversus mathematicos*, VII, 199.

affection of the body or of the flesh (τοῦ σώματος, τῆς σαρκός) [27] and probably as an index of normal organic conditions.[28] At any rate, they stoutly maintained that pleasure, even though arising from the most unbecoming causes, is always good, and pain, evil; since, apart from perversion (διαστροφή), every man involuntarily, by a natural instinct (ἀπροαίρετος), pursues and rests satisfied in the one and seeks escape from and avoids the other. They denied that pleasure is caused by past or anticipated good fortune, for the mind's movement, they said, is terminated by time; meaning, apparently, that it is always a temporally present fact. Nevertheless, they admitted other than the immediate sensation in its production, otherwise we should be unable to account for the fact that we get pleasure from the " representation " of grief, but not when we see it in real life. And they acknowledged the existence of ideal pleasures, such as that which a man takes in the prosperity of his country, or in his own.[29] But how in detail they connected these various denials, admissions, and requirements, is not clear. In any event, since all pleasure is bodily, the distinction between bodily and ideal pleasures is only logical; qualitatively, pleasure is always one and the same.

We at length reach Plato (427–347 B.C.) who here as elsewhere largely reflects the opinions of his predecessors. In him the streams of tendency from both the physical and the ethical philosophers meet and blend; he carries

---

[27] Sextus Empiricus, *Hypotyposcon Pyrrhoncorum*, I, 215.

[28] γένεσις εἰς φύσιν αἰσθητή (production perceived in a natural way), *Ethica Nicomachea*, VII, 12, 1152 b 12. A Lafontaine observes *Le plaisir d'après Platon et Aristote*, 50, that the Cyrenaic definitions of pleasure and pain indicate only the intimate nature of the process in each and must not be taken to mean that the one is according to nature and the other contrary. The conceptions, however, are nearly related and the evidence suggests that the Cyrenaics held both. Cf. E. Zeller, *loc. cit.*

[29] Diogenes Laertius, *op. cit.*, II, 88–90.

forward and in a measure completes their work, he pre-
pares the way for the ampler investigations of Aristotle,
and by the distinctions and points of view which he
himself develops, he determines to a large extent, positively and negatively, both the thought of Aristotle on
this subject and that of many succeeding generations.
The question in which he is primarily interested is the
relation of pleasure to good, its place in an ideal scheme
of life. It is as contributory to this that he undertakes a
thorough examination of its origin and nature. In addition, he touches at various points on other problems of
the affective life; one has only to recall his masterly descriptions of the various forms of the passion of love in the
Phaedrus and the *Symposium*. And he relates the affections not only to ethical and metaphysical interests, but
also, in part, quite definitely, to their bodily conditions.

On the general question of the relation of pleasure and
good — to speak of this in passing — Plato's accounts
vary. In the *Protagoras* the Socrates of the dialogue assumes as the basis of his argument that all actions are to
be regarded as honorable and useful, the tendency of which
is to make life pleasant and painless; or, expressed bluntly,
" that the pleasant is the good and the painful evil." [30]
Since no man voluntarily chooses evil, all that appears
necessary to the conduct of life is the art, based on knowledge, of calculating and weighing different pleasures, and
pleasures as against pains, so as to determine in what
course of action lies the greatest amount of pleasure. In
the *Gorgias,* on the other hand, the pleasant and the good
are sharply contrasted and the advocate of pleasure, being
forced to admit a distinction between good pleasures and
bad, the conclusion is drawn that pleasure, like everything

[30] *Protagoras,* 358 (*Dialogues,* I, 182).

else, is to be sought for the sake of good, and not good for the sake of pleasure; pleasure, like its opposite pain, being in itself considered ethically indifferent.[31] In the *Republic,* and still more definitely in the *Philebus,* distinctions are drawn which lead to the inclusion of pleasure, qualified as to its kinds, as an essential element in the good. The highest form of life is here represented as one in which wisdom, pleasure, and truth are symmetrically combined; the defining principle of symmetry or order being that which renders the mixture both virtuous and beautiful.[32] These differences of representation are largely explicable by reference to the aims of the respective dialogues, the nature of the opposing contentions, and the characters of the persons with whom the arguments are supposed to be carried on. They must not be exaggerated. It might even perhaps be shown, with due allowance for difference of emphasis, that Plato's doctrine concerning the relation of pleasure and good is substantially the same throughout.[33] They point, however, to a development in the conception of pleasure as it appears in the analysis of its nature, kinds, and conditions in the later dialogues. To this we now turn.

The discussion of pleasure in the *Philebus* begins with the assertion of the common-sense view that pleasure is not one, but manifold; in other words, that there are various sorts of pleasure, or the pleasure is of too ambiguous a nature to be determined as good, since it is experienced alike by the temperate and the intemperate, by the wise man and by the fool. This view, which strikes at the root of hedonism, the dialogue seeks ultimately to define and defend. It is objected — and the objection expresses the

---

[31] *Gorgias,* 477 f.; 499 B (*Dialogues,* II, 362, 389).
[32] *Philebus,* 64 f. (*Dialogues,* IV, 641 f.).
[33] Cf. E. Friedrichs, *Platons Lehre von der Lust im Gorgias und Philebus,* I, D.

"scientific" doctrine of the Cyrenaics — that the various pleasures do not differ as pleasures, but only in respect to their sources. Instead of meeting this objection directly by appeal to experience, Plato has recourse, in the first instance, to logic and dialectic. We must not, he says in effect, be misled by the use of a common name. We speak, for example, of "science," yet nobody would claim that one science is exactly like another. And the same may be true of "pleasure." We need, he says, to consider the relation of the one and the many, not only in the realm of sensible things, but also in the realm of ideas. This theme he proceeds to develop in some detail.[34]

The ground being thus cleared, a framework is furnished for the positive construction in a classification of all existents into four divisions: (1) the indeterminate ($ἄπειρον$); (2) the determinate ($πέρας$); (3) the union of the two; and (4) the cause of the union. Pleasure, and with it pain, as something indefinitely capable of more and less, is placed in the first or lowest class, as mind or reason is placed in the highest; but with respect to their origin, both pleasure and pain are assigned to the third class. In other words, while it is impossible to ascribe a positive character to these quantitatively indefinite affections in themselves, or, as we are now accustomed to say, they cannot be defined, but only directly experienced, we

---

[34] *Philebus*, 12–16 (*Dialogues*, IV, 576 f.). It should be noted that the logical and metaphysical interest of the discussion of the relations of "Ideas" in the latter part of this section is entirely subordinate to the purpose of indicating the necessity of a classification of pleasures and a division of pleasure into its kinds. This disposes of G. Grote's criticism, *Plato*, II, 561, that the main points raised are untouched by the explanation: a criticism, moreover, which rests on the vulgar interpretation of the Platonic "Idea" as a sort of metaphysical entity on all fours with a sensible "thing," instead of what it really is: the postulated objective of a perfect scientific definition, such as is symbolized, e.g., in the mathematical formula which defines the character of a curve and which is realized in every instance of the curve's construction.

are able to do so if we look to the way in which they are generated. What then, from this point of view, are pleasure and pain? Plato answers: pain is the destroying, or breaking up of the natural union of the determinate and indeterminate factors in the healthy organism, and pleasure is the process of its restoration; or, in simpler terms, pain is due to the dissolution and pleasure to the restoration of the natural organic harmony.[35] Two things in this definition are especially to be noted. First, pleasure and pain are, or originate in processes and, indeed, bodily processes.[36] Where there is no process of dissolution or restoration, or where the changes are too slight or too gradual to be noticed, the state is neutral.[37] This is the Cyrenaic element in the doctrine; the affections are recognized as bodily processes and a neutral state is distinguished along with pleasure and pain. The conception of pleasure as a process or movement towards an end is later used as an argument against hedonism, which regards it as the supreme end, Plato sarcastically remarking that the author of the definition was " clearly one who laughs at the notion of pleasure being a good." [38] The second thing to note is that the definition appears to make pain a condition of pleasure. This is the Cynic element.[39]

[35] *Philebus*, 31 E ff.; cf. 25 E f. (*Dialogues*, IV, 591, 599); *Cratylus*, 419 C (*Dialogues*, I, 364).

[36] Plato's language is inexact; the conscious " feeling " ($a\"\iota\sigma\theta\eta\sigma\iota\varsigma$) of pleasure or pain is in the soul. Cf. J. I. Beare, *Greek Theories of Elementary Cognition*, 212. Bodily affections, to be felt, must be propagated to the mind ($\phi\rho\acute{o}\nu\iota\mu\sigma\nu$), cf. *Timaeus*, 64 B (*Dialogues*, III, 485), or to the soul ($\mu\acute{e}\chi\rho\iota\ \tau\hat{\eta}\varsigma\ \psi\upsilon\chi\hat{\eta}\varsigma$). Cf. *Laws*, 673 A (*Dialogues* V, 75); *Philebus*, 33 D (*Dialogues*, IV, 602); *Republic*, 462 C, 584 C (*Dialogues*, III, 156, 296).

[37] *Philebus*, 32 E, 43 C (*Dialogues*, IV, 601, 615).

[38] *Ibid.*, 53.

[39] Plato repeatedly remarks on the close connection of pleasure with pain: two bodies with a single head, *Phaedo*, 60 B (*Dialogues*, II, 197); bodily pleasures were almost always conditioned by antecedent pains, *Phaedrus*, 258 E (*Dialogues*, I, 465). Cf. *Republic*, IX, 583 B ff. (*Dialogues*, III, 294 f.).

The doctrine is further developed in the *Timaeus*. There we are told that pleasure and pain must be conceived as follows: " An impression produced in us contrary to nature and violent, if sudden, is painful; and, again, the sudden return to nature is pleasant; but a gentle and gradual return is imperceptible, and *vice versa.*" Here the suddenness and violence of the excitement are emphasized. If the impression is produced easily, no affection results; Plato cites in illustration the visual stream (ὄψις, ὄψεως ῥεῦμα), which, according to his theory of vision, is a sensitive emanation of the subtlest and most mobile particles; and this, he says, may be cut or burned without discomfort, nor is there any pleasure in its return to the natural state. The affections, therefore, have no essential connection with the acuteness of perception. A certain resistance is demanded requiring a certain appreciable amount of force to overcome it. This leads to an explicit qualification of the doctrine that pleasure is preceded by pain. If the " withdrawings and emptyings " are too gradual to be noticed, while the corresponding replenishments are great and sudden, we are sensible of the pleasure without being sensible of antecedent pain; Plato finds this illustrated by sweet smells. The opposite case of sudden change with gradual and difficult return to the normal, is exemplified by the sheer pains of bodily wounds.[40] A little further on he adopts the general and commonly accepted thesis that what is contrary to nature is painful and what is according to nature is pleasant, using the principle to explain the alleged pleasurableness — not, be it noted, the mere painlessness — of death from old age, as contrasted with its painfulness when due to accident or disease; [41]

[40] *Timaeus,* 64 f. (*Dialogues,* III, 485 f.).
[41] *Ibid.,* 81 E.

an evident departure from the doctrine that pleasure is due to organic replenishment.

Returning to the *Philebus* we find that the above account applies directly only to bodily pleasures and pains. But there is another kind of affection which is only of the soul and which originates in ideational processes. Such, e.g., are the pleasures of remembering and of anticipating pleasure.[42] The question then arises, how far does the previous account, especially that part of it which conceives of pleasure as a process of restoration of disturbed equilibrium, hold for them? Now Plato considers the description entirely applicable so far as the pleasure is derived from the satisfaction of desire. For desire, he says, implies want and its satisfaction, replenishment: the one is admittedly painful, the other pleasant. If the person, while actually suffering, calls to mind past pleasures which, if present, would afford relief, his state may be described either as one of mixed pleasure and pain, or of a double pain, according as he has the sure hope of satisfied relief or is in despair.[43] On the other hand, apart from desire or bodily disturbance, mental pleasures and pains are said to be " pure," i.e., there is no admixture of one with the other; neither is conditioned on the other.[44] Here it is difficult to see how the conception of pleasure as replenishment would apply, and Plato does not elucidate the point.

[42] *Philebus,* 32 B f. (*Dialogues,* IV, 600 f.). As already pointed out, the " seat " of *all* the affections as consciously experienced is, for Plato, the soul. Bodily and mental pleasures and pains are distinguished with reference to their immediate origin, the latter being regarded as independent of the body. Cf. P. Shorey, *The Unity of Plato's Thought,* 46.

[43] *Ibid.,* 36. The conditions might be variously complicated. G. Grote, *op. cit.,* II, 569 n., gives the case in which, while tasting a pleasure, we have the desire and sure hope of its continuance, and says that here, instead of a combination of pleasure and pain or of two pains, we have a combination of pleasures. The question turns in part on the affective coloring of desire; Plato too readily assumes its universal unpleasantness.

[44] *Ibid.,* 32 C.

The distinction of pure pleasure and pleasure mixed with pain is forthwith taken up into that of true and false.[45] This is an important distinction in Plato's argument, but one of questionable psychological value. Those pleasures and pains are characterized as false which are wrongly judged in respect to their objects, their quality and amount, or their intrinsic constitution. In the first case the feeling is regarded as infected with the falsity of the opinion concerning its object; in the second, the illusions are analogous to those arising in sense perception, the feelings being viewed at different distances, in different perspectives, and being subject to all the modifying effects of comparison; in the third, the pleasures are false because they are not pure, but are mixed with, or conditioned on, pain. " Mixed " pleasures, accordingly, in this reference, are a species of " false " pleasures. It is on these mixed pleasures that, in this connection, Plato particularly dwells; for they include the typical sensual pleasures, which, as the most intense, hedonism in its extreme form commends. Plato will not go so far in his opposition as to say that such pleasures are merely negative. He adopts rather, as we have seen, the Cyrenaic view that pleasure and pain are both movements, the absence of either of which, and even their presence in a slight degree, would be practically neutral. But the followers of Antisthenes, he thinks, discerned a great truth in finding in these intensest of physical pleasures the evidence of a diseased condition of both body and soul. The fact on which he here insists, however, is that these morbid pleasures are of a mixed character: a blending, and oftentimes a very subtle blending, of pleasure and pain. But they are not the only mixed pleasures. Plato enumerates three classes of such pleasures: (1) those of

---

[45] *Ibid.,* 36 C ff.

the body only, as relief of itching by scratching; (2) those in which affections of the body and the mind are combined, such as bodily pains accompanied by the hope of relief; and (3) those of the mind only, as in anger, fear, desire, sorrow, love, emulation, malice (φθόνος), and the like. Over against these are set three classes of pure and true pleasures, namely: (1) those of simple qualities absolutely beautiful, such as straight lines and circles, pure elementary colors, smooth and clear sounds, sweet tastes; (2) those of an analogous sort unattended by pain, however and wherever experienced; and (3) the pleasures of knowledge (τὰς περὶ τὰ μαθήματα). As purity is a quality independent of intensity, Plato concludes that " a small pleasure or a small amount of pleasure, if pure and unalloyed with pain, is always pleasanter as well as truer and fairer than a great pleasure or a great amount of pleasure of another kind." [46]

Incidentally in illustrating mixed pleasures by the feelings associated with tragedy and comedy, Plato makes what is probably the first recorded attempt by a European writer at a psychology of the comic.[47] A man is ridiculous, he explains, when, through ignorance, he entertains a false conceit of his wealth, beauty, or wisdom, and is not powerful enough to be dangerous. If he is powerful his ignorance is an occasion of hatred and dread. But if he is harmless, his friends take a malicious pleasure in laughing at him; they express the spite, malice, or offense (φθόνος) excited by his pretensions in laughter, the pleas-

[46] *Ibid.*, 51 ff. Although (1) and (2) seem to be explicitly distinguished as " two kinds," to which the pleasures of knowledge are added, Plato's illustrations refer only to the pure pleasures of sense and the pure pleasures of the mind. Complex aesthetic pleasures are excluded and, strange to say, no mention is made here of those pure moral pleasures which are said later (*Ibid.*, 63 E) to " accompany health and temperance, and which every virtue, like a goddess, has in her train."

[47] *Ibid.*, 48 D ff.

ure of which, accordingly, in Plato's view, arises from and is combined with pain.[48]

In the *Republic* we meet with the same distinctions of pure and mixed and of true and false pleasures as in the *Philebus,* with, if possible, even greater emphasis on the superior truth and purity of the " higher " pleasures, though here too there is incidental recognition of pure pleasures of sense. The superiority of the mental and moral pleasures is here argued on the metaphysical principle that what is filled with the more real being is more really filled than what is filled with the less.[49] Pleasure, thus, like color, is regarded as having degrees of saturation. Now these distinctions are for Plato fundamental. As long as all pleasure is held to be identical in quality, the pleasure of thinking will not differ, except possibly in amount, from the pleasure of drinking, and the question as to which kind of life is the pleasantest, the question which interests Plato, is either meaningless or incapable of any but an individual solution. Plato himself appeals on occasion to the judgment of the man who has experienced the various kinds, that is, to the philosopher. But he seeks also to determine it on general principles. And while his argument is partly metaphysical, it rests for the main part on the sound psychological presumption that an item of consciousness is qualified by its relations to other items of consciousness and by the whole content and context of its appearance.

---

[48] Grote is right (*op. cit.,* II, 574 n.) in suggesting that φθόνος here can hardly mean " envy " or " jealousy " in our sense of the terms. But we have only to turn to Aristotle's definition of it, *Rhetorica,* II, 10, 1387 b 22 as pain at the sight of the prosperity of others resembling ourselves solely because of their prosperity, to see that, apart from any personal desire for possession, the word could have the wider meaning of displeasure or offense at the spectacle of others' advantages. What Plato fails to explain is why we should take offense at the pretension of advantages which we do not believe to exist, and, still more, why that which offends us should, nevertheless, excite pleasure.

[49] *Republic,* IX, 583 ff., esp. 585 D (*Dialogues,* III, 294 ff.).

Hence his discussion brings to light a number of important psychological facts, such as the influence of pleasure and pain on one another, their co-existence in the same state of consciousness, the various effects of their comparison and contrast, and their relations to past and future time. He proves that unless all such facts are taken into consideration, we are subject to mistake in judging the experience and that, in this sense, the pleasure may be said to be illusory. But he does not prove that the pleasure as experienced does not exist as a psychological fact or is not, as pleasure, precisely what it is felt to be. Hence the distinctions, which seemed to him so important, could not be maintained. Aristotle continued to speak of pure and true pleasures, but in a different sense. Plato's doctrine that some pleasures were essentially pleasant, while others, in spite of the evidence of feeling, were only illusory appearances of pleasure, was criticized and rejected by Theophrastus and, although defended by the Neoplatonists, survives only as its terms are reflected in the estimative vocabulary of religion and ethics.[50]

To sum up: Plato's doctrine of pleasure and pain was developed in relation to the ethical controversies of his time and conditioned by current conceptions as well as by his whole ethical and metaphysical philosophy. He inquires into the nature of pleasure and pain with more thoroughness than his predecessors, but his analyses and inductions are imperfect and his conclusions inconsistent. Unable to accept the extreme Cynic view that pleasure is only negative, he adopts the Cyrenaic opinion that both pleasure and pain are motions or transitional processes to be distinguished from the neutral state in which they are absent;

[50] For a modern defense of Plato's doctrine, see H. H. Joachim, " The Platonic Distinction between ' True ' and ' False ' Pleasures and Pains," *Philos. Rev.,* XX (1911), 471–497.

but he advances beyond the crude conceptions of them as smooth and rough by relating them more definitely to the conception of organic harmony. Pain is the process of the dissolution of this harmony, pleasure the process of its restoration; the perfect undisturbed harmony itself is neutral. Some support for this view could be found in the broad facts of organic experience, especially the facts of nutrition and bodily pain, but it is hardly a mistake to suppose that it commended itself to Plato by its conformity to some of his cherished ideals. The ideal for him was everywhere and always perfect harmony, and the life which frequently appeals to him as best is the life of complete calm, neutral as regards both joy and sorrow. This he represents as the condition of the gods, and a similar state, he says, may be maintained by one who chooses the godlike life of wisdom.[51] But the theory relates, in the first instance, only to bodily pleasures and pains, whereas, according to Plato, there are some affections which are of the mind only, apart from the body. Moreover, it implies, or seems to imply, that pleasure is conditioned on antecedent pain, and this Plato sees cannot be universally maintained even in the case of bodily pleasures. Finally, in the interests of ethics itself, he finds it important to show that the life of wisdom is, after all, not neutral, but the pleasantest life of all. These various facts and demands require a modification of the theory. The case of painless bodily pleasures is made to conform to the hypothesis by assuming that there is an antecedent process of dissolution, but that it is too slight or too gradual to be perceived. The conditions of pleasure and pain are seen to be complicated. These affections depend not simply on phenomena of exhaustion and replenishment, but on the

[51] *Philebus,* 32 E (*Dialogues,* IV, 600).

intensity and rapidity of the process and on the amount
of resistance offered in either direction. In one case, indeed, that of pleasurable death from old age, the mere
naturalness of the process is held to be a sufficient explanation of the pleasure, a return to normal organic conditions being here evidently excluded. As to mental pleasures
which follow the satisfaction of desire, they are referred
to the principle of want and replenishment; but this,
except in so far as bodily processes are involved, is only
an analogy. The pure mental pleasures which are not
based either on a bodily process of restoration to organic harmony or on the satisfaction of a want require,
in order to be even remotely connected with the theory,
the extension of the analogy beyond all bounds of psychology: an extension which Plato makes in representing the pleasures of knowledge as due to the " filling " of
the soul with reality.

The more complex affections, the emotions and passions,
are regarded in part as modifications of pleasure and pain,
and in part as distinct.[52] To the immortal soul, νοῦς or
reason, located in the head, without, however, being made
dependent on the functions of the brain, Plato assigns its
own spiritual impulses and enjoyments, in particular the
philosophical ἔρος and intellectual love of beauty: the
stages in the development of which he has described in
the language of genius in the *Diotima* passage of the *Symposium*. The ordinary emotional excitements he connects
with the mortal part of the soul distributed over the body:
θυμός, that " part of the mortal soul which is endowed
with courage and passion and loves contention," being
placed in the chest; τὸ ἐπιθυμητικόν, the faculty of the

---

[52] *Ibid.*, 32 B f., 39 C, joy and hope are species of pleasure; grief and
fear, of pain, — a grouping in which H. Siebeck, *Geschichte der Psychologie*,
I, 232, finds the germ of the later fourfold classification of the emotions.

bodily appetites, below the midriff. We have here the
basis of the famous medieval classification of the " irascible " and the " concupiscible " affections. This mortal
soul is " subject to terrible and irresistible affections," —
pleasure and pain, rashness and fear, anger and hope and
" all-daring love." [53] The awakening of this love in the perception of beauty, the onrush of bodily appetite, the violent
struggle of the latter against the resistance of the higher impulses, the part played by reason in calling to mind its
ideals, the gradual subsidence of the passion and its transformation into a love of benevolent affection exciting a re-
sponsive love, with mutual delight in the presence of the beloved and longing in absence: all this is vividly portrayed
in the great myth of the *Phaedrus*. In the *Timaeus* these and
similar perturbations are connected in the spirit, and
doubtless under the influence of Hippocrates,[54] with organic disturbances, particularly in the heart, the lungs, the
liver, and the various fluids and more mobile substances of
the body. Thus the heart, excited by the vital heat, palpitates in fear and is turgid in anger; for which reason, says
Plato, the gods placed about the heart the soft, bloodless
and spongy lungs in order that, when passion was rife, the
heart might beat against a yielding body and get cooled.[55]
In unregulated appetite the bitter gall is diffused through
the liver producing a wrinkling and roughening of its
surface, twisting and contorting its lobes, constricting and
stopping its passages, the whole being attended with pain
and loathing; whereas when reason controls, it makes use
of the liver's natural sweetness to render the part of the
soul there resident happy and cheerful.[56] Disorders in the

---

[53] *Timaeus*, 69 f. (*Dialogues*, III, 490).
[54] Cf. F. Poschenrieder, *Die platonischen Dialoge*, 48.
[55] *Timaeus*, 70 C (*Dialogues*, III, 491).
[56] *Ibid.*, 71 B f.

distribution and consistency of the fluids and like mobile substances also engender morbid affections. The intemperance of the passion of love, for example, is declared to be " a disease of the soul due to the moisture and fluidity produced in one of the elements by the loose consistency of the bones," Plato's idea being, apparently, that by reason of this " looseness " the semen, which, according to him, is formed in the spinal marrow, is not properly held in check. Again, infinite varieties of ill-temper, melancholy, rashness, and cowardice, as well as of disturbances in the intellectual functions, are produced by the wandering through the body of " acid and briny phlegm and other bitter and bilious humors," whose vapors thus blend with the motions of the soul.[57] But not only can the body affect the soul, the soul also affects the body; excited arguments produce rheums; an impassioned soul, more powerful than the body, convulses and fills with disorder the whole nature of man. A harmonious proportion between soul and body is the foundation principle of health and sanity.[58]

No one will be deceived as to the significance of these beginnings of a scientific treatment of the emotions. Their outlines are vague. They rest on no such independent examination, no such attempted isolation and classification of the phenomena as Plato attempted in the case of pleasure. He could describe the play of emotions in individual characters in particular situations with the skill of a supreme artist. But what he has to say on emotions in general is fragmentary and on its physiological side, to all appearances, a reflection of current medical opinion on the nature of disease. Such expression as he gives of the best scientific thought of his time on this subject only makes

[57] *Ibid.*, 86 f.; cf. *Philebus*, 42 (*Dialogues*, IV, 613).
[58] *Ibid.*, 87 ff.

manifest the necessity for fresh beginnings and further developments. These we have in Aristotle (384–322 B.C.), who not only gives us a new theory of pleasure, but also the first connected and relatively systematic study of the emotions and passions.

CHAPTER II

THE DOCTRINE OF PLEASURE, PAIN, AND EMOTION IN ARISTOTLE

Aristotle's treatment of the affections, like Plato's, is conditioned throughout by other than purely psychological interests. His principal discussion of pleasure is in the tenth book of the *Nicomachean Ethics*, where the primary aim is to define the relation of pleasure to the pursuit of the moral end; and his principal discussion of the emotions is in the second book of the *Rhetoric*, where the main object is to relate the emotional susceptibilities of an audience to the art of persuasion. In the *De anima*, where psychological problems are handled more from the point of view of a philosophy of mind, with the emphasis on cognition, references to the phenomena of the affective life are few and incidental. Nevertheless, wherever Aristotle does treat of these phenomena, whether incidentally or in a connected discussion subordinate to an ulterior purpose, he seems to be genuinely interested in the facts. His inventory of the facts is far fuller than Plato's, his analyses more thorough. In constructing a theory there is always a certain selection of the material, a guiding idea, and a mutual adaptation and molding of the two as the theory develops. But the emphasis may be now on the one factor, and now on the other. Plato's emphasis is on the ideal factor; Aristotle is more careful in the manipulation of the material. Thus in the doctrine of pleasure Aristotle's theory seems to be more molded on the facts, whereas Plato makes the impression of fitting the facts to the requirements of ideas. The antithesis is not absolute; both writers deal reflectively with experience, and neither succeeds in clearly discriminating the psychological from logical and practical points of view. But Aristotle comes the nearest to such discrimination of any ancient writer, and although, as has been said, " he studied psychology as a philosopher and was chiefly interested in it as it bore upon philosophical problems," [1] he nevertheless exhibits in a remarkable degree the spirit of scientific detachment in surveying and handling his material. Hence his account of the emotions, imperfect as it is, and particularly his conception of pleasure as a concomitant of the normal exercise of vital functions, though that too is incomplete, are not only of importance historically, but contain large elements of permanent psychological value.

Aristotle begins the discussion of pleasure by criticizing the definition of it as a kind of motion ($\kappa\acute{\iota}\nu\eta\sigma\iota\varsigma$), especially Plato's view of it as the origin of a process ($\gamma\acute{\epsilon}\nu\epsilon\sigma\iota\varsigma$) of the replenishment of a deficiency, and, therefore, as conditioned on a state of pain. Pleasure cannot be a motion, he argues, for motion implies rate; but while the transition to pleasure may be quick or slow, these terms are not applicable to the pleasure itself. The conception of it as a process of replenishment and as conditioned on pain was suggested, he thinks, by the pains and pleasures of nutrition, such as hunger and thirst and the satisfaction of these wants. But this conception, besides making pleasure a bodily state, is plainly inadequate to meet the case of many pleasures in which no pain of want precedes.[2] Plato, as we have seen, admitted and glorified these pure painless pleasures without, however, being able

---

[1] R. D. Hicks, *Aristotle's De anima*, lxxii.
[2] *Ethica Nicomachea*, X, 3, 4–7, 1174 ff. Cf. *Magna moralia*, II, 7, 1204 b 5; *Ethica Nicomachea*, VII, 15, 1154 b 27.

to explain them in terms of his original theory. As against the view that pleasure is a motion or process, Aristotle maintains that it is something which at any moment of its actual existence is naturally complete. Duration is essential to motion, but not to pleasure; even a momentary pleasure is wholly and entirely pleasure. Like the act of vision or a mathematical point, pleasure is without beginning, middle, or end.[3]

This criticism is not, of course, meant to deny that pleasures exist in time, that they persist for a longer or shorter time, that within a given extent of time they may vary in intensity; nor does it necessarily deny that all pleasure rests upon and is connected with some kind of organic movement. Aristotle is not here looking at the psychical process, a movement in the flow of consciousness to be observed and described, nor is he dealing with a physiological theory of such a process. He is simply isolating a moment or element in immediate experience and inquiring into its logical definition. His point is that, when thus isolated, the moment in question is seen to be improperly defined as a motion or transition to an end beyond itself, but is itself a fully realized mode of conscious being, whatever its conditions and however manifold its relations. The contention may seem futile, ignoring the element of truth in the opinions criticized, which, though crudely identifying a psychical content with a physical change, had at least the merit of indicating conditions of the origin and fluctuations of the experience. But the criticism had the value of exposing precisely this crudity and of bringing the discussion onto psychological ground; it showed the necessity of avoiding hasty generalizations and misleading analogies; and it formed an indispensable beginning in

[3] *Ibid.*, X, 4, 4, 1174.

the construction of Aristotle's own more inclusive and penetrating theory.

Here, however, we are confronted by an apparent contradiction in Aristotle himself. In the passages cited above he denies that pleasure is a movement or process, but in a passage in the *Rhetoric* he himself describes it as " a certain motion of the soul and a sudden and sensible settling into the normal state," [4] pain being the opposite — a description strikingly similar to Plato's. [5] The difficulty may be met in various ways. We might explain it, for instance, by Aristotle's broad use of the term " motion " (κίνησις) as including any sort of change. [6] Aristotle, it may be said, does not deny in the *Ethics* that pleasure can be regarded as a " motion " from any and every point of view; all that he insists on is that it is not a " motion " in a sense that would conflict with the conception of it as a fully realized state of consciousness. Pleasure and pain certainly imply change; they are, according to Aristotle elsewhere, " qualitative changes of the faculty of sense," [7] and he notes that pleasure, in man at least, cannot be continued uninterruptedly. [8] Or we may refer to Aristotle's technical conception of motion as not mere transition to an end, but as a process in which the quality of the end is imminent. On this reading of the passage pleasure would here be defined by metonymy in terms of the process of its attainment: the end and the process being " formally " the same thing in different stages of its attainment. Frequently the latter part of the description is taken as epexegetical, the " motion of the soul " being interpreted as *consisting in*

[4] *Rhetorica* I, 11, 1369 b 33: κίνησίν τινα τῆς ψυχῆς καὶ κατάστασιν ἀθρόαν καὶ αἰσθητὴν εἰς τὴν ὑπάρχουσαν φύσιν.
[5] *Timaeus*, 64 D (*Dialogues*, III, 485).
[6] Cf. H. Bonitz, *Index aristotelicus* (*Aristotelis Opera*, V) for κίνησις.
[7] ἀλλοιώσεις τοῦ αἰσθητικοῦ, *Physica*, VII, 3, 247 a 15.
[8] *Ethica Nicomachea*, X, 4, 9, 1174.

" the sudden and sensible settling into the natural state ";
and this is even supposed to mark the critical difference
between Aristotle's doctrine and Plato's; the " motion "
with Aristotle being, it is said, not, as with Plato, a " process of origination," but an " unmediated consciousness." [9]
All such explanations assume that we have here to do with
a precisely worded scientific definition. But what if the
wording were not intended to be scientifically exact?
Aristotle, when careful in his language, plainly distinguishes between the changes which introduce a quality and
the quality itself.[10] Here the distinction is obliterated. If
now we compare this passage in the *Rhetoric* with the
corresponding passage in the *Timaeus* of Plato, we can
hardly escape the conviction that both passages express
substantially the same doctrine. Dogmatically, therefore,
the teaching of the *Rhetoric* would be at variance with
that of the *Ethics*. But it is to be observed that the description in the *Rhetoric* is not put forth dogmatically, but in
the form of an assumption.[11] Hence we may conclude with
a fair degree of probability that Aristotle did not intend
that it should be taken as a formally precise definition, but
that he adopted it as sufficiently exact for the purpose in
hand, the purpose, namely, of the rhetorician: a proposition generally understood and a conception more or less
currently accepted, especially by Platonists. In any case

[9] " *Das* ἀθρόα *soll hier eben die* κίνησις *in dem Sinne erklären, dass mit
letzterer nicht wie bei Plato eine* γένεσις, *ein Entstehungsprozess, gemeint
sei, sondern ein unvermitteltes Bewusstsein des naturgemässen Zustandes.*'
H. Siebeck, *Geschichte der Psychologie*, 489. But ἀθρόον is the very term
used by Plato in the passage cited. A. Lafontaine, *Le plaisir d'après Platon e
Aristote*, 54, interprets : " Pleasure is *as it were* a movement of the soul
or rather a sudden and sensible return *of the soul* to its proper state." The
gloss is indicated by the italics.

[10] *Physica*, VII, 3, 247 a 19.

[11] ὑποκείσθω ἡμῖν κ. τ. λ., " let us assume that," etc. The view taken in
the text was suggested by E. M. Cope, *Introduction to Aristotle's Rhetoric*
who, in Appendix D to Book I, 234 ff., treats fully of the whole subject o
Aristotle's varying expressions concerning the nature of pleasure and pain

it is to be noted that in the discussion which follows, the emphasis falls not on the idea of pleasure as a process, or as a sudden settling, but on the normal and natural conditions in connection with which the affection arises.

Setting aside, then, the questionable definition as, except for this emphasis, relatively unimportant, we are now prepared for the further positive statement of Aristotle's doctrine of pleasure. The doctrine in the briefest and simplest terms is this: pleasure is the concomitant of the normal exercise of the faculties of a living, conscious being. The exercise or actual realization (ἐνεργεῖν, ἐνέργεια) of any faculty, or of the natural potentialities of life as a whole, is pleasant, and the pleasure is proportioned to the completeness of the realization. On the other hand, any impediment experienced in the process of realizing a faculty, of expressing a function, is felt as pain. Thus in order to experience pleasure, the faculty must be in good condition and the object of its activity appropriate. When the faculty is in the best condition and the object affords the fullest scope to its exercise, the pleasure relative to that faculty is the greatest possible.[12] In the exercise, for example, of the perceptive faculties there are certain conditions of proportion in the constituents of the object and a certain normal ratio between the object and the faculty which may not be transgressed with impunity: if it is exceeded, the result is less pleasure, or pain, or in extreme cases the destruction of the sense itself. In the exercise of thought there is a similar adaptation of the object to the faculty, but without any such limitation; for the more intellectual the object, the more it stimulates the faculty, and the greater, consequently, is the pleasure.[13] No faculty,

---

[12] *Ethica Nicomachea*, X, 4, 7, 1174.
[13] *De anima*, III, 2, 426 b 3 ff.; II, 11, 424 b 28.

however, is capable of continuous exercise, for as the novelty wears off, the activity is relaxed and the pleasure is correspondingly diminished. But the general principle applies not only to the special activities of the cognitive faculties, but to the totality of the individual's vital functions, life being described by Aristotle as a perpetually renewed exercise of faculties. Pleasure is the accompaniment of the free, unimpeded expression of the natural capacities, pain the accompaniment of conditions detrimental to such expression. This, in terms of faculty and function, is Aristotle's new rendering of the old doctrine that pleasure is according to nature and pain contrary to nature.[14]

Three things in this theory are particularly worthy of remark. (1) Pleasure (and by inference pain) is not a special faculty or the realized expression of such faculty. There is no special sense of pleasure the exercise of which is required by the conditions of life.[15] It is an accompaniment, a complement, something superadded and attached, when the normal functions of life are being fulfilled. Aristotle puts it thus: " Pleasure completes the activity . . . as a kind of supervenient finality, like the bloom that is set on youth." [16] As the peculiar charm which belongs to the

---

[14] *Ethica Nicomachea*, X, 4, 9 f., 1174.

[15] *Ibid.*, X, 5, 7, 1175.

[16] *Ibid.*, X, 4, 8, 1174: τελειοῖ δὲ τὴν ἐνέργειαν ἡ ἡδονή . . . . ὡς ἐπιγιγνόμενόν τι τέλος οἷον τοῖς ἀκμαίοις ἡ ὥρα. There is an apparent conflict between the assertion in this chapter that pleasure is ἐν ἐνεργείᾳ (in activity) (cf. X, 5, 11, 1176 a 26; X, 5, 6, 1175 b 26), but not itself ἐνέργεια (activity), and what is said of it in VII, 12, 1152. There we read: " Wherefore it is not proper to call pleasure a perceived process of origination (γένεσις), it should rather (ἀλλὰ μᾶλλον) be described as a realization of normally constituted faculty (ἐνέργειαν τῆς κατὰ φύσιν ἕξεως), with the substitution of 'unimpeded' for 'perceived.' " The contradiction may be toned down by considering the nature of the antithesis and what is implied in the ἀλλὰ μᾶλλον. The probability, however, is that Book VII, which parallels the discussion of pleasure in Book X with various modifications in doctrine, is not Aristotle's, but is derived, along with Books V and VI, from the *Ethics* of Eudemus. Cf. J. A. Stewart, Notes on the *Nicomachean Ethics*, II, 218 ff.

heyday of life is not any one or all of the powers which co-
operate to create the charm, so pleasure is not identical
with, but an incident of the exercise of the faculties to
which it gives an added touch of perfection. The chief significance of this idea lies in its bearing on hedonism, which
it is taken to refute. Psychologically it asserts the universal dependence of pleasure and pain on other functions
of the organism. But it must not, on that account, be
identified with any particular form of modern analytical
theory, and especially not with that with which at first
sight it may seem to have the closest affinity: the theory
namely, which makes these affections general " attributes " of sensation or of other forms of " consciousness."
Modern theory and discussion rest in the main on a conception of mental " elements " of which the psychology
of Aristotle, perhaps to its credit, knows nothing. (2)
Aristotle's doctrine is an " activity " doctrine; pleasure is
a concomitant of the active exercise of the faculties. " The
exercise of every sense is attended with pleasure, and so
is the exercise of reason and the speculative faculty; and
it is pleasantest when it is most complete." [17] The emphasis on the connection of pleasure with the realization
of faculties is so strong that one is tempted to charge Aristotle with exaggeration and with failure to take account
of the large class of pleasures connected with recreation
and repose. It is quite true that he does not take them
sufficiently into account; he does not develop his doctrine
in this direction. He does, however, notice them, telling us,
for instance, that " all conditions of ease, comfort, or in-
attention, amusements, recreations, and sleep " are pleasures. And the explanation he seems to give of them is
that they rest on processes which fulfil either natural or
acquired tendencies and conform to the general conditions

[17] *Ethica Nicomachea*, X, 4, 1174 b 20. (F. H. Peters' translation.)

of life.[18] If, therefore, we are to characterize Aristotle's doctrine of pleasure as an " activity " doctrine, it must be, apparently, in the broad sense in which " activity " denotes any unimpeded vital process whatsoever. In the *Ethics* he emphasizes the pleasures of the cognitive processes, which afford, indeed, the readiest illustration of the thesis that pleasure is an accompaniment of function and not the function itself, and especially that it is not a mere process of restoration of a natural state previously impaired. But he nowhere denies that a process of the latter sort is pleasant. His theory rather requires that it should be pleasant, so far, namely, as it can be regarded as an expression of the latent capacities of life and as going on without obstruction; similarly of all other processes that can be viewed as realizing in any way any of the manifold conditions of normal life. Pleasure, he explains, completes the exercise of all the vital powers, and so completes life itself; pleasure and life seem constantly conjoined.[19] (3) Aristotle's doctrine is thus fundamentally " biological." But, it must be well noted, not in any narrow sense. The " soul " is, indeed, the " entelechy " of the body, but not its product; it is the formal and final " cause " of the physiological functions, not their efficiently produced " effect." Bodily processes, the " matter " of the psychical, are not the sole condition of the affections; and the intellect, although in man intimately bound up with sensible experience, is in its essential nature a thing apart. Aristotle's point of view is dynamic: life is for him a complex of functions, and the affections are related to these functions. It is wholly a secondary matter whether or not the functions of life are embodied. The

---

[18] *Rhetorica*, I, 11, 1369 ; cf. *Problemata*, 878 b 11 : " The way to what is natural is sweet, if only it be perceived."
[19] *Ethica Nicomachea*, X, 4, 7, 1174.

incorporeal Deity, whose life is one of perfect and un-
interrupted intellectual activity, experiences, according to
Aristotle, the greatest and purest joy.[20] It is only, therefore, with this understanding that we may see in the doctrine that pleasure is a concomitant of the normal exercise
of the faculties, and pain the contrary, the original of the
modern view that pleasure is an index of favorable conditions and pain an index of disturbance in some or all of
the vital processes of the organism. There are, it is well
known, many objections to this view of which Aristotle
was ignorant. The one obvious objection to his own view,
the case of pathological pleasures, he does not appear to
feel as an objection; they seem to him sufficiently explained by diseased conditions of the body or perverted
dispositions of the mind.[21]

Aristotle, like Plato, holds that pleasures differ in kind.
But while this view in Plato rests primarily on an ethical
appreciation and is developed in the distinctions of pure
and mixed pleasures and pleasures true and false, in Aristotle it appears as a consequence of the conception of
pleasure as a concomitant and completion of the exercise
of the faculties. As there are specific differences among the
faculties, so, he argues, there must be corresponding differences among the pleasures arising from their exercise,
for each pleasure perfects the use of its own faculty. To
this abstract logical consideration others are added of a
more empirical character. Thus it is observed that pleasure

[20] *Ibid.*, X, 7, 3, 1176; *Metaphysica*, XI, 7, 1072 b 14 f.
[21] He treats the question from the ethical point of view, assuming a
normal man, ἀγαθὸς ἀνήρ, as a standard. "In all matters of this kind," he
says, "we assume that things are what they appear to be to the perfect
man." Hence he declares base pleasures, like perverted tastes in sickness,
to be not pleasures at all "except to corrupt men"; *Ethica Nicomachea*,
X, 5, 10 f., 1175. This is his version of Plato's "false" pleasures. Aristotle,
it should be added, has other principles of explanation, namely, specific and
individual constitutional differences (cf. *Ethica Nicomachea, loc. cit.*) and
habit, a "second nature."

has a facilitating effect on the specific kind of activity it accompanies and an inhibitory effect on rival activities. If we take pleasure in any pursuit, such as music or geometry, we are much more likely to acquire proficiency in it. On the other hand, a lover of the flute, whenever he hears the sound of it, can hardly be made to attend to an argument. And, in general, the pleasanter activity so preoccupies the mind that attention at the time to any other subject less pleasant is difficult. Such pleasure, says Aristotle, has almost the same effect on the rival activity as its own proper pain.[22] The argument makes plain that what Aristotle means by pleasure is the various ways of being pleased, the actual sense of agreeable hearing, seeing, remembering, thinking, etc. There are various ways of being pleased, consequently various kinds of pleasure. The " pleasure " that is common to the different experiences is an abstraction, like " color," and has not actual existence. The pleasure that Aristotle has in mind is that which is specifically realized in specific modes of activity, and such pleasure is manifold. The dynamic effects of which he speaks are strictly, therefore, effects of the whole pleasant experience considered functionally. This functional view of pleasure, which reappears in various places in Aristotle, makes it difficult to maintain rigidly the doctrine that pleasure exists only *in* the realization of function and is not itself the realization of a function, as in the seventh book of the *Ethics* it is declared to be.

Pleasures differ in purity, the degrees of purity being measured by corresponding differences in the functions with which they are connected. Thus, sight is purer than touch, hearing and smell than taste, intellection than any activity of sense. Consequently the pleasures of the intel-

[22] *Ibid.*, X, 5, 1–5, 1175.

lect are purer than those of any sense, and the pleasures of the senses differ according to their kind. Evidently the criterion of " purity " here is not, as with Plato, freedom from admixture with pain, but freedom from " matter." [23] Independently of this distinction Aristotle also admits mixed states of pleasure and pain, the most conspicuous illustrations of which are found in the emotions, e.g., the " tragic " emotions of pity and fear. Considerations similar to those which derive differences in pleasure from the particular functions they attach to lead to the conception of differences of pleasure relative to the life function of one species of sentient being as compared with another and of individual differences among members of the same species; but the facts are noted only as a background for the conception of a normal life function for man, and to mark the ethical distinction between the pleasures proper to it and the " false " pleasures of the profligate.[24] Aristotle further accepts the current distinction between bodily pleasures and pleasures of the soul. Under the former he includes those connected with a purely human exercise of the senses, what we may call aesthetic pleasures, as well as those common to all animals and related to conservation and reproduction, such as the pleasures of eating, drinking, and the sexual appetite. Under the latter he includes such pleasures as those arising from gratified ambition and the love of learning, the pleasure of successful revenge (its failure is unpleasant), of victory (since it gives us a sense of superiority), of honor and good reputation in the opinion of the competent, of flattery, and the pleasure in things similar and cognate.[25] Aristotle curiously derives self-love from this last, since, as he says,

[23] Cf. J. A. Stewart, *op. cit.*, II, 435.
[24] *Ethica Nichomachea*, X, 5, 10 f., 1175.
[25] *Ibid.*, III, 10, 2–11, 8, 1115–1116; *Rhetorica*, I, 11, 1369.

everyone directs the relation of the similar and the cognate in a pre-eminent degree towards himself.[26]

As a psychical experience all pleasure is, of course, an " affection of the soul." [27] The part of the soul to which it is referred is sense ($\alpha \check{\iota} \sigma \theta \eta \sigma \iota s$), the Greek term, be it remembered, having all the breadth and indefiniteness of our " feeling." The admission of pure pleasures of the speculative intellect would seem to imply an intellective or spiritual feeling. Sometimes, however, Aristotle insists on the relation of all pleasure to bodily sensation. For pleasure, he says, is either in present action, in which case it is a direct sensible experience excited by a sensibly perceived object, or in memory or anticipation, which are dependent upon such experience. The objects of memory are pleasant not only if they were pleasant at the time, but also if they were pleasant in their consequences. Objects of anticipation are pleasant if pleasant consequences are expected from them. But whether relating to a present object or to one past or future, pleasure itself is a sensible experience, the ideal feeling differing from the actual only in degree.[28]

Besides the relations of pleasure and pain to the cognitive processes, they are also intimately connected with conation. Mere sensation, says Aristotle, is like bare thinking, or the simple uttering of words; but if it is pleasant or painful, the soul, as if affirming or denying, pursues or avoids it. Being pleased or pained is thus being active in

---

[26] T. Gomperz, *Griechische Denker*, III, 336, cites this as illustrating a certain *Verschrobenheit* in Aristotle which is further exemplified by his artificial deduction of the pleasure of a reputation for wisdom from the power it gives us over others, since we all like to rule. Gomperz remarks that it does not always have this effect and that Aristotle might have derived the pleasure more directly from the pleasure of superiority, of which he had previously spoken.

[27] *Ethica Nichomachea*, I, 8, 10, 1098.

[28] *Physica*, VII, 3, 247 a 7 f.; *Rhetorica* I, 11, 1369.

respect to good and bad in the medium of sense.[29] Indeed,
so intimate is the connection of these feelings with active
tendency that they are expressly assigned, on occasion, to
the sense faculty of appetition.[30] But besides sensuous
conation Aristotle recognizes a conation of the rational
will. In the contemplation of an intelligible object the mind
is affected by a spiritual pleasure inseparable from a spiritual conation. There is a similar relation of pleasure, pain,
and conation through imagination. The pleasure that arises
from the normal exercise of any function and the pain
that arises from excess or defect in its exercise set up movements of approach or avoidance, beget tendencies of desire or aversion, the satisfaction or thwarting of which
are themselves attended with pleasure or pain. Thus under
the influence of these affections the manifold impulses, inclinations, and desires are created, strengthened, checked,
organized, developed, and expressed. Every man, says
Aristotle, is actively concerned with the things he chiefly
loves; in these he takes pleasure; and the pleasure completes the activity and the life whose tendency it manifests.[31] It is this which makes the regulation of pleasure
so important ethically; pleasure consolidates or suppresses
tendencies, but does not of itself determine what tendencies it is desirable to further or inhibit or how the different tendencies are to be related in an ideally perfect human
life. We are not concerned here with Aristotle's ethics; the
point of psychological interest is that pleasures and pains
are regarded as capable of voluntary control, pleasure

---

[29] *De anima*, III, 7, 431 a 8 ff.; cf. II, 3, 414 b 4; *Politica*, I, 2, 12, 1252.
[30] *Topica*, IV, 5, 126 a 9: ἐν τῷ ἐπιθυμητικῷ. In the same context
shame (αἰσχύνη) is connected with the thinking faculty (τὸ λογιστικόν)
and fear and anger with the spirited faculty (τὸ θυμοειδές). This division
of faculties — Plato's — Aristotle in his doctrine of affection usually disregards.
[31] *Ethica Nicomachea*, X, 4, 1174 b 20; I, 8, 10, 1098.

more easily, it is held, than intense pain.[32] How more precisely the control is brought about is something of a mystery. Aristotle's disposition to separate the powers of the
soul into distinct faculties obscures the conception of organic relations between the different mental processes
and between these and the bodily processes which under-
lies his view of psychology as a whole, and which it was
his great merit to have introduced in his designation of
the soul as the body's form and entelechy. His conception
of pleasure and pain as concomitants respectively of free
or impeded vital function remains as a permanent acquisition of scientific psychology, needing, however, more concrete definition through observation of all the facts without
neglect of the negative instances. Much of what he says
concerning the relations of pleasure and pain to other
aspects of mental and bodily life also remains, though the
subtlety of the connections and the continuity in the processes require a formulation free from the disturbing suggestions of distinct and separate faculties.

Turning now to the subject of the emotions or passions,
we find Aristotle including under the term πάθη (feeling)
a variety of affectional states, dispositions, and qualities
for the grouping together of which it is not easy to discover a principle. Fifteen of these are treated in some detail in the second book of the *Rhetoric*, where they are
arranged mostly in pairs: anger and placability, love and
hate, fear and confidence, shame and shamelessness, benevolence and churlishness, pity and resentment. The last
three, envy, emulation, and contempt, are also correlated,
emulation being regarded as in a sort the reverse of envy,
and contempt the antithesis of emulation. The list is not,
and is not intended to be complete, for in other connections

[32] *Ibid.,* X, 7, 1175.

we find, e.g., joy and longing, enthusiasm and " spirit "
(θυμός), of which anger and resentment would be expressions, and even appetite (ἐπιθυμία) used to illustrate
the same general kind of mental fact.[33] It is difficult to distinguish some of these " passions " from the virtues and
vices which are said not to be " passions " (πάθη), but
formed habits of the soul (ἕξεις). Nor, does Aristotle
himself appear to be wholly consistent. Thus gentleness
(πραότης, πράϋνσις) is treated in the *Rhetoric* as a passion, whereas in the *Ethics* it is classed with the moral
virtues and discussed as such, being defined as a kind of
moderation in respect to anger, with the vice of wrathful-
ness as its opposite. Benevolence, one would suppose,
would be regarded as a virtue in any theory; yet it is entirely absent from the list of the virtues treated in the
Ethics (II–IV) and is grouped with the passions in the
Rhetoric (II, 7), where it is described as that which leads
one to render a disinterested service to another in the hour
of need. Modesty or shame (αἰδώς) is discussed in the
Ethics (IV, 9) in connection with the virtues, the reason
given being that the modest person is praised as maintaining the mean between bashful shyness and shamelessness.
Here shamelessness, which in the *Rhetoric* figures as a
passion, appears as a sort of vice. The opposite, shame,
however, is declared not to be, in the strict sense, a virtue,
" since it resembles a passion (πάθος) rather than a
formed habit of soul (ἕξις) "; it is held, in fact, to be
a sort of physical instinct, "a kind of fear of disgrace
with effects resembling those of the fear aroused by danger: men blush when ashamed, when terrified they turn

---

[33] *Ethica Nicomachea,* II, 4, 5, 1105 b 20 ff.; *De anima,* I, 1, 403 a 16 f.;
Politica, VIII, 5, 1340 a 11. Cf. *Magna moralia,* I, 7, 8, 1186; *Ethica
Eudemia,* II, 2, 1220 b 10 ff.

pale." [34] We are not surprised, therefore, to find that in the *Rhetoric* shame is treated along with its opposite among the passions.[35] Resentment or virtuous indignatiòn (νέμεσις) appears both as a virtue and as a passion.[36]

This apparent confusion is partly due to the ambiguities of language, the same term being used to designate different things, or the same thing viewed in different ways. Back of it lies a genuine attempt on Aristotle's part to distinguish these differences. " There are," he says, " three sorts of mental facts (τὰ ἐν τῇ ψυχῇ γιγνόμενα), passions (or affections, πάθη), faculties (capacities, potentialities, δυνάμεις), and formed habits (dispositions, characters, ἕξεις). By (1) 'passions' I mean appetite, anger, fear, confidence, envy, joy, love, hate, longing, emulation, pity, and, in general, states accompanied by pleasure and pain. (2) A ' faculty ' is that in respect of which we are said to be capable of being affected in any of these ways, e.g., in respect of being angered or pained or feeling pity. (3) A ' formed habit ' is that in respect of which we are well or ill regulated in our ' passions,' for example, as regards anger we are ill regulated if we are either too violent or too slack, but we are well regulated if our anger is in moderation; and so with the rest." [37] According to this the passions occupy a mean between the predisposing susceptibilities and the habits which are formed by their repeated exercise. Habits are also capacities of behavior, but capacities formed and fixed as features of character. They show how well or how little the passions in a man are under the control of an ideal principle and are hence subjects of

---

[34] *Ethica Nicomachea*, IV, 9, 1 f., 1125; cf. II, 7, 1108 a 21.
[35] *Rhetorica*, II, 6, 1383.
[36] *Ethica Nicomachea*, IV, 7, 1108 b 1 ff.; *Rhetorica*, II, 9, 1386 b 9 ff.
[37] *Ethica Nicomachea*, II, 4, 5, 1105 b 20 ff.; cf. *Magna moralia*, I, 7, 8, 1186. *Ethica Eudemia*, II, 2, 1220 b 10 ff. Cf. C. Plutarch, *De virtute morali*, 4 (*Moralia*, III, 151).

the moral attributes of praise or blame, virtue or vice. It
is easy to understand, therefore, how Aristotle can say
that the virtues are not passions, and yet declare that the
two have much in common.[38] The distinction is not always represented by the name; the same name may be
applied to both. But there is one thing which characterizes
every virtue that is not characteristic of the passions, and
that is the element of choice. " The virtues are in a sort
choices, or at least they are not independent of choice "
(προαίρεσις), they result in part from determinations
of the will, whereas we may, e.g., " be afraid or angry
involuntarily " (ἀπροαιρέτως). Aristotle speaks of the
"irrational" passions (τὰ ἄλογα πάθη) and frequently
contrasts a life that is according to passion (κατὰ πάθος)
with one that is conformed to reason (κατὰ λόγον); but
he is far from suggesting the Stoic inference that the passions must be suppressed; he regards them rather as so
much material to be brought under rational control.[39]

With all this, however, we are still far from a positive
conception of " passion." It arises from a " faculty," but
so in a way does every other manifestation of the psychic
life. It is not a " habit," from which we conclude that it is
a temporary and transient expression of its capacity; but
this is true of the actual expression of every mental power.
Why are not the expressions of the habits passions? What
difference does it make to the nature of a passion to be
frequently repeated so that its original potentiality becomes fixed in a disposition of the character? Well, there

---

[38] *Ethica Nicomachea*, II, 4, 5, 1106 a 3; X, 8, 1178 a 15. Hence remarks on the passions are naturally included in the chapters III, 6 — IV,
which treat of the moral virtues. W. Wundt, *Grundzüge der physiologischen
Psychologie*, III, 239, finds in these chapters the beginning of a psychology
of the emotions, but omits to mention the fuller treatment in *Rhetorica*, II,
1, 1377 ff.

[39] *Ethica Nicomachea*, III, 3, 1111 a 1; cf. I, 1, 1095 a 8; VIII, 3,
1156 a 32, etc.

is a difference, especially in the case of the virtuous dispositions, as Aristotle clearly points out. This habit is not formed merely by repetition; it is formed in relation to the whole organization of experience, the developing knowledge of the individual, and the pressure of the social environment. It is formed in the light, used or misused, of ideals, and it is these which give to it its moral character. Hence there is a difference, for example, between the resentment or benevolence which springs up sporadically from a natural inclination and the resentment or benevolence arising from settled habits developed under the guidance of ideas. Nevertheless, if we abstract from the relations, occasions, and manner of their manifestation, it can hardly be denied that the phenomena in the two cases present a psychological identity, an identity particularly manifest in the ill regulated vices as compared with the life phenomena before they acquired moral character. Aristotle himself calls enthusiasm a passion of the " ethical " part of the soul and pity and indignation passions of virtue.[40] We are ready to conclude, then, that although primary potentialities or " faculties " and formed habits of soul are distinct as regards both originality and organization, the phenomena called "passions " which are said to arise from the one may and do arise from the other also. None possibly ever occurs unless grounded in some constitutional tendency; but not every expression of a native tendency appears to be regarded by Aristotle as a " passion." What, then, determines the class to which he gives the name?

To this question he supplies no satisfactory answer. He defines " passions " in the passage quoted by naming a number of the things he regards as such and by a general reference to states attended with pleasure and pain. In

---

[40] *Politica,* VIII, 5, 1340 a 11.

the *Rhetoric* he defines them also, primarily as states that radically affect judgment, a feature which especially commends them to the rhetorician and the student of politics.[41] The particular "passions" are defined very largely as species of pleasure and pain. But they differ from pleasure and pain as such in that, besides being evidently more complex, they are "motions of the soul," and not mere complements of a function.[42] Some of them are defined as pains *or* perturbations. Many of them have a markedly conative character; they express appetites, tendencies, strivings; they include "appetite" (ἐπιθυμία) and "spirit" (θυμός), into which Plato had distributed the whole of the "mortal" soul, and these impulses expand into account; thus — to use Aristotle's own illustration all "materialized notions" (λόγοι ἔνυλοι), i.e., mental states or processes so connected with bodily processes that they can be described as being either the one or the other, while to be fully described both aspects must be taken into account; thus, — to use Aristotle's own illustration — anger is defined "logically" as a propension to retaliation, but "physically" as an ebullition of the blood about the heart.[44] Along with this, however, we have a special class of "somatic passions" (σωματικὰ πάθη) to which the pains of want and the pleasures of replenishment are referred and which may reasonably be supposed to include the appetites of hunger, thirst, and sex; [45] and although the corresponding term "psychic passions" does not oc-

---

[41] *Rhetorica*, II, 1, 1378 a 20 f.; *Politica*, III, 15, 1286 a 33.

[42] κινήσεις ψυχῆς *Politica*, VIII, 7, 1342 a 8; cf. 5; also *De memoria*, I, 450 b 1.

[43] The summary statement, "By πάθη I mean anger, appetite, and the like" is in this connection not without significance, *Rhetorica*, II, 12, 1388 b 33.

[44] *De anima*, I, 1, 10, 403 a 25, b 8.

[45] *Ethica Nicomachea*, X, 3, 6, 1173 b 9. The term σωματικὰ πάθη is also used in another sense, namely, of such determinations of body as largeness, smallness, softness, roughness, etc., *De partibus animalium*, I, 4, 644 a 13.

cur, it seems to be implied in the description of the passions in the *Rhetoric:* they are what in the discussion of pleasure Aristotle called pleasures (and pains) of the soul.[46] But from all this we get no clear idea of a distinct class of mental phenomena such as might conceivably be derived from a careful psychological analysis. Much of what is said applies generally to all mental phenomena, e.g., to sense perception. What we find is rather a broad classification with indications of subordinate groupings in which, however, conations of various kinds, pleasure and pain, emotion, passion and sentiment are confused. The explanation of this lies deep in Aristotle's logical way of thinking in approaching the problems of psychology. The soul is for him a real entity ($o\vec{v}\sigma\acute{\iota}a$) with a definable essence which actively expresses itself in modes ($\vec{e}v\acute{e}\rho\gamma\epsilon\iota a\iota$) which are the realization of its proper function or end ($\vec{e}\rho\gamma o\nu$, $\tau\acute{e}\lambda o\varsigma$). Now the passions ($\pi\acute{a}\theta\eta$) do not belong to the "essence" of the soul; they are rather ways in which it is "affected." Hence, although Aristotle warns us that we must not neglect the passions, since they reflect light on the essence, it evidently depends very much on our prior conception of the soul's essence what we decide to contradistinguish from it as its passions. Aristotle's conception leads him to a very wide use of the latter term, one of its uses being to designate roughly what we, also for the most part very roughly, are accustomed to call emotions. But as we have seen, and as will further appear from the definitions to be presently given, this class of "passions," often spoken of as the passions generally, is of varied nature and indeterminate extent.[47]

[46] Cf. E. M. Cope, *Aristotle's Rhetoric,* note on II, 1, 8.

[47] On Aristotle's use of the terms $\pi\acute{a}\theta o\varsigma$ and $\pi\acute{a}\theta\eta\mu a$, see H. Bonitz, *Index Aristotelicus.* Etymology has suggested the use of "passions" in the text; the broader term would be "affections." The historical student of

In discussing the passions selected for special examination in the *Rhetoric,* Aristotle does not pretend to give a complete scientific account of them, such as would satisfy his own conception of scientific method; much less does he approach the subject from the point of view of a modern analytical psychologist. He neglects altogether the physical aspects of the passions and deals with them logically by definition and description with reference to their usual objects, occasions, and circumstances in a manner suited to the purposes of the rhetorician. His point of view, therefore, is that of a keen observer of human nature arranging his observations in some kind of classified order. For this sort of descriptive writing he sets the standard. Later writers, whether accepting or modifying his definitions, followed in the main his method for centuries. Certain of the passions, as, e.g., anger, were treated more fully and the passions in general were more systematically classified. Classification was pre-eminently the work of the Stoics. But so thoroughly did Aristotle do his work that in writings still extant we find none which surpasses it in abundance and sharpness of detail till we come in the Middle Ages to the great treatment of the subject by Thomas Aquinas.

In what follows it must suffice to note the definitions and a few of the more important observations. *Anger* (ὀργή) is " an impulse attended with pain to avenge openly an undeserved slight openly manifested towards ourselves or our friends." [48] The pain, however, which arises from the consciousness of frustrated desire, is only the predominant affection; there is besides an element of pleasure in the expectation of revenge. The objects of anger are individu-

psychology will not overlook the connection of both these terms with Aristotle's conception of the soul as οὐσία (an entity).

[48] *Rhetorica,* II, 2 ff., 1378 ff.

als; the slight may be contempt, spite, or insolence. Seasons, times, temperaments, and periods of life condition the passion. *Gentleness* or placability (πράϋνσις) is "a settling or quiescence of anger," arising, e.g., from lapse of time, or from the mood induced by mirth or prosperity, or from pity on seeing the object of our anger suffer greater injury than the anger itself would have inflicted. *Love* or friendliness (φιλία) consists in "wishing a person all the things you consider good, not for your sake, but for his, and readiness, so far as in you lies, to bring them about." *Hate* or enmity (ἔχθρα) is the opposite. Hate differs from anger in several respects. In anger we are moved by personal offenses; we may hate a man solely for his character. Anger is concerned with individuals; hatred may be directed towards a class. Anger seeks to make the evil it inflicts manifest; to hate, the exhibition of the evil is indifferent. Anger is necessarily painful, not so hate. Anger, finally, is not inconsistent with compassion; but if you hate a man, you aim at his destruction.

Fear (φόβος) is "a kind of pain or perturbation arising from the idea of impending evil hurtful to life or at least painful." Aristotle dwells particularly on the different circumstances which excite this feeling towards persons, such as their criminality, enmity, rivalry; he notes too an indirect source of it in compassion: what excites compassion when it happens or threatens to happen to others appears, generally speaking, as a thing formidable to ourselves. Aristotle makes use of this fact in his theory of tragedy. *Confidence* (θάρσος) is the opposite of fear, being a kind of hope attended with the idea of things salutary as at hand and of things formidable as either absent or remote. *Shame* (αἰσχύνη) is "a kind of pain or perturbation in reference to evils past, present, or future, that are thought to tend to discredit " (ἀδοξία). *Shame-lessness* (ἀναισχυντία) is disregard of and indifference to such things. Shame may be excited not only by acts which we condemn ourselves, but also by those deemed disgraceful by others. Before intimates we are ashamed only of things really shameful, before strangers of things that are conventionally so. But we must hold the persons and their good opinion in some regard; we do not feel shame before those whose opinions we despise. Regard for the consequences of others' opinions is also, in Aristotle's view, a potent factor, for we feel shame, he says, in the presence of slanderers and telltales, satirists, and comic poets. *Benevolence* (χάρις) is the feeling "which leads one to render service to another in time of need, not to repay past services or to obtain future rewards, but solely for his benefit." Past services, however, may be the occasion of its exercise, in which case it is gratitude. Its opposite is ill-will or churlishness.[49] *Pity* or compassion (ἔλεος) is "a kind of pain at the sight of great and undeserved misfortune in another, such as we deem liable to befall ourselves or any of our friends or relatives, and especially when it appears imminent." It is not felt either by the utterly miserable or by those who are enjoying supreme felicity; it requires a sense of liability to suffer and is found in those who have experienced suffering, are somewhat advanced in years, are physically weak or constitutionally timid, who have parents, wife, or children living, etc., and it implies belief in the existence of human virtue. Further, its object must not be too nearly related to us, for then the feeling is akin to that which we should have in similar circumstances for ourselves, namely, fear or horror. Aristotle tells the story of a Persian general who

[49] χαρίσεσθαι καὶ ἀχαριστεῖν, *Rhetorica*, II, 7, 1385 b 10.

wept at the sight of his friend's beggary, but not when he saw his own son led out to death. *Resentment* or indignation (νεμεσᾶν, νέμεσις), the correlative of pity, is pain at the sight of unmerited prosperity. This is a noble sentiment, not found in slavish, mean, or unambitious natures. It is, therefore, sharply differentiated from *Envy* or malice (φθόνος), where the feeling of pain at the prosperity has no regard to the merit of its possessor, but solely to the fact that another, our equal or similar, enjoys certain advantages. Envy is not especially limited to the poor; it is found in the ambitious and mean-minded, including persons engaged in important affairs or highly prosperous, but who think that the world is robbing them of their dues; and it is directed towards those who are near to us in time, place, age, or reputation, who are our rivals, who have attained a rapid success, whose success is our reproach, etc. *Emulation* (ζῆλος) is "a kind of pain at the sight of goods which we value and might acquire, when possessed by another naturally resembling ourselves, not because he possesses them, but because we do not." This, like resentment, is also a noble passion, being a spur to increased activity in the pursuit of worthy ends. The antithesis of emulation is a supercilious *Contempt* (καταφρόνησις).[50]

Following these definitions and observations Aristotle treats of the influence on the passions of the different periods of life, giving an admirable popular description of the common emotional characteristics of each, especially those of youth and old age; he notes, among other things, how the same emotion may spring up in different periods from different impulses: pity, for example, from generous good nature in youth, from feebleness and a

[50] *Ibid.*, II, 2–10, 1378–1387.

disposition to fear all manner of evils to themselves in the old.[51] But it must suffice to refer to this in passing. There is one other topic which must be touched on before concluding this part of our subject: Aristotle's teaching concerning the peculiar emotional effect of tragedy. What he says on this topic is tantalizing in its brevity. It is simply this, that tragedy, by exciting pity and fear, aims at a κάθαρσις of such emotions,[52] one of its effects being to alleviate these usually painful feelings with pleasure (κουφίζεσθαι μεθ' ἡδονῆς). Much has been written to elucidate the meaning of this teaching and the controversy is still from time to time renewed. Since the thoroughgoing investigation of the subject by Bernays, this much at least may now be regarded as settled: we must not follow Lessing in referring the *katharsis* to a moral purification of the character in respect to pity and fear and emotions of a similar nature generally, but must take the term in the medical sense, and the process indicated as limited to the emotions excited at the time by the tragedy itself.[53] The rest is largely conjecture. Aristotle possibly had in mind the teaching of the Hippocratean school regarding the process which takes place in the cure of disease; this school held that disease was eliminated by the morbid matter being " concocted out," it being thereby first raised to a condition of more intense activity.[54] Aristotle seems to be thinking of this analogy when he speaks

[51] *Ibid.*, II, 11 f., 1387 f.

[52] *Poetica*, 6, 1449: δι' ἐλέου καὶ φόβου περαίνουσα τὴν τῶν τοιούτων παθημάτων κάθαρσιν.

[53] J. Bernays, *Grundzüge der verlorenen Abhandlung des Aristoteles über die Wirkung der Tragödie* and a number of subsequent writings. Cf. G. E. Lessing, *Hamburgische Dramaturgie*, 75–78. Bernays' interpretation does not necessarily deny an effect on the character; only it was not of this that Aristotle was thinking.

[54] A view also found in Plato. Cf. H. Siebeck, *op. cit.*, 94 f. with references to Hippocrates, *Œuvres*, I, 444; Plato, *Republic*, X, 606 A (*Dialogues*, III, 321); *Laws*, VII, 790 A (*Dialogues*, V, 172).

of the effect of orgiastic music on persons suffering from
religious frenzy; he represents the music as effecting a
purgation ($\kappa\acute{\alpha}\theta\alpha\rho\sigma\iota\varsigma$) of the morbid state and a consequent alleviation of soul; and music, he says, has a similar
effect on pity and fear and other emotions.[55] If he conceived the action of tragedy in a similar way, his thought
would be something like this: the spectators enter the
theater with susceptibilities to certain emotions which in
real life are painful and burdensome; the tragedy represented on the stage excites these emotions in a very high
degree; but, if properly constructed and acted, it excites
them in such a way that the painful element is purged
away and the final result is pleasing and satisfying. It is
not necessary to suppose that he regarded pity and fear
as literally diseases; the analogy must not be pressed.
And it will be generally admitted that a true tragedy does
produce some such effects quite apart from the antiquated
medical analogy. But it is also obvious that we have here
no adequate account of the psychology of the process.
Even if we allow that the tragic pathos contains as its
essential ingredients pity and fear, or rather commisera-
tion and horror, we find no explanation of the all-important
difference between these feelings as aesthetically experienced and similar feelings when aroused by the dread
events of real life. Aristotle may possibly have conceived
the relief as brought about " by an appropriate adjustment of responsibilities and actions " exhibited in the development of the characters and the plot; [56] but this is
doubtful. Probably he thought no small part of it due to
the representation as such, for he elsewhere in the *Poetics*

---

[55] *Politica*, VIII, 7, 1342 a.
[56] As maintained, e.g., by A. W. Benn, " Aristotle's Theory of Tragic
Emotion," *Mind*, N.S., XXIII (1914), 84–90.

observes that we naturally take pleasure in imitation;[57] but this is clearly insufficient.

Turning now from the logical to the physical side of the emotional process, we find little on the subject in the genuine writings of Aristotle, but a good deal in the *Problemata,* which reflect the Peripatetic tradition, and in the works of other adherents of the school whose opinions it will be convenient to indicate in a general way here. The special contribution made by Aristotle himself was in the development of the doctrine of the pneuma. He holds the pneuma to be the congenital source of all vital power in the organism. By its spontaneous contraction and expansion it moves the limbs of the body mechanically.[58] It is the vitalizing material principle, the source of the animal heat, with its special seat in the heart, the power also by which the parts of the organism are differentiated in the embryo, and with its differences are correlated the differences of honor and dishonor in souls. It is not composed of the ordinary corporeal elements, but is of a nature akin to that of the stars.[59] As the source of heat, it is naturally bound up with the blood, and differences in the quality of the blood, according as it is warm or cold, thick or thin, and, especially, pure or impure, affect the whole mental and physical constitution.[60] Timidity is due to a thin, watery condition of the blood; the chill of fear comes from the congelation of the water. Bloodless animals are as a rule more timid than sanguine-

[57] *Poetica,* 6 ff.; 1449 b 24; 1453 b 12.

[58] *De motu animalium,* 10, 703 a 6 ff., reading κινοῦν, not κινεῖν (Bonitz, *op. cit.*).

[59] Namely, ether. *De generatione animalium,* II, 3, 741 b 37; 736 b 29 ff.

[60] *De partibus animalium,* II, 4, 651 a 12 ff.; cf. 667 a 9 ff. where Aristotle speaks of the influence of the anatomical character of the heart as affected by the vital heat on the emotional dispositions of courage and timidity.

ous and show the symptoms of fear in a marked degree; they become motionless, discharge the excrements, and, in some cases, change color.[61]

The *Problemata* give a list of the symptoms of fear in man that rivals in extent that found in Darwin or any other modern writer: cold and shivering, pallor of countenance, trembling of the body, of the hands, of the lower lip, trembling and shrilling of the voice, thirst, disturbed action of the heart — the pulsations becoming rapid (πυκνή) and pricking (νυγματώδης) — the drying up of the saliva, paralysis of the tongue, abnormal secretions of bile, puckering of the skin in the body generally and, in particular, in the scrotum, loosening and discharge of the bowels and bladder, breaking of wind, contraction of the testicles, and emission of semen. The prominent cause assigned to all these phenomena is a redistribution of the vital heat consequent on the withdrawal of the blood from the upper to the lower parts of the body and from the surface to the interior, the result being that the former parts are abnormally chilled, the latter abnormally heated. Thus the trembling of the voice is explained by the spasmodic action of the heart as the sustaining heat is withdrawn, causing a rapid succession of pulsations to be sent to the vocal organs instead of a single stroke. The shrilling of the voice is due to inability to set a sufficient quantity of air in motion, this loss of power being involved in the diminution of the vital heat. The thirst of fear arises from the excessive heating of the parts in the region of the stomach; the relaxation and discharge of the bowels and bladder come from a like excess of heat in the lower viscera, heat tending to liquefy as cold to solidify. A difficulty was found in the fact that different emotions have the same

[61] *Ibid.*, 650 b 20 ff.

or similar symptoms. Thus the heart is disturbed not only
in fear, but in rage. But there is a difference, it was said.
In fear the heat is withdrawing downwards, hence the
rapid, pricking movements; in rage, on the other hand, it
is crowding in upon the heart, hence the ebullition and
tumult of the passion. Again, there is trembling of the voice
due to departure of heat from the heart not only in fear,
but in grief or distress (ἀγωνία); but with this difference, it is said, that in fear the pitch of the voice is high,
in distress low. The ingenious explanation assigned for
this difference is that the heat in distress mounts upwards
instead of descending as in fear, evidence for this being
found in the blush of shame, a species of distress; but
when the heat ascends, it compacts the vital breath
(pneuma) used in vocal utterance and that, being more
slowly emitted, gives a lower pitch.[62] Another point in
which fear and distress agree — and also anger — is in the
matter of thirst; but it is noted that in fear, e.g., in
the panic of soldiers, the thirst demands abundance of
liquid for its satisfaction, whereas in distress, and also in
anger, all that is required is a swallow or a rinsing out
of the mouth. The explanation is that in distress and anger
the thirst is due to the withdrawing of the blood from
the tongue and is, therefore, only a quasi-thirst and not the
real thirst due to the exhaustion of the liquids in the
stomach, as in the case of fear. The cardinal point to be
explained, of course, was the movement and direction of
the heat. Why, for example, does it withdraw downwards
and inwards in fear? The answer is that the vital heat is
animated, and so, like a living creature, seeks to escape

[62] It may be noted that Zeno the Stoic is reported to have regarded voice
as a special faculty due to the pneuma stretching from the ruling faculty
of reason or intelligence to the vocal organs. Nemesius, *De natura hominis*,
96; Aetius, *Opera*, IV, 21, 4.

from that which threatens it; but as the object of fear is outside the body, the heat naturally moves inwards.[63]

Aristotle must not be held responsible for these special observations and explanations, though we may fairly ascribe to him the general direction which they follow and which was followed in the school for generations. Thus in the *Problems* falsely ascribed to Alexander of Aphrodisia (*ca.* 200 B.C.) we find a number of the same and similar questions raised and essentially the same principles used to solve them. Here " nature," which, following the usage of Hippocrates, appears as the synonym of the pneuma or physical soul, plays a prominent part in the crude teleologico-biological explanations. We turn pale in fear because " nature " and the provident force of the body seek the body's safety by retreating downwards; as we, when in danger, take refuge in our houses. We color in joy because " nature," self-taught, goes out to meet the object of pleasure, as we go to meet a friend or a child. We blush in shame because " nature," with a certain instinctive consciousness of evil, decently retires, like a well-born maiden, to the interior and inferior part of the body; and the blood, separating and diffusing itself, invests the body like a covering veil, as the maiden covers her face with her hands. Fantastic as these speculations appear, they nevertheless contain the germs of the idea that the organic expressions of the emotions are essential parts of the phenomena to be studied and that they arise in the main instinctively and spontaneously with reference to the welfare of the organism. This idea could not be duly developed until for notions of hot and cold, dry and moist, " nature," pneuma, vital heat, and the physical soul, there were substituted more precise conceptions of the nervous

[63] *Problemata*, XI, 31, 32, 902; XXVII, 9, 948.

system with its sensory, motor, and vaso-motor functions, and of the whole organism as related to its environment through a process of evolution. But this is a late achievement of the present time, and we are still far from the solution of the problems of emotion. The imperfect physiology of the ancients naturally led to much futile writing; on the other hand, the interest taken in the study of the phenomena led to some not unimportant observations of fact and not infrequently to explanations which were correct in principle. The same writer who compares the blush of shame to a girl's hiding of her face with her hands notes with scientific acuteness the closing or semi-closing of the eyes in the enjoyment of voluptuous pleasure, ascribing the phenomenon to the withdrawal of energy, or as we should say attention, from external perception and its absorption in the voluptuous sensations themselves; and explains the sighs of grief, love, and anger as phenomena of physical oppression and relief involving at once the condition of the lungs and of the heart.[64]

[64] The numbers in the Pseudo-Alexander *Problemata* treating of the physical phenomena of the emotions are I, 11–16, 19–21, 31, 102, 105, 118; II, 26, 35. (*Theophrastus et Aristoteles,* 257–267.)

CHAPTER III

ANCIENT THEORIES OF THE AFFECTIONS

Psychological interest in ancient doctrines of the affections — using the term broadly to denote what are popularly called the feelings, including emotions — naturally
attaches itself chiefly to the teachings of Plato and Aristotle. Nevertheless, to the historical student the discussions in this field in the post-Aristotelian schools are far
from negligible. To begin with, there is no subject in
psychology on which more came to be written. The direction taken by philosophy, which now seeks, characteristically, to find for the individual a way to happiness and
security of soul in the midst of a changing and troubled
world, brought with it an increased interest in his pleasures, pains, and so-called passions. In literary output the
lead is taken by the Stoics. Treatises on the passions are
ascribed to Zeno,[1] Chrysippus,[2] Posidonius,[3] Hecato,[4]
Herillus,[5] and Sphaerus.[6] Cleanthes wrote one on pleasure.[7] Dionysius Heracleota also wrote one on pleasure in
four books and another in two books on freedom from
passion ($\pi\epsilon\rho\lambda$ $\dot{\alpha}\pi\alpha\theta\epsilon\dot{\iota}\alpha s$).[8] Seneca composed a treatise
in three books on the single passion of anger.[9] All the
Stoics deal with the passions in their ethics. Indirectly
also they contributed largely to the discussion by arousing

---

[1] Diogenes Laertius, *Works,* VII, 4, 110.
[2] C. Galen, *Opera omnia,* V, 404. Diogenes Laertius, *op. cit.,* VII, 111.
[3] C. Galen, *loc. cit.*
[4] Diogenes Laertius, *op. cit.,* VII, 110.
[5] *Ibid.,* 166.
[6] *Ibid.,* 178.
[7] *Ibid.,* 175.
[8] *Ibid.,* 175.
[9] *De ira* (*Opera,* I, 1–154).

opposition. The principal controversy turned on the question whether the passions were, or were not, " contrary to nature." The Stoics — to speak broadly — said that they were and should therefore be extirpated; the Peripatetics denied this and required only that they should be controlled. Here, as throughout the ancient period, and, for that matter, throughout almost every period, the motive underlying the examination of the affections is practical. In post-Aristotelian philosophy the ethical interest, and along with this the religious, is everywhere paramount. The primary question relates to the worth and place of the affections in an ideal scheme of life; it is for the sake of this alone that any inquiry is undertaken as to their nature and conditions. This interest vitiates the scientific analysis and perplexes the psychological theory. But, in spite of this, an advance is made in several directions. The complexities of the phenomena are more fully realized; distinctions are recognized that had previously been overlooked; new aspects of mental life are brought to light in respect to the attitude the mind is capable of taking towards its affections; and some new views are developed regarding their function. Now for the first time a serious attempt is made to classify them, and the connections of the affections with the bodily processes, if not more satisfactorily explained than heretofore in detail, are in some respects more precisely conceived in theory.

An illustration of this advance may be found in the Epicurean doctrine of pleasure. Regarding pleasure as an affection proper to the animal nature and pain as alien thereto,[10] Epicurus (341–270 B.C.) agreed with Aristippus (*ca.* 435–356 B.C.), the founder of ancient hedonism, in holding that all pleasure is good and that to attain the

---

[10] Diogenes Laertius, *op. cit.,* X, 34.

greatest amount of pleasure is the supreme aim of life. But he observed, as bearing on this question of the greatest amount, what seemed to him an important difference among pleasures. Admitting that all pleasures are alike in intrinsic quality, as pleasures, he called attention to the fact that they are not all alike in intensity or durability. Some are intense, but transitory, others tranquil, but more lasting. Aristippus, followed by Plato, had made all pleasure consist in motion. Epicurus finds two distinct kinds of pleasure; one consists in motion ($\dot{\eta}$ κατὰ κίνησιν), and one is a state of rest ($\dot{\eta}$ καταστηματική). To the former he reckoned bodily pleasures and the more boisterous emotions, to the latter the calmer pleasures of the mind.[11] This distinction is of the utmost importance for him in its bearing on the question of the best life. The Cyrenaics held that bodily pains were worse and bodily pleasures greater than mental. Epicurus maintains the opposite. He notes, in the first place, what Plato had made the basis of his condemnation of (bodily) pleasure as illusory, the contrast effects in the experience of the bodily affections as tending to diminish the force of the argument for their intrinsic intensities. He notes, further, a difference in the time relations of bodily and mental affections: bodily pain, he says, is acute but transient, whereas the mind feels grief with reference not only to the present, but also to the past and future; and similarly of pleasures.[12] The mental, therefore, possesses the wider range as well as the greater independence. But his main argument against the Cyrenaics is derived from considerations regarding the varying relations of pleasure, pain, and desire. Desire is want and want is painful; abolish or moderate the desire and you therewith abolish or moderate the pain. Now if pain is taken away

[11] *Ibid.*, 136.   [12] *Ibid., 29*, 140.

we rejoice though no bodily pleasure follows, while if pleasure is removed, pain does not necessarily follow.[13] Again, it is only when we are pained at the absence of pleasure that we feel the need of pleasure, but when we feel no pain, we no longer need pleasure.[14] Herein lies the condemnation of unnecessary and inordinate desires. Desires which, if unsatisfied, do not lead to pain are unnecessary; if, on the other hand, the natural desires, failure to satisfy which is painful, are violent and obstinate, that is sure proof that they are mixed with false opinion.[15] All this points to an ideal of felicity conceived as consisting in freedom from pain and intemperate desire and all disturbing affections of the soul. This is the famous Epicurean imperturbability (ἀταραξία). "By pleasure," writes Epicurus in a letter to Menoeceus, "we mean the absence of pain in the body and trouble in the soul. It is not an unbroken succession of drinking feasts and of revelry, not sexual love, not the enjoyment of fish and other delicacies of a luxurious table that produce a pleasant life; it is sober reasoning, searching out the grounds of every choice and avoidance, and banishing those beliefs through which the greatest tumults take possession of the soul." [16] Such pleasure is unaffected by time; infinite and finite time both have equal pleasure, if we measure the magnitude of pleasure by reason; the man who has found the true happiness would not have that happiness increased though he lived forever. Nor is it added to by the pleasures of the flesh; it is only diversified.[17]

The psychological significance of this teaching lies not

[13] M. T. Cicero, *De finibus bonorum et malorum,* I, 56 (*Opera,* VI, 103).
[14] Diogenes Laertius, *op. cit.,* X, 20, 128.
[15] *Ibid.,* 149 f. Maxims 30–32.
[16] *Ibid.,* 131 f. The letter to Menoeceus has been translated by R. D. Hicks, *Stoic and Epicurean,* 172.
[17] *Ibid.,* 144 f. Maxims 17, 19.

in its attempt to measure the quantity of one kind of pleasure as compared with another, nor in its attempt to fix the limit to the variations of pleasure in intensity; it lies rather in its suggestion of a sort of generalized pleasure consisting in a habit or frame of mind. Aristippus had made the best life consist in a sum of pleasures strung along in a series; according to Epicurus it is not found in any sum or succession of pleasures, but in a stable disposition of soul which meets with the same cheerful serenity all the vicissitudes of life. This disposition is molded by philosophy. Particularly interesting is the psychology involved in a famous application of this teaching. " Even in the hour of death, when ushered out of existence by circumstances, the mind does not fail to enjoy the best life," [18] writes Epicurus; even if the wise man were put to the torture, he would still be happy. Even in the bull of Phalaris, Cicero quotes him as saying the wise man would exclaim, " How sweet, how indifferent this is to me! " [19] Something of this Epicurus himself claims to have experienced. Writing to a friend from his death bed, he tells him that the disease — the acutely painful malady of renal calculus — had reached its height, but it is all outweighed, he says, by the mental pleasure derived from the memory of a life devoted to philosophy.[20] It is easy to accuse him of exaggeration. The doctrine at least is plain: the mind habituated to reflection has the power, by voluntarily dwelling on the memories of past pleasures, of detaching itself from present ills and thrusting them aside. As, according to another Epicurean doctrine, vulgar fears produce all manner of disturbances in the body and

[18] *Ibid.*, Maxim 20.
[19] *Tusculanae Disputationes*, II, 7 (*Opera*, VI, 287). Cf. Diogenes Laertius, *op. cit.*, X, 118.
[20] H. Usener, *Epicurea*, 143.

are only to be eradicated by enlightenment, so contrariwise the pains of the body may be surmounted and suppressed by the tranquil soul: the sage can enjoy felicity
even on the rack. Marcus Tullius Cicero (106–43 B.C.)
found in this doctrine a subject of pleasantry; modern psychology, better acquainted with the facts, is disposed to
admit the experience among the possibilities of suggestion
and of the imagination.[21] We shall meet with a similar
doctrine in the Stoics and in Plotinus, the latter of whom
speaks for the mystics generally.

Regarding the physical basis and bodily symptoms of
the affections Epicurus has nothing to say worth record-
ing. He thought of the soul as an assemblage of atoms
within the body, the irrational part distributed throughout the body, the rational more especially in the chest; [22]
and this perhaps made it possible for him to conceive of
the mind as rationally affected apart from the participation of the rest of the body. Titus Lucretius (*ca.* 98–55
B.C.) gives a vivid description of the more striking symptoms of fear and anger, but his explanations do not go beyond a superficial use of the recognized Hippocratean
principles.[23]

Of the other doctrines of Epicurus about the affections,
the best known is that which places them among the
criteria of truth; but this appears to amount only to the
assertion that their presence points to a corresponding
object to be approached or shunned.[24] Less well known,
but more significant, is his contribution to the theory of

---

[21] Cf. V. Brochard, "La morale d'Épicure," *L'Année philos.* (1903),
8–12; F. Pillon, "Sur l'imagination affective," *Rev. philos.* LXIII, 240 ff.

[22] Diogenes Laertius, *op. cit.,* X, 66.

[23] *De rerum natura,* III, 152–160, 288–306; IV, 859 ff.

[24] Diogenes Laertius, *op. cit.,* X, 31; Sextus Empiricus, *Adversus
Mathematicos,* VII, 203. Cf. E. Zeller, *Philosophie der Griechen,* III, 1,
386, n. 2.

the origin of language, a subject in which the Greeks had for some time shown a lively interest. Was language " natural " or " conventional "? The question is discussed at length by Plato in the *Cratylus*. The view of Epicurus was that " the names of things were not originally due to convention, but in several tribes under the influence of special feelings and special presentations of sense primitive man uttered cries. The air thus emitted was molded by their individual feelings or sense presentations and differed according to the differences in the regions which the tribes inhabited. Subsequently whole tribes adopted their own special names " for convenience in communication.[25] This vague anticipation of modern teaching is in principle as far as any ancient writer on the subject went, but we do not know how far Epicurus carried it out, if at all, in detail.

We turn now to the Stoics. The peculiar theme of the Stoics is the passions. In reporting their doctrines it is even less possible than elsewhere to keep the psychological aspects free from the ethical, for a condemnation of the " passions " is contained in their very definition. A " passion," namely, was defined, in general, as a perturbation of soul ($\pi\tau o\iota\alpha$ $\psi\upsilon\chi\dot{\eta}s$) which consisted in an excessive or overpowering impulse ($\dot{o}\rho\mu\dot{\eta}$ $\pi\lambda\epsilon o\nu\dot{\alpha}\zeta o\upsilon\sigma a$, $\dot{\epsilon}\kappa\phi\epsilon\rho o\mu\dot{\epsilon}\nu\eta$), such movement or process being irrational or insubordinate to reason ($\ddot{\alpha}\lambda o\gamma os$, $\dot{\alpha}\pi\epsilon\iota\theta\dot{\eta}s$ $\lambda\dot{o}\gamma\omega$) and contrary to nature ($\pi a\rho\dot{\alpha}$ $\phi\dot{\upsilon}\sigma\iota\nu$).[26] It is a phenomenon of un-

[25] Diogenes Laertius, *op. cit.*, X, 75; Letter to Herodotus has been translated by R. D. Hicks, *op. cit.*, 275.

[26] J. Stobaeus, *Eclogae*, II, 7, 1, p. 39, 5 W (quoting from Zeno); 7, 2, p. 44, 4. Clement of Alexandria, *Stromateis*, II, 460; Diogenes Laertius, *op. cit.*, VII, 110; Cicero, *Tusculanae Disputationes*, IV, 11, 47 (*Opera*, VI, 343 ff.). Cf. Aspasius, *Aristotelis Ethica Nicomachea*, 12, 44. G. Heylbut, *Commentaria in Aristotelem graeca*, XIX, 1, $\dot{o}\rho\mu\dot{\eta}\nu$ $\sigma\phi o\delta\rho\dot{\alpha}\nu$ $\ddot{\eta}$ $\dot{o}\rho\mu\dot{\eta}\nu$ $\ddot{\alpha}\lambda o\gamma o\nu$, $\lambda a\mu\beta\dot{\alpha}\nu o\nu\tau\epsilon s$ $\tau\dot{o}$ $\dot{\epsilon}\nu a\nu\tau\dot{\iota}o\nu$ $\tau\hat{\omega}$ $\dot{o}\rho\theta\hat{\omega}$ $\lambda\dot{o}\gamma\omega$, (understanding a violent impulse or an unregulated one as the opposite of normal thought).

regulated impulse. That it was irrational and contrary to
nature was implied in the Stoic conception of reason and
nature, for this — the two are one — allowed of no excess. The term here translated impulse (ὁρμή) nearly
corresponds in the Stoic terminology to what Aristotle
called ὄρεξις (which the Stoics made a species of ὁρμή)
denoting all instinctive tendencies to action. In itself it is
necessary, normal, and natural.[27] But " passion " is by
definition excessive impulse, one not conforming to the
natural ends of life; it is a movement by which the subject
of it is violently carried away. Hence it is contrary to that
inner thought (λόγος) that rational order, or principle
of order, which the Stoics regarded as constitutive of
" nature " generally, and the essence of reason, they
conceived, was free from its disturbance. The word by
which they designated this freedom — " apathy " (ἀπά-
θεια) — must not be taken to mean what we mean by
the term; it does not mean a pathological state devoid of
all feeling. It meant rather a settled state of freedom from
the perturbations which prevent the exercise of the normal
functions in fulfilling the rational aims of human living.
Apathy is, therefore, not itself the end, but the negative
condition of its attainment.

The question at issue between the Stoics and their opponents was not whether such perturbations were evil and
freedom from them good, but whether the disturbances
which they named as such — anger, fear, love, hate, etc. —
were of such a nature that, in order to secure the best life,
every disposition to these affections must be, as they held,

---

[27] *Scholia ad Lucian, Luciani Samosatensis Opera,* IV, 211, ὁρμῆς
μὲν κινητικὰ ὅσα κατὰ φύσιν. Stobaeus, *op. cit.,* II, 160, 162, φορὰ ψυχῆς
ἐπί τι τῶν ἐν τῷ πράττειν, φορὰ διανοίας (the product of the soul
in its activity becoming the product of the intellect), quoted by A. E.
Chaignet, *Histoire de la psychologie des Grecs,* II, 140 f. Cf. Cicero, *De
finibus bonorum et malorum,* III, 16 ff. (*Opera,* VI, 157 ff.).

eradicated, or whether by suitable discipline they might not be converted into occasions of virtue. The Stoic view was that the soul which is subject to passions is in a condition of weakness, is lacking in " tone." The passions are diseases of the soul analogous to those of the body, and like the latter may be distinguished as to constitutional morbid propensity, the state of disease itself, and the incidental sickness or infirmity.[28] Freed from the passions, the soul is all strength ($\mathit{i}\sigma\chi\acute{\upsilon}s$), force ($\kappa\rho\acute{\alpha}\tau os$), tone ($\tau\acute{o}vos$), in good tone ($\varepsilon\mathit{\dot{\upsilon}}\tau ov\acute{\iota}a$), and mistress of itself ($\mathit{\dot{\varepsilon}}\gamma\kappa\rho\acute{\alpha}\tau\varepsilon\iota a$).[29]

That the condemnation of the passions did not involve the repudiation of every affection is seen in the admission by the Stoics of a class of " good affections " ($\varepsilon\mathit{\dot{\upsilon}}\pi\acute{\alpha}\theta\varepsilon\iota a\iota$, Cicero, constantiae). They included under this term cheerfulness ($\chi a\rho\acute{\alpha}$), discreetness ($\varepsilon\mathit{\dot{\upsilon}}\lambda\acute{\alpha}\beta\varepsilon\iota a$), and a virtuous habit of will ($\beta o\acute{\upsilon}\lambda\eta\sigma\iota s$), each with subdivisions. Thus under virtuous will we have good will or benevolence ($\varepsilon\mathit{\dot{\upsilon}}vo\acute{\iota}a$), affability ($\varepsilon\mathit{\dot{\upsilon}}\mu\acute{\varepsilon}v\varepsilon\iota a$), cordiality ($\mathit{\dot{\alpha}}\sigma\pi a\sigma\mu\acute{o}s$), and affectionateness ($\mathit{\dot{\alpha}}\gamma\acute{\alpha}\pi\eta\sigma\iota s$); under discreetness, shame or the fear of dishonor ($a\mathit{\dot{\iota}}\delta\acute{\omega}s$), and purity ($\mathit{\dot{\alpha}}\gamma v\varepsilon\acute{\iota}a$); under cheerfulness, wholesome pleasure in the use of the higher senses ($\tau\acute{\varepsilon}\rho\psi\iota s$), good-fellowship ($\varepsilon\mathit{\dot{\upsilon}}\phi\rho o\sigma\acute{\upsilon}v\eta$), and good temper ($\varepsilon\mathit{\dot{\upsilon}}\theta\upsilon\mu\acute{\iota}a$).[30] These vari-

---

[28] Regarding the distinction of these factors: $\varepsilon\mathit{\dot{\upsilon}}\varepsilon\mu\pi\tau\omega\sigma\acute{\iota}a$ $v\acute{o}\sigma\eta\mu a$, and $\mathit{\dot{\alpha}}\rho\rho\acute{\omega}\sigma\tau\eta\mu a$, see Stobaeus, op. cit., II, 93, 1; Diogenes Laertius, op. cit., VII, 115; Cicero, Tusculanae Disputationes, IV, 12, 13, 26 (Opera, VI, 341 ff.).

[29] Cf. A. E. Chaignet, op. cit., II, 149.

[30] Diogenes Laertius, loc. cit. The English terms translating the Greek in the text are at best only approximately equivalent; in both languages the terms are equivocal. Alexander of Aphrodicias, Commentaries in Aristotelis Topica, II, 96, 181, says that the first to distinguish $\mathit{\dot{\eta}}\delta ov\acute{\eta}$, $\chi a\rho\acute{\alpha}$, $\varepsilon\mathit{\dot{\upsilon}}\phi\rho o\sigma\acute{\upsilon}v\eta$, and $\tau\acute{\varepsilon}\rho\psi\iota s$ was the Sophist Prodicus. He himself regards the words as all meaning substantially the same thing. The Stoics, he says, distinguished $\mathit{\dot{\eta}}\delta ov\acute{\eta}$, an irrational elation; $\tau\acute{\varepsilon}\rho\psi\iota s$, pleasure from hearing; $\varepsilon\mathit{\dot{\upsilon}}\phi\rho o\sigma\acute{\upsilon}v\eta$, pleasure from discourse. Others, however, stated the distinctions somewhat differently; thus Andronicus, $\Pi\varepsilon\rho\grave{\iota}$ $\Pi a\theta\mathit{\tilde{\omega}}v$ (J. v. Arnim, Stoicorum veterum fragmenta, III, 97,) defines $\tau\acute{\varepsilon}\rho\psi\iota s$ as "pleasure from sight or hearing." Cf. L. A. Seneca, Epistolae ad Lucilium, 59, 2 (Opera, II, 265).

ous affections and dispositions, regarded as habits or general modes of feeling and behavior, are set over against the turbulent " passions " as species of quiet emotion befitting the wise.[31] In addition to these two classes of " passions " and " good affections," the one remorselessly condemned, the other approved, the Stoics recognized two other classes of affections: the natural affections arising from kinship, companionship, etc., and physical pleasures and pains as distinguished from the elation or depression of mind attending them. The former, although not having the character of good affections as dispositions of a virtuous will, were regarded by the Stoics as good, or at least as not in themselves evil, and the latter as at least necessary; but as to the goodness or badness of bodily pleasures and pains, opinions differed.[32]

Understanding, then, that the passions formed only one class of affectional states, we return to their definition. As already described, they are regarded by the Stoics as commotions arising in unbridled, irrational impulse, and therefore contrary to nature. It was agreed on all hands that such ebullitions of impulse had a disturbing effect on the intellectual processes, and this was considered a reason why the wise man would seek to be rid of them.[33] But they not only disastrously affect judgment, they take their rise, according to the Stoics, in judgment, and from this point of view the various passions are described as kinds of judgment or opinion. The Stoic psychology thus recognizes in a " passion " the three elements or aspects of judgment, feeling, and impulse, without, however,

[31] Cicero, *Tusculanae Disputationes*, IV, 12 f. (*Opera*, VI, 341 f.).

[32] On this difference of opinion see Stobaeus, *op. cit.*, II, 58, 3 ; Sextus Empiricus, *op. cit.*, XI, 73. On the fourfold distinction of affectional states made by the Stoics, cf. R. D. Hicks, *op. cit.*, 102.

[33] Themistius, *Aristotelis de anima*, 90 b. (*Paraphrases Aristotelis librorum quae supersunt*, II, 197, 24) ; Cicero, *Academicorum posteriorum*, I, 38 (*Opera*, VI, 77).

sharply discriminating between them. The aspect at first emphasized was the movement of the soul towards or away from the object, that is, the impulse; but this movement had to be accounted for, and the most obvious explanation was that the mind entertained a certain opinion concerning the good or evil nature of the object. At any rate they looked upon this opinion as an integral and essential part of the process. Accordingly the " passion " itself came to be defined as primarily an opinion or judgment. Here is the origin of the intellectualistic theory of emotion which has prevailed in the schools even down to recent times.

This intellectualistic tendency was more especially developed by Chrysippus (280–209 B.C.).[34] The passions, according to him, are erroneous, ill-founded judgments (κρίσεις, in Cicero's phrase, *judicia levitatis*).[35] Another form of the doctrine spoke of the passion as a " sudden " or " fresh " — meaning, perhaps, hasty — opinion (δόξα πρόσφατος; Cicero, *Opinio recens*).[36] But Chrysippus went still further. Regarding the whole soul as rational, he refused to allow that the passions were affections of the lower part of our nature which reason had to control, as Plato had taught, and boldly declared them to be diseases of the reason itself. As Plutarch (*ca.* 46–120) states the doctrine, lust, anger, fear, etc., were perverse opinions

[34] In his work *On the Passions,* numerous fragments of which are preserved in C. Galen, *De Hippocratis et Platonis Decretis,* (*Opera omnia,* V, 181 ff.).

[35] Cicero, *De finibus bonorum et malorum,* III, 31 (*Opera,* VI, 163). Cf. Themistius, in *Aristotelis de anima* (*op. cit.,* III, 5).

[36] Posidonius, whom Galen, *op. cit.,* V, 416, follows, interprets the phrase as referring to the suddenness or imminence of the falsely opined good or evil; Cicero, *Tusculanae Disputationes,* III, 75 (*Opera,* VI, 335), interprets it as referring to the fresh vigor of the judgment. The text suggests that a " snap " judgment would come near to expressing its meaning; it is at any rate an immature opinion, the opposite of the calm, reflective judgment of the wise man. Cf. H. Siebeck, *Geschichte der Psychologie,* I, 233.

and false judgments, not formed in some inferior faculty, but such motions back and forth, such operations and energies of the whole directive faculty, as are ready to be turned with the greatest ease this way or that, " like the sudden motions and eruptions in children, the violence and impetuosity whereof, by reason of their imbecility and weakness, are very fleeting and inconstant." [37]

A consequence of the Stoic conception of the passions as judgments, or as essentially involving judgment, and as perversions of reason, or at least hostile to reason, was that passions in the proper sense of the term were denied to brutes. " For," they argued, " all disorders and perturbations of the mind arise from a disregard of reason; hence they arise only in men; for though beasts act similarly, they are not similarly perturbed." [38] Seneca, in denying that brutes have anger while allowing them ferocity, puts the general contention neatly by saying " dumb brutes do not have human affections, but have similar impulses (*similes illis quosdam impulsus*)." [39]

The doctrine of Chrysippus that the " passions " are affections of the reason was vigorously criticized by Posidonius (130–46 B.C.), who represents the mediating tendency of the later Stoicism, which sought to reconcile the general spirit of the teachings of the Porch with those of the Academy and the Lyceum.[40] It seemed impossible to Posidonius to use this theory to account for the origin of

---

[37] *De virtute morali,* 7 (*Morals,* III, 478). Cicero, *Tusculanae Disputationes,* IV, 22 (*Opera,* VI, 347). Zeno seems to have been content with the traditional view of the faculties, distinguishing three according to Q. S. F. Tertullian, *De anima,* XIV, eight according to Nemesius, *De natura hominis,* 96.

[38] Cicero, *Tusculanae Disputationes,* IV, 31 (*Opera,* VI, 349.)

[39] *De ira,* I, 3 (*Opera,* I, 6.)

[40] A full report of his arguments is given by Galen, *De Hippocratis et Platonis Decretis,* IV, and V ; cf. Sextus Empiricus, *Adversus Mathematicos,* VII, 93.

a passion. How can that which is irrational spring from reason? It is incredible that a faculty should give rise to a movement whereby its own action is impeded. Moreover, the doctrine fails to explain the accepted facts: why, e.g., ideas of even the greatest good and evil arouse no passions in the wise, while fools are upset by the most trivial things; why the same or similar ideas excite different persons differently; why emotion should be so much influenced by habit. Why, further, should a " recent " or " sudden " opinion cause passion, and one old and familiar not? And how is it possible to suppose that reason at one and the same time knows a thing to be evil and yet falsely opines it to be good? For these and other reasons Posidonius reverted to the Platonic tripartite division of the soul, emphasizing the dualism of the rational and irrational faculties and ascribing the passions to the latter. He regarded, moreover, the " concupiscible " and " irascible " susceptibilities from which the passions spring as determined by the constitution of the body. Thus the passions are neither judgments nor necessary consequences of judgments; they often arise from a movement in the " passional " side of our nature without any judgment at all. Posidonius has, therefore, no difficulty in ascribing passions to the lower animals. The basis of the passional disposition lies in the congenital constitution: the broad-chested and warm are courageous; the broad-hipped and cold, timid in men and in brutes. And similarly of the other passions.[41]

The tendency of the later Stoics to adopt the views of their opponents in explaining the operations of the passions is well illustrated by a story told by Aulus Gellius.[42] He

---

[41] Cf. E. Zeller, *Die Philosophie der Griechen*, IV, 579 ff.; H. Siebeck, *Geschichte der Psychologie*, I, 234 f.
[42] *Noctes Atticae*, XIX, 1, 592.

was once in the company of an eminent Stoic philosopher during a storm at sea. The passengers were much interested to see how a Stoic philosopher would behave under such circumstances, and even forgot their own peril as they watched him grow pale with fear. After the storm was over, one of the passengers, a luxurious Asiatic, asked him banteringly why he, a philosopher, had shown fear, while he himself had been unmoved. To this the philosopher replied by citing the answer given on a similar occasion to a questioner of similar character by Aristippus the Socratic: " You had no cause for anxiety for the life of a miserable profligate, but I had reason to be alarmed for the life of Aristippus." But when Aulus asked him seriously for the explanation, he replied by taking from his wallet a book of Epictetus in which he read that, according to the Stoics, certain impressions called *phantasiae* are made on the soul by certain objects and that it is not in our power to determine whether or when we shall be invaded by them, so that the soul, even of the wise man, may be moved for a time by grief or fear; but this does not imply that the soul accepts, approves, or consents to these impressions. It is within our power to refuse to do so, and the difference between the fool and the wise man lies precisely in this, that the one yields and consents to them and the other does not. Augustine, who repeats the tale, concludes that there is no difference, or next to none, between the opinion of the Stoics regarding the passions and that of other philosophers; for all agree, he says, in holding that the mind and reason of the wise man is not subject to them.[43]

There are, however, four ways at least in which this freedom from subjection to the passions may be conceived. (1) The wise man does not experience them at all; his

[43] *De civitate Dei*, IX, 5.

whole mind is one perpetual calm. This was the orthodox Stoic view as popularly understood. (2) The perfect man experiences them, but always as expressions of his virtuous character, always at the right time, in the right way, towards the right objects. This represents the Peripatetic ideal. (3) The good man is temporarily affected, but quickly recovers and through the exercise of habits of control and considerations of reason moderates the force of the passion and shortens and deflects its course. This may be called the common-sense view; it is the one suggested on the surface by the story of Aulus Gellius. (4) The man both is and is not affected by the passion. The passion is a natural phenomenon which takes place in him and of which he is aware, while at the same time he himself, or some deep underlying part of himself, remains unmoved by it; in the midst of his fears he is fearless, his ebullitions of anger leave him calm. His attitude towards his emotions is detached. This may be called the mystic view. Epicurus maintained it, as we have seen, in respect to pain. Plotinus, as we are soon to see, maintains it on the basis of his metaphysical conception of the soul. It naturally connects itself with the dualism of the Platonic-Aristotelian philosophy in sharply separating the reason from the other faculties; so far as this separation was made by the Stoics, it fell in very well with certain of their tendencies also. There is a suggestion of it beneath the surface in the narrative of Aulus Gellius. Plotinus uses the very conception of the *phantasiae* there referred to in explaining the turbulence of emotions such as fear. The view thus recurrent in the ancient world persists to be dealt with by modern psychology in the light thrown upon the facts chiefly, it must be admitted, from the region of the abnormal, though it does not follow that they are to be themselves regarded as pathological.

A great deal of ingenuity was expended by the Stoics on the classification of the passions. This, along with the definitions they gave of the several kinds, was their most distinctive contribution to the psychology of the subject on its systematic-formal side. All the passions, they held, were fundamentally four: appetite, or desire (ἐπιθυμία, Lat., *libido*), fear (φόβος, Lat., *metus*), pleasure, or delight (ἡδονή, Lat., *voluptas, laetitia*), and pain, or grief (λύπη, Lat., *aegritudo*). As irrational impulses (ὁρμαί) they were defined as follows: appetite (desire) is an irrational inclination towards (ὄρεξις); fear, an irrational recoil from (ἔκκλισις); pleasure (delight), an irrational expansion or elation of mind (ἔπαρσις); pain (grief), an irrational contraction or depression of mind (συστολή).[44] On the theory that the passions were, or had their roots in judgments or opinions regarding good and evil in their objects, they were defined, typically, in this way: appetite is an opinion of coming good, which, if already present, would be of advantage; fear is an opinion of impending evil which seems intolerable; pleasure (delight, joy) is a " recent " opinion of a present good wherein it seems right to the mind to be elated; pain (grief, sadness) is a " recent " opinion of a present evil wherein it seems right to the mind to be dejected and contracted.[45] Over against three of these " irrational passions " were set the three " good affections " as rational feeling-tendencies: cheerfulness is opposed to pleasure as rational elation, discreetness to fear as rational disinclination, will to appetite as rational inclination. No good affection corresponded to grief.

[44] Andronicus of Rhodes, Περὶ Παθῶν, 1, 11; Stobaeus, *op. cit.*, II, 90, 7 W. The germs of this fourfold division are in Plato, *Philebus*, 32 B, 39 C (*Dialogues*, III, 168, 177). It is unfortunate that the same words, ἡδονή and λύπη, here used for emotions, have also to do duty with the Stoics for simple sensory pleasure and pain.

[45] Cicero, *Tusculanae Disputationes*, IV, 7, 14 (*Opera*, VI, 342 ff.). Cf. Stobaeus, *op. cit.*, II, 88, 6 W.

Under the four fundamental passions the Stoics included all manner of emotions and emotional dispositions of which they disapproved. Andronicus of Rhodes (*ca.* 70 B.C.) enumerates twenty-seven kinds of appetite, thirteen of fear, five of joy and twenty-five of sadness or grief.[46] Other lists were shorter. We may take as representative the classification of Johannes Stobaeus (*ca.* 450). Here under appetite are grouped anger and its varieties (resentment, rage, wrath, spite, bitterness), passionate love, longing, yearning, love of pleasure, wealth, honor, etc.; under fear, timidity, anxiety, consternation, shame, confusion, religious fear, awe, and dread; under the pleasure-passion, malevolent pleasure, joy in unexpected good fortune, pleasure in magic tricks (γοητεῖαι), etc.; under the pain-passion, envy, emulation, jealousy, pity, mourning, heaviness of spirit, dumb grief, trouble, anguish, poignant grief, distress. Stobaeus remarks that some of these terms, e.g., pity, envy, and malevolence, point to the source of the emotion, while others, like poignant grief and dread, refer to some peculiarity in the emotion itself.[47]

As already indicated, the definition of the class varies according as the passion is conceived more prominently as " impulse " or as " opinion." Thus fear is defined as " an opinion of impending evil that seems intolerable," but also as " an avoidance of evils without reason accompanied by a low and broken condition of the vital energies." [48] Sometimes the two conceptions are combined as in the definition of fear as " a recoil by reason out of control arising from

---

[46] J. v. Arnim, *op. cit.*, III, 96 f. For other lists see Diogenes Laertius, *op. cit.*, VII, 111 f.; Cicero, *Tusculanae Disputationes*, IV, 7 (*Opera*, VI, 342); Nemesius, *De natura hominis,* 19–21.

[47] *Eclogae*, II, 90, 7; 92, 18. The definitions help to suggest the corresponding English terms, but as already suggested there can be no thought of exact equivalence.

[48] Both given by Cicero, *Tusculanae Disputationes*, IV, 6, 13; 7, 15 (*Opera*, VI, 342 ff.). Cf. Diogenes Laertius, *op. cit.*, VII, 116.

an opinion of impending evil." [49] The different passions included in each class are defined in general by adding to the class name the specific difference. Thus, to illustrate, envy is defined as grief at another's prosperity, that prosperity causing no injury to the envious person; jealousy, as grief at another's possessing what one has desired for oneself; pity, as grief at the misfortune of one whose suffering is undeserved; mourning, as grief at the death of one dear to us. [50] Such definitions, which follow in the main the model set by Aristotle, we feel to be largely verbal and only at the best the rough preliminaries of a psychology; and it must be admitted that the Stoics are more concerned with discriminating and fixing the meanings of terms than with the analysis of the states of mind for which the terms stand. It was recognized, indeed, that the distinctions were made from different points of view, but the analysis in this direction is not carried very far. [51] Nevertheless, we should not underestimate the attempt to classify the emotions, to reduce them to a few fundamental forms, to group under each form its several varieties, and to take the terms used in common speech to denote the diversities of emotional experience and stamp them with a precise, technical meaning. Such an undertaking is an essential part of science. Even the discrimination of synonyms involves a certain amount of psychological analysis. Down to the end of the seventeenth century the classical writers on emotions all followed the lead of the Stoics in seeking to reduce, classify, and logically define them. Nor is the problem wholly foreign to the psychology of our own time, though we are probably more keenly aware of the limitations of language to express the subtle shadings of feeling and find other as-

---

[49] Stobaeus, *op. cit.*, II, 172. Cf. H. Siebeck, *op. cit.*, I, 504.
[50] Cicero, *Tusculanae Disputationes*, IV, 17 f. (*Opera*, VI, 345).
[51] Cf. H. Siebeck, *op. cit.*, I, 2, p. 233.

pects of the psychological problem both more important and more fruitful. Along with its obvious shortcomings it must, however, be regarded as a conspicuous merit of the first attempt of this sort that it selected as the basis of classification such fundamental characteristics of the emotional process as the antitheses of elation and depression and the opposed tendencies of approach and recoil, rather than the simple qualities of pleasantness and unpleasantness.

Occasionally a single passion was made the subject of more extended discussion. The most famous work of this kind was the treatise by Lucius A. Seneca (*ca.* 4 B.C.–65 A.D.) in three books on anger.[52] Seneca, after giving other explanations, defines anger with considerable psychological insight as " a sudden and powerful agitation of the mind moving straight forward to the execution of vengeance, an agitation combined with will and judgment." [53] He disregards the distinctions drawn by Greek writers between the different kinds of anger, because of the lack of corresponding Latin terms to express them, and skillfully marks off the differences himself by such epithets as bitter, sharp, peevish, clamorous, etc.[54] In the process itself he distinguishes the involuntary arousal of the impulse, the conscious idea that what has been felt or perceived demands punishment, and the arrest of the reason in the further development of the passion.[55] Along with these and other observations of permanent psychological value Seneca interestingly notes the manifestations of anger in the mob.[56]

[52] Among other works on the same subject we have Plutarch, *De cohibenda ira* (*Opera moralia*, III, 178–208), and a treatise, Περὶ 'Οργῆς, discovered at Herculaneum, the author of which was the Epicurean Philodemus, a contemporary of Cicero's (*De ira*, 164–165).
[53] *De ira*, II, 3 (*Opera*, I, 43).   [54] *Ibid.*, I, 4 (*Opera*, I, 9).
[55] *Ibid.*, II, 1 ff. (*Opera*, I, 40). Cf. H. Siebeck, *loc. cit.*
[56] *Ibid.*, III, 2 (*Opera*, I, 93).

The physiological side of the affections receives more or less explicit recognition in all the schools. On the basis of principles expounded in the medical writers of his time Plato goes into details in the *Timaeus;* illustrations abound in the pseudo-Aristotelian *Problemata.* Theophrastus, Strato, Alexander of Aphrodisia, and other Peripatetic writers, while upholding the doctrines of the master in other respects against divergent views of Platonists and Stoics, follow and develop his teaching in this direction also.[57] The Stoics seem to have the material for a more special development in the form peculiar to them of the doctrine of the " pneuma." They held the pneuma to be the very soul and substance of the universe, a substance possessing the highest degree of vital energy, perfect in " tone," with power to expand spontaneously and disperse itself without loss. It is in nature akin to air and fire which form, as it were, the soul of the physical world, as earth and water form its body. The soul of man consists of pneuma, an ethereal substance present in the generative seed and continually nourished by exhalations from the blood.[58] This pneuma soul is not, as the Epicureans held the soul to be, merely contained within the body; it pervades the body and is the vitalizing principle which holds its parts together. Now the obvious application of these conceptions

[57] For illustration see H. Siebeck, *op. cit.,* I, 3, pp. 224 ff.

[58] Cf. Chalcidius, *Timaeus Platonis,* (*ca.* 220); Epiphanius, *Adversus haereses,* III, 2, 9: πολυχρόνιον πνεῦμα, (everlasting breath, soul); Galen, *De placitis Hippocratis et Platonis,* II, 8, reported the ascription by Diogenes the Babylonian of the view that the soul was pneuma and nourished by the blood, to all three founders of the school; Eusebius, *Praeparatio evangelica,* XV, 21, 3; 20, 2, and Theodoretus, *De curandis graecorum affectionibus,* V, 2, referred to the soul-pneuma as a sensitive exhalation (ἀναθυμίασις), a view ascribed to Zeno and Cleanthes. Souls were supposed to be continually generated from moist substances, a conception connected apparently with the doctrine of Heraclitus of the "way up and down," (Diogenes Laertius, *op. cit.,* IX, 8). Justus Lipsius in his *Physiologiae Stoicorum,* III, Diss. VI and IX, quotes numerous passages from Stoic writers and their doxographers which show that the identification of the soul with the material pneuma was a common doctrine of the Stoics in all periods of their history.

in a doctrine of the passions would be to say that, so far
as the passions appear as disturbances in the soul, they are
the transcription and counterpart of actual physical movements or of qualitative changes of the pneuma; then the
doctrine might be called upon to point out the particular
modifications of the pneuma corresponding to each kind of
passion and the relation of these modifications of the
pneuma to those states of the body which it pervades and
controls. This program is not carried out. What we find
are merely such general indications as those which follow.

Chrysippus represented the modifications of the pneuma
that take place in emotion as modifications of tone. The
tone of the soul is either normal or defective. This must be
taken literally; the reference is not merely to consciousness, but to the material, conscious pneuma; i.e., either in
good tone or lacking in tone (εὐτονία, ἀτονία), just as the
nerves or tendons are either tonic or relaxed. Chrysippus
uses this analogy: there is that in the soul, he says, which
resembles the nerves or tendons, so that we can say metaphorically (κατὰ μεταφοράν) that it is " nerved up " or
" enervated." Now when one is struck with terror or suc-
cumbs at the prospect of gain or loss, the soul, i.e., the
pneuma, is enervated; it is in a state of weakness, and it is
from this weakness that evil actions arise.[59] In another
passage he draws the analogy from general bodily conditions. As in the body there is strength and weakness, good
tone and poor tone, and, relative to these conditions, health
and disease, so the soul is said to be strong or weak, firm or
flabby, etc.[60] In addition, comparison is made with the
balance of the constituent elements of the body. As health
consists in a normal, disease in a disproportionate relation

[59] Galen, *op. cit.*, IV, 6. Cf. J. v. Arnim, *op. cit.*, III, 123.
[60] *Ibid.*, V, 2. Cf. J. v. Arnim, *op. cit.*, III, 120.

of the hot, cold, moist, and dry elements, so the soul is fair or foul according as the reason is thus or thus disposed with reference to its proper parts.[61] This conception of the soul's tone is perfectly general; it neither tells us what particular differences of tone correspond to the different passions nor how these differences are brought about. When, going beyond this, Stoic writers treat of the physical phenomena of emotion, they, like the writers of other schools, make use of common observation and current medical theory.

Seneca, in a passage which sums up much of the ancient speculation and which seems to be the source of a great deal of the later writing on the subject, connects the dispositions to specific emotional reactions with the body's temperament and the various periods and conditions of life. As is the prevailing temperament of the body, so is the character of the man. Heat in excess makes men irascible, cold disposes them to timidity. Dealing with the passion of anger, Seneca remarks that the common opinion that anger is excited by effervescence of the blood about the heart is due simply to the fact that the breast is of all parts of the body the hottest. Where the moist element abounds, anger develops gradually, time being required to generate the requisite heat. Thus in women and children anger is sharp, but of little consistency at first, though it may swell in volume as the movement continues. In middle life — the dry period of life — anger is vehement and robust, but is not likely to be greatly augmented. The aged, sick, and convalescent are rather irritable and querulous than angry, the heat being diminished by lassitude and loss of blood. Wine increases anger because it inflames; people of a florid complexion are irascible because of their heat.[62] Plutarch,

---

[61] *Ibid.*, V, 2 ff. Cf. J. v. Arnim, *op. cit.*, III, 121 f.
[62] *De ira*, II, 19 (*Opera*, I, 63).

eclectic, platonizing, writes in a similar vein, picturesquely describing also the visible effects of anger on gait and voice, on the color and aspect of the countenance, which it " doth swell and puff very indecently," on gesture, and on speech.[63]

All this falls short of a thoroughgoing theory of the relation of the conscious affection to its bodily conditions, concomitants, and expressions. Hot, cold, dry, moist, and pneuma seem to be so many independent principles each of which is called upon in turn to play its part, but the intimate, organic connections of which, if any such exist, are not made plain. No doubt it lay in the spirit of Stoic metaphysics to regard these principles not as independent, but as differentiated modes of the all-pervading world-substance, and accordingly to view the affections as ultimately conscious modes of an organic cosmic process and more immediately of the bodily processes in the individual organism. But so far as appears, no Stoic writer develops this doctrine or avails himself of the general conception in his observations and explanations in detail. That the emotions were in a sense physical must, of course, have been the opinion of all the philosophers who held the soul to be a material substance or composed of material substances; although if conceived, as the Epicureans conceived it, as merely contained within the body, it was always possible to think of its motions as arising spontaneously and as unaffected by general somatic influences. That all ordinary emotions took their rise in the body and had a bodily aspect, was a natural inference from Plato's doctrine of the mortal soul, was implied in Aristotle's doctrine of the soul

---

[63] *De cohibenda ira*, 6, 10 (*Opera moralia*, III, 185, 192). According to orthodox Stoic doctrine all the passions have their seat in the heart, the center of the psychic life. Nemesius, *op. cit.*, 19, 20, makes the organ of grief the orifice of the stomach.

as the body's " entelechy " and his explicit statement of
the twofold way in which an emotion may be viewed, and
was expressly asserted by adherents of the Peripatetic
school.[64] But the most pronounced formulation of the doctrine in antiquity is found in a writer in whom perhaps we
should least expect to find it, namely, in Plotinus (*ca.* 204–
270), who teaches emphatically and unqualifiedly that all
ordinary affections of the soul are nothing but the soul's
consciousness of the affections of its body and that an emotion, for example, was, in modern phrase, simply the consciousness of the bodily changes, or the emotion's " expressions," as they occur. In the way in which he connects this
doctrine with a metaphysical conception of the soul, he is
far enough removed from the metaphysical reserve commonly professed by modern physiological psychology, but
his teaching is for that reason perhaps all the more illuminating. It is at any rate sufficiently interesting both in
itself and as the final term of the historical development in
the ancient world to attract our attention.

The interest of Plotinus in the affections is metaphysical
and ethical; he seeks to vindicate in his theory his conception of the soul's essential independence and impassivity.
The soul is in the body, he holds, not as a body is in space,
or an attribute in a substance, or a part in the whole, or the
whole in a part, or sensible form in sensible matter, but as
the power exerted by an agent is in its instruments, as
" fire " is in the warmed and illuminated air. It energizes
and animates the whole body and in specific ways the different parts of the body, giving to them thereby a " trace "
or " impress " ($\H{\iota}\chi\nu o s$, $\H{\iota}\nu\delta a\lambda\mu a$) of itself. In virtue of its
intimate connection with the body the soul is conscious of
the body's affections and may identify itself with them and

[64] Cf. H. Siebeck, *op. cit.,* 225.

with their tendencies; but we must not think of the soul as affected nor, on the other hand, suppose the body sensibly affected without the soul. On this basis Plotinus enunciates the following specific doctrine of pleasure and pain. " Pain," he says, " is awareness ($\gamma\nu\hat{\omega}\sigma\iota\varsigma$) of the recoil ($\dot{\alpha}\pi\alpha\gamma\omega\gamma\dot{\eta}$) of the body in the process of being deprived of the impress of the soul; pleasure is the living being's awareness of the process of restoration of the harmony of the impress of the soul in the body." [65] When, for instance, the body is wounded, the affection is perceived and localized, and we say, e.g., that the finger feels pain and that the man feels pain, since it is the man's finger. But we cannot properly say, according to Plotinus, that the mere awareness of the sensation is pain. The consciousness is cognition having pain for its object, and the cognition, he urges, is not affected, otherwise it would not be able to give a true account of the affection. Pleasure and pain, then, are not affections of the soul, but of the living body. In the living body, similarly, arise the appetites which spring from these affections. This is shown by the varying character and strength they assume in the different periods of life. But although the soul is not in itself affected, still as the " nature " operating in the process and seeking to direct the appetites, it is cónscious of the body's limitations and identifies itself, as it were, with its longings. Plotinus follows Plato in making the seat of the bodily appetites the region about the liver and the seat of the nobler impulses of defense in the heart.[66]

Passions or emotions, defined broadly as states accompanied by pleasure or pain, originate, according to Plo-

---

[65] *Enneades*, IV, 4, 19. In 18 pain is referred to the unsuccessful struggle of the inferior nature to achieve a firm union with the superior.
[66] *Ibid.*, IV, 4, 20, 21, 28.

tinus, in two ways. Some arise in ideas (ἐπὶ δόξαις), e.g.,
fear from the thought that one is at the point of death, joy
from expectation of good fortune. But some arise independently of ideas and themselves take the lead, involuntarily
exciting the opinion.[67] Idiopathic emotion is recognized by
other ancient writers; Posidonius, for example, makes use
of it in criticizing the Stoics; but in no ancient writer perhaps is it so explicitly intimated as in Plotinus that the
emotion thus arising independently of ideas goes on to complete itself by developing its own motive or justification.
Plotinus insists, further, that an opinion is not an emotion
in the faculty or process of thinking (ἐπὶ τῷ δοξάζειν);
thought and emotion belong to quite distinct spheres
(ἐν ἄλλῳ . . . ἐν ἄλλῳ). Nevertheless the two are intimately related in the emotional process. The idiopathic
emotion, as we have seen, gives rise to an opinion and an
opinion may be the starting point for an emotional disturbance which, when occurring, produces a certain consciousness of itself with which the opinion is conjoined.[68]

If now we ask, what is the cause of the feeling, e.g., of
fear, it is not enough to say, as is commonly alleged, a disturbance arising from anticipated evil; for how can any
disturbance arise directly from an opinion? An opinion, the
representation (φαντασία), e.g., that some evil is about to
befall, is a pure act of cognition and is neither itself an emotion, nor, apart from accessory conditions, capable of exciting one. Plotinus finds these accessory conditions in an

---

[67] *Ibid.*, III, 6, 4: τὰ δέ ἐστιν ὡς ἡγησάμενα αὐτὰ ἀπροαιρέτως ἐμποιεῖν,
ἐν τῷ πεφυκότι δοξάζειν τὴν δόξαν.
[68] Cf. *Ibid.*, IV, 4, 23 (ὁ δ'ἐκτὸς τῆς δόξης φόβος ἐλθὼν ἄνωθεν αὖ ἀπὸ τῆς
δόξης οἷον σύνησίν τινα παρασχὼν τῷ λεγομένῳ τῆς ψυχῆς φοβεῖσθαι).
If ἄνωθεν κ.τ.λ. is taken with ἐλθών, the main assertion appears to mean
that the feeling of fear is consciously taken note of, but if, as seems
possible, the clause goes with παρασχών, we have the more interesting view
indicated that the conscious emotion is determined and defined by the idea
of its object as the exciting cause.

unconscious or subconscious psychical process mediating certain changes in the body — a kind of obscure thought and indistinct imagination (ἀμυδρὰ οἷον δόξα καὶ ἀνεπί-κριτος φαντασία) operating in the organism, and to be compared with the blind force of Nature producing the particulars of existence. The modern psychologist, according to his predilection, will think here of associational processes, psychical or psychophysical dispositions, instincts, Freudian complexes, etc.; Plotinus contents himself with the simple general conception of a blindly working function of the "psyche" animating the body. What he urges is that the whole process thus far considered, the whole process short of the bodily changes, consists not of "passions," but of the soul's activities. But what follows (τὸ δ'ἀπὸ τούτων) is a complex of bodily affections — trembling, paling, speechlessness, etc. In the last resort it is not the soul which is perturbed, but the animated body. The soul is immediately, sensibly aware of this perturbation and associates with it the idea of impending evil. In this synthesis the emotional process is completed.[69]

A similar explanation is given of anger. We are angry, indeed, not only at our own body's sufferings, but also at the sufferings of our friends and at violations of the proprieties generally. Perception and understanding, therefore, play a part in the emotion, and we might consequently be tempted to look for the origin of the impulse outside of the merely vital energies of the organism. On the other hand, we cannot help noticing that the disposition to anger follows the constitution and condition of the body. In animals as in men the hot-blooded and bilious are quick to take offense, the cold-blooded and those deficient in bile,

---

[69] Ibid., III, 6, 5 : καὶ συνέζευκται τῇ ταραχῇ ἡ τοῦ προσδοκωμένου κακοῦ εἰκών.

slow; and the very same person is more disposed to the emotion in sickness than in health, when hungry than when sated. These facts make it clear, in the view of Plotinus, that the beginnings of anger are due to the bodily constitution and that the liver and the blood are, as it were, the animating principles of its motions. When, therefore, the predisposed body is affected, the immediate effect is a stirring up of the blood and the bile. Now the soul perceives this, and the imagination which unites the soul with the state of its body, allows reason to become conscious of the pain — the breaking up of the natural harmony of the animated body — and the soul which, from its own superior point of view, looks on injustice or injury of any sort in a calmly rational manner and is not inclined of itself to enter into the affections of the body, is made the ally of the passion. This view of the origin of anger is confirmed by the observation that those who are little inclined to indulge their bodily appetites and, in general, pay slight attention to the body, are relatively less disposed to this and other similar affections. Let it not be objected that if the principle of the passion is placed in the vital forces of the organism — in the terminology of Plotinus, the vegetative soul — then trees ought to feel anger. The obvious reply is that trees have neither blood nor bile; if they had, but were without sensation, there would only be an effervescence of these humors, but if sensation were added, then doubtless there would also be an impulse to repel the injury.[70]

Although thus referring bodily pleasures and pains and emotions like fear and anger to the physical organism, Plotinus admits spiritual feelings and impulses, such as the longing for knowledge and pleasure in its possession, excited by the mind itself.[71] The rational soul is thus not ab-

[70] *Ibid.*, IV, 4, 28.   [71] Cf. H. Siebeck, *op. cit.*, I, 2, p. 328 f.

solutely impassive. In particular he contends for a state of happiness (τὸ εὐδαιμονεῖν) possible to one who finds pleasure in the good. He who has within himself the unchangeable good will not be moved by common griefs, happiness will not fail him even in the bull of Phalaris.[72] This doctrine of a source of feeling independent of the body is common to many ancient writers, from whom it passes over to the Church Fathers, being, we may say, a practically indispensable component of any orthodox interpretation of Christian doctrine. Also the doctrine of the power, latent in such a transcendent source of feeling, of resisting ordinary afflictions and annulling the force of physical pain, plays a not inconsiderable part in the psychology of the mystics and in thinkers generally who, from Plato and Aristotle down, mark a sharp cleavage between the rational or spiritual part of our nature and the sensible. We have already noticed the part it plays in the teachings of Epicurus and the Stoics.

In concluding this study of affective psychology in writers after Aristotle it may not be inappropriate to sum up briefly the impressions left by a survey of the work of Greek writers generally in this field. The whole movement, as already observed, is controlled by practical interests and the results are conditioned in no small degree by ethical and metaphysical considerations which to the modern mind lie outside of psychology, but which, nevertheless, are constantly tending, explicitly or implicitly, to intrude themselves. In ancient writers the intrusion is explicit; it furnishes the motive, sustains the inquiry. In spite of this we have here the fruitful beginnings of a science.

---

[72] *Enneades* I, 4. Cf. Dionysius Areopagita, *De divinis nominibus*, II, 9, quoted by Thomas Aquinas, *Summa Theologica*, q. XXII, a. 3, Prima secundae partis: *non solum discens, sed etiam patiens, divina* (divine not only while learning, but also while undergoing hardship).

Human nature is subjected to observation and analysis, theories regarding human affections are developed of wide-reaching influence. The conspicuous illustrations are the doctrines of Plato and Aristotle concerning pleasure and pain. Sir William Hamilton held that all theories of pleasure and pain were modifications of these two, and much might be said for this opinion.[73] Even Kant held with Plato that all sense pleasure is conditioned on pain.[74] The affinity of modern biological theories of pleasure and pain to the views of Aristotle is so obvious as to have become a commonplace. On the formal logical side the emotions are treated by the Greeks with unusual fullness, not altogether to advantage. This is particularly conspicuous in the endeavor of the Stoics to define and classify them. On the other hand, much attention is given to the physical phenomena, the tendency being to regard the bodily commotion as of the very essence of the emotional " affect." And although the Hippocratean physiology employed to explain the more striking phenomena of the coarser emotions is now antiquated, the influence of conceptions like those of the body's humors, vapors, and temperatures, and particularly of the pneuma, is seen throughout the whole of the Middle Ages, in the psychology of the Renaissance, in the " animal spirits " of Descartes and Malebranche, and in still later writers, as well as in current forms of popular speech. Finally, there appears in these ancient writers a growing sense of the complexity of the problems: states of feeling are mixed and compounded, pass into one another, variously influence and are in turn influenced by thought and action, develop into habits and dispositions, inhibit one another, grow out of and react on bodily condi-

---

[73] *Lectures on Metaphysics*, I, 444 f.
[74] *Anthropologie in pragmatischer Hinsicht* (*Werke*, VII, 58).

tions and are no less manifestly related to conditions in the social environment. The facts are noticed and partly accounted for. Some of them, as, e.g., the apparent detachment of mystical feeling, to a marked degree, and all of them to a certain extent, evidently contain problems that point to the future, to a more developed psychology and to a more developed physiology.

CHAPTER IV

Patristic and Medieval Doctrines of the Affections

Christianity created, along with a new world of ideas and a new attitude towards life, a new order of emotional experiences. The Christian religion is rich in sentiment; the Christian life, as well in its beginning as in the various stages of its development, realizes some of the profoundest and some of the subtlest stirrings of feeling of which the human soul is capable. These phenomena, taking their place beside, or grafted upon, the other phenomena of the reflective life, are of the greatest psychological interest. But the interest they aroused was in the first instance not psychological, but practical. And even as objects of mere scientific reflection, the practical point of view is never absent in the treatment of them throughout the period with which we have now to deal. In the broadest sense of the term psychology, indeed, becomes one of the leading interests of the period. For as the soul and its concerns are of chief importance in the Christian salvation, attention was naturally directed to the soul and the things belonging to it as objects of special reflection. Along with its theology the Church developed its anthropology. But it is the first characteristic of the thinking of the period that the two go together and that in the combination of the two theology takes the lead. Psychology and anthropology enter the circle of the theological and the therewith connected metaphysical disciplines. What is true of psychology in general is true in particular of the treatment of the affections. In ultimate reference the discussion has regard to the content of the Christian faith and the aims of the Christian life. A second characteristic of the treatment of psychological questions in this period is its dependence on conceptions derived from the Greeks. In adapting the material to the Christian system both the matter and the form had to be reshaped, but the fundamental framework on which this new pattern was woven was supplied by Plato and the Stoics and, after the twelfth century, by Aristotle. The physiological doctrines were derived from the Hippocratean tradition, which Galen systematized. In spite of this dependence, first on the presuppositions of Christian doctrine, then on the psychological and physiological conceptions of the Greeks, the period was not altogether unfruitful in original observations, particularly on the matter furnished by religious experience, nor altogether lacking in theoretical considerations of importance. In both of these regards Augustine is pre-eminent. In the Middle Ages Bonaventura, the Victorines, and the mystics of a later time often show noteworthy appreciation of the psychological relations of the religious affections. Over and above this, we find in the Schoolmen attempts to reduce the chaos of emotional phenomena to order. In this regard the name pre-eminent above all others is that of Thomas Aquinas. To be sure the great systems are largely schematizations in which matter is sacrificed to form.

The most and almost the only systematic account of the affections in the Patristic period is that given by Nemesius, Bishop of Emesa in Phoenicia, probably in the second half of the fourth century. As this account is typical and to a large extent the prototype of the medieval constructions, it may here serve to give a brief report of it with incidental notice of some of the opinions of the other Fathers, reserving only a special place for St. Augustine. The work of

Nemesius, *De natura hominis,* formerly ascribed to Gregory of Nyssa, consists of forty-four chapters dealing with the whole nature of man, the soul, the union of the soul and the body, the constitution of the body, the powers of the soul, the freedom of the will, and divine providence.[1] Chapters 16–21 treat of appetition, desire, pleasure (joy), pain (sorrow), fear, and anger. The author shows familiarity with the leading scientific, anthropological, and psychological conceptions of the Greeks and makes a not unskillful use of them in the development of his own views, which are eclectic. The soul is divided into two parts, the rational and the irrational. This formal distinction is the generally accepted doctrine of the Fathers and the Schoolmen. The irrational part has two divisions, one subject to reason (λόγῳ ἐπιπειθές), the other not. By the latter is meant the so-called vegetative faculty, the power regulative of waste, repair, etc. in the physical organism. The part subject to reason is subdivided into the " concupiscible " faculty of appetite or desire (τὸ ἐπιθυμητικόν) and the " irascible " faculty of anger, resentment, or resistance of evil (τὸ θυμόν), both being forms or modes of the " orectic " conative activity, the *vis appetitiva* of the Schoolmen. This Platonic division was also a generally accepted doctrine. The reference, however, of the passions or affections to the concupiscible and irascible appetites and the limitation of the latter to the irrational part of the soul, introduced for Christian thinking a difficulty. While Clement of Alexandria (150–211) could speak of the passions as " demons " and look to an ascetic ideal in the release and separation of the soul from the body,[2] his contemporary at Carthage,

---

[1] J. P. Migne, *Patrologiae, graeca,* XL, 803–818, with additional notes to p. 843. For a critical account of Nemesius' psychology see B. Domanski, *Die Psychologie des Nemesius.*

[2] Cf. P. Siegert, *Die Psychologie des T. Flavius Clemens Alexandrinas,* 45 ff.

Quintus S. F. Tertullian (160–220), protests against the invariable attribution of the irascible and concupiscible faculties to the irrational nature on the ground that our Lord possessed both and that righteous anger belongs to God.[3] Firmianus Lactantius (*ca.* 325) carried this view still further, distinguishing between affections that are peculiar to man and are grounded in human infirmity, such as fear, envy, bodily pleasure, and carnal appetites, and those which, like graciousness, anger, and pity, belong also to God.[4] Either expressly or by implication an irascible faculty is quite generally ascribed to the Deity by Christian writers, and in the course of time both an irascible and a concupiscible appetite are assigned by some to the rational part of the soul.[5]

Nemesius regards the passions or affections (πάθη) as belonging to the very constitution of a living being (συστατικὰ τῆς ζωώδους οὐσίας) and essential to its existence. This view was the one generally held. The Fathers as a rule combatted what they understood to be the Stoic doctrine, that the passions were naturally evil. They become evil only in combination with reason and will. But the natural impulses in which they arise are given to the animals for defense.[6] Man in addition possesses for a similar end, according to Lactantius, a benevolent impulse, an affection of piety, *humanitas*.[7] And not only so, but as he, and

---

[3] *De anima,* 16.

[4] *De ira Dei,* 15, 8–12.

[5] The division of opinion on the question whether in passion the whole soul, including the reason, is affected, is seen by contrasting, e.g., the Neoplatonic view of Synesius (early fifth century) that the mind is in perpetual repose, *Oratio de regno,* 10, with that of Tertullian, who holds that mind, soul, and body are all involved in the emotional process, *De anima,* 12.

[6] Lactantius, *Institutiones divinae,* VI, 18, 22 f. A curious detail in the doctrine of Lactantius is that he denies all pleasure to the lower animals, *praeter unam voluptatem, quae ad generandum pertinet* (except the one enjoyment which relates to reproduction), *ibid.,* 20, 2. Cf. for a similar view of a natural teleology of the passions, Gregory of Nyssa, *De hominis opificio,* 18.

[7] *Op. cit.,* VI, 10, 3; III, 23, 9, 10. *Epitome Institutionum,* 38, 8.

especially Theodoret (386–457) insist, the affections are incentives and material not only to vice, but to virtue.[8] The ambiguity in the conception of this term affections (πάθος, *affectus*) is commented on in this connection by Nemesius. He distinguishes between affections of the body and those of the soul. The general conception of " animal affection " is that of a state accompanied by pleasure or pain; a " psychical affection " is specifically a movement of the appetitive faculty, or an irrational movement of the soul, sensed under the idea of apprehension of good or evil. Similar distinctions are made by Basil the Great (*ca.* 330–379).[9] Nemesius further distinguishes between passion as a movement contrary to nature induced by some alien influence (παρὰ φύσιν, ἐξ ἑτέρον ἐν ἑτέρῳ) and a normal fulfillment of function (ἐνέργεια κατὰ φύσιν). The same term, e.g., anger, may express a state or process of either sort, just as the beating of the heart may denote either a natural function or, when excessive, an abnormal affection. In this general distinction, in the definition of *passio* or *motus contra naturam* and in the classification and definitions of the several passions, Nemesius is closely followed by John of Damascus (*ca.* 754) who appears from frequent references to have been the chief medium for the transmission of his influence to the Middle Ages.[10]

Of the two forms of the orectic faculty, the *concupiscibilis* is divided into pleasure and pain, according as the appe-

---

[8] Lactantius, *Fragmenta* (F. S. Brandt and G. Laubmann, *Fragmenta in corpore scriptorum ecclesiasticorum latina*, XXVII, 157). Cf. F. Marbach, *Die Psychologie des Firmianus Lactantius*, 56–61 ; Theodoretus, *De curandis graecorum affectionibus* (J. P. Migne, *Patrologiae, graeca*, LXXXIII, 844–951).

[9] *Epistolae*, CCLXI : " it is the property of the flesh to undergo division, diminution, dissolution ; of flesh endowed with soul to feel weariness, pain, hunger, thirst, and to be overcome with sleep ; of soul using body to feel grief, heaviness, anxiety, and such like. Of these some are natural and necessary . . . others come of evil will."

[10] John of Damascus, *Institutio elementaris*, 9 ; *Expositio fidei orthodoxae*, II, 13–16.

tite is fulfilled or thwarted. But with reference to good and evil the division is fourfold, a separate passion arising according as each of these objects is apprehended as present or as future. Good expected is desire; present, pleasure; evil expected is fear; present, pain. Thus the Stoic division of the passions, familiar to the Fathers,[11] is here referred to the concupiscible faculty; anger (θυμός) being thus separated from desire (ἐπιθυμία), of which it was regarded by the Stoics as a species. But in this separation Nemesius naturally falls into a certain embarrassment, for anger is, or at least sometimes includes, an impulse to retaliation. If it is thus defined, he says, it is thought of as *combined* with desire; he thinks that the distinction of the two is sufficiently secured by defining anger proper in physiological terms as an ebullition of the blood about the heart arising from evaporation and troubling of the bile. In other respects he somewhat simplifies the Stoic classification, naming only three species of anger, four of pain (sadness), and six of fear. His definition of pleasure is Aristotle's; from Plato he adopts the distinction of pleasures true and false.[12]

As was to be expected, we find nothing original in the Fathers on the physiology of emotion, although the subject occasionally engages their attention. Nemesius, e.g., accepts from Galen the opinion that the seat of grief is in the orifice of the stomach.[13] Lactantius records that anger was assigned by some to the gall-bladder, fear to the heart, joy

---

[11] Cf. Jerome, *In Ezechielem*, I, 7.

[12] That an affection must necessarily be referred either to the concupiscible or to the irascible appetite exclusively is recognized as false by Gregory of Nyssa: pain and pleasure, he shows, derive their material from both: *De anima et ressurectione*, 56. This agrees with the twofold division of Nemesius; but the latter is evidently inconsistent with a fourfold division in which pleasure and pain figure as only two of the varieties. The confusion arises from the ambiguity of the Greek terms for pleasure (ἡδονή) and pain (λυπή), the same terms being used for the feelings generally and also for the special emotions of joy and grief and their congeners.

[13] *De natura hominis*, 20.

to the spleen, and sexual pleasures to the liver, but prudently refrains from expressing an opinion of his own, considering the whole matter too obscure to admit of any settled conclusion.[14] Probably the most interesting deliverance on this subject in the Patristic period is found in Gregory of Nyssa (331–394). In criticizing the doctrine that the soul is seated in the heart, he mentions as the principal support for this view the affection of the heart in emotion. But the best medical opinion, he says, is that the affection of the heart in emotion is secondary and derived and that the primary phenomenon is the contraction or dilatation of the vessels conveying the bodily fluids. He then goes on to indicate how the theory is applied to the phenomena of grief. In this, as in every painful emotion, the vessels are contracted. The first effect of this is to check the normal process of evaporation and force the contained substances into the lower cavities; hence deep breathing, sighs, and groans, the object being to relieve the pressure on the lungs. The palpitation of the heart is caused by the action of the gall which, owing to the general contraction of the vessels, is driven into the orifice of the stomach; hence too the sufferer's pale and yellow look. Weeping is due to the fact that the evaporations in the vessels being checked and their functions in the viscera impeded, they rise to the head, accumulate as moisture and descending to the eyes are pressed out by the eyelids as tears. In joy we have opposite effects. The vessels are dilated and all the viscera conspire to enhance the vitality. In particular, respiration is invigorated, the volume of air inhaled is increased, as indicated by the puffed-out cheeks; to facilitate its passage nature provides for its expulsion through the mouth; and this, according to the representation, is laughter.[15] Crude as it is,

---

[14] *De ira Dei,* 14, 4 ff.   [15] *De hominis opificio, 12.*

a pronounced vasomotor theory of this sort appearing at this time is not without historical importance.

We now turn to Augustine (*ca.* 430). Like the other Fathers of the Church, but to a still greater degree, his interest in psychology was practical. He will know nothing but God and the soul, and the sole object, he declares, of studying the soul is to learn one's own weakness and God's perfection. He does not treat of the affections in any systematic fashion; he touches upon them only incidentally, either in connection with his description of his own experiences in the *Confessions* or in the course of expositions of Christian doctrines or matters pertaining to the religious life. And yet Augustine possesses for our subject unusual interest. As no other among the Church Fathers, he emphasized the worth of the individual soul and gave expression to its inner conflicts, its deeper discontent. Himself a man of strong passions, he was also gifted beyond all the writers of the Patristic period with the power of introspection. He complains that the Platonists and other philosophers, when they speak of the passions, argue more about words than things.[16] He knows them from experience. Although under evident obligations to his predecessors, especially to Plato, his attitude towards the tradition is relatively free. He makes his own observations, penetrating and original, of which the following may serve as specimens: remarks on the difference between emotional experiences at the time of their occurrence and when viewed in memory — the sorrow of remembered pleasure, the pleasure of remembered sorrow; [17] recognition of " mixed " feelings — of pleasure combined with pain, as in losses attended with a feeling of relief, as in grief which finds assuagement in tears and lam-

---

[16] *De civitate Dei,* IX, XIV.
[17] *Confessiones,* X, 14, 21.

entations, as in tragedy; [18] of the combination of such diverse emotions as joy and fear; [19] descriptions of the growth of the mind in the child, of how knowledge is acquired under the guidance of pleasure and pain and of how language, at first the involuntary expression of feeling, is developed by imitation and association; [20] of how, while pleasure may be the object of our striving, pain may be voluntarily sought in order to enrich experience.[21]

In treating specifically of the affections (*affectiones, affectus*) as the soul's motions (*motus animorum*), he distinguishes the passions (*passiones*) as those perturbing motions of the soul which are contrary to nature, accepting the Stoic classification and including under them every form of moral evil. Passions, therefore, are not to be ascribed to God or to the angels. On the other hand they are not to be referred to the body, for they exist in discarnate evil spirits. Nor are they to be referred in the first instance to false opinion. The root of all the affections, including the passions, according to Augustine, lies in the will. " For what," he asks, " are desire and joy but a volition of consent to the things we wish? And what are fear and sadness but a volition of aversion to the things we do not wish? When consent takes the form of seeking to possess the things we wish, it is called desire; when it takes the form of enjoying the things we wish, it is called joy. In like manner when we turn with aversion from that which we do not wish to happen, this volition is termed fear; and when we turn away from that which has happened against our will, this sort of will is called sorrow. And generally, in respect of all that we seek or shun, as a man's will is attracted or

[18] *Ibid.*, IV, 5, 10 f.; III, 2, 3.
[19] *Enarratio in Psalmum*, LXXXV.
[20] *Confessiones*, I, 6, 7; 7, 11.
[21] *Ibid.*, X, 35, 54 f.

repelled, so it is changed into these several affections." [22]
With this reduction of the affections to the will, a reduction
in which, to be sure, the distinction between feeling and
inclination is obliterated, Augustine is now prepared to
find for the whole affective life a common principle in what
for him is the fundamental character of the will in respect
to its inclinations, and that principle is love (*amor, dilec-
tio*). To love and to will are, in his view, identical. Thus in
representing the soul as the image of the Trinity, he parallels the order of its faculties, *memoria, intelligentia, voluntas* (memory, intelligence, will) with the order *mens,
notitia, amor* (mind, knowledge, love). Love is the universal motive power in human life, the " hand " of the soul,
the " foot " of the mind in its journey towards God. Nothing escapes it, the very impulse to cognition is an expression of it; [23] nothing is too hard for it to overcome. It is the
direction of this affection, according as it is well placed
or ill placed, which determines the character. Augustine re-
jects the Stoic doctrine of the " good affections " ($\epsilon\dot{v}\pi\dot{a}$-
$\theta\epsilon\iota\alpha\iota$), as though only the good man could firmly will, be
cheerful and prudent; and what the Stoics called passions
he regarded as capable of expressing, under the conditions
of the mortal life, a proper state of will. In the City of God
the members fear and desire, grieve and rejoice, and these
affections of theirs are right because their love is rightly
placed. To be without affections would be the loss of all
humanity; on the other hand the perfection of love and
felicity involves in the life immortal a sort of transformation of the human into the divine. [24]

In spite of the theological coloring of these doctrines,
neither their intrinsic significance nor their historical im-

[22] *De civitate Dei*, XIV, 5 f.
[23] *De trinitate*, IX, 8.
[24] *De civitate Dei*, XIV, 7–9. *Enarratio in Psalmum*, XXXV.

portance is to be lightly estimated. In his vivid realization of the facts of the emotional life, in his clear and decided grounding of them in the will, in his reduction of them to the single principle of love, in the whole emphasis and value he places on the affections with a corresponding subordination of what is merely cognitive, the influence of Augustine is directed against a too exclusive intellectualism and ultimately in favor of an independent, empirical psychology. Till the rise of scholastic Aristotelianism, he was, though not the only, yet the chief authority in the psychological teaching of the Middle Ages and in the latter part of the period his influence co-operated with other factors, particularly the voluntarism of Duns Scotus and the new Nominalism, in preparing the way for the transition to the modern age.[25]

In the Middle Ages the basis of all psychological doctrine, as already observed, was the Platonic division of the soul into parts rational, concupiscible, and irascible. This division is found in all the principal writers down to the middle of the twelfth century. At that time the distinctions were conceived by Isaac of Stella as follows: the rational is that by which the soul is capable of being enlightened in regard to objects of knowledge below, in, or beside itself; it is the source of the soul's " sense " (*sensus,* awareness) of anything; the concupiscible and irascible are faculties by which it is capable of being affected (*affici*) to the pursuit or avoidance, to the love or hatred of anything. According as the object is apprehended as present or future, the affections (*affectus*) of love are respectively joy and hope; those of hatred, sorrow, and fear. The first two were referred to the concupiscible faculty, the last two to the irascible.[26] This scheme, which, as a schematization is clearly an improvement on that of Nemesius, is modified by Richard of St. Victor (*ca.* 1173) in the twofold division of *ratio,* by which we discern or apprehend, and *affectio,* by which we love; seven principal emotions being ascribed to the latter — hope, fear, joy, grief, hate, love, and shame — corresponding to the seven principal virtues.[27] In the following century Johannes Bonaventura (1221–1274) recognizes this division under the names *vis cognitiva* (the power to know) and *vis affectiva* (the power to feel), subdividing the latter into *concupiscibilis* and *irascibilis,* which may or may not be opposed to the *rationalis.* The distinction between the concupiscible and the irascible is that the one is related *ad voluptatem* (to pleasure), the other *ad sensuitatem* (to sense awareness).[28] When these are united with the *rationalis,* which pertains *ad claritatem* (to understanding), we have will (*voluntas*) which Bonaventura declares to be nothing else than *affectus sive appetitus ratiocinatus* (a feeling or a desire rationalized).[29] The affections, as having respect to

[26] Isaac Stellensis, *De anima* (J. P. Migne, *Patrologiae, latina,* CXCIV, 1878). Isaac's teaching on this subject was copied verbatim by Alcher of Clairvaux, *De spiritu et anima,* IV, XXVI (J. P. Migne, *Patrologiae, latina,* XL, 781, 798). The four passions here mentioned differ from the Stoic list in the substitution of "hope" for "desire" (ἐπιθυμία) now giving its name to the whole concupiscible faculty. This substitution goes back to Boethius (*ca.* 480–525), whose verses (*De consulatione philosophiae,* I, 7, J. P. Migne, *Patrologiae, latina,* LXIII, 552) are often quoted:

"Gaudia pelle,	Drive away joys,
Pelle timorem,	Drive away fear,
Spemque fugate,	Banish hope too,
Nec dolor adsit."	Nor let grief appear.

The same author sometimes gives one list in one connection, the other in another. So Albertus Magnus, who in his *Ethics,* III, 3, 5, quotes Aspasius for the Stoic list and in his *Summa Theologiae,* II, 18, Paschasius Radbertus for the later list. See "*passio,*" in Index.

[27] *De praeparatione animi ad contemplationem,* 3, 7.

[28] *Sententiae,* III, d. 25, a. 2, q. 5 concl.

[29] *Ibid.,* d. 33, q. 3, concl.

good and evil, he reduces ultimately to two, love and fear, making love the originating principle, though not the sole cause of them all.[30] In John Gerson (1363–1429) a century and a half later we meet with the same main division, each subdivided into three special powers.[31] With writers of a less mystical tendency, the term *vis affectiva*, was replaced by that of *vis appetitiva*, and in the great systems ingenuity was well-nigh exhausted in splitting up the *vis cognitiva, vis apprehensiva*, and the *vis appetitiva* into a multitude of particular *vires*, and in the attempt to define their exact relations. Sometimes a special *vis aestimativa* is introduced to mediate between the pure apprehension and the feelings of inclination and disinclination.[32] Ordinarily each main division was subdivided into a sensitive and an intellectual part, the question then arising whether the concupiscible and irascible faculties and their respective affections belonged only to the sensitive appetite or were carried up also into the intellective. A characteristic solution is given by Albertus Magnus (1193–1280) who explains that in the general sense of the terms the intellective appetite is both concupiscible and irascible, but that in the strict sense these terms can only be applied to the sensitive.[33]

Under the affections (*affectiones, affectus*) and passions (*passiones*) assigned to the appetitive faculty are included

[30] *Ibid.*, d. 33, q. 1, concl., 2. The doctrine is Augustine's and for his combination of love and fear, cf. *Enarratio in Psalmum*, LXXIX, 17, n. 13.

[31] *Mystica theologia*, 9, 13, 21.

[32] Albertus Magnus and Thomas Aquinas, cf. H. Siebeck, " Zur Psychologie der Scholastik." (*Arch. f. Gesch. d. Phil.* II, 189 f.)

[33] *Summa theologiae*, II, 5, q. 25. Similarly Thomas Aquinas, cf. F. Suarez, *De angelorum natura*, III, 1. The unity of the intellective appetite is also maintained by Aegidius Romanus (*ca.* 1316). The contrary view is found in Bonaventura, *Sententiae*, III, d. 33, q. 3 concl. (*Opera*, III, 717). Henricus Gandovensis, *Quodlibeta*, VIII, 15, contends for the proper applicability of the terms to the rational appetite, but thinks that in it the irascible is more a force of the concupiscible, whereas in the sensitive appetite the two faculties are more distinct. Henry, however, denies any *vis concupiscibilis* to God.

very diverse psychological phenomena — pleasure and pain, sudden and transient emotions, more or less permanent tendencies, dispositions, habits, both of feeling and of behavior, virtues, and vices. We read, for example, of *affectus voluntatis* (the feeling of wishing), *orandi* (of supplicating), *fidei* (of trust), *virtutis* (of virtue), and an *affectio pia* (a pious feeling), regarded as a habit, more perfect than religion, abiding even in the will of the sinner.[34] On the other hand the seven mortal sins, avarice, pride, lust, gluttony, anger, envy, and sloth have the names of passions, and sometimes a writer's whole psychology of the affections is incidental to their treatment.[35] The terms have in fact all the ambiguity of the Greek πάθος and like it are related to the conception of the soul's " substance." This ambiguity is formally recognized, with a very imperfect recognition, however, of the psychological differences involved. Bonaventura distinguishes four meanings of the term *affectio,* one of which includes *passio,* and a twofold *affectus,* one *naturalis,* the other *deliberativus.*[36] Thomas Aquinas distinguishes three senses of the term *passio,* the strictest being that in which the soul " suffers " under the action of an alien power and passes into a condition for the worse.[37] Manifold distinctions are drawn to square the conception with ethical demands.[38] Frequently *passio* is regarded, with Augustine and John of Damascus, as an *affectio, motus,* or appetite *contra naturam* or *ra-*

[34] Cf. F. Suarez, *De oratione mentali* (*Opera,* XIV, 139, 148). See " *affectio*" in Index (ed. Vives).

[35] As e.g., in Roger Bacon, *Opus Majus,* Part VII.

[36] *Sententiae* (*Opera,* III, 318 d 2; 375 d 1). The *affectus naturalis* was subdivided into an *appetitus justi* and an *appetitus commodi;* e.g.. John of Salisbury (*ca.* 1180), *Policraticus,* VIII, 5; Hugo of St. Victor (*ca.* 1141), *De sacramentis,* I, 7, c. 11. Cf. A. Stöckl, *Geschichte der Philosophie des Mittelalters,* I, 344.

[37] *Summa,* I–II, q. 22 a. 1.

[38] E.g., between " natural " and " necessary," " innate " and " illate," with subdivisions. Albertus Magnus, *Ethica,* V, 3, 6. 61.

tionem.[39] In most writers of the middle period it is limited to the sense appetite. Francis Suarez (1548–1617) applies the term to every act of that appetite.[40] For emotion in the more specific modern sense, Bonaventura employs the term *propassio,* defined as *" subitus motus, cui ex ratione non consentitur "* [41] (a sudden motion which is not determined upon deliberately). Rarely is an attempt made to distinguish the purely affective side of the phenomena; we find this, however, indicated in the distinctions drawn by Johannes Duns Scotus (1270–1308) and a few others between passions as acts elicited by the appetite, and affections as states produced in the appetite by something else, as, e.g., pleasure and pain. Suarez criticizes this on the ground that there is nothing in the appetite which is purely passive.[42] The one thing that stands out most prominently throughout this whole period, the one thing in which all the principal writers agree, is the doctrine that affections and passions are intimately connected with — most indeed make them identical with — modifications of conative tendencies.[43] As regards their relation to cognition, there is a diversity of view, or at least diversity of emphasis. All agree that apprehension accompanies the modification, but while some writers show a disposition to regard the apprehension of some good or evil as an antecedent condition of the emotion, others lay stress on the " intention " of the

[39] Interpreted by Bonaventura in a specifically theological sense as *contra naturalem appetitum salutis, Sententiae,* III, d. 18, a. 1, q. 3, concl. 4.

[40] *De actionibus qui vocantur passiones,* sec. 1, 1–3.

[41] *Sententiae* (*Opera,* III, 342 d. 4).

[42] *Loc. cit.* Besides Duns Scotus, Suarez ascribes the opinion criticized to Bassolis, Maironius, and Andifax. When in section 5 of the treatise he distinguishes between the complacency of love and the desires that spring from it, he comes near to recognizing the difference himself.

[43] An extreme but interesting statement as regards passion is Abelard's: *Nusque enim passio esse potest, nisi ubi contra voluntatem aliquid fit* (there cannot be any passion unless something is done involuntarily), *Ethica, scito te ipsum,* III. Cf. the modern doctrine of Paulhan and others that emotion is a phenomenon of arrested tendencies.

object, that is, its favorable or unfavorable relation to tendencies in the individual, and dwell on the function of apprehension in promoting or checking these tendencies.[44] One of the most significant expressions in medieval literature of the general relations of the cognitive and the affective-appetitive powers is found in John Gerson, who considered that the powers in both faculties were like lights which not only illuminate, but warm. There is no cognition, he holds, which is not also, formally or virtually, affection; no affection which is not also accompanied by some degree of cognition. The two operate together and are perfected together.[45]

As an illustration of the scholastic method of dealing with a special psychological problem, we may take as characteristic and representative Richard of Middletown's discussion of the question whether one pleasure (*delectatio*) is contrary, or opposed, to another.[46] A modern writer would probably either settle the question offhand by illustrations drawn from common experience, or he would undertake and report experiments under test conditions. Not so Richard. His method is dialectical, formal. He first states briefly, with reference to the opinions of Aristotle, the arguments *pro* and *con. Against* the supposition of contrarity of pleasures, there are two arguments: (1) The opposite of pleasure is not pleasure, but pain (*tristitia*); the pleasure of contemplation is free from even this opposition (Aristotle); still less, therefore, can one pleasure be op-

---

[44] For this latter emphasis, especially as regards pain, see Henricus Gandovensis, *Quodlibeta,* XI, q. 8 and 9. The real cause of a passion, which formally belongs to appetite, not to apprehension, lies in the *intentiones* of the object as felt or imagined.

[45] *Mystica theologia,* 15 ; quoted by A. Stöckl, *Geschichte der Philosophie des Mittelalters,* II, 1090 n.

[46] *Super Sententiis,* III, d. 27 a. 4 q. 2. Middletown, an Englishman (*ca.* 1285), is a singularly lucid writer and his descriptions of particular emotions in the book referred to are about as full, and often as illuminating, as those in many modern treatises of psychology.

posed to another pleasure. (2) For pleasures to be opposed their objects must be opposed, but the object of pleasure is good, and one good cannot be opposed to another good (Aristotle). On the other hand, *for* the supposition is the argument that if no pleasure were contrary to another, one pleasure could not impede another, and such impediment Aristotle admits.[47] Richard next states his conclusion: As the objects of certain pleasures appear to be contraries, with respect even to that in which they please, so it comes about that one pleasure is contrary to another. This thesis is then argued, first with reference to the special case of sense pleasures, then generally with reference to the two arguments against it already stated. As regards sense pleasures it may be said that though their objects are contrary, they are not contrary in respect to that in which they are pleasant: for instance, heat is pleasant to a freezing man and cold to one who is too hot, but the abolition of heat in the one case and of cold in the other do not seem to be contrary, since the quality in either case is reduced to a mean. To this it is replied (1) that contrary things are pleasant to appetite for contrary reasons, the pleasantness of different foods, e.g., depends on the bodily constitution; and (2) in the illustration used for the opposite contention, the pleasure is due in the one case to the reduction to normal proportions of the excessive heat, in the other of excessive cold, but a normal degree of heat is contrary to a normal degree of cold, as well as an excessive amount of the one to an excessive amount of the other. This argument is supported by an exposition and application of Aristotle's doctrine of the opposition of states of rest in *termini* of contrary motions. Coming now to the general arguments against the thesis, it is replied to 1: (*a*) that the major is true only where the pleasure and pain are opposed *secun-*

[47] *Ethica Nicomachea*, X, 5, 1175 f.

dum speciem; (*b*) that the minor holds only so far as the pleasure of contemplation is not opposed by a pain of the same kind; there is no object of contemplation which is unpleasant, but the act itself may be lacking or hindered in its exercise, and although contemplation is pleasant *per se,* it may be painful *per accidens* owing to the labor of the body and the senses in maintaining it. And it is replied to 2 : that one good is at times contrary to another, as heat, which is good for fire, is contrary to cold, which is good for water; the reference to Aristotle in this connection being out of place, for the goods of which he speaks as not opposed are specifically the virtues. From this refutation of objections, with its appeal to logic and experience, Richard concludes that his thesis has been established. It was by such controversial methods that the Schoolmen sought results in science; experience is not ignored, but it is not carefully investigated: logical considerations and logical points of view predominate.

The crowning achievement of medieval thought on our subject in this direction was the great systematic exposition of the passions by Thomas Aquinas (1225–1274).[48] Distinguishing the different senses of the term *passio* Thomas explains that, in the stricter sense, the soul is " passively " affected only *per accidens*, i.e., through its connection with the body. Here the movement may be in either direction, from the body to the soul, or from the soul to the body; in

---

[48] Questions XXII–XLVIII of the First Division of the Second Part of the *Summa*, commonly called the *Prima Secundae*. Thomas treats the same subject at considerable length in the ten articles of Q. XXVI of the *De veritate*. Other medieval works, besides those already mentioned, were Aspasius, *De passionibus;* Vincentius Belvacensis (*ca.* 1268) in Book XXVIII, 62–75 of his *Speculum Naturale;* Fracastorius Hieronymus, *De Sympathia* (chiefly medical) ; and Simon Portius, *De dolore*. The important work of Ludovicus Vives will occupy us in the next chapter. The majority of the theologians, as Suarez remarks, *De actionibus qui vocantur passiones* (*Opera*, IV, 455), *pauca dicunt et in variis locis* (say little and that in various places).

the first case we have *passio corporalis,* e.g., a wound; in the second, *passio animalis,* e.g., anger or fear.[49] The latter term may be applied to states of the soul which are only in· directly, if at all, connected with bodily change, but· strictly, *passio animalis* is a movement of the soul which re· sults in a bodily change, and most strictly, one which re- sults in a harmful bodily change. It is defined as a movement of the sense appetite resulting in a corresponding change in the body.[50] Analogous states in the intellective appetite are not passions, though often called by the same names, and they may result in passions, that is, in sensible bodily disturbances, *per modum redundantiae,*[51] through overflow of energy affecting the sense appetite. While the intellective appetite, which always has regard to universal good (*sub communi ratione boni*), is simple, the sensitive appetite, which always has regard to particular good and evil, is differentiated into *appetitus concupiscibilis* and *ap- petitus irascibilis.* The former relates to sensible good and evil, i.e., pleasure and pain, as such; the latter to some quality in the circumstance which makes the satisfaction of the appetite difficult.[52] On this basis Thomas gives the following classification of the passions: [53]

[49] *Summa Theologica,* Q. XXII, a. 1; *De Veritate,* Q. XXVI, a. 1. 2. Similarly Bonaventura, *Sententiae,* IV, d. 44; P., 2, a. 3. q. 2, concl.

[50] *Summa Theologica,* Q. XXII, a. 2, ad 3.

[51] *Ibid.,* a. 3, ad 3. Love, joy, etc. in God, angels and men, so far as they are in the intellective appetite, are, therefore, not passions but acts of will. Cf. Q. XXIV, a. 3 ad 1.

[52] *Ibid.* I, Q. LXXXII, a. 5. This scheme differs both in its assertion of the simplicity of the intellective appetite and in its conceptions of the two powers of the sensitive, and leads to a different classification of the passions from what we generally find in earlier writers. Even Albertus Magnus conceives of the concupiscible as referring to the pursuit of the pleasant, and the irascible (following Avicenna) to the repelling of the harmful, *Summa de creaturis,* Q. 66, 1; Q. 67, 1, although he also defines the latter as *insurrectio appetitus contra malum et in arduum* (a revolt of desire against evil under difficulties). Cf. *Summa Theologica,* II, Q. 23. Later we find Thomas' distinctions adopted, e.g., by Richard of Middletown, *op. cit.,* III, d. 26, a. 2, q. 1. [53] *Summa Theologica,* XXIII, a. 4.

PASSIONS

CONCUPISCIBLE		IRASCIBLE	
relating to		relating to	
Good	*Evil*	*Good*	*Evil*
Love	Hate	Hope	Fear
Desire	Aversion	Despair	Courage
Pleasure (joy)	Pain (sorrow)		Anger

The passions of the concupiscible faculty regard good or evil absolutely, those of the irascible regard good or evil as something arduous, something to be attained or avoided with a certain difficulty.[54] The primary passion and the source of all the rest is love, since all movement relative to good and evil presupposes an inclination of the appetite towards the good. Love is defined as aptitude or proportion of the appetite to good, a complacency in good; hate is the contrary, a certain dissonance of the appetite with what is apprehended as repugnant and injurious. But it is only because of a natural love of the congruent that there can be any dissatisfaction; hence love is the principle of hate and only contrary to it in respect to the same object, while in respect to contrary objects each implies the other.[55] From the love of an object follows the movement towards it, which is desire; and from the attainment of it, the rest in it, which is pleasure, or joy (*delectatio*).[56] There is a con-

[54] *Ibid.*, a. 1, ad. 1.
[55] *Ibid.*, Q. XXV, a. 2; Q. XXIX, a. 1.
[56] Thomas remarks on the objection to placing pleasure, defined as rest in a good, in the appetitive faculty, and meets it by saying that though the movement to accomplish ceases, there is an impression in the appetite by reason of which pleasure is a sort of movement: he quotes Aristotle's definition of pleasure (*Rhetoric*, I, 11) as the movement of "a sudden and sensible settlement into the natural state," *Ibid.*, Q. XXXI, a. 2; Q. XXV, a. 2. It would have been simpler to have said that our "rest" in pleasure is a form of tendency to retain the state, or the source of fresh tendencies, e.g., for its increase or recurrence. But Thomas, not clearly distinguishing the affection from the conation, thinks that the former is sufficiently shown to belong to the latter when it is conceived as a kind of movement, with a corroboration of this conception from the imperfectly understood Aristotle.

trary movement in the case of the antithetic passions of the concupiscible faculty relating to evil. Although love is the primary passion, the faculty, it is explained, takes its name from desire (*concupiscentia*) rather than from love, because desire is the passion most keenly felt. For a similar reason, although hope is the first of the irascible passions, the name of the class is derived from anger (*ira*).[57] Anger is the only one of the passions which is without a corresponding opposite.[58] As the irascible appetite has its source and end in the concupiscible, being concerned with the overcoming of obstructions in the way of securing good (pleasure) or avoiding evil (pain), so the irascible passions, which are modifications of the appetite, take their rise in the concupiscible and in the concupiscible come to rest. Love is the principle, pleasure the final end. If love passing into desire, or hate into aversion, finds a difficulty in the attainment of its object, a passion of the irascible is excited according to circumstances; anger if a present, courage if an impending evil is apprehended as superable; fear if avoidance of an impending evil seems difficult; hope if a future good, not easily acquired, seems possible; despair if it seems impossible. The classification, therefore, is meant to be, and is, not merely formal, but suggests at the same time a geneological relation of the emotions. It is in this regard that Thomas, although enumerating eleven passions, subscribed to the time-honored doctrine that there are only four principal passions, pleasure and pain, hope and fear, the first two being the terminals of all the pas-

---

[57] *Ibid.*, Q. XXV, a. 2, ad 1; a. 3, ad 1. Cf. Augustine, *De Trinitate*, X, 12: *Amor magis sentitur quum eum prodit indigentia* (love is felt more when need prompts it).

[58] Aristotle made "placability" its opposite. J. B. Bossuet afterwards suggested, *De la connaissance de Dieu et de soi-même* (*Œuvres*, V, 25), the inclination to do good to one who has put us under obligation, but pointed out that this was rather a virtue than a passion. Neither falls within the irascible appetite as Thomas defines it.

sions, the last two the terminals of the actual movements of appetite, — love, e.g., passes through desire to hope, hate through aversion to fear.[59]

This classification was widely accepted; even after its rejection by Vives, Descartes, and others, it reappears in Catholic writers down to the beginning of the eighteenth century,[60] and is even still praised and defended by scholastically-minded commentators.[61] But even among the Schoolmen there are indications of a consciousness of its inadequacy, particularly in assigning certain emotions to one or the other of the two divisions of the appetitive faculty exclusively. Thus Duns Scotus, regarding the concupiscible and the irascible appetites as *realiter* distinct, refutes in detail the opinion of Henry of Ghent (Gandovensis, 1217–1293) that love belongs to the concupiscible, hope to the irascible part, Henry himself admitting that the function of hope was not to repel the hurtful, which is the proper function of the irascible, but to strengthen the concupiscible and prevent it from drawing back in the pursuit of an arduous good.[62] And there are other indications in Duns Scotus of a tendency to treat the relations of the several passions as fluent.[63] Suarez criticizes Thomas' distinction between the two forms of appetite as related to good, namely, that the concupiscible has regard to good absolutely and the irascible to " arduous " good, showing (1) that in any of the senses in which the term arduous

[59] *Op. cit.,* Q. XXV, a. 4. Cf. the similar attempt at relating the passions genetically, Richard of Middletown, *Super Sententiis,* III, d. 26, q. 2; a. 2.

[60] J. B. Bossuet, *De la connaissance de Dieu et de soi-même* (*Œuvres,* V, 26).

[61] E.g., by J. Gardair, *Philosophie de St. Thomas: les passions et la volonté,* 60 ff.

[62] Duns Scotus, " De primo principio," *Report. Paris.,* III, d. 26, Schol. The reference is particularly to hope and love as theological virtues, but the discussion suggests the difficulty of operating with the accepted distinctions of appetite.

[63] Cf. H. Siebeck, *op. cit., Ztschr. f. Phil.,* XCV, 256 f.

may be taken, the good thus qualified may be the object of concupiscent love or desire, and (2) that an irascible passion does not always seem to its subject to be concerned with what is difficult.[64] Further, while impartially enumerating the different reductions of the passions, Suarez observes that a classification of them can be made from four different points of view. From one point of view, he holds, they can be reduced to six; from another, their number is indefinite; Thomas' classification belongs to a third; the fourth can be accommodated to various schemes. He retains the scheme of Thomas because of its general acceptance and because, as he thinks, it enables one to explain most easily the origin and connection of the passions.[65]

Thomas' exposition includes a detailed discussion of each of the eleven passions, considering its nature and varieties, its causes and its effects. Though lacking the originality of Aristotle's treatment of the same subject in the *Rhetoric,* that of Thomas Aquinas is incomparably its superior in elaboration and systematic arrangement. It is the representative exposition of the medieval doctrine of the affections, and affords the most conspicuous illustration of at once the strength and weakness of its logical method. It will suffice, perhaps, to indicate briefly the character of the treatment from what is said concerning love, the principle of all the passions, and pleasure, the end in which all the appetites seek to rest.

Thomas distinguishes two kinds of love, *amor concupiscentiae,* whose object is a good, and *amor amicitiae,* whose object is a person for whom the good is desired. Self may be, directly or indirectly, the object of either kind. Primarily the cause of love is its object, a good, which perfects being, because containing something of the Primal

---

[64] *De actionibus qui vocantur passiones,* sec. II.
[65] *Ibid.,* sec. XII, 1, 2.

Good; evil is never loved *nisi sub ratione boni*[66] (except for some good purpose). Beauty is also a primary cause of love, because beauty is the same as good, the difference being only in regarding the object's relation to the appetite in the one case, in the other to the apprehension.[67] But besides this primary cause, there are secondary causes of love, such as similarity and knowledge. If the similarity consists in identity of attribute, we have the love of friendship, or benevolence; if in the possession by the one of what is potential in the other, the love of desire, or friendship based on pleasure or utility. In the latter case each man loves himself; but in the former case also, since each is likest to himself, every man naturally loves himself more than another. Hence similarity may be as hostile to love as favorable: "two of a trade can never agree." Love, therefore, is the principle of rivalry. Knowledge is a cause of love, because although there is an inapprehensive *amor naturalis* which inclines one being to another, as in plants, there is no love as an animal passion which is not based on an apprehension of the good. But love is not commensurate with knowledge; the intensity of the love of God, for example, is out of all proportion to the perfection of our apprehension of Him.[68] Among the effects of love Thomas mentions union (also regarded as a cause of love and as love itself), transport, jealousy, injury to the lover (in *formal* reference good, the object of love, naturally perfects the lover; only an improper good alters him, in this respect, for the worse; but in *material* reference "we do find that love wastes and wears a man away," and this may happen *per accidens* even from the exercise of a spiritual faculty), all the lover's acts, and indeed all acts whatsoever, so far

[66] *Summa Theologica*, Q. XXVII, a. 1 and ad 1.
[67] *Ibid.*, ad 3.
[68] *Ibid.*, a. 2.

as they express an inclination to a desired end.[69] Pleasure, the rest of the appetite in good attained, follows immediately the sensible apprehension of the congruent object, the movement to seek which is due to the stirring of the appetite by the " aestimative " faculty.[70] The movement of pleasure is *totum simul,* not a temporal process; hence pleasure, though not a passion, may be ascribed to God. It is temporal only *per accidens,* one pleasure following on another. Logic therefore seems to require that what we speak of as a continued pleasure must be resolved into a succession of pleasures, each fully complete.[71] Joy (*gaudium*) is a species of pleasure conscious of its reason. In the sensible appetite pleasure is accompanied by bodily change, in the intellective it is a pure movement of the will.[72] Intellectual pleasures are greater than sensible in some respects, in others not. Although pleasure corresponds to a good *secundum naturam,* what is contrary to reason and the natural constitution may please *per accidens* an individual whose nature is corrupt.[73] Among the causes of pleasure Thomas mentions first activity and its products; not all activity, but only that which is proportionate and connatural to the agent.[74] Then he mentions change not conflicting with habit, which is second nature, but such as relieves the strain of an activity too long continued.[75] Hope and memory are causes of pleasure, even sorrow on occasion when allied with memory; while the memory of past sorrows often adds to present enjoyment.[76] The actions of others procuring us good, praising us, loving us, give pleasure, as satisfying our self-love, and this explains our pleas-

[69] *Ibid.,* Q. XXVIII, a. 1–6.
[70] Cf. J. Gardair, *Philosophie de St. Thomas,* 125 ff.
[71] *Op. cit.,* Q. XXXI, a. 2 corp. and ad 1.
[72] *Ibid.,* ad 3 and 4.
[73] *Ibid.,* a. 7.
[74] *Ibid.,* Q. XXXII, a. 1, ad 3.
[75] *Ibid.,* a. 2 and ad 3.
[76] *Ibid.,* a. 4.

ure in the excellences of our friends. Self-love is also at the root of a man's pleasure in his own beneficence, " inasmuch as thereby he gets an imagination of an overflowing source of good existing in himself; " it too, and not the doing of evil, explains why it is pleasant to conquer, confute, punish.[77] Likeness and similitude are causes of pleasure — *similitudo est quaedam unitas* — but not invariably, for the reason previously mentioned; and often unlikeness rather than likeness is its cause, as in the case of a pleasant distraction.[78] Finally, *admiratio* is a source of pleasure, especially of aesthetic pleasure, and in conjunction with sympathy can render even pain or grief aesthetically enjoyable.[79] The effects of pleasure are expansion of being, thirst, or desire, of which the ultimate object is self, obstruction in the exercise of reason, also the perfection of an activity, both as its complement (Aristotle's " bloom of youth ") and as leading to its more earnest and diligent employment.[80] In most of all this Thomas appears as the diligent systematizer of doctrines that go back to Augustine and Aristotle.

It has several times been suggested that, according to Thomas, the soul is not *per se*, the subject of passions, but only *per accidens* through its connection with the body. *Videntur passiones omnes esse cum corpore*,[81] (all passions seem to be in connection with the body). Three things, indeed, are requisite to a passion — apprehension, appetite, and bodily change, and the normal order of their relations is as follows: the apprehension of good and evil excites the appetite, the appetite induces the bodily changes. Passion cannot properly be ascribed to the apprehensive sense

[77] *Ibid.*, a. 6 and ad 3.
[78] *Ibid.*, ad 2.
[79] *Ibid.*, a. 8 ; Q. XXXV, a. 3, ad 2.
[80] *Ibid.*, Q. XXXIII, a. 1–4.
[81] *Commentaries in Aristotelis De anima*, I, sec. II.

whose modifications vary with those of the body,[82] nor can "animal" passion be ascribed to the body alone apart from the soul. It is ascribed, as we have seen, to the sense appetite; but this, conceived in abstraction from the bodily movements of which it is the principle, is but one side of the process. The full process is constituted by the dual movement of the appetite and the body. Fear, hope, and courage, says Thomas, consist (*consistunt*), as passions, in a movement of the appetite and in a certain corporeal transmutation; and a similar relation, a proportional relation of form and matter, is found in the passions generally.[83] Hence not only is the body's "complexion" a predisposing cause of passion, but the bodily accompaniments of a passion, by which it is defined, are also spoken of as its "cause." [84] We are not, however, to conclude that Thomas conceived of the passion on its psychical side as the "effect" of the bodily changes, the mere consciousness of them as they arise. The bodily changes are the "cause" of the passion only in the sense that they are its material embodiment. The "moving" cause of the bodily changes is the appetite excited by the apprehension of good or evil and seeking satisfaction. The process is to be conceived as a movement of the soul in the body rather than as a movement of the body in the soul. "The affections of the soul," says Thomas, "are not caused by changes in the heart, but rather cause them. . . . A man does not seek vengeance because the blood about the heart is inflamed; by this he is disposed to anger: but the anger itself comes from the appetite of vengeance." [85] Similarly in speaking of the effects of fear, he ascribes the "contraction" it imparts to the in-

---

[82] *De veritate*, Q. XXVI, a. 3, ad 11.

[83] *Summa Theologica*, I–II, Q. XLV, a. 3 ; Q. XXXVII, a. 4 corp.

[84] *Commentaries in Aristotelis De anima, loc. cit.; Summa Theologica*, I–II, Q. XLV.

[85] *Irascitur ex appetitu vindictae, Opusc.* 35, *De motu cordis, ca.* fin.

efficiency of the appetite to cope with the impending evil, the consequent contraction of the appetite being followed *secundum similitudinem et rationem* by a corresponding alteration in the body.[86] While, therefore, he makes the bodily changes essential to the constitution of a passion, he nowhere regards the sensation of those changes as essential to its psychical constitution. His general representation is that of a process of apprehension and appetite on the one side resulting in expressive bodily movements on the other, the relation of the two being conceived in Aristotelian terms as one of " form " to " matter," so that the phenomenon may be described by either, but is best described, of course, by the determining factor, the form. He does not recognize that the sensations aroused by the bodily alterations may so react on the form of an " animal " passion as to become essential ingredients of it. Even when he undertakes to explain how the soul, which *per se* is incapable of passion, may be said to be affected in anger, fear, etc., he goes no further than to state that such passions are brought about by the soul's apprehension and appetite, on which a bodily modification follows, and that the body being modified, the soul is said to be affected *per accidens*.[87] Nor may we infer that Thomas supposed this affection of the soul in anger, fear, etc. due to the perception of the bodily modification; for in the content in which the above explanation is given he expressly distinguishes the " animal " passion as one which terminates in the body from the " corporeal " passion which, starting from the body, terminates in the soul united with the body as its

[86] *Summa Theologica,* II, Q. XLIV, 1.

[87] *Nam hujusmodi per apprehensionem et appetitum animae peraguntur, ad quae sequitur corporis transmutatio. . . . Et sic corpore transmutato per alterationem aliquem, ipsa anima pati dicitur per accidens, De veritate,* Q. XXVI, a. 2 corp.

" form." [88] We may reasonably conclude that for Thomas
the sensations of the bodily changes were merely corporeal passions, and that while he may have conceived them
as the invariable accompaniments of the animal passions,
fear, anger, etc., he did not consider them as adding anything essential to their psychical constitution: essential,
that is, in the same way as, according to him, the bodily
modifications themselves are essential to the constitution
of the concrete phenomenon. [89] The physiological process
itself Thomas conceives of as primarily connected with the
movements of the heart as affected by the appetite resident
there and the organically connected " animal spirits "
which, he says, are the substrate (*subjectum*) of all the
passions and the proximate instrument of the soul in its
operations through the body. In anger the heart becomes
warm, in fear, cold and constricted. Pleasure involves an
adaptation of the spirits both in quantity and in quality. [90]
Thomas describes how, e.g., in fear there is an afflux of
spirits inwards and downwards, and how contrariwise in
anger, they surge about the heart and mount upwards to
the head; and these movements are taken to account for
other phenomena. But in all this he is only following a tradition which goes back to the Aristotelian *Problemata* and
the teachings of Hippocrates. And as no other medieval

---

[88] *Dupliciter ergo passio corporis attribuitur animae per accidens. Uno
modo ita quod passio incipiat a corpore et terminetur in anima, secundum
quod unitur corpori ut forma; et haec est quaedam passio corporalis. . . .
Alio modo ita quod incipiat ab anima, in quantum est corporis motor, et
terminetur in corpore . . . et haec dicitur passio animalis. Loc. cit.*

[89] Thomas Duboscq, *Les émotions d'après St. Thomas,* seeks to prove the
substantial identity of the doctrine of Thomas with the James-Lange theory.
But the essence of that theory is that the emotion as psychical " affect " is
consequent and dependent on the bodily changes. If the interpretation given
in the text is correct, this is not the Aquinate view.

[90] *De veritate,* Q. XXVI, a. 3 corp, *ca.* fin. ; *Commentaries in Sententias,*
IV, d. 49, q. 3, a. 2.

writer appears to have done more, this account must suffice as typical.[91]

[91] A doctrine of the " spirits " was common property in the twelfth and following centuries. It was derived from Latin translations from the Arabs who in their anthropology were disciples of Galen. Cf. F. Dieterici, *Die Philosophie der Araber*, VII, 14 f. Among the earliest to reflect the new, yet ancient, physiology of the Arabs in psychology were Constantine of Carthage (for whose doctrine of the passions, see *Opera*, IV, 8, p. 90 f.) and William of Conches, who, in his *Physica*, distinguishes with Galen a natural, spiritual, and animal spirit, referred respectively to the three Platonic organs of the soul : the liver, the heart, and the head. Cf. K. Werner, *Der Entwicklungsgang der mittelalterlichen Psychologie.* One influential work on the subject, cited by Albertus Magnus, was Costa-ben Luca's *De differentia animae et spiritus* translated by Johannes Hispalensis, and incorporated in Book II of the *De anima* ascribed to Hugo of St. Victor. Costa is followed by Alfred, a contemporary of Roger Bacon. He rejects in his *De motu cordis* Galen's threefold distinction, and speaks of only two : " vital spirit " elaborated in the heart, and " animal spirit," a sublimation of the former, elaborated in the ventricles of the brain ; cf. C. S. Barach, *Excerpta e libro Alfredi Anglici.* The connection of " animal spirits " with the brain was sometimes developed into a crude localization theory, the spirit in the anterior, middle, and posterior ventricles being connected respectively with the functions of imagination, reason, and memory, e.g., Alcher of Clairvaux, *De spiritu et anima*, 21 f. Augustine, to whom Alcher refers, localizes sense, memory, and motion respectively in the fore, middle, and hind parts of the brain, *De genesi ad literam*, 7, 18. There is a very full discussion of the subject by Albertus Magnus in *Parva naturalia*, Tract. I and II. Albert accepts the threefold distinction, but as derived by specific modifications of the one spirit generated in the heart. There was a difference of opinion as to whether it was more akin in its nature to air or to fire. Albert regards it as a composite of elements having the form of air, but a mean between air and water, with something of the nature of fire, with hardly anything of that of earth. Thomas Aquinas thinks of it as a *vapor tenuis diffusus per membra ad motus* (a delicate vapor diffused through the limbs for the purpose of producing motion). Cf. L. Schütz, *Thomas Lexicon*, " spirits." The functions assigned to it as an " instrument " of the soul were analogous to those afterwards ascribed to the nervous " fluid," and it is this which makes a theory of the passions, like that of Thomas', in which it appears as the substrate of all passions, interesting, as bearing a certain resemblance to modern physiological theories.

CHAPTER V

AFFECTIVE PSYCHOLOGY IN THE PERIOD OF THE RENAISSANCE

There is no break between the Middle Ages and the period of the Renaissance, nor between that and times commonly called modern. We are accustomed to reckon Descartes, Malebranche, Hobbes, and Spinoza among modern philosophers; their doctrines of the emotions may equally well, or better, be regarded as the systematic culmination of the teaching of the Renaissance, and that to a large extent continues, while modifying, the traditions derived from antiquity and the Middle Ages. It is, therefore, with a certain arbitrariness and from considerations of convenience that we reserve for subsequent exposition the systems of the passions or affections, as they are variously named, developed by the philosophers mentioned. In the present chapter we shall call attention to certain characteristics in the treatment of the subject by other writers, and particularly writers of the sixteenth century, whose importance in this field has not been as generally recognized.

The very amount of the writing on the affections at this time is significant. Not to mention on the one hand the academic disputations in which they were a frequent theme, nor on the other the great systems of the passions in the works of the seventeenth century philosophers, we find the affective life and related topics extensively discussed. These were partly included within a wider range of subjects, partly independent with reference to certain as-

pects, now from the medical, ethical, or philosophical point
of view, now more from the point of view of the observant
man of the world. They appeared in numerous textbooks,
essays, and treatises, of which the *De anima* (1538) of J.
Ludovicus Vives, the *De anima* (1540) of Philipp Melanchthon, the *De rerum natura juxta propria principia*
(1565) of Bernardinus Telesius, the *Psychologia anthropologica* (1594) of Otto Casmannus, the *De noscendis et
emendandis animi affectionibus* (1597) of Laelius Peregrinus, the *De voluptate et dolore, de risu et fletu, somno
et vigilia* (1603) of Nicandrus Jossius, the works of M.
Equicola, *Libro di natura d'amore* (1526), of A. Niphus,
De pulchro et amore libri (1529), of Léon l'Hébreu,
Dialoghi di amore (1565), of John de Indagine and J. Baptista Porta in *De humana physiognomia* (1586), the *De-
conjectandis cuiusque moribus et habitantibus animi affectibus* (1625) in ten books by S. Claramontius, a whole
series of works of a similar import by the French physician, de la Chambre: *Les caractères des passions* (1658),
L'art de connoistre les hommes (1660), and *Le système de
l'âme* (1665); and, in another direction, Michel de Montaigne's *Essais* (1580), B. Gracian's *L'homme de cour*
(1646), and La Rouchefoucauld's *Réflexions; sentences et
maximes morales* (1665) — to mention only a few names
— may serve as examples. The age itself was one of strong
passions and striking individual characters, an age rich.
in feeling and forceful in action. A new world of sentiment
had been discovered with freedom to move about in it and
men entered eagerly in to possess and enjoy it. The science
of the time reflects the life of the age. Man comes to be a
more special object of interest and in man the things that
excite the liveliest interest are those that pertain to his inner
states of happiness or misery and his showing of himself

in character and deed. It is these things — emotion, passion, striving, will, temperament, character, and their expressions — which now attract attention and, relatively even to the intellectual powers, fill a conspicuously large place in anthropology and psychology. We must take these words in the broad historical sense of the time.

" Very little," says the author of a monograph on the subject at once erudite and illuminating, " has been learned in addition to what the sixteenth and seventeenth centuries accomplished in the doctrine of the emotions; whereas, on the other hand, extraordinarily much of it has been forgotten." [1] It is easy to exaggerate. There is no doubt that much has been forgotten. How much was accomplished, how much has since been accomplished, remains to be seen. Certainly we shall be disappointed if we expect to find in the affective psychology of the Renaissance either a fulfillment of our present demands or a complete reversal of methods and results already familiar. On the contrary, what perhaps impresses us most at first is the extent to which it merely reproduces ancient and medieval teaching. Plato, Aristotle particularly, Plutarch, and, in physiology, Galen are very largely the masters of those that know in this department of science, while the influence of the Middle Ages is seen in many special doctrines, in formal arrangements, and in the pursuit of logical distinctions with a corresponding overestimation of their value for promoting knowledge of the facts. The amount of this dependence on the tradition, however, differs very greatly with different writers, and this implies that the reproduction of ancient doctrines is only one of the characteristics to be

---

[1] M. Steinitzer, *Die menschlichen und tierischen Gemütsbewegungen als Gegenstand der Wissenschaft. Ein Beitrag zur Geschichte des neueren Geisteslebens.* This work is particularly valuable for the literature, but in the absence of direct references should be used with a good deal of caution.

noted. Another more significant feature is the attempt to break away from the tradition, to assert independence, to square tradition with facts, to strike out into new paths and, in general, to draw material and inspiration from the living well of experience. The old distinctions, the old classifications, no longer satisfy; new combinations are proposed, new theories propounded: some sober, some, like that which ascribes hereditary dispositions to the influences of the stars, fantastic in the extreme.

The sense of new beginnings finds repeated expression in the complaints of leading writers, not without ignorance or misconception of the facts, that no proper attention had hitherto been given to the emotions or that previous accounts of them were radically defective. It is thus that Vives, who never mentions Thomas Aquinas, introduces his discussion of them; a similar complaint is voiced by Bacon, who knows nothing of either Thomas or Vives and is amazed that Aristotle's treatment of the subject is so slight; Descartes begins his work on the passions by declaring that nothing of any value had hitherto been written about them, and Spinoza recommends his own exposition with a like judgment on the treatise of Descartes. It belongs to this tendency of reconstruction that psychology now achieves its emancipation from theology, so that the affective life can be viewed, and at times is viewed, entirely apart from theological or even moral considerations. With it too are connected an increased interest in the pure description of the phenomena as they present themselves to observation in the everyday life of men and a finer appreciation of their wealth and intricacy. Finally, as evidence of the more realistic temper of the age, we note a marked preference for physiological conceptions and explanations, the " spirits," a development of the old pneuma doctrine, playing here, even more decidedly than in the Middle Ages, the leading role.

In illustrating these various characteristics we shall speak (1) of the general doctrine of the affections in the period of the Renaissance, their conception and definition, their mental and bodily conditions, their classification and description; then (2), briefly, of special topics, such as love, laughter and weeping, and the physiognomy of emotional dispositions, to which the age was attracted; then (3), and more particularly, as symptomatic of the modern spirit, of the beginning of an empirical science of human emotion and character of which Bacon drew up the program. Further illustrations will be found in the chapters following which treat of the systems of the emotions in the philosophers of the seventeenth century.

As in the Middle Ages, so in the period of the Renaissance, the terms used to denote affective phenomena are various and of varying import. In the broadest sense *affectio* was the name for any modification, as distinct from the " essence," of body or of mind; in the narrower sense, it stands for the emotions and passions; in the narrowest, for the gentler emotions and sentiments. In the best writings of the sixteenth century the word used for emotion in the present generally accepted use of the term, was *affectus*. Ludovicus Vives (1492–1540) uses both words interchangeably, *affectus sive affectiones*. The old term passions, as designating the class, tends to desuetude, to be revived again, but not altogether with the old connotation, by Descartes, and the Cartesians. Vives, followed by Laelius Peregrinus, considers *passiones* as a term appropriate to only the more violent emotions. Both these writers hold that the mind is not merely " passive " in emotion, or that only the body " suffers; " the mind shares the experience *per accidens*. The emotions are *actus* (Vives) or *actiones* (Peregrinus), even if not " pure " acts, of the soul's faculties; and this view, reflected in the terminology, though by no means universal, certainly marks an advance.[2] Sense pleasure and pain were usually treated as distinct from emotion, the former, as Philipp Melanchthon (1497–1560) explains, belonging to the sensitive appetite *per contactum* (when aroused by an external stimulus), the latter *sine contactu* (without such a stimulus).[3] This leads to a distinction between *voluptas* or *delectatio* and *dolor* on the one hand (*dolor* being at times limited to the pain of touch) and *laetitia* (joy) and *tristitia* (sadness), with their synonyms, on the other. But the distinctions were not maintained, *delectatio* especially appearing now as a sense pleasure, now as an emotion. Nicandrus Jossius, regarding the limitation of *dolor* to pains of touch as absurd, uses *voluptas* and *dolor* as designating in general the *affectiones contrariae* of pleasure and pain found " in every sense, in mind and in opinion." [4]

Concerning the nature of pleasure and pain the Renaissance adds little to the doctrine of the ancients. Marsilius Ficinus (1433–1499) repeats and defends the teaching of Plato; Girolamus Cardanus (1501–1576), too, and after him Michel de Montaigne (1533–1592) held that all pleasure is rooted in a preceding pain.[5] Bernardinus Telesius (1508–1588) roundly and rightly denied that all pleasure is connected with a return to equilibrium on the

[2] J. L. Vives, *De anima et vita* (*Opera*, II, 551 f.) ; L. Peregrinus, *De affectionibus*, 9.
[3] Melanchthon, however, does not apparently restrict pleasure and pain to sensations of external touch, for he speaks of these feelings as in the ventricles or nerves or other bodily parts in distinction from the emotions, which have their seat in the heart, *De anima*, 1.
[4] *De voluptate*, IV, 39 f.
[5] Ficinus, *De voluptate*, 2 ; Cardanus, *De subtilitate*, XIII (Sir William Hamilton, *Metaphysics*, XLIII, 458) ; M. de Montaigne, *Essais*, II, 12.

ground that pleasure is also found in movement and appropriate action.[6] This conflict of opinion is representative. The definitions given of these states were often purely verbal, as some of the writers themselves observe.[7] The more significant were physiological, with an emphasis on the teleology of the phenomena. Thus Melanchthon defines pleasure as " the perception (*perceptio*) in the nerves or nerve coating of a congruent object (*objecti convenientis*), a perception not injuring or lacerating the nerves, but naturally adapted to their conservation; " contrariwise pain is " a lesion or laceration of the nerves or nerve coating due to a non-congruent object." The susceptibility of the nerves to these affections he regarded as an ultimate not further explicable fact of their constitution.[8] Telesius connects them respectively with the moderate and gentle and the immoderate and violent contraction or expansion of the animated physical " spirit," and considers it as perfectly obvious (*liquido patet*) that pleasure is the feeling of conservation and pain the feeling of corruption and destruction.[9] How on this so generally accepted theory pleasure could ever be an evil, was a question by which the more ethically-minded were not a little disturbed. Montaigne, with characteristic freedom, boldly asserted — and the doctrine has psychological, as well as ethical interest — that pleasure, instead of relaxing the mind, actually strengthened it.[10] Of other details, mention may be made of Julius Caesar Scaliger's (1484–1558) reference to local pain which is not felt, one among many indications that might be adduced of how little the contrast between the conscious and the unconscious was appreciated prior to

[6] *Principia*, VII, 4, 5.
[7] E.g., O. Casmannus, *Psychologia anthropologica*, I, chap. 15.
[8] *De anima* (not paged), under section *Quid est potentia adpetitiva*.
[9] *Principia*, V. 9; VII, 3.   [10] *Essais*, III, 13.

Descartes.[11] The same author denied that pleasure and pain are perceived by sense, the argument, as reported and criticized by Otto Casmannus, being that they are *sensiones*, but *sensio non sentitur* (a sensation that is not perceived).[12] Casmannus' insistence that pains (*dolores*) differ *inter se realiter*, shows that for him, as for others, pain (the same would be true of pleasure) was a class name for concrete experiences and not the name of an abstraction, the identity or diversity of which, as never found in experience, can only be speculatively asserted or denied.[13] The attempt of Peregrinus to give a complete list of all the causes of pleasure provides a résumé from Aristotle and others, including seventeen kinds: one illustration of the tendency of the age to formal elaboration, of which no use is made as an inductive basis for further analysis and theory.[14]

Pleasure and pain were often assigned to the appetitive faculty, but others, and notably Jossius, rejected this view, considering that they were derived immediately from cognitions and that the appetitions followed as their effects.[15] The opinion derived from the Middle Ages that the emotions belonging to the appetitive, and more particularly to the sense-appetitive, faculty was still generally adopted, but it also received important modifications. Thus Vives defines them as " acts of the faculties by which our minds are endowed by nature for seeking good and avoiding or combatting evil," and Peregrinus similarly, as " commotions derived from the appetent faculty in its very self (*in*

---

[11] *De subtilitate ad Cardanum,* 391 b. One is reminded of Lotze's question as to what a toothache would be like if nobody felt it.

[12] *Psychologia anthropologia,* I, chap. 15. The word *sensio* here used denotes the apprehensive act.

[13] *Ibid.,* p. 311.

[14] *De affectionibus,* 107–128.

[15] *De voluptate,* II, 16.

se ipsa) excited by a judgment of good or evil relatively to something to be pursued or averted." [16] Neither definition expressly mentions the sense appetite, the distinction between which and the intellective appetite, as though the nature of desire and aversion essentially depended on the difference in their objects, is clearly breaking down. Vives, indeed, definitely rejects a limitation to the sense appetite of *amor* and *delectatio,* which he defines as functions of the will (*voluntas*). Other definitions of emotions made them motions in the organism. Thus Melanchthon says that they are motions of the heart following an idea (*notitia*) pursuing or avoiding objects; pleasure or pain accompanies them according as they help or harm the constitution (*natura*); and Casmannus writes " emotions are motions of the heart proceeding from the animal motor faculty, the heart being thereby affected by an internal commotion of blood and spirits consequent on cognition and the appetition of sense." [17] Here the emotion is connected with the sense appetite, only, however, to be the more definitely distinguished from it as its consequent. Other writers make appetition, as Jossius does in pleasure and pain, the consequence of the affection. The order, according to Scaliger, is first affection, then appetite, then the incitement of appetite to act, then the act. Repetition of acts generates a habit, which often bears the same name as the affection and operates like it, the process being circular.[18] Even those writers, who in their general definitions most closely connect emotion and appetite, frequently ignore the connection in defining particular emotions conceived now predominantly as perturbations, now as pleasures or pains. All this points to the necessity of a revision.

[16] Vives, *op. cit.,* 551 f.; Peregrinus, *op. cit.,* 8.
[17] Vives, *op. cit.,* 554; Melanchthon, *loc. cit.;* Casmannus, *op. cit.,* 406.
[18] *De subtilitate,* 391.

The connection of emotion and appetite is too plain to be disregarded, but there is as yet no clear discrimination between inclination and feeling, feeling and will, or even between will and idea; consequently the relations between them, speaking generally, are confused.[19]

In most accounts a judgment of good or evil — approbation or disapprobation — is represented as preceding and instigating the emotion, but Vives admits that this judgment is usually determined more by imagination than by reason and is often so rapid as to be hardly noticed.[20] J. C. Scaliger, with that appeal to experience characteristic of the acutest psychological critic of his age, blames Vives for admitting it at all in certain cases, such as the delight occasioned by the sight of a friend.[21] And even Vives notes the pathological origin of grief: the melancholics, whom no evil otherwise afflicts, being themselves unable to account for their depression.[22]

Striking testimony to the new spirit at work in the affective psychology of the Renaissance is afforded by the dropping of the distinction of " concupiscible " and " irascible " as the main basis of the division in the classification of the emotions. The best illustration of independence in resisting the fascination of this powerful tradition is, in the sixteenth century, Vives, the more so as in many respects his classification nearly resembles that of Thomas Aquinas. Vives, in accordance with his conception of emotion as activity directed to the attainment of good or to avoiding or resisting evil, divides the simple emotions into three groups, those relating to good (*ad bonum*), those relating to evil (*ad malum*), and those actively combatting

[19] On this confusion cf. M. Steinitzer, *Die menschlichen und tierischen Gemütsbewegungen,* 17–26.

[20] *Op. cit.,* 551.

[21] *De subtilitate,* 429.

[22] Vives, *op. cit.,* 584.

evil (*contra malum*), his classification, compared with that of Thomas, being as follows: [23]

VIVES	THOMAS AQUINAS
A. *Affectus ad bonum*	I. *Passiones concupiscibiles*
1. *ad bonum per se: allubescentia, amor favor, reverentia.*	1. *bonum per se: amor*
2. *ad bonum praesens: laetitia, delectatio.*	2. *bonum praesens: delectatio*
3. *ad bonum futurum: cupiditas, spes*	3. *bonum futurum: desiderium*
B. *Affectus ad malum*	
1. *ad malum per se: offensio, odium*	4. *malum per se, recessum: odium*
2. *a malo praesenti: moeror*	5. *malum praesens, recessum: tristitia*
3. *a malo futuro: metus*	6. *malum futurum, recessum: fuga*
C. *Affectus contra malum*	II. *Passiones irascibiles*
1. *contra malum praesens: ira, invidia, indignatio*	1. *bonum futurum, accessum: spes*
2. *contra malum futurum: fiducia, audacia*	2. *bonum futurum, recessum: desperatio*
	3. *malum praesens, accessum: ira*
	4. *malum futurum, accessum: audacia*
	5. *malum futurum, recessum: timor*

[23] The comparison is adapted from the table given by R. Pade, *Die Affectenlehre des Joh. Lud. Vives,* 42. It may be observed that in the scholastic terminology *accessum* denotes a movement towards the good, *recessum* one away from evil.

On the basis of the assumptions common to him and Thomas, the classification of Vives is certainly the simpler and more natural. He is not required to explain by an artifice how, e.g., hope and anger have to do with a " difficult " object, while hate and grief do not; nor why hope and fear are irascible affections, whereas, love and hate — for the most general aspects of which, moreover, he chooses the better terms of liking (*allubescentia*) and disliking (*offensio,* contrariety) — are concupiscible. He makes no mention of despair, whose place would be among the " mixed " emotions, that is, emotions compounded of the simpler emotions and constituting a fourth class in his scheme. Although his classification relates the emotions only to good and evil as such and to present and future good and evil, Vives recognizes that they may equally well relate to the past, and not only to actual objects, but to objects merely possible and imaginary; but these objects he treats as good or evil present or future to imagination.[24] Again, with a recognition of differences obscured even by Aristotle and confused in many subsequent representations, he distinguishes from the emotions proper such dispositions or habits as equanimity, gentleness, and *securitas*,[25] which he regards as states of rest rather than as motions of the mind.

The significance of Vives in the history of the psychology of the emotions is not confined to his classification. His descriptive work is equally representative of the spirit

[24] Vives, *op. cit.,* 553.

[25] In spite of Vives' dropping of the distinction of concupiscible and irascible, we find it resumed again by Peregrinus, who classifies the emotions, with an evident desire to combine Aristotle with Aquinas, as (1) in the *concupiscent* faculty, — love, hate, desire, aversion, joy, sorrow; (2) in the *irascent* faculty, — hope, fear, courage, despair, anger, gentleness; (3) in both (mixed), — modesty, immodesty, jealousy, contempt, pity, indignation, envy, malignant pleasure. Peregrinus, *De affectionibus,* 16 f.

of the time. Regarding the emotions as in closest connection with the body, *adjuncti atque adhaerentes,* he points out both how the judgment of good and evil involved in them is affected ʾby bodily states and how the emotions themselves affect judgment, sensation, and states of the body generally. He speaks too of their influence on one another, of how one emotion grows out of another, how they combine, conflict, collide; augmenting, diminishing, or overwhelming one another, like the waves of the sea. It is only, he holds, by affection that affection can be controlled, and in the struggle, it is not the quality of the affection which counts, but only its strength, a strength derived partly from natural endowment, partly from circumstances, chiefly from the bodily constitution. Like the other writers of the time Vives draws largely on Greek and Latin sources for his material, but he uses it as if reporting the facts as he himself found them. With illustrations taken from wide reading, he mingles others that have the stamp of personal observation.[26] As an example of the way he deals with a particular emotion, we may refer to his account of shame, which is almost entirely independent of both Aristotle and Thomas Aquinas. Including under *pudor,* along with shame, modesty, and bashfulness, he defines it as *" metus dedecoris, ex quo non sequitur damnum."* [27] Its objects are things monstrous and unnatural: expressions in word and deed of sexual matters considered as disgraceful — a reason assigned being that we do not have full control of the sexual organs and are ashamed of their disobedience — the mention of things disgusting to the senses, especially to taste and smell, and whatever is

---

[26] As when, e.g., he says that a lie which would be strongly resented when spoken for another, is grateful when employed in our own behalf, because agreeable to the tendencies of the will; *op. cit.,* 573.

[27] *Ibid.,* 589.

opposed to convention and to general requirement and expectation (e.g., ignorance in a scholar, cowardice in a sol-
dier). We feel shame, moreover, not only on account of
disgrace attaching directly to ourselves, but also at that
which attaches to our relatives, and especially to our parents, as though it connected itself with us by heredity. The
Cynic view that we ought not to be ashamed to speak of
acts that are natural, while not hesitating to speak of vices
and crimes, is refuted by the difference in the two cases in
the excitement of the imagination. We are more strongly
affected in this emotion by what we see than by what we
hear and by the visible display of our own disgraces than
by the mere report of them. Hence the movements of con-
cealment in the downcast, averted, closed, or covered eyes;
hence too the fact that we experience the feeling less in the
dark or when alone. Its disturbing effects are described as
similar to, though less violent than, those of fear. This is
the substance of what Vives says, and neither its force nor
its insufficiency requires special comment. Its principal
defect, from a modern point of view, is its lack of a genetic
standpoint; in other respects it compares favorably not
only with what we find in Spinoza and Descartes, but also
with much that has been written on the same subject since.

The organ to which the emotions were particularly assigned by writers of the Renaissance period was, commonly, the heart. It is to the credit of Vives that he does
not adopt this opinion. A distinction, however, had been
drawn by the Schoolmen between the heart as a muscular
organ automatically pulsating and the heart as organically connected with the animal spirit. All agree that the
emotions are intimately bound up with the motions of this
spirit. Questions concerning the latter were eagerly discussed: whether it was of a celestial nature, or like that of

the ordinary elements; whether it was the bond which connected soul and body, or the soul itself; whether it was one or more, how it was generated, how nourished; whether it was identical with, or distinct from, the animal heat — all questions handed down from the Middle Ages.[28] We have not to report the divergent opinions on these questions. It is enough to say that the generally accepted doctrine, represented, e.g., by Melanchthon, was that to the " vital spirit," derived from the purest blood in the heart, and to the " animal spirit," derived from the " vital spirit " by further elaboration in the brain, in whose ventricles, and, according to some accounts, in whose very substance, it is stored, while at the same time disseminated and diffused through all the nerves of the body, belong the sum total of the functions of the psychophysical individual — conservation of life, generation, nutrition, sensation, thought, and affection. Melanchthon himself asks whether the soul and the spirits are not identical, seeing that the operations usually ascribed to the former as the animating principle of the body are also attributed to the latter. Although he goes no farther than to adopt the cautious opinion of Galen that they either are the soul or the soul's immediate instrument, he expresses his sense of their wonderful nature by declaring that they surpass by their light the light of sun and stars and that they can mingle with the spirit of God and become more glorious still, or on the other hand with the spirit of the devil and become corrupted and defiled.[29] A basis for more definite ideas concerning the connection of the brain and the heart in emotion was laid in about the middle of the century by

[28] The above questions are treated in the order named by Casmannus, *Psychologia anthropologica*, Part II, 62–121.

[29] Melanchthon, *De anima* (under *ventriculi cerebri* and *de spiritibus*).

B. Eustachius (*ca.* 1574), who gave a description of the
nervus vagus; [30] and in the seventeenth century by more
extended knowledge of the capillaries and the circulation
of the blood. But the connection of the brain and the heart
was long thought of as a mysterious sort of *sympathia* and
the conception of the relation of the " spirits " to the circulation of the blood in the textbooks of the Renaissance was
indefinite in the extreme.

Along with the " spirits " the " humors " played a leading part in the physiological explanation of emotion.
Melanchthon expresses the traditional opinion in teaching
that when the red (yellow) bile is in excess, we have
irritability, proneness to violent but quickly subsiding outbursts of anger, ferocity in inflicting injury, turbulent
foolish impulses of various sorts, much gesticulation, in-
effective loquacity, etc.; when the black bile is in excess,
melancholy, taciturnity, persistence in execution, morose-
ness, suspicion, obstinacy; with an unhappy mixture of the
red and black bile, monstrous natures full of pride, malevolence, poison, and fraud; with excess of phlegm, natures
sluggish, lazy, and fond of pleasure. Individual differences
are derived both from the temperaments of the parents and
the influence of the planets.[31] Some points in the traditional
doctrine of the temperaments, however, were occasionally
criticized, as, for instance, by Scaliger who, by citation of
contrary instances, denied that abundance of heat necessarily predisposed to anger.[32]

---

[30] *Opuscula anatomica,* 1564.

[31] " *Multo generosior est melancholia, si conjunctione Saturni et Jovis
in Libra temperetur . . . quam si confusa sit Saturni, Martis, et Lunae
congressu in Scorpio* " (melancholy is felt to a much greater degree if it
is influenced by the coming together of Saturn and Jupiter in the constellation Balance, . . . than if it is confused by the grouping of Saturn, Mars,
and the moon in the constellation Scorpion) ; *De anima* (under *de hu-
moribus*).

[32] *De subtilitate,* 347–350.

What particularly interests us in all this is the absence of any consciousness of a dualism between the affections of the mind and those of the body. There were metaphysical dualists before Descartes and, in the period with which we are now dealing, a writer like Marsilius Ficinus (1433–1499) can contrast as sharply as anyone the immaterial *animus* with the corporeal *spiritus*.[33] But in general, while fully recognizing the existence of a divine faculty and an immortal soul, Renaissance writers made no use of it in treating of functions like emotion, which could be most naturally ascribed to the animated body. They were not materialists, but on the other hand they regarded the movements of the mind and the movements of the body, in particular the " spirits," as, in certain cases, one and inseparable, and found no difficulty in passing freely from the one to the other and either describing the same thing in either terms, or ascribing the same predicates to both. The affections are in the heart *or* the will. The heart dilates or contracts, so does the *anima*. The " spirits " expand or withdraw, are gloomy or bright, cheerful or depressed, and the same is true of the soul. Bernardinus Telesius (1508–1588) explains all the affections by reference to the movements of the sensitive *spiritus e semine eductus*.[34] The conception of consciousness, so familiar to ourselves, is not yet developed, the consequence being that to us much of the writing of the time, while in principle in accord with modern physiological tendencies, appears from the psychological point of view confused and unintelligible.[35]

[33] *De voluptate* (*Opera* I, 1039).
[34] *De rerum natura*, V, 177.
[35] Textbooks like Melanchthon's *De anima*, J. Sperling's *Anthropologia physica* and Casmannus' *Psychologia anthropologica* indicate in their very make-up how little the psychology of the time was separated from its physiology. Nearly a third of Melanchthon's work is taken up with an inventory of the parts of the body and includes serious discussion of such curious questions as why the number of the ribs should be the same in

We must omit the details of the physiological explanation, but note in passing one of those curious anticipations of modern doctrine so often met with in the history of science, frequently combined, as here, with ideas long antiquated. Scipio Claramontius (1565–1653), namely, held that the most reliable signs of emotion were to be found in pulse and respiration; his reason, however, for this opinion is that these give the clearest indications of the heat of the heart.[36] So far as the heart was regarded as the principal seat of the emotions, a certain primacy was naturally given to what we should now call the vasomotor phenomena. In general the interpretation was biological, teleological. This was a consequence involved in the conception of the emotions as expressions of the tendency to seek good and avoid evil. Telesius, Peregrinus, and others represent them as indications of furtherances or hindrances to the fundamental tendency to self-conservation.[37] Vives explains how the characteristic phenomena of fear — pallor, cold, trembling of the limbs, stammering, etc. — all arise from weakened action of the heart and the consequent rush of the blood to the aid of that organ from the periphery. This explanation of the physiological reflexes is paralleled by the conception of the emotion as felt as a warning to the subject experiencing it to

---

men and women, seeing that one was taken from Adam in the making of Eve! Casmannus' work was published in Hanover in two parts, the first with the subtitle, *sive animae humanae doctrinae,* in 1594, the second, with the explanation, *hoc est, Fabrica humani corporis,* in 1596. This second part is wholly anatomical, but bears on the even pages the running title, *Psychologiae Pars II.* The author had previously made the better division of *Anthropologia* into (1) *psychologia* and (2) *somatomia.* But even in Part I, the more psychological part, we find discussed at great length, under the "alogical" faculty, subjects connected with generation, nutrition, and growth, in agreement with Aristotle's conception of "soul" as the vital principle of the body.

[36] *De affectibus,* 165.
[37] Telesius, *op. cit.,* IX, 362 f.; Peregrinus, *De affectionibus,* 11.

take the requisite measures for defence.[38] Needless to say, this teleological view was carried out only imperfectly in detail.

Among the favorite subjects of discussion by Renaissance writers on the affections were laughter and weeping. These topics had been frequently treated in antiquity and in the Middle Ages. Cicero confesses that he did not know what laughter was, nor its cause; *et optime,* says Duns Scotus in reporting him, *quia conjecturis incertis cognosci potest* (the only knowledge attainable is by uncertain conjectures).[39] The more obvious muscular movements were described and referred, in general, to a diffusion of the blood and spirits; the psychological cause was disputed, some holding pleasure alone sufficient, the stock illustration being tickling, some requiring in addition an element of suddenness and surprise, the stock counterargument being that we do not laugh when we tickle ourselves.[40] There was no serious attempt to analyze the ludicrous, it being enough, apparently, to recognize that we laugh when we are suddenly and pleasantly surprised or when anything strikes us as funny.[41] In the period of the Renaissance the subject is repeatedly discussed and elaborated, both in works of general psychology, in which it sometimes fills a place altogether disproportionate, as in Johann Sperling's *Anthropologia physica* (1656), where it is the exclusive topic in one of the six chapters on the soul, and in special treatises, one of the best of which is

---

[38] *Op. cit.,* 508.

[39] Cicero, *De oratione, 2* ; Duns Scotus, *Report. Paris* (*Opera* III, 693 a).

[40] Cf. F. Suarez, *De appetitu sensitivo,* V, 7–10 (*Opera,* III, 766).

[41] Cf. Duns Scotus, *loc. cit.:* " *Objectum risus est res nova repentina, levis, vel ludicra, habens facetiam vel argutiam, quibus animi utuntur, ut si quis vane et profane incedens in lutum incideret* " (the object of laughter is a novel, sudden, trivial, or ludicrous thing, having wit or subtility, which minds enjoy, as when a person, walking carelessly and inattentively, falls down in the mud).

the *De risu* of Antonius Laurentius in two books of over a hundred and forty pages, published in 1603 along with the essays of Jossius, which also include one on laughter and weeping. Laurentius, who seems to be thoroughly versed in the anatomy and physiology of his time, makes a much more detailed analysis of the physical movements in laughter than his predecessors, and distinguishes among its various kinds some less commonly remarked on, such as sardonic laughter and laughter from sudden fear. The " spirits " play a large part in his physiological explanations; on the psychological side he lays stress on the intellectual significance of the ordinarily exciting causes and holds, with the best of the Schoolmen, *quod homo sit resibilis quia rationalis* [42] (man laughs because he is rational). The most modern account of the subject was given by Sieur de la Chambre in an admirably written section of his *Les caractères des passions* (1658). De la Chambre finds in his time not two, but seven different theories of the psychological theory of laughter, all of which he criticizes. In his own view three things are essential: the soul must be " taken in " (*décue*) and surprised, the surprise must be gentle, not such as to astonish and stun, and it must be agreeable. But ordinarily a further condition is required, it must have witnesses. The insistence on the social factor, the recognition that laughter is a phenomenon most commonly appearing in company, and the attempt to appreciate the psychological significance of this fact, is perhaps the most noteworthy feature in De la Chambre's treatment. We laugh, he holds, because, according to a theory of the ludicrous since often repeated, we thereby give expression to the feeling of our own superiority. Animals do not laugh because they have neither

[42] *De risu,* II, 368 ff. (N. Jossius, *Tractatus novus*).

a sense of their own excellence nor a developed social consciousness. The expressions of laughter De la Chambre represents as all ultimately derived from pleasure and surprise: the sparkle in the eyes, the color in the face, the tears, come chiefly from pleasure; all the rest, from surprise. The physical processes involved he describes with such fullness of knowledge of mechanical relations and organic interdependence of functions as we might expect to find in one of the best educated physicians of his time.[43]

The subject of weeping forms a shorter chapter. A common opinion was that weeping was an expression of grief having for its object the procuring of aid to the sufferer through the arousal of sympathy. It is recognized, nevertheless, without apparently any sense of contradiction, that there are tears of joy, shame, anger, and pity, as well as of grief, and that the deepest grief is often tearless. Tears are regarded as humors distilled from the moist and soft brain, sometimes as a subtler sort of blood exuded by reason of congelation.[44] Tears flow profusely, Vives explains, when the brain is filled with moisture, as when a man is drunk, or when it is soft and tender, as in boys, young women, and the sick. But when for any reason it is greatly heated or the moisture in it dried up, as in the hot anger of men, melancholia, and prolonged grief, there are no tears to flow.[45]

The interest in the expression of the emotions in gesture and countenance, which began in a scientific form with Leonardo da Vinci,[46] was developed in a pseudo-

[43] *Les caractères des passions,* 138–169.   [44] *Ibid.,* 63.
[45] The traditional opinion is well represented by Vives, *De anima et vita* (*Opera* II, 584 f.).
[46] Leonardo da Vinci, in *Treatise on Painting* in 1551 remarked particularly on the variety of the expressions, conditioned on temperament, corresponding to every variety of idea and feeling, requiring the painter to draw his material from direct observation of them as they spontaneously arise in the living situations of experience.

scientific form in the extensive physiognomic literature of the later Renaissance. This sought evidence of the individual's native dispositions in the more permanent features of his countenance and other bodily parts, sometimes, in connection with astrological notions, from particular parts alone, such as the face and brow (metoposcopy) and the hand (cheiromancy).[47] Of the general works, all of which go back to the Aristotelian *Physiognomica,* the most celebrated was J. Baptista Porta's *De humana physiognomia,* published at Naples in 1586 and frequently reprinted. The fundamental principle of this curious book is that any element in a man's character may be gathered from his resemblance to an animal possessing the same characteristic. If, for example, we have inductively established the major premise, every animal with broad extremities is strong and courageous, we easily complete the " physiognomic syllogism," when we have observed as our minor premise that Hector has broad extremities.[48] The ingenious artist who illustrated the book succeeded in producing the most amazing resemblances in the features of men and beasts by the simple expedient of assimilating them according to his fancy.

Among the many disquisitions on love [49] — a word ambiguous enough to embrace, along with the sexual passion, the *amor Dei,* the virtue of *caritas,* and every form of benevolent affection, all positively defined conative tend-

[47] For the literature and its character, see M. Steinitzer, *Die menschlichen und tierischen Gemütsbewegungen,* 53–60.

[48] *De humana physiognomia,* I, c. 18. Another more plausible principle of the " science " was that the resemblance of a man's ordinary expression to that of one temporarily experiencing a certain passion indicated a characteristic disposition to that passion.

[49] M. Equicola in his *Libro di natura d'amore,* in six books, reports the opinions on this subject of eighteen different authors of the late Middle Ages and early Renaissance. For the still earlier interest in the passion of sex love, see Hjalmar Crobus, " Zur Geschichte der Liebe als Krankheit," *Arch. f. Kulturgesch.,* III, 66–86.

encies, and the natural attractions of plants and minerals — probably the most remarkable of the period under review were the connected *De pulchro et amore libri* dedicated in 1529 by their author, the Roman physician and scholar, Augustinus Niphus (1473–1546), to the young queen Joanna of Aragon. In the first book Niphus develops the theory that nothing can properly be called beautiful which does not excite sensuous desire for its enjoyment, in a way to refuse this predicate alike to intellectual objects and to the objects of external nature, and to attach it particularly to the physical charms, heightened by modesty and the *morum concrimitas* of women. The beauty of woman appeals to the combined senses of sight, touch, and smell, and there can be no perfect enjoyment of it without all three. The question whether the desire for its enjoyment, by which all men are naturally impelled, can exist *sine appetitu Veneris,* raised in the first treatise, is answered in the second in the negative; but the appetite can be controlled, as the author illustrates from his own experience; assuring the fair Joanna, the beauty of whose person he describes in minute detail from head to foot and the concordant excellencies of whose mind he repeatedly extols, that he spent many days at the palace in her company without falling into a love of that kind. The *De amore* deals with the various phases of the sexual passion, normal and abnormal, in the spirit at once of the scientific writer and of the courtier and man of the world.

In the elaborate program which Francis Bacon (1561–1626) drew up in the second book of the *Advancement of Learning* for the establishment of a science of man, which, he says, while only a portion of the science of nature, is the end and term of human knowledge, we find one part dealing with the characters and affections. It is characteristic of Bacon that he places this study in the practical part of " Moral Knowledge," the part which he calls the " Georgics, or Culture of the Mind." This part has two divisions, the doctrine concerning the mind's characters, the affections, and the remedies and cures. Bacon considers it strange that this part, considering its excellence, has not yet been reduced to writing. Proceeding to sketch out some of its principal heads, he names as the first " the different characters of natures and dispositions." The best material for this article, he thinks, is to be derived from the depiction of characters in the wiser sort of historians. " Wherefore out of these materials (which are surely rich and abundant) let a full and careful treatise be constructed." " And not only should the characters of dispositions which are impressed by nature be received into this thesis, but those also which are impressed on the mind by sex, by age, by region, by health and sickness, by beauty and deformity, and the like; and again those which are caused by fortune, as sovereignty, nobility, obscure birth, riches, want, magistracy, privateness, prosperity, adversity, and the like." [50] The next requirement is " knowledge touching the affections and perturbations," i.e., the emotions, which, following the tradition, Bacon calls diseases of the mind. In this connection he refers to Aristotle's treatment of the passions in the *Rhetoric* as acute and good " for the quantity thereof," but says, rightly, that there they were only handled collaterally, with reference to their being moved or excited by speech; he is surprised that Aristotle should not have included a discussion of them as a principal portion of his *Ethics*.[51] The Stoics, he observes, took better pains, but on their work he makes the apt criti-

[50] *Advancement of Learning*, VII, 3 (*Works* V, 22).
[51] *Ibid.*, 24.

cism that it abounds " rather in subtlety of definitions than in any full and ample description." He also refers to other writings " of an elegant nature " about which particular affections had been written. But these do not satisfy. What is wanted is accurate description and analysis. As the best " doctors of this knowledge " Bacon refers us to the poets and historians, in whose writings we find vividly set forth and dissected how the affections are kindled and excited, how pacified and restrained; how they disclose themselves, though repressed and concealed; how they work and vary; how they are enwrapped one within another; how they conflict, etc., the thing of special value in moral and civil matters taught by them being how to set affection against affection and use one to master another.[52] Bacon goes on to speak of the influence of custom and habit on the affections, lays down a number of precepts touching their regulation and concludes with remarks on the relation or conformity that there seems to be between the good of the mind and the welfare of the body.

Bacon was not the only writer of the period to conceive the idea of a science of human nature in which the affections and the propensities to them, regarded as the elements of character, occupied a principal place. The characteristic form which this idea took was that of a science which should afford a practical understanding of human nature as it manifested itself in daily life. This was the idea underlying the elaborate work of Claramontius (1565–1653) designated " Moral Semeiotic," [53] a work which contains a very painstaking systematization of the views on this subject most current in the sixteenth century. The same idea was conceived, but very imperfectly carried

[52] *Ibid.*, 25 f.
[53] Another title for his *De conjectandis affectibus.*

out, towards the end of the seventeenth century by Christian Thomasius (1655–1728) in his *New Discovery of a well-grounded and for the community most necessary Science of the Knowledge of the Secrets of the Heart of other men from daily conversation, even against their will.*[54] The most extended and in many respects most interesting attempt to establish such a science was made by Sieur de la Chambre, physician to the Chancellor and afterwards royal counsellor and physician-in-ordinary to Louis XV. De la Chambre's *Les caractères des passions*, published in Paris, 1648–59 and in Amsterdam, 1658–63, consists of five small, but closely printed, volumes of over 1300 pages. This work was intended as but the beginning, the first of seven parts, of a *magnum opus* designed to include an examination of the characters of the passions, virtues, and vices, of the nature of animals so far as it bore on the science, of male and female beauty and the inclinations corresponding, of the physical and mental differences of different peoples, of the temperaments and their mental and bodily effects, of the interconnection of passions and habits, concluding with an ordered collection of the signs derived from these sources and exposition of their uses: the whole constituting *The Art of Knowing Men*. This program was never carried out. In 1660 the author published a small volume of 278 pages, besides the table of contents, under the title, *L'art de connoistre les hommes*, which, with a good deal on physiognomy, cheiromancy, and metoposcopy, partly makes good the defect, but is more a sketch

---

[54] This is a tract of only 47 pages, dated 1691. It was followed in 1692 by another short work of 281 pages, entitled *Further Elucidation by different examples of the recent Proposal for a New Science for obtaining a Knowledge of other men's minds,* cf. M. Steinitzer, *op. cit.*, 233 f. Thomasius' not unimportant doctrines of the affections are expounded in a work with a long title beginning, *Von der Artzeney wider die unvernünftige Liebe*, 1696, where he appears as a vigorous critic of the teaching of Descartes.

than a treatise. In the preface to his *Le systeme de l'ame* (*sic*, without accents), published in 1665, he confesses that to complete *The Art of Knowing Men* exceeded both his powers and the years of his life.

De la Chambre's work is a most extraordinary mixture of medieval tradition and modern learning, of naïve credulity combined with acute observation and critical independence of judgment. Nowhere perhaps is the struggle of the new and the old, or, if we choose to so regard it, their innocent juxtaposition, so perfectly represented as in his writings. No writings of the kind bear more the stamp of their author's personality. He does not merely report the traditional views, he assimilates them and reproduces them as though they were his own discovery. Along with this, he is constantly relieving the prolixity of his fluent style with original observations, or observations from novel points of view. He will evidently see things with his own eyes. Speaking of fear, he says, after citing and criticizing a number of definitions, it is better not to stop with the opinions of men, but to consult nature and see what she has to teach us concerning this passion.[55] He criticizes among other points in Aristotle's account the view that the only evils capable of exciting fear are those which threaten physical injury or some great affliction, such as the loss of honor, goods, friends; as a matter of fact, he says, there is no evil which cannot inspire this passion, provided only its *malice* is known. " If a man but knew the injury that vice and ignorance bring, he would fear them more than the greatest perils that could menace his life or fortune." He criticizes with equal emphasis the opinion of the schools that an evil, to cause fear, must be " difficult " and shows, generally, that " difficulty " has no special connection with

[55] *Les caractères des passions*, V, 122.

the passions of the irascible appetite, but can equally well, on occasion, condition those of the concupiscible as well.[56] His account of the several passions under the heads of description, nature, effects, and causes are the most systematic and complete to be found in any writer of the period.

A point that will interest the modern reader is the view De la Chambre repeatedly urges that each passion has its own peculiar characteristic mode of expression. He finds an *a priori* necessity for this in the teleology of the emotional process, as he conceives it. As in every passion the appetite has a particular motion and end, the means employed to carry it out must also be particular.[57] The means are mainly the spirits and humors and the voluntary muscles. De la Chambre seeks to describe these movements in each several passion. It is not enough for him to say of love, for instance, that it is a movement of the sense appetite whereby the soul unites itself to what seems to it to be good; he wants to know the particular agitation which the appetite gives itself to effect this union, and how it differs from that in joy, desire, and hope, whereby the soul also seeks, apparently, to unite itself with a represented good. Naturally he does not succeed in discovering these particulars from observation in every detail. His descriptions are drawn partly from observation, partly they are based on the physiological assumptions of his time, while back of these assumptions lies his own peculiar view of the nature of the soul and the relations of the soul and the body. He considers, namely, that the soul is a spiritual substance having extension, parts, figure, and size permeating the body and moving literally in and with its movements,[58] and criticizes, without naming him, the opinion of his contem-

---

[56] *Ibid.,* 131 ff.   [57] *Ibid.,* I, 12.
[58] *Système de l'âme,* I, 374.

porary, Descartes, for allowing the soul to act on the body
only through the movements of the pineal gland.[59] The idea
that the soul moves only metaphorically, he scornfully rejects, maintaining, on the contrary, that the movements of
the body are only crude and imperfect images of those of
the soul which cause them and which they accompany.[60]
It is the soul, therefore, in the fulfillment of its own ends,
which determines the movements in the body by which,
literally, the particular passion is expressed. Thus De la
Chambre explains the assumed stability and steadiness of
the " spirits " in fortitude by saying that the soul " flows
and insinuates itself into all their parts and, having the
power to place them as it pleases, arrests them in the order
it desires and holds them, as by the hand, in the place it
assigns them ": it acts, in fact, on the " spirits " — such is.
the illustration by which the author seeks to bring his conception nearer to our comprehension — in the same manner as the angels in giving stability to the air and other
fluid bodies.[61] This *outrée* teleology is elsewhere qualified
by the admission not only that the movements ordered by
the soul in the judgment that they are necessary to execute
its passion, are often useless, but also that a large number
of the movements arise from the pure necessity of nature.[62]
The general character of the movements, indiscriminately
referred in this theory to the soul, appetite and " spirits,"
is represented, in a modification of the old Stoic-scholastic
doctrine of *accessum* and *recessum,* as being fundamentally of four kinds: movement outwards and withdrawal
inwards, expansion and contraction. The simple, as distinguished from the mixed, passions of the concupiscible
faculty show the first in love, the second in hate, the third

[59] *Les caractères des passions,* VI, 497 f.
[60] *Ibid.,* I, 33.
[61] *Ibid.,* II, 394.
[62] *Ibid.,* I, 57.

in joy, and the fourth in sorrow; similarly the irascible faculty is tense in fortitude, relaxes in despair, goes out beyond itself in daring, and withdraws into itself in fear.[63] Along with a great deal of mythology of this sort, we do nevertheless find in De la Chambre not a little in the way of good and accurate description. It is this combination which makes him so especially interesting, so faithful a mirror of his age. Descartes and Malebranche, Hobbes and Spinoza were more sober and restrained; there is scarcely another writer of the time more genial and entertaining. The program of the great Bacon was not executed, and never has been executed according to the letter. But it can be said for De la Chambre that, with all his shortcomings, he at least seriously conceived and sincerely attempted to inaugurate an independent science of human nature, and that he upheld the idea of such a science in a century which was tending to absorb the interest in man, so powerfully stimulated by the Renaissance, into the construction of systems of metaphysics.

[63] *Ibid.*, V, 134.

CHAPTER VI

SYSTEMS OF THE " PASSIONS " IN THE SEVENTEENTH
CENTURY: DESCARTES AND MALEBRANCHE

We come now to the more distinctive systems of the
emotions, passions, or " affects," as they were sometimes
called, in the seventeenth century. Of these there are
four of historical importance, which may be divided into
two groups, the first containing the closely related doctrines of Descartes and Malebranche, the second the
partly related, partly contrasting doctrines of Hobbes and
Spinoza. Reserving for the end of our exposition a general comparison and estimate, we proceed to trace in the
two following chapters the main outlines of the systems
of the passions developed by these writers.

We consider first Descartes (1596–1650). Descartes'
treatise, *Les passions de l'âme,* published in 1649, grew
out of a correspondence on the subject five years earlier
between the philosopher and his favorite pupil, Princess
Elizabeth of the Palatinate, and was the revision and expansion of a shorter treatise written for her in the winter
of 1645–46. The work is of considerable extent, consisting of over two hundred articles. It is divided into three
parts, the first part treating of the passions in general, with
reference to their place and origin in man's dual nature;
the second, of their number and order, and especially of
the six primary passions; and the third, of various modifications and combinations of these primary passions. The
main emphasis in the treatise is on a psychophysiological
theory of the passions illustrated from the point of view

of a thoroughgoing mechanism of the bodily processes and a thoroughgoing dualism in the relation of the body to the soul. The foundations of this theory were laid by Descartes in his earlier work, *On Man*.[1] Besides this general theory which was set forth in the first part and applied in greater or less detail throughout, the most notable and characteristic points in Descartes' teaching appear in *Les passions de l'âme:* the selection of the sex passions which were regarded as primary and especially the introduction of *admiratio* [2] with the place assigned it as the first of these; the deduction of the other passions from them, as set forth in the second and third parts; and, incidentally, the reference to experiences in the early life of the individual as the practically exclusive principle for explaining individual differences in emotional susceptibility. Like all similar investigations of the period, the final aim of the *Traité de l'homme* is ethical; this final aim, occasionally suggested in the first part, comes out more clearly in the second, and fully appears in the third part; indicating how the passions, on which all good and evil in the present life are represented as depending, may be controlled by reason. Benedictus de Spinoza (1632–1677), while judging the attempt a brilliant failure, correctly interprets Descartes' main purpose when he says that Descartes aimed " both to explain human passions by their causes and to show the way thereby the mind might come to a perfect mastery of them." [3]

Descartes claims for his work the highest degree of originality and independence. The ancients, he says,

[1] *Traité de l'homme* was outlined by him in 1633 but it was not published until 1662, twelve years after his death.

[2] This term, not meaning what we understand by " admiration," is less misleading in its Latin form than in the French. The Latin form is therefore adopted in this chapter.

[3] *Ethics*, III, Praef.

treated the subject meagerly, and what little they did
teach concerning it has but little to commend it; he, therefore, is obliged to deal with it as though no one had ever
touched on it before. His independence will not be disputed. Originality, however, is a relative term, and it can
hardly be denied that in the judgment he passes on his
predecessors, Descartes shows both ignorance and lack of
appreciation. On the purely descriptive side his work
shows no advance on that of Aristotle, of St. Thomas, of
Vives. His main emphasis is on the physiological conditions of the passions. But this was nothing new. If our
previous studies have made anything clear, it is this: all
the leading discussions have recognized, and some of
them, in the assertion of the soul's essential impassivity,
have even exaggerated the part played by the body in the
emotional process. It is absurd, therefore, to assert, as is
sometimes done,[4] that antiquity saw in the passions merely
psychical processes, and to claim as the new and decisive
achievement of Descartes his attempts to find the roots of
passive mental states in bodily conditions and to give due
play to the bodily factor in the life of the soul. If modern
psychology has followed in this respect the special lead of
Descartes, it is only because of his peculiar influence in
establishing a still more ancient tradition. Moreover, the
main elements of his anthropology were largely derived
from ancient and medieval sources. This holds particularly of that conception of the " spirits " which plays so
prominent a part in his explanations, notwithstanding the
fact that the best physiology even of his own time had rejected it. The essentially original feature in his system is
a theory of the passions based on a dualistic conception

---

[4] E.g., by A. Koch, *Die Psychologie Descartes' systematisch und historisch-kritisch bearbeitet*, 185, 205.

of the relations of the soul and the body and a strictly mechanical conception of physiological phenomena. The ancients, speaking generally, had either regarded the soul as a material entity or as a function of some or all of the vital processes, or they had considered the vital processes as the functions of the all-animating soul. Descartes conceives of the living body as altogether a machine, independent of the soul, and of the soul as a distinct substance independent of the body, which it nevertheless influenced and was influenced by in causal interaction. This conception was certainly new and in so far the theory of the emotions founded on it was new also. But it is precisely this conception which has proved the crucial difficulty in Descartes' philosophy, a difficulty which modern psychology largely escapes by the device of not formulating with the same degree of definiteness its presuppositions.

To proceed, however, with the exposition of the Cartesian doctrine, we have first to ask, what does Descartes understand by its subject matter? What does he mean by a " passion of the soul "? The term passion, he explains, in its broadest psychological acceptation, denotes any new experience of which the soul is the subject. But where the soul is not only the subject, but the cause of the experience, the latter is called an action, and not a passion, taking its name from the higher faculty.[5] A passion, therefore, properly speaking, is an experience of the soul derived from an alien cause. As the immediate cause of the soul's passive experience in this sense is some impression or modification in the brain, the passions generally are explained as embracing all " thought " (*pensées, cogitationes*), that is, all conscious phenomena (Descartes' *pensée* being used in the same broad meaning as Locke's "idea") which are ex-

[5] *Les passions de l'âme*, I, 19, 20.

cited in the soul solely by impressions in the brain without
the co-operation, directly or indirectly, of the will.[6] Such
" thoughts " include the whole realm of sensible experience, within which Descartes distinguishes perceptions referred to external objects, organic sensations, and the natural bodily appetites, and finally passions referred to the
soul. The " passions of the soul," therefore, require a
stricter definition. This Descartes gives as follows: passions of the soul, he says, are " perceptions of feelings or
emotions of the soul which we refer especially to it " (and
not to external objects, as in ordinary perceptions, nor to
the body, as in the case of organic sensations and the
bodily appetites) " and which are caused, supported, and
corroborated by some movement of the spirits." [7] The
triple designation, perceptions, feelings, and emotions, apparently refer to distinct modes of experience, but may
perhaps be taken as applying to the same experience from
different points of view. A passion perception is explained
as a " thought " (*pensée*, state of consciousness) which is
neither a clear cognition nor an act of will; a passion feeling (*sentiment*) as something of which the soul is receptive
in the same way as it is receptive of objects of external
sense; and a passion emotion as a " thought " by which the
soul is more than ordinarily agitated and disturbed. Descartes' " passion " is thus broader than our " emotion," in
the narrower sense, and knows nothing of the distinction
between the two terms as used in later psychology. Yet although as agitating experiences all passions of the soul are
emotions, they are not all emotional in the same degree.
Moreover, not all emotions are passions in the sense defined, for some are held to be voluntary and intellectual,
caused solely by the soul itself. As illustrating a purely

[6] *Epistolae*, I, 8.   [7] *Les passions de l'âme*, I, 27.

spiritual emotion Descartes, like many of his ancient and scholastic predecessors, refers to the coexistence of a sweet joy along with experiences of a deep sorrow and to the intellectual pleasure accompanying the passions excited by tragic drama, assuming, to establish the distinction, that the one is, while the other is not, in our own power.[8] His antithesis of intellect and sense, indeed, is even more absolute than the scholastic, since he makes the body, the source of all sensible experience, more completely independent of the soul.

The essential elements, thus, in the definition of a passion of the soul are (1) the relating of the experience to the soul as *its* passion — the soul, not the body, loves, hates, etc., and (2) the explanation of the experience is due to some movement of the " spirits " agitating the brain and sustaining the impression.[9]

Descartes' conception of the " spirits," sometimes called " animal spirits," is, as already remarked, wholly traditional. He thinks of them as a certain air or breath consisting of the most lively and subtle parts of the blood rarefied by the heat in the heart, very minute and very mobile, like the flame of a torch. They may be conceived, it has been suggested, after the analogy of the molecules in the modern theory of gasses: small, extremely mobile, material particles capable of permeating the finest pores and intensified in their velocity and energy by heat.[10] While the rest of the blood is distributed by the veins and arteries over the body, only the " spirits " are fine enough to enter the capillaries of the brain, where they fill the ventricles and whence they pass by pores in the nerves to the muscles.[11] This

[8] *Ibid.*, II, 147.   [9] *Ibid.*, I, 27–29.
[10] Paul Pleassner, *Die Lehre von den Leidenschaften bei Descartes,* I, D, 15.
[11] *Les passions de l'âme,* I, 7, 10.

conception, of hoary lineage, had already received its mortal wound by Harvey's discovery of the circulation of the blood.[12] Descartes had himself accepted this discovery as early as 1637, but he did not realize its full consequences. Harvey, however, had rightly condemned the " spirits " as *deus ex machina* and the resort to them in physiology as an *asylum ignorantiae*. The doctrine was also sharply attacked by one of Harvey's earliest disciples, Jacob Buck, in a work on the heart published in Rotterdam in 1648. In 1666 the Jesuit Father Fabri, criticizing in his *Cursus physicus* the teachings of Descartes, argues with effect that to explain the passions by " spirits " is to explain the obscure by the more obscure; that the movements of the pineal gland attributed by Descartes to the percussion of the "spirits" are anatomically impossible; that the nerves are not hollow and that not only has no one ever discovered any " spirits " in them, but that there is no need or ground for assuming any.[13]

Descartes, however, making this assumption without empirical justification, with a conception of a physiological mechanism strictly that of mechanical physics and, relying on the authority of the tradition, ascribes to the " spirits," in common with his predecessors, the functions now commonly attributed to the energies of the nervous system. He regards them, namely, as the media by which other stimuli, whether organic or extraorganic, make their impressions on the brain, by which the " traces " left by these impressions are revived, and by which movements, both the voluntary and the involuntary, are produced in the muscles. His distinctive use of the conception is bound up

[12] William Harvey, *Exercitatio anatomica de motu cordis et sanguinis,* 1628.

[13] Cf. M. Steinitzer, *Die menschlichen und tierischen Gemütsbewegungen,* 139–141.

with his mechanical view of the physiological processes and his dualistic view of the relations of the soul and the body. His conception of the bodily mechanism led him to seek a definite anatomical connection for every observable bodily movement, and where such a connection had not been discovered, to imagine one in terms not anatomically impossible. In treating of the passions, this leads to a good deal of hypothetical physiology, which, nevertheless, is in so far sound in principle, as it expresses the demand for definite constructions, as opposed to mere abstract generalities. The "spirits," moreover, determinant as their function is as regards all movements proceeding from the brain or destined to act upon it, have a relatively subordinate function in the fundamental economy of life, for the ultimate source of bodily movement lies, according to Descartes, in the vital heat.[14] Descartes uses this principle to refute the ancient and scholastic theory which ascribed the vital heat and all bodily movements to the soul. As to the relation of the soul to the body, he formally subscribes to the generally accepted view that the soul is united to all parts of the body conjointly and cannot be said with propriety to be in any one part to the exclusion of the rest. But he makes no practical use of this conception. On the contrary, he operates entirely with his novel idea that the commerce of the soul with the body is carried on through the medium of the "animal spirits," especially in the pineal gland, an idea with which he also negatively disposes of both sides of the ancient controversy which held, the one that the seat of the soul was in the brain, the other that it was in the heart.[15]

So much for Descartes' general conception of a passion, meaning more particularly a "passion of the soul," and

---

[14] *Les passions de l'âme*, I, 8.   [15] *Ibid.*, I, 30, 31.

for the general character and foundation of his theory. The whole complex of the bodily organs constitutes a machine by which, through the medium of the "animal spirits," the soul, having its principal seat in the pineal gland, is influenced. But this influence extends, as we have seen, not only to the passions in the strict sense, but also to external perceptions, to natural appetites like hunger and thirst, and to general sensations like pain and tickling, in which last Descartes finds an analogy to pleasure. It also extends to the temperaments, about which a word must be said in passing, since they are closely related to the passions and to which they predispose. By "temperaments" we understand all the states variously designated by Descartes as *inclinationes naturales, ingeniorum et morum diversitas, propensiones, habitus et indoles* (natural inclinations, various temperaments and characters, desires, habits, and inborn dispositions). These all, together with the passions, with the exception of *admiratio,* are connected more particularly with the functioning of the nerves about the heart.[16] But the ultimately important factors in the explanation are the quantity and quality of the "animal spirits" as affected by the blood and the food and the organs concerned in digestion, respiration, and circulation.[17] The temperaments, however, are distinguished on the physical side from the passions proper by the fact that they are derived from the *cursus spirituum ordinarius,* a purely physical process resulting from the constitution of all the bodily organs and their reactions to the supply of food and drink. Individual differences are due to differences in the physical character of the "spirits" according as they are more or less abundant, coarser or finer, more

[16] *Principia philosophiae,* IV, 190; *De homine,* IV, 56.
[17] *De homine,* IV, 56–61.

or less active, or more or less homogeneous.[18] The " passions of the soul " on the other hand, although depending on the same physical conditions, require a special agitation of the " spirits," *particularis aliqua spirituum agitatio*, a movement which, as registered in the *conarium*, generates a particular commotion in the soul.[19]

What now, we have to ask, is the nature of this latter process? How is the production of an emotion to be conceived? We may take as typical Descartes' account of the way fear is excited by the perception of some strange and frightful animal.[20] The mere perception of the animal is accounted for by the convergence on the *conarium* of the movements of the " spirits " excited by the corresponding visual impressions in the eyes.[21] But the object appears not merely as object, but as having a certain relation to us: it is strange and frightful. If it were strange only, it might agitate the spirits in an unwonted manner, indeed, but we should have, along with the deepened impression, the arrested attention and the adaptation of the sense organs: simply the feeling of *admiratio*.[22] But it is also frightful. Descartes explains this to mean that it is closely akin in character to things that have been found in previous experience to be harmful, that is, he explains it on the principle of association. This association, or assimilation, involves a special movement of the " spirits " and imports a corresponding apprehension of the threatening danger. But the passion to be excited is so far indeterminate. The apprehension or mistrust (*crainte*) may be followed either by

[18] Cf. *Epistolae*, I, 8 ; *Les passions de l'âme*, I, 15.
[19] *Epistolae*, I, 8 ; *Les passions de l'âme*, I, 27, 28, 36, 46. For details of Descartes' doctrine of the appetites and temperaments, see A. Koch, *Die Psychologie Descartes'*, 170 ff.
[20] *Les passions de l'âme*, I, 36.
[21] *Ibid.*, I, 35.
[22] *Ibid.*, II, 70.

boldness (*hardiesse*) or by fear (*peur*) or terror (*épou-
vante*). That depends upon further conditions. It depends
on the temperament of the body, the force of the soul —
the will, in Descartes' system, having the power to determine the *course* of the " animal spirits " and thus to control
the passion — and the attitude which has been found useful on previous occasions in securing protection against
similar dangers. It happens, however, as Descartes says,
that in some men the brain is so disposed that the " spirits " are reflected from the gland into the nerves in such a
way that some are distributed to the muscles which turn
the back or move the legs, and some to those which contract or dilate the orifices of the heart, or which convey
them to other viscera which supply blood or fluids affecting
the blood to the heart. The critical phenomena in the genesis of the emotion are those which follow from the discharge of the " spirits " into the viscera, Descartes appearing to attribute little or no importance in this regard to the
direct action of the external muscles. The unusual visceral
excitement produces an unusual modification in the rare-
faction of the blood in the region of the heart, with the consequence, it is assumed, that fresh " spirits " are sent back
to the brain of a kind adapted to keep open or, as the case
may be, to reopen the same minute passages by which they
were transmitted to the nerves and muscles specifically involved in the bodily disturbance. The result, in the case
supposed, is, to use Descartes' expression, to " maintain
and strengthen " the emotion of fear. For in entering the
passages in question, they set up in the gland that peculiar
movement which is " instituted by nature " to cause the
feeling of fear.[23]

It might be inferred from this account that an emotion,

[23] *Ibid.,* I, 36.

according to Descartes, is constituted, always excepting *admiratio,* by the totality of organic sensations arising from the visceral disturbance. Some support may be found for this interpretation in the fact that he speaks of the passions as felt most acutely in the heart, which, as far as they arise from the body, may even be regarded as their principal seat.[24] But it is not to be supposed that in Descartes' view localizable organic sensations, such as palpitations, congestions, coldness, heat, tonicity, or flaccidity of muscles, played any part in the constitution of an emotion. He recognizes the existence of organic sensations as a species of passion, but distinguishes them, psychologically, as referred to the body, from passions of the soul. Nor does he ever speak of the former as constituent elements of the latter. His language and his doctrine are consistently to the effect that certain motions are produced in the pineal gland by the action of " spirits " generated in consequence of the visceral disturbance and, ascending to the brain, these motions maintain and strengthen an impression already existing. These " spirits " keep open, or reopen, the passages by which the " spirits " were conveyed to specific nerves and muscles in the discharge which set up the bodily disturbances. Descartes' idea seems to be that the movements they excite in the gland correspond to, though not necessarily exactly reproduce, the complex of movements due to the totality of conditions affecting the opening and closing of the passages that determine the direction of the original discharge: movements by which the gland, and consequently the soul, are peculiarly affected already.[25] It is the reinforcement of this original impression as a consequence, rather than the added sense, of bodily dis-

---

[24] *Epistolae,* I, 84: *affectuum, quatenus ad corpus pertinent, sedes prae-cipue est in corde; Les passions de l'âme,* I, 33.

[25] *Les passions de l'âme,* I, 34.

turbance which, in Descartes' theory, constitutes the " passion." Thus in speaking of love, after describing hypotheti-
cally the discharge of " spirits " by the vagus nerve to the
stomach and intestines and the consequent inflaming of the
heart by the force and abundance of the gastric juice, he
tells us that the " spirits " which the heart thereupon sends
to the brain " strengthen the impression made by the first
thought of the beloved object and oblige the soul to dwell
on this thought." He adds that in this dwelling on the
thought, not, be it observed, in the accession of a new set
of organic sensations, " consists the passion of love." Contrariwise in hate, the thought of the object exciting aversion causes the " spirits " to descend to the stomach and
intestines in such a way that the flow of the gastric juice is
impeded and the blood from the spleen and liver respectively very unevenly heated and rarefied; consequently the
" spirits " which rise thence to the brain are very un-
equal and have very extraordinary movements which
" strengthen the ideas of hate already imprinted there."
Descartes similarly explains the bodily movements in
other passions: the process in each case, with the exception
of *admiratio,* is a specific discharge of " spirits " from the
brain to the viscera, specific modifications in the production of fresh " spirits " from the blood, an afflux of these
" spirits " to the brain causing specific movements in the
gland, therewith reinforcing and sustaining the emotional
impression due to the complex of conditions exciting the
original discharge.[26] To state the theory in more sensational terms would be to transform it. It is true, of course,
that for Descartes the passion, as distinguished from the
pure emotion, is a sensible phenomenon, since it is
" caused, maintained, and strengthened " by an agitation

[26] *Ibid.,* II, 102–106.

of the " animal spirits," an agitation due in all but one case to a widely extended somatic disturbance.[27] He does not conceive the consciousness thus aroused as a mere report of the bodily disturbance, a sum of distinguishable sensations, or even a *coenaesthesia*, which makes us aware of the body's state, but as a sensible and vivid feeling of the soul's reaction to the object as determined by the soul's connection with the body. The agitation of the *conarium* produced by the concussion of the " spirits " is one instituted by nature to produce this feeling, just as the movement due to the affection of the eyes by the external object is naturally adapted to produce the perception of the object. Descartes does not push the analysis further, but his distinction of organic sensations " referred to the body " and passions of the soul " referred to the soul " is sufficiently precise to justify the conclusion, however difficult it may be to maintain in fact, that he did not suppose the former as essential constituents of the latter but regarded them rather as incidental accompaniments, conditions, or effects.[28]

The body, however, is the primary object of the passions. They are all, according to Descartes, related in the first instance to bodily welfare. If they are excited by external objects, it is not in virtue of any objective quality, but because of differences in the relation of the objects to our profit and hurt; and the agitation of the " spirits " which customarily causes them is of a sort to dispose the body to movements adapted to its life. This is the natural

[27] *Ibid.*, II, 147.

[28] I cannot, therefore, agree with Irons in holding that Descartes anticipated the James-Lange theory in maintaining " that emotion is caused by physical change," or that he worked out the theory " with a completeness that is not to be found in the modern presentations of the same general point of view." Cf. D. Irons, " Descartes and Modern Theories of Emotion," *Phil. Rev.*, IV, 291. Cf. E. B. Titchener, " Notes on the James-Lange Theory of Emotion," *Am. J. of Psych.*, XXV, 428.

teleology of the passions, and the important practical inference Descartes derives from it is that the sole use of the
passions is to dispose the soul to will persistently the things
which nature declares to be useful.[29] He was neither aware
of the modern biological foundations for the principle nor
of the many modern objections to its all-sufficiency.

The habitual connection of a given emotion with certain
definite movements he explains, in connection with this
theory, by association, the original mechanism being constituted in the early life of the individual. He assumes that
the first passions were joy and sorrow, the latter, insti-
gated by pain and developing into hate and the desire of
deliverance, being regarded as of the two the more primary
and necessary.[30] The genesis of the emotional mechanism
is conceived as follows: among the earliest experiences
arising after the union of the soul with the body would be
various modifications in the alimentation of the vital heat.
Sometimes the blood or other fluid entering the heart would
be more than ordinarily suitable, sometimes it would be of
a character to impede the process. In the first case vitality
would be enhanced, in the second place it would be low-
ered; in the one the soul would feel pleasure,[31] in the
other, pain. As a consequence of the feeling of enhanced
vitality the soul, according to Descartes, would voluntarily
unite itself with the *aliment* exciting it, in other words,
would " love " it, and the " spirits " (by virtue, apparently,
of the natural teleology not further to be accounted for)
would flow from the brain to the muscles of the appropriate organs to cause more *aliment* of the same sort to be
sent to the heart. These organs are the stomach and the

---

[29] *Les passions de l'âme*, II, 52.

[30] *Ibid.*, II, 137.

[31] *Epistolae*, I, 6: *tota nostra voluptas posita est tantum in perceptione
alicujus nostrae perfectionis* (all our pleasure depends so much upon the
perception of some form of our well-being).

intestines, the liver and the lungs. In this first passion of
love, therefore, the whole circulatory, digestive, and respiratory mechanism is peculiarly affected. " And this,"
says Descartes, " is why this same movement of the spirits
has always accompanied the passion of love since." The
basis is laid in the individual's experience and the principle
of association (the principle that when an idea and a movement have once been united, the recurrence of the one involves the reinstatement of the other) accounts for the
rest. In the opposite case we should have opposite effects,
the movements now usually associated with hate. Similarly of the other passions: their characteristic movements
originate in an association early- established in the life of
the individual between a certain type of experience and
a specific set of organic changes adapted to promote the
bodily welfare.[32] Descartes uses the same ontogenetic principle to account for certain individual peculiarities in affective experience, such as his own fondness for persons
with squint eyes. In the treatise on the passions he refers
to one of those curious phenomena which are still something of an enigma: the one he mentions is the aversion to
the odor of roses. There is no doubt in his mind that this is
due either to some early individual association or to some
experience of the mother during pregnancy influencing the
unborn child.[33] In a letter to the Princess Elizabeth he
states as a fact that in some men sorrow diminishes, while
in others it increases appetite. He explains this difference
by supposing that in early life the latter experienced grief
at insufficient, the former at unpalatable or otherwise unsuitable food.[34] The ingenuity of Descartes and his followers in the use of this principle might not have been pushed

[32] *Les passions de l'âme*, II, 107–111.
[33] *Ibid.*, II, 136.
[34] *Epistolae*, I, 11.

so far had they been aware of its corrective and complement in the conception of biological evolution.

The absence of a phylogenetic principle, combined with
inadequate physiological knowledge, makes itself especially felt when Descartes comes to treat of the external
expressions of the emotions. His discussion of these
" signs " is lengthy and painstaking.[35] Yet he only regards
them as incidental effects of the emotions due to the nature,
amount, and direction of the blood and " spirits " generated in each particular case. Joy, for example, causes
reddening, grief pallor, by respectively dilating and contracting the orifices of the heart, though grief may exist
with flushing when accompanied by other passions, such
as desire and hate. Trembling is due to the fact either that
too few " spirits " are transmitted to the nerves, or too
many: the first cause operating in grief and fear, the
second in ardent desire and violent anger. Languor arises
from paucity of " spirits " impelled to the muscles generally, and may be caused by various passions according to
circumstances. Laughter consists in the vigorous expulsion of the air in the lungs by the sudden, spasmodic filling
of the lungs by blood pumped from the right cavity of the
heart. The muscular contractions of the diaphragm, chest,
and throat are secondary effects, and on these depend the
mimic expressions in the face. There are two, and only
two, causes of the sudden expansion of the lungs: the surprise of *admiratio* combined with joy, and the infusion of
some liquid into the blood to make it rarer; Descartes
thinks that in certain passions this liquid is the more fluid
part of the blood, resembling vinegar. Tears he conceives
are formed from vapors akin to sweat; they are changed
into water when the normal evaporation is interrupted, by

[35] *Les passions de l'âme*, II, 112–136.

a process like that in the formation of rain. Weeping is not continuous, and it does not occur in extreme grief, but arises from the alternation of grief with love or joy: grief contracting the pores of the eyes, love and joy sending more blood to the heart and so increasing the quantity of the vapors. These and similar explanations of other signs evidently show no advance in principle beyond those given by Hippocrates and Galen. Even if we substitute for " spirits " the more modern conception of nervous energy, the descriptions would in many points be scientifically defective. But what we miss above all things is any attempt to relate in detail the manifold expressions of the emotions to the assumed teleology of the emotional process as a whole or to bring under a common point of view their various external signs and the visceral changes by which, on the theory, they are caused, strengthened, and sustained. It is true, indeed, that, in a general way, Descartes has explained the primary discharge of the " spirits " to the external muscles as an adaptive reaction of the organism, but he does not apply the principle to the explanation of the signs in particular. He treats them rather as incidental by-products, mechanically produced; but as regards the interpretation of the emotional experience, meaningless.

In the above account the passion is represented as starting in a perception or idea involving the apprehension of the good or ill relation of an object. This, however, is not always the case; sometimes it arises solely from impressions on the brain directly due to somatic conditions. Descartes notes an origin of this sort in certain cases of joy and grief.[36] An exception to the general rule which requires visceral changes and a fresh accession of " spirits " from the heart in order to reinforce the original impressions and

[36] *Ibid.*, II, 93.

so fully constitute the passions, is, as already repeatedly observed, the case of *admiratio*. The nearest English equivalent for this term is astonishment, or, perhaps, surprise. Descartes defines it as " a sudden seizure (*surprise;* Lat., *occupatio*) of the soul causing it to consider attentively objects that appear to it rare and unusual." [37] Its excess is amazement, or consternation, in which degree, by preventing knowledge, its natural end is defeated. Among its species Descartes reckons esteem and contempt. The cause of *admiratio* is an impression on the brain representing the object as rare and, therefore, worthy of regard, and an agitation of the " spirits " conserving and strengthening this impression. At the same time " spirits " flow to the muscles which adapt the sense organ to a closer inspection of the object. Its exceptional position among the passions consists in the fact that it involves no change in the heart or blood. The reason assigned for this is that its object has no relation to bodily welfare, but only to knowledge. It is pre-eminently an " intellectual passion," its purpose being to fix attention and store the memory; it has its dangers, however, for it may lead us to dwell too much on things which do not merit such regard. In denying its relation to bodily welfare, Descartes makes a decided break with his general doctrine. It does not occur to him to consider the first appearance of surprise as a shock akin to fear, or to observe and interpret the widespread bodily effects which accompany it. He takes as original an intellectualized form of the feeling, the feeling of astonishment, we may almost say of wonder, and he shows no adequate appreciation of the fact that our primary interest in novel objects is practical. Here, again, the lack of a genetic point of view is keenly felt by the modern student.

[37] *Ibid.,* II, 70.

Admiratio is the first in Descartes' classification of the
" primary passions," which are six: *admiratio*, love, hate,
desire, joy, and grief. All other passions are held to be
either modifications or combinations of these.[38] With the
exception of *admiratio*, which is added, and *aversio*, which
is omitted, the above list is identical with that ascribed by
Thomas Aquinas to the concupiscible appetite.[39] The distinction between the concupiscible and the irascible parts
of sense appetite as a basis for classification, quickly
dropped by Vives, is expressly rejected by Descartes, first
on the ground that the soul as *res cogitans* has no such
" parts," and secondly, because he finds no reason why all
the passions of the soul should be referred to its two faculties of desire and repugnance (*se fâcher*). [40] The first argument is a verbal quibble, and the second would have less
force if the emotions had been more definitely connected,
as they were by the Stoics and as they are by many more
recent writers, with opposite motor tendencies. However,
in excluding from his list of primary passions those of the
irascible appetite, Descartes but carries to a conclusion the
scholastic recognition that they were subordinate to, and
dependent on those of the concupiscible. He omits aversion on the ground that it is only the negative form of desire.[41] His boldest departure from the tradition is his introduction of *admiratio* into the list, the uniform scholastic
doctrine being that this was not a passion, but an intellectual act. Descartes is himself forced to admit that its
position among the passions is exceptional. His doctrine
was sharply attacked by Thomasius.[42]

---

[38] *Ibid.*, II, 69.
[39] See above Chapter IV, Thomas Aquinas' classification.
[40] *Les passions de l'âme*, II, 68.
[41] *Ibid.*, II, 87.
[42] C. Thomasius, *Von der Artzeney wider die unvernünftige Liebe*, 2.
De la Chambre included *admiration* among the " mixed " passions in his list

The passions are all naturally good and useful, but whether they are actually so to us or not, depends on the use we make of them, for they are also, when ill-regulated, the sources of the greatest misery. Descartes' theory of the control of the passions rests, psychologically, on his conception of the freedom of the will, its power to evoke ideas, and the inhibition of bodily movements through other movements arising from the habitual association of ideas and movements. The will has no power either to excite or to allay a passion directly. But it can exercise control indirectly by calling to mind the ideas which are customarily conjoined with the emotion we desire to have and contrary to that of which we wish to be rid. When an emotion arises suddenly and strongly, we cannot help experiencing its effects, but we can refuse to consent to them and thereby check the movement to which it disposes. All the special rules and suggestions for control mentioned by Descartes rest on the principle of association between ideas and movements and the free power of the will to summon up and put into operation its ideas; the secret of control lies in having the right ideas and in bringing them into play at the right time. There is no conflict between higher and lower parts in the soul; this so-called conflict really consists in the opposition between movements which the will tends to excite and those which at the same time are excited in the pineal gland by the " spirits." The latter movements cannot be voluntarily eradicated, but they can be subordinated to associations which embody and fulfil rational desires. The chief use of wisdom is to make us masters of our passions and so to manage them " that the

---

in *Les caractères*, etc., Pref., but omitted it from the corresponding list in *L'Art de connoistre les hommes,* 85. N. Malebranche calls it an " imperfect passion." *De la recherche de la vérité,* V, 7.

evils they cause may become endurable and that we may even extract joy from all." [43]

Such is Descartes' doctrine of the passions, a doctrine probably as influential as any propounded in modern times. His views were adopted and in part developed by his most attached disciples, Louis de la Forge and Pierre Régis, the former of whom translated into Latin Descartes' *Traité de l'homme* and in a *Traité de l'esprit de l'homme* published in the same year (1666) includes a discussion of the emotions in which he notes more particularly their double origin and course, according as the lead is taken by the agitation of the " spirits " or by the disposition of the will. Régis (1632–1707) who in 1690 published a system of philosophy on Cartesian principles in three quarto volumes,[44] reduces all the passions to the principle of self-love. But the disquisitions of these men are far outclassed in interest and historical importance by those of the philosopher Malebranche, whose treatment of the subject, faithful to the spirit of Descartes, is worked out with great ability and with the independence of an original genius.

Nicolas Malebranche (1638–1715) treats of the passions in the *De la recherche de la vérité* (1674) in intimate connection with the inclinations. The discussion of these two topics fills a third of the entire work (Books IV and V). His main object is to discover how the passions help and hinder the discovery of truth, that truth the apprehension of which is in his view so fundamentally important for our felicity. His interest in the topic is more pronouncedly ethical than Descartes', and his treatment of it is pervaded by a religious spirit and interspersed with allusions to spe-

[43] *Les passions de l'âme,* I, 45–47 ; III, 211, 212.
[44] P. S. Régis, *Cours entier de philosophie ou système général selon les principes de Descartes,* I, Book 2 ; II, Book 6.

cifically theological ideas, entirely absent from that of his predecessor. The celebrated idealism into which he developed the Cartesian metaphysics forms for the discussion a general background, indicated by an occasional reference to impressions made by God on the soul and to the continual action of God in connecting the movements of our will with those of the body and the movements of the body with the passions, but it does not essentially affect the main outlines of his theory. His language in general is that of common-sense dualism. His physiology of the passions, apart from the metaphysical interpretation of the causal relationship, is substantially identical with that of Descartes, except that he no longer conceives of a special commerce of the soul with the body through movements of the pineal gland. The physical organ of consciousness is rather the brain in its entirety. But there is a similar emphasis on the role of the visceral phenomena and on the action of the "spirits" on the brain. For the rest, his analysis of the emotional process is more precise than Descartes' and serves to clear up some points which the latter had left obscure.

The inclinations are the conative tendencies, as original endowments of our nature, seeking satisfaction in the attainment of some good. Their fundamental principle is a tendency to good in general, and this for Malebranche means an implicit movement of the soul towards God. This is the principle of all our restlessness, our curiosity, our striving, the inmost essence of our will which, as Malebranche says, is nothing "but the continual impression of the author of nature leading the mind of man to good in general." [45] The principle, derived by Malebranche from the idea that God can have no other end in creation than

[45] *De la recherche de la vérité*, IV, c. 1, sec. 3 (T. II, 199).

His own glory, is clearly identical with the *synderesis* of Bonaventura and the Victorines and recalls the still older thought of Augustine, to whom for his theory of the passions he is perhaps as fully indebted as to Descartes: " Thou hast made us for Thyself and our hearts are restless until they find their rest in Thee." To this general tendency there are two that are subordinate: (1) a natural inclination of self-love, disposing to self-preservation and happiness, and (2) a natural social inclination, disposing us favorably towards our fellows; and there are many special inclinations dependent on these. All the natural inclinations exist in us now as they existed originally in Adam, but their exercise has been disordered by the Fall, the consequences of which can only be effectually remedied by divine grace.

The distinction between the natural inclinations and the passions is this: the former are defined with reference only to the soul, the latter are causally connected with and related, directly or indirectly, to the body. In Malebranche's words, " the inclinations are impressions of the author of nature which lead us chiefly to love Him as sovereign good and our neighbor without regard to the body; " " the passions of the soul are impressions of the author of nature which incline us to love our body and everything useful to its preservation." [46] The natural or " occasional " cause of these impressions is the movement of the " animal spirits." But the distinction is not absolute. Both inclinations and passions express conative tendencies. The passions are sensible, the natural inclinations spiritual; but the former are not to be conceived as affections of a special sense appetite independent of a special intellectual appetite. The latter are also accompanied by

[46] *Ibid.*, V, c. 1 (T. II, 405 f.).

movements of the " animal spirits " which render them
sensible, just as intellectual cognition is accompanied by
imagery. The passions are rooted in the inclinations; we
are capable of experiencing a sensible love and hate only
because we are capable of experiencing a spiritual. Indeed, the passions as defined appear to be little more than
feelings with impulsive tendencies expressing a special direction of the inclination of self-love. Moreover, they relate not only to the apparent good of the body, but also to
that of the mind. They are definable, in fact, from various
points of view and are so treated by Malebranche in the
free course of his discussion. They are modes in which we
feel the relation of things to our welfare and our consequent modes of reaction, and their empire is as vast as this
relation extends in our humanity.[47]

Malebranche's list of primary passions differs only
verbally from that of Descartes in that what Descartes
called " hate," he calls " aversion." The list is: astonishment (*admiration*), love, aversion, desire, joy, and sorrow.
These six he divides into three groups: first, astonishment,
which stands apart, an " imperfect " passion excited only
by novelty and not, like the rest, by the feeling of good and
ill; secondly, love and aversion — the terms propension
and aversion, or liking and disliking would, perhaps, have
been better — which are the " mother passions "; finally
the " general passions " of desire, joy, and sorrow. All the
passions proper are derived from the " mother passions,"
and ultimately — in this Malebranche agrees with Augustine and the orthodox scholastic tradition — from love,
which aversion, its contrary, is never without. Thus the
passions are derived from a generating passion which
springs from the natural inclination which is the deepest

[47] *Ibid.*, V, c. 2 (T. II, 412–429).

principle of our will. The idea of good possessed causes the love of joy; of good not possessed, that of desire; of good neither possessed nor hoped for, at least without the loss of some other, that of sorrow (*amour de tristesse*). Hope, usually denominated a passion, is regarded, apart from joy or desire, as a mere judgment of expectation. And as these three simple or primary passions have regard to good, so, conversely, with reference to the same three modes of time, they have regard to evil: we have joy when the good is present or the evil past, sorrow when the good is past or the evil present, desire when the good or evil is future. These " general " passions are variously modified and combined into " particular " passions. Passions are the more composite according as the ideas of good and evil exciting them are accompanied by a larger number of accessory ideas or as the good or evil is, relatively to us, more elaborately conditioned. The passions depend on a multitude of circumstances such as age, sex, occupation, social status, mental development, and bodily temperament, and vary in such an infinity of ways according to association of ideas and bodily peculiarities that it is not improbable that any two men have ever been moved by precisely the same passion in all respects.[48] But the effects of the conditions are practically determinate. If we knew them all, " we should perhaps," says Malebranche, " have less difficulty in divining the greater part of human actions than astronomers have in predicting eclipses. For although men are free, they rarely use their freedom to resist their natural inclinations and their violent passions." [49]

The definite connection established by Malebranche between the passions and the innate dispositions, the inclinations, together with the reduction of both to a common

---

[48] *Ibid.*, V, c. 7 (T. II, 516).   [49] *Ibid.*, V, c. 2 (T. II, 425).

principle with the will, marks a decided advance on the
exposition of Descartes. But the most conspicuous improvement in this respect is in the clearness with which
Malebranche analyzes the emotional process. Excepting
astonishment which, not being directly concerned with
good and evil, is regarded, as we have seen, as an " imperfect " passion, every passion normally exhibits, according to Malebranche, seven distinct phases. This he illustrates in detail by the typical case of anger, as Descartes
had illustrated his more summary analysis by that of fear.
The seven phases are as follows: (1) There is the perception, confused or distinct, of the object's relation to us,
e.g., of the affront. (2) This view of the object causes a
specific determination of the will: new if the object appears
good, but merely augmented in the direction of the threatened good, if it appears evil, the intensity of the movement
being proportional to the conceived strength of the opposition. This movement is accompanied by feelings respectively of agreeableness (*douceur*) and disagreeableness
(*douleur*), which are often confounded with, but must be
distinguished from, the emotions.[50] (3) The natural consequence of this movement is, according to circumstances, a
feeling of love, aversion, desire, joy, or sorrow, — in the
case supposed, it is the feeling of hate. This feeling is not
the mere consciousness of the movement of the will; that
is the same, namely towards the good, in hate as in love.
But the feelings are different. " The movements are actions
of the will, the feelings are modifications of the mind
(*esprit*)." [51] But the former are natural causes of the latter
under the conditions (1) and (2), and pass over into their
determination.

So far we have feelings and spiritual emotions, but not

---

[50] *Ibid.*, V, c. 3 (T. II, 429 f.).　　　　[51] *Ibid.*, (T. II, 440).

sensible passions. The phases (1)–(3) might conceivably take place in a pure unbodied spirit. But in man as a composite being the movements of the mind are communicated to the body and those of the body to the mind. Hence (4) the modifications of the mind, and particularly the new determination of the will, referred to above, naturally produce a change in the movements of the " animal spirits." Before the perception of the object of the passion, the " spirits " were distributed over the body for its general conservation. This economy is now disturbed. If the cerebral excitement due to the view of the object is sufficiently intense, the major part of the " spirits " is vigorously impelled to the muscles of the arms, legs, face, and other external parts to give to the body the disposition demanded by the passions, the attitude fitted to acquire the good or avoid the evil, and to the countenance the appropriate " air." The intensity, extent, and rapidity of this discharge is proportional to the strength of the impression made by the object on the brain and the vigor of the imagination; its character will also depend on the ability of the individual to cope with the situation. For if, e.g., he is strong enough to conquer his enemy, his " air " will be menacing and proud, whereas if he is too weak to resist, it will be humble and submissive, calculated to excite compassion and secure assistance by arousing a sympathetic response in the spectator.[52]

Now the production and maintenance of an image sufficiently lively and an excitement sufficiently strong to give rise to such forced and unusual expressions of the body require a superabundance of " spirits," while the variety and promptness of the changes manifested in the different passions must also be provided for by a special mechan-

[52] *Ibid.*, (T. II, 441 f.).

ism. These demands Malebranche conceives of as met by
a distribution of the " spirits " to the nerves communicat-
ing with the interior organs, the innervations thus affected
resulting as follows: (*a*) stimulation of the liver, spleen,
pancreas, etc., to supply the heart with the humors needed
for an abundant production of the " spirits "; (*b*) regulation of the rate of supply of these humors to the heart by
dilation and contraction of the conveying vessels; (*c*) regulation of the rate of their fermentation by nervous control
of the pulse; (*d*) further regulation of the fermentation by
nervous control of respiration, affecting the aeration of the
blood; finally (*e*) rapid distribution of the blood in the
specific manner appropriate to the circumstances by dilation and contraction of the arteries by which it is conveyed
to the brain and to other parts of the body. It is admitted
that these processes cannot be demonstrated with the
desirable exactness in detail, owing to the imperfect development of the sciences of physics and physiology. Malebranche does not speculate minutely on their physiological relations, nor does he attempt, with Descartes, to trace
out the differences of the processes in the different passions. For the explanation of these differences he contents
himself with a general reference to the circumstances of
the excitement — the view of the object determining the
will, with the concomitant disturbance of the brain and
propulsion of the " spirits " — and to the teleology of the
emotional process as a whole, the adaptation of the organism to the conditions. It is enough, he holds, for his purpose
if the general idea is not false. The primary phenomena, it
should be remembered, are not vasomotor and visceral,
important as these are, but the attitudes due to the discharge of the " spirits " to the peripheral muscles. For, as
already observed, the major part of the " spirits " is im-

pelled to these muscles under the influence of the cerebral
excitement in order to "put the body in the disposition
suited to the passion and to give it the expression and
movement necessary for the acquisition of the good or
avoidance of the evil." [53] The function of the visceral and
vasomotor phenomena is to meet the unwonted demands
on the organism by furnishing an adequate supply of properly qualified " spirits " and by a prompt and appropriate
distribution of the blood.[54]

Accompanying, and as a consequence of, this agitation
of the " spirits," we have (5) a " sensible emotion," or
agitation, in the soul. It is important to note that Malebranche does not represent this emotion as consisting in,
or as caused by, the sensations derived from the organic
changes. He represents it rather as due to the perturbation
of the brain and violent discharge of the " spirits " to the
periphery and intestines consequent on the movement in
the soul following the view of the exciting object. It is this
unwonted overflow (*débordement*) by which the soul
feels agitated. " At the very instant the animal spirits are
discharged from the brain the soul is impelled towards the
good it perceives, and that the more energetically the more
vigorously the spirits proceed from the brain, for it is the
same perturbation of the brain which agitates the soul and
the animal spirits." [55] So far, indeed, is his theory from
being " peripheral " that, not to speak of his ignorance of
the specific functions of the afferent and efferent nerves,
he does not even expressly consider that factor in the

---

[53] *Ibid.*, (T. II, 452 f.).

[54] C. Lange, *Sindsbewegelser*, add. 22, cited by R. Lagerborg, *Das
Gefühlsproblem*, 38, finds in Malebranche anticipations of his vasomotor
theory of the emotions, even in details. Neither Malebranche, however, nor
Descartes, whose doctrine in this respect is not essentially different, makes
the vascular phenomena primary in Lange's sense, nor conceives the emotion
as consisting solely in the bodily disturbances and the resulting sensations.

[55] *De la recherche*, etc., V, c. 3 (T. II, p. 456).

process which Descartes regarded as critical, namely the fresh accession of " spirits " to the brain reinforcing and sustaining the original impression. This factor is no doubt implied in the theory, but it is not insisted on. Occasionally and incidentally the passion is ascribed to the agitation of the blood.[56] But there is no dwelling on the circularity of the process. The point is that the agitation of the brain corresponding to the perception of the object's relation to us and the impulse to seek or conserve good and escape evil leading to movements adapted to bodily conservation, is sensibly experienced and that thereby the view of the good and the impulse towards it are sensibly augmented. Malebranche makes no allusion to the concomitant organic sensations as such. Nor does he regard the " emotion in the soul," of which he speaks, as a merely added cerebral *coenaesthesia*. Nor, again, does he regard it as itself the feeling of love, hate, fear, etc. His analysis is incomplete, but he leaves us in no uncertainty as to his meaning. The " emotions in the soul " are identical, he tells us, with those which follow immediately the intellectual view of the good, except that they are stronger and more lively. This character they derive from the union of the soul with the body and the fact that they are produced no longer by a view merely intellectual, but by one that is sensible, implicated namely — for so we are to interpret the statement — in the cerebral changes which find expression in movements adapted to organic welfare.[57]

Then (6) there is the feeling of the passion of love, aversion, joy, sorrow, etc. This also is identical with the feeling already referred to as following the intellectual perception and impulse, only stronger and more vivid by reason of the cerebral disturbance which makes it sensible. Thus

[56] E.g., *Ibid.*, 459 f.   [57] *Ibid.*, 457 f.

the phases (2) and (3) are repeated in phases (5) and (6), in which they appear sensibly strengthened and transformed by the modifications of consciousness brought about by the movements in the brain referred to under (4). Phase (1), though not separately noted, is also repeated and transformed under the same influence as a sensible view of the body's good. Usually the whole process begins with (1), but there are cases where the passion is primarily excited by bodily movements. In horror and antipathy and in agreement and sympathy, indeed, the attractions and repulsions are so prompt and at the same time so sensible that no reason can be assigned for them, and Malebranche, who has no evolutionary principle for explaining these reactions, properly leaves them unexplained.

Finally (7) the process fulfills itself in an attendant feeling of " joy " or sweetness (*douceur*), the agreeableness which attests the suitableness of the state to the requirements of the situation. Every emotion, whatever its character in other respects, is, in Malebranche's view, pleasant. This novel conception is regarded as a necessary consequence of the reaction. The movement of the " spirits," whether flowing to the peripheral muscles or to the intestines, is in the direction of adapting the organism to meet the conditions of stimulation. But the body is never in the condition proper to it without satisfaction, or in a contrary state without pain. Hence, when we follow the movements of the " spirits," we receive an interior satisfaction, whereas if we arrest them, e.g., from a sense of duty, we feel distress. This satisfaction is regarded by Malebranche as the greatest source of moral and religious danger, for all that it attests is the good estate of the body, of which it is the confused feeling. But the good of the body is, or may be, contrary to the good of the soul, which is clearly discerned by reason. Moreover, this sensible joy is not solid, but restless and inconstant and is almost never accompanied by any joy of the spirit; whereas the latter is almost always accompanied by a very great joy of the senses. But for the natural man the bodily pleasures are the more intense, and as the movements in the passions are mechanically produced and the freedom to give or withhold assent to them is impaired in its exercise by the corruption of " original sin," he naturally yields to his passions and thus becomes more and more estranged from his true good, which is God. From this slavery he can only be rescued by grace.

We have not to follow Malebranche in the ethical and theological developments of his doctrine. Involved with ideas of reason, free will, sin, grace, and the like, he seems to recognize forms of emotional experience which are not strictly passions, but spiritual affections, whose end is the good, not of the body, but of the soul. It is impossible to distinguish in them any difference of psychological process, except in so far as they are determined by reflective ideas or by impressions of a supernatural origin. Every view of good or ill is accompanied by some emotion in the soul and some change in the body.[58] On the other hand, the passions include states of very varying psychological complexion, not only sudden invasions of the mind with widespread bodily effects, as in anger and fear, but such a feeling as " admiration " with, it is assumed, restricted bodily changes, and such more or less permanent and organized dispositions as a " passion for poetry, for history, for mathematics, for the chase, and for the dance." [59] Both in its wider and in its narrower use the term denotes concretely all the moments in the analysis given above,

[58] *Ibid.,* V, c. 10, 575 f.   [59] *Ibid.,* V, c. 7, 512.

though the name of a given passion frequently emphasizes some one phase of the process, standing as an abbreviated expression of the whole.

Malebranche dwells at length on the influence of the passions on judgment, on which subject he has much to say of value for a psychology of affective reasoning,[60] though his point of view is mainly moral and religious. The distinction is drawn between the judgment which precedes and that which follows the passion. The former, he says, is almost always false in some respect, being usually sustained by perceptions of the objects as related to the soul, and not as they are in themselves; while the latter, as being entirely dependent on perceptions of those relations, are false every way. The important principle is that all the passions tend to justify themselves; hence the perversity of reliance on them alone in the search for truth. Like Descartes Malebranche seeks the control of them in the illumination of the understanding, especially that furnished by metaphysics and religion, and explains by essentially the same psychological mechanism — the association of ideas and of ideas with movements — the method of control.[61]

[60] Especially in V, Chapter 6 and following.
[61] *Ibid.*, V, c. 8, 559 f.

CHAPTER VII

SYSTEMS OF THE " PASSIONS " IN THE SEVENTEENTH CENTURY: HOBBES AND SPINOZA

Thomas Hobbes's interest in the passions appears to have been derived in large part from his interest in politics. Long before he conceived the plan of a philosophical system, he had been an anxious observer of the political movements of his time and a close student of the springs of action from which they arose. His plan of a philosophical system was formed comparatively late in life after he had made the discovery of mathematics and had become acquainted with the physical sciences as they were then being developed on strictly mechanical principles. The new scientific insight revolutionized, or at least fashioned and fixed his thinking. His chief problem was the origin, nature, and constitution of civil and political society. That problem could only be solved by an interpretation of human nature. But back of that lay a more general conception of the nature of the universe, of which human nature was a part. This conception was frankly materialistic. The real world is composed of bodies, precisely as the physicist conceives it; and the affections of bodies are motions transmitted from body to body by actual contact. Human nature is itself thus constituted. The psychical life consists really of mechanically propagated motions of the particles of the organism.[1]

---

[1] T. Hobbes (1588–1679) formulated a system which was not executed in the order planned. The *De corpore* was not published till 1654. Seventeen years earlier, on returning from the continent, Hobbes had been led by the political unrest which he found in England to write the *Elementes of Law*

The clue to human nature Hobbes found in the passions. No writer of the period attributes to them such significance for the whole life of man as he. They are omnipresent; in the drama of man's life they occupy the center of the stage. They sustain thought, essentially constitute will, determine the intellectual no less than the moral character, and are the sole springs of action. Without passion the train of our thoughts would be unregulated; direction is given by a desired end. The power of passion to regulate the flow of our thoughts is found in the strength and permanence of the impressions made upon us by such things as we desire or fear. From desire arises the thought of the means to its fulfillment, and from that the thought of the means to the means, and so on, " till we come to some beginning in our own power." And if our thoughts wander, it is the greatness of the impression of the end which brings them back to consecutiveness.² Since passion is thus the guide of thought, Hobbes naturally finds in it the explanation of the differences of men's evils. These differences, he holds, are largely due to the greater or less desire for power or for its species, the desire for riches, for knowledge, and for honor. " A man who has no great passion for any of these things . . . cannot possibly have either a great fancy or much judgment, . . . for as to have no desires is to be dead, so to have weak passions is dullness." On the physical side the differences are due, not to the temper of the brain, which Hobbes assumes to be practically alike in

---

Naturall and Politique, the dedicatory epistle of which is dated May 9, 1640. This treatise was published in two parts separately in 1650, the one entitled *Human Nature,* the other, *De corpore politico. Leviathan* appeared in 1651.

The chief sources in Hobbes's doctrine of the passions are: *Human Nature,* cc. VII–X (E. W. IV, 31–59) and *Leviathan,* Part I, c. VI (E. W. III, 38–51). Cf. also *De homine,* cc. XI–XIII (L. W. II, 94–118) and *De corpore politico,* IV, 25 (L. W. I, 331–334).

² *Leviathan,* I, c. 3 (E. W. III, 12 ff.).

all men, but to the character and movements of the " spirits " about the heart.[3] The passions are also the beginning
of voluntary motion; will, in fact, is itself a passion and
was wrongly defined as a rational appetite. Deliberation
is simply an alternation of appetites and aversions, hopes
and fears, the last appetite in the series being the will.[4] As
the passions are the beginning of voluntary movement, so
they are the beginning of speech, the motion of the tongue;
speech arising from the desire of men to show to others
the knowledge, opinions, conceptions, and passions which
are in themselves.[5] The passions, being of the very essence
of human nature, are also the basis of civil society. For as
the natural condition of warfare among men is an effect of
their passions, so the social order which ends this warfare
is due to the passions which incline them to peace. While
passion is power, it is also, Hobbes teaches, limited power.
It is not, therefore, to be ascribed to the Deity. The dangers arising to the commonwealth from the inflaming of the
passions in public assemblies is used as an argument in
favor of monarchy; the single ruler, it is held, being less
subject to passion than the multitude.[6]

The nature of the passions of the mind, which are thus
found so significant in human life, is defined by Hobbes
prominently in terms of endeavor. Except pure pleasure
and pain, " which are a certain fruition of good and evil,"
they all consist of appetite and aversion.[7] Appetite, or desire, is endeavor towards; aversion, endeavor away from.

[3] *Ibid.*, I, c. 8 (E. W. III, 61 f.) ; *Human Nature*, c. 10 (E. W. IV,
55).
[4] *De homine*, II, 11, 2 (L. W. II, 94) ; *appetitus ultimus, sive faciendi
sive omittendi, qui actionem vel omissionem immediate producit, proprie
voluntas dicitur.*
[5] *Human Nature*, c. 5 (E. W. IV, 25).
[6] *Leviathan*, I, c. 13 (E. W. III, 116) ; II, c. 17 (E. W. III, 153) ;
II, c. 25 f. (E. W. III, 248 f.) ; *De corpore politico*, II, 5 (E. W. IV, 166 f.).
[7] *Physics*, IV, 25, sec. 13 (E. W. I, 409 f.).

As what men desire or are averse to they are also said to love or hate, love and hate are synonyms of desire and aversion, except that we commonly use the latter terms when the object is absent, the former, when it is present. The object of appetite is called good, that of aversion, evil. According as the good or evil is viewed in the promise, in the effect, or as a means, the one is designated respectively *pulchrum, jucundum, utile,* the other, *turpe, molestum, inutile.* Nothing is good simply. The distinction between real and apparent good depends on whether the chain of experiences is good, that is, satisfies desire on the whole; and in this regard inexperience may easily lead to mistakes. The primary and greatest good is the being's own conservation, the greatest evil, its destruction.[8] Besides appetite and aversion as the root passions, Hobbes posits as a third fundamental but derived passion, contempt, the object of which we neither desire nor hate, but the action of which we resist. He defines it as an immobility or contumacy of heart in resisting the action of certain things when the heart is already otherwise moved, that is, fixed in its set of appetite or aversion. Directly connected with appetite and aversion are delight (pleasure) and molestation (displeasure) in the fruition of good and evil, and joy and grief in their expectation.

We have now before us all the passions of the mind which Hobbes designates as " simple ": namely, appetite, desire, love, aversion, joy, and grief — a list strongly reminiscent of the concupiscible passions of the Schoolmen and, excepting *admiratio,* more or less akin to those of Descartes and Malebranche. It is noteworthy that appetite and desire, while commonly used as synonyms, are here distinguished and that delight and molestation do not ap-

[8] *De homine,* II, 11, 5 (L. W. II, 95 f.).

pear; neither does contempt. From these simple, although not equally primary, passions — since the roots of all the passions are appetite and aversion — Hobbes derives, without attempting an exhaustive enumeration (the passions, in fact, are innumerable) a multitude of emotional states, qualities, and dispositions, which are, in his view, but different names of these same simple passions due to diverse considerations: namely, (1) the opinion entertained of the prospect of the fulfillment of the desire, (2) the object loved or hated, (3) the coexistence of these passions, and (4) their alteration or succession. Thus hope is defined as appetite with opinion of attainment; despair as appetite without this attainment; fear as aversion with opinion of hurt from the object; courage as aversion with hope of avoiding the hurt by resistance; anger as sudden courage. In certain cases the passion in question is defined by contrast as a species of contempt. Thus magnanimity is contempt of little helps and hindrances as over against pusillanimity, a combination of desire of things little conducive to our ends and fear of things of but little hindrance; cruelty is contempt of the calamity of others in contrast with pity, which is grief at such calamity. The definitions are all short and often arbitrary, as, e.g., that of anger as sudden courage and that of diffidence as constant despair. It is to be noted also that Hobbes includes indiscriminately among the passions, besides emotional shocks, affectively interested processes of various sorts and, more particularly, permanent dispositions and habits of character. Thus, along with such states as anger and fear, he reckons as passions covetousness and luxury, curiosity and ambition, good nature, religion, superstition, deliberation, and will. His main interest, we remember, is not psychological analysis, but the development of a concep-

tion of human nature which would explain men's actions
and afford an intelligible basis for civil institutions and political government. His account of the passions in the treatise on *Human Nature* culminates, therefore, in the famous
comparison of the life of man to a race in which men
moved by the fundamental ambition of power are strug-
gling to be foremost. And as all effort, success, or failure in
this race arises from or gives rise to passions, very many
passions are redefined by Hobbes from this point of view.
Thus in this race, to endeavor is appetite; to be remiss, sen-
suality; to consider those behind, glory; to consider those
ahead, humility; and so on through a long list.[9]

While the passions are thus, in common with the medieval psychology, conceived fundamentally as conations,
and not, as in some later systems, as forms of feeling, they
nevertheless are closely connected with the affective elements of pleasure and displeasure, although Hobbes himself does not draw this distinction. Pleasure and pain, as we
have seen, are, according to him, the fruition of good and
evil, that is, of the objects of appetite and aversion. Pleasure, or delight, is thus defined as the *apparence,* or sense of
good; molestation, or displeasure, as the *apparence,* or
sense of evil. But these experiences give rise to fresh appetites and aversions. Indeed, the only distinction which
Hobbes appears willing to draw between pleasure-pain
and conation is that the former is always a present experience while the latter relates to the future. Appetition, he
says, is pleasure and aversion displeasure, the one from
expected pleasant, the other from expected unpleasant
experience. On the other hand, pleasure and displeasure,
though called *sensiones,* are distinguished from ordinary

9 *The Elements of Law,* I, ix, 21 (ed. Tönnies, 47).

sensations having external reference, as internal conations (*conatus introrsi*) [10] consisting in passions.

The real doctrine of Hobbes by which this is to be interpreted is that pleasure, pain, and passions generally are bodily motions. All change whatsoever, he assumes, is motion or endeavor, and endeavor is " the small beginnings " of motion. Sensation, therefore, he argues is nothing but motion in the " sentient " generated by the object and propagated through the various media to the innermost organ of sense, combined with the motion, or endeavor outward of the organ, or organs, which it affects or excites. The psychical content, or *phantasm,* is the *apparence* of this action and reaction. Hobbes conceives of the heart in its organic connection with the head as the true ultimate organ of sense, so that if the motion is only propagated to the head, or if the connection between that organ and the heart is interrupted, sensation is absent. The motions thus excited subside or decay gradually. Decaying sense is imagination or fancy, under which term are included both memory and expectation.[11] While sensation is thus referred to the heart, in the sense, presumably, that, unless the motion is continued to the heart, the sensory process is incomplete, the intellectual contents, the " conceptions " and " apparitions " are referred to the head, and the distinction between the two organs is used to specifically define the bodily seat of the passions. In the treatise on *Human Nature* the various conceptions which are said to consist in the " motion and agitation of the brain " are divided into those of sense, remembrance, and expectation, and to each severally Hobbes seeks to attach the passions

[10] *De homine,* II, 11, 1 (L. W. II, 94).
[11] *De corpore,* IV, 25, 2 (L. W. I, 331 f.).

that we " commonly take notice of," and which are nothing but the former motion " continued to the heart." [12] The effect of the propagation of motion to the heart must be either to help or to hinder, quicken or slacken the " vital " motion, that is, the motion of the perpetually circulating blood. When this motion is helped, it is called delight, contentment, or pleasure, and with reference to the object, love; when it is hindered, it is called pain, and, with reference to the object, hatred. As pleasure and pain are each a solicitation, or provocation to or from the object present or imagined, we have in these same modifications of circulation the real phenomena of appetite, aversion, fear, and, indeed, so far as these are the root or simple passions, of the passions generally.[13] The furtherance of vital motion is sustained by the " spirits." This process, with its accompanying feeling, takes place even in the embryo. In the appetite and aversion arising from the motions of pleasure and pain, modifications of " vital " motion, we have the first beginnings of " animal " motion; the passional movements being accompanied by corresponding movements of the " spirits " flowing into or withdrawing from the nerves, which then act on the muscles. According to Hobbes very few of our appetites and aversions are congenital, the majority being acquired through individual experiences of pleasure and pain.[14]

Unlike Descartes, Hobbes makes no attempt to trace the specific changes which constitute the specific passions of fear, anger, etc. The details of the doctrine are left

---

[12] *Human Nature,* c. 8 (E. W. IV, 34 ff.).

[13] *Human Nature,* c. 7 (E. W. IV, 31). The affects consist in diverse motions of the blood and animal spirits, so far as they variously now expand, now withdraw to the source; the causes of which motions are the *phantasmata* excited in the mind by objects as regards good and evil, *De homine,* II, 12, 1 (L. W. II, 98 f.).

[14] *De corpore,* IV, 25, 12 (L. W. I, 335 f.) ; *De homine,* II, 11, 3.

vague. Its significance lies in its general theoretical simplicity. Body and soul are a unity and the real factors are bodily movements. No purely psychical factor intervenes; there is no causal interaction between soul and body, as between two things. When Hobbes uses language which seems to imply such interaction, it must be interpreted in the metaphysical sense of his materialism. When, for example, he speaks of " extraordinary and extravagant passion " as sometimes proceeding from the evil constitution of the body, and, on the other hand, of " the hurt and indisposition of the organs " as " caused by the vehemence and long continuance of the passion," [15] this can only refer to contrasts and effects within differently conditioned movements of the body, and not at all to any interaction of the body and the mind. The psychical element, which is declared to be in reality nothing but motion in certain parts of the body, is accounted for by ascribing to human nature definite psychical capacities, and these Hobbes conceives as called into exercise by the appropriate bodily movements, which give to them their content and are the bearers of the whole psychical dynamism. When, for example, the external object has affected the organs of sense, the motion being propagated to the brain excites the cognitive power and we have, in virtue of its association with the traces left by past experience, both a *phantasm* of the object and the idea of good or evil to be expected from it. The motion being continued to the heart becomes or excites a passion, that is, a pleasure or pain together with the connected impulses felt as such of withdrawal or approach. If the blood and spirits are decisively determined, the action takes place at once — the vital motion passes over into animal motion; but if the idea of anticipated pleasure

[15] *Leviathan*, I, c. 8 (E. W. III, 62).

from the exhibition of our power alternates with that of unpleasantness attendant on diminished power, a mechanical process of " deliberation " is set up terminating in, let us say, flight. Somewhere in this process occurs the emotion, for example, fear, connected with the changes in circulation brought about by the affection of the heart. We may suppose it to be the feeling of the tension of the manifold impulses. But Hobbes is vague on this point, and we must leave his theory, with its general advance towards simplicity, its effort to get rid of dualism, as we find it.

A similar simplicity, with more explicit recognition of the dual aspects of human nature expressed in a doctrine of philosophical parallelism, and with much more systematic elaboration of the material, is found in Benedictus de Spinoza (1632–1677) who devotes the third part of his *Ethics* to a consideration, a demonstration *more geometrico,* of the *Origin and Nature of the Emotions (affectuum).* This account of the passions is spoken of as Spinoza's masterpiece, and has been much admired.[16] His profession of a scientific attitude in approaching the subject is certainly admirable. Men generally, he writes, are wont to cry out against the vices and follies of men as opposed to reason; he, on the other hand, is convinced that " nothing happens in nature which can be attributed to any vice of nature, for she is always the same and everywhere one." [17] The passions are natural phenomena and follow the necessities which other natural phenomena follow. This is Spinoza's just assumption, which in a modern writer would result in an attempt impartially to describe and ex-

---

[16] Cf. F. Pollock, *Spinoza, His Life and Philosophy,* 201. As evidence Pollock cites the opinion of J. P. Müller, who declares that it is impossible to give any better account of the relations of the passions to one another, apart from their physiological conditions, " than that which Spinoza has laid down with unsurpassed mastery," *Physiologie des Menschen,* II, 543.

[17] *Ethics,* Part III Pref.

plain the observed facts. But Spinoza's conception of scientific method is to deduce, or at any rate develop, the facts
more geometrico. " I shall treat of the nature and strength
of the passions," he writes, " and the power of the mind
over them, by the same method as I have treated of God
and the mind in the foregoing parts; and I shall consider
human actions and desires after the same sort as if the inquiry were concerned with lines, surfaces, and solids." [18]
He criticizes Descartes' attempt to explain them, that is,
Descartes' physiological theory, and his account of the way
the mind attains mastery over them as unsuccessful, except as showing the acuteness of his great intellect. His
own attempt, it is feared, and with greater reason, must
be similarly criticized.

It is obvious that Spinoza cannot deduce the emotions
more geometrico without appeal to experience. He makes
a show of such deduction by assuming certain metaphysical principles, as e.g., that of parallelism (supposed to have
been demonstrated earlier in the treatise) and certain
others, as e.g., that of the *conatus* of self-preservation, as
constituting the essence of a thing. His deductions are all
supposed to agree with experience, of course, and they
often in fact do. But we must distinguish the facts from
the reasons Spinoza assigns for them and be prepared for
many cases where the facts are sacrificed to the logic. Take,
for example, the demonstration of Proposition 17. The
proposition asserts that " if we imagine that a thing which
is wont to affect us unpleasantly (*tristitiae affectu*) is like
another which usually affects us very pleasantly (*magno
laetitiae affectu*), we shall at the same time both hate it
and love it." The proof that we shall hate it is that we hate,
as explained in an earlier theorem, whatever gives us pain;

[18] *Loc. cit.*

the proof that we shall love it is derived from the preceding Proposition 16, which declares that any object imagined as resembling one that usually affects us in a certain way will affect us in a similar way, — a proposition which rests on the abstract argument that the imagination of an object affects us in the same way as the object itself. The logic may be flawless, but what are the facts? Is it not true that in certain cases the very resemblance of a hated object to an object that we love, the very possession by it of qualities that are in themselves admirable, is an added reason for hate? Such would usually, perhaps, and certainly might very well be the case. For example, in respect to one whom we regarded as a polished but dangerous hypocrite, we do not necessarily abstract the graces and develop a " fluctuation of the mind " between delight in them and pain at the hypocrisy: we may rather reject and renounce and hate *en bloc,* and the more vigorously the more we see in the polished speech and manners only indications of the villainy. Spinoza fails to consider the total complexion of the affect. Another example of the fallacy of deducing facts from logic is found in Proposition 32. " If we imagine," the proposition asserts, " that anyone delights in anything which only one can possess, we shall try to bring it about that he shall not possess that thing." That this is not necessarily true is obvious; as a critic pointed out long ago, we do not normally try to prevent a man's sole possession and enjoyment of his wife.[19] How then does Spinoza demonstrate the proposition? His proof is simple. If, he says, we imagine that another takes delight in anything, that will be a reason for our loving and delighting in the same thing. This, empirically, is of course by no means true, but Spinoza proves it by his theory of sympathy, according to

[19] Christoph Vittichius, *Anti-Spinoza.*

which the *imagination* of another's state is a partial reproduction in us of his physical and mental affection, this theory being derived from his doctrine of parallelism. Now by
hypothesis, Spinoza continues, we imagine that his delighting in a thing is an obstacle to our pleasure, and therefore,
he concludes, we endeavor to prevent his possessing it.
Possibly, we reflect, if we make the hypothesis, though not
necessarily even then. But the hypothesis is not necessary
under the circumstances, nor is it clear that it was made
except in the proposition to be proved, and which, by a
process of circular demonstration, it is now used to prove!
As a fact, we not infrequently rejoice in the pleasure of
others which we can only imaginatively share, not being at
all able to share the possession of the thing they delight in.
Spinoza begins the *Scholium* on this proposition by saying,
" we see, therefore, that it is the nature of men generally
to pity those in adversity and to envy those in prosperity."
That is, we do not find this to be a fact by observation and
generalization, but see it through the medium and as the
consequence of a logical (and fallacious) argument! After
finding in the same argument grounds for other supposed
facts of human nature, Spinoza complacently adds that " if
we will consult experience, we shall find that she teaches
the same doctrine " — the reference to experience being
secondary.

It has been contended that Spinoza himself does not consider the geometrical method of exposition an infallible
method of discovery, but uses it as the most perfect type of
scientific method to indicate his determination to conduct
the investigation in a purely scientific spirit.[20] But it is hard
to escape the impression of instances like the foregoing,
and, indeed, of the whole tenor of the discussion, that

---

[20] F. Pollock, *Spinoza, his Life and Philosophy*, 201.

Spinoza really does mean to deduce consequences from principles and to construct human nature *a priori,* in part at least. Certain facts are for him necessarily implied in the laws of nature and these follow from the metaphysical principles of its constitution. What he actually does for the most part is to express familiar experiences in abstract terms and then by a logical artifice to weave such connections between them as to give the illusory appearance of a demonstration.[21] With this proviso we are prepared to admit and admire the acuteness and accuracy of many of his observations, which have the force of laws, but of empirical laws. An illustration is the following: " If a man has begun to hate an object of his love, so that love is thoroughly destroyed, he will, causes being equal, regard it with more hatred than if he had never loved it, and his hatred will be in proportion to the strength of his former love." [22]

The taproot of Spinoza's doctrine of the passions is his conception of the striving of each particular thing to maintain its own existence. This striving is no mere property, but the thing's very essence.[23] Viewed with regard to the mind only it is called " will "; with regard to both body and mind, " appetite," which, when conscious, is called

[21] M. Steinitzer remarks, *Die menschlichen und tierischen Gemütsbewegungen,* 174, that Spinoza's demonstration that the consequences of a passion follow from its nature with mathematical necessity is often in a given case nothing but the further exposition of the thesis which already contains the beginning and end of a psychic process, the connecting links of which then furnish the " proof."

[22] *Ethics,* III, Proposition 38. The proposition is cited by A. F. Shand, *The Foundations of Character,* 73, as a model of what such laws should be.

[23] *Ethics,* III, Proposition 6. When Spinoza declares that the *conatus* in question is nothing *praeter ipsius rei actualem essentiam,* he excludes (as Pollock points out) the interpretation of it as a *vis insita* or as a power back of the individual and acting through it. It seems almost to be his principle of individuation and suggests a dynamic pluralistic-monistic view of his metaphysics. But how reconcile it with the doctrine that the individual is a mere *modus* of the Substance? Is, *e.g.,* the body's " extension " an essential attribute — to be conceived as the expression of its effort *in suo esse perseverare?*

" desire." The things which further existence and determine action are relative to this striving; we do not will, desire, strive for a thing because we deem it good, but contrariwise we deem it good because we will, desire, or strive for it.[24]

The doctrine that the passions are essentially conative is common to all writers of the period and goes back to Aristotle and the Stoics. It is especially prominent in Malebranche, who finds them rooted in the natural inclination of man to the good, and in Hobbes, who connects them empirically with the two antithetic forms of endeavor, appetite and aversion. It remained, however, for Spinoza to reduce the conative tendencies which find expression in emotion to the one fundamental striving of self-conservation, to conceive this striving as the individual's very being, and to derive from it all human actions and passions. How is this deduction brought about?

It is brought about in the first place by associating with this *conatus* in the form of desire the phenomena of pleasure and pain. All the passions consist in, or are compounded of, pleasure, pain, and desire. This is Spinoza's simplification of the Cartesian scheme of the primary passions. " I know no other primary *affectus*," he says, " but these three," and he proposes to show that the others are derived (*oriri*) from them.[25] Indeed, he goes even further and declares the different emotions to be but desire, pleasure, and pain differently named " after the diverse presentments and tokens of them in outward operation." This simplification plausibly combines the classical representation of them in all systems which operate mainly with logical definitions, where they invariably appear either as

[24] *Ibid.,* Proposition 9, *Scholium.*
[25] *Ibid.,* Proposition 11, *Scholium.*

forms of conation or as forms of pleasure and pain. But with this simplification Spinoza, in the second place, goes beyond the bare idea of self-conservation to that of perfection. Pleasure, joy, or delight, *laetitia*, — the term embraces all varieties of pleasant experience — is defined as a passion whereby the mind passes to a greater perfection; pain, displeasure, or sorrow, *tristitia*, — the term embraces all varieties of unpleasant experience — is defined as a passion whereby the mind passes to a lesser perfection; or, as stated elsewhere, with emphasis on the transitional character of the phenomena and on the indication of the complex nature of the subject, pleasure is the *passage* of a *man* (body as well as mind) from less to greater perfection; pain is the passage of a man from greater to less perfection.[26] By "perfection" here we are to understand a relative degree of the "power of acting" which is identified with "power of existing" or, simply, "reality." Thus emotion (*affectus*) is defined as consisting in "the affections of the body whereby the body's power of acting is increased or diminished . . . together with the ideas of these affections," while a passion (*pathema*), distinguished from an action, when referred solely to the mind, is defined in part as a confused idea whereby the mind affirms a greater or less power of existing (*existendi vis*) in its body, or some part of its body than it had previously. The mind's power of thinking corresponds, of course, on the parallelistic principles of Spinoza's philosophy, to its body's power of existing. Spinoza explains the alleged increase or diminution in the former as merely meaning that the mind forms an idea of its body, or some part thereof,

[26] *Ibid.* and articles 2 and 3 in the Recapitulation following Proposition 59.

expressing more or less reality than before.[27] Perfection, existence, reality, and power of acting are thus convertible terms; it is by identifying these conceptions that Spinoza builds up his system of the emotions as checking or furthering the development of the individual to the freedom of self-realization, while concealing from himself the fact that the tendencies involved are anything more than modifications of the fundamental tendency of every individual to self-conservation.

All affective phenomena in man, then, are phenomena of pleasure, pain, and desire. Of these, as we have seen, pleasure and pain are by definition — it does not occur to Spinoza that there is here any question of fact — the experienced transition to a greater or less perfection, that is, to a greater or less power of acting or existing. These states are related not only to the soul's passions in the narrower sense, that is, to the restriction of its reality expressed in confused ideas, but also to its "actions" expressed in adequate ideas. Desire, as conscious appetite, is the man's actual essence, his fundamental striving to maintain his existence. If this is to be called a passion, then passion is of the very essence of the man, and the old Scholastic-Aristotelian distinction between οὐσία and πάθη disappears.

We have now to see how this doctrine is carried out. The most important species of pleasure and pain, according to Spinoza, are love and hate, love being pleasure and hate pain accompanied by the idea of its external cause. Striving for the presence and preservation of the beloved object is a " consequence "; and similarly, of hate.[28] Inclination (*propensio*) and aversion, devotion and derision are vari-

---

[27] *Ibid.*, Def. I–III. Proposition 16, Dem., speaks of an *affectus* by which the mind's power of action is neither increased nor diminished.

[28] *Ibid.*, Proposition 13, *Scholium.*

eties; the first two arise — the description is plainly arbitrary — when we regard the cause as accidental (or, perhaps, incidental, *per accidens*); devotion is love towards
one whom we admire; derision (*irrisio*), pleasure from
imagining in an object of our hate something that we despise. *Admiratio,* which Descartes reckoned among the primary passions, Spinoza does not regard as emotional at all,
" since this distraction of the mind ariseth from no positive
cause drawing the mind away from other things, but
merely from the absence of a cause, determining the mind
to think on other things." It is defined as " the imagination
of something on which the mind remains fixed because that
particular imagination is unconnected with others." [29] Contempt, a prominent form of passion with Hobbes, is similarly defined as " imagination of an object so little affecting
the mind that the mind is moved by its presence to imagine
those qualities which are not in it rather than those that
are." In this connection Spinoza mentions reverence (*ven-
eratio*) and scorn, but declines to define them " since there
are no emotions to my knowledge named after them."
Cheerfulness, merriment, melancholy, and grief are also
undefined, but for an opposite reason: not because of their
intellectual character, but " because they have rather the
nature of bodily affections, and are but kinds of pleasure
or pain." [30] The intellectualism and arbitrariness of Spinoza's procedure is here very manifest.

Another group of passions defined in terms of pleasure
and pain are those which have reference to past and future
time. This group includes hope, an inconstant pleasure

[29] *Ibid.,* Proposition 59, Def. IV. Steinitzer, *op. cit.,* 175 notes that in
the *Short Treatise* Spinoza had regarded wonder (*admiratio*) as more affective than intellectual ; if a country bumpkin, he said, were to hear an animal
bark other than a dog, he would be as much astonished as an Aristotle,
although no train of reflection preceded.

[30] *Ibid.,* Proposition 59, Def. III and V.

from the idea of something future or past, of the issue of which we are in doubt; fear an inconstant pain similarly aroused; confidence, a pleasure, and despair, a pain, when the cause of doubt is removed; joy, pleasure with the idea of something that has happened beyond our expectation, and gnawing grief (*conscientiae morsus*),[31] pain similarly attended.

These emotions are, in a way, aroused by association of ideas. Affective association is a frequent cause of emotion. " If the mind has at any time been simultaneously affected by two objects, whenever it is afterwards affected by one of them, it will also be affected by the other " (Proposition 14). Resemblance operates similarly (Proposition 16). Hence objects which are in themselves indifferent may excite emotion *per accidens* (Proposition 15). Hence too the possibility of emotional conflicts; an object causing present pain may be attended by memories of equal or greater pleasure, so that we may at the same time both love it and hate it (Proposition 17). Or the conflict may arise directly either from the complexity of the body, one part of which is affected in one way, another in another, or from the complexity in the relations of the object, which being itself diversely affected by things external to it may diversely affect the same part of the body. The state of mind induced Spinoza calls vacillation, *animi fluctuatio*, a state related to emotion as *dubitatio* to imagination, differing, in fact, from the latter only in degree (*secundum majus et minus*). Spinoza seems not to distinguish between this explanation (in the *Scholium*), which suggests a phenomenon analogous to retinal rivalry, and the doctrine of

[31] *Ibid.*, Proposition 59, Def. XII–XV. Pollock translates this " disappointment or grief "; White and Stirling in their translation of the *Ethics* render it by " remorse." " Disappointment " satisfies the definition, but seems too weak a word for the term. Neither it nor " remorse " seems the proper antithesis to joy, *gaudium*.

" mixed " emotions implied in the proposition (17). Principles of association are used to explain affections based on
sympathy. Sympathy arises from the imagination of another constituted like ourselves, it being impossible, in
Spinoza's view, to imagine such a being as affected in any
way without reproducing a similar affection in ourselves
(Proposition 27). His demonstration of this thesis is metaphysical and farfetched; instead of consulting experience,
he assumes as a metaphysical necessity that " the idea of
the imagined external body will imply an affection of our
own body like to that of the external body," and from this
he concludes that if we imagine another like ourselves as
emotionally affected, the imagination will be the conscious
expression of a similar affection in our own body, in other
words, that we shall feel a similar emotion.[32] Why the
emotion should be sympathetically felt as another's, Spinoza does not clearly explain. Nor does he make it altogether evident why the affections in us which are based on
sympathy should be in so many cases different from the
emotions which we imagine in their objects. Among these
affections he reckons pity, approval, indignation, overestimation and disparagement of others, envy, and compassion. Here as elsewhere the definitions are formal and more
or less arbitrary. Thus pity (*commiseratio*) is defined as
pain accompanied by the idea of evil happening to another
thought of as resembling ourselves, but compassion (*mi-
sericordia*), as a kind of love, namely that which disposes
us to rejoice in another's good fortune and to be sorry at
his ill fortune. The other affections mentioned are defined
as species of love and hate.

A number of what in distinction from the foregoing may
be called self-regarding affections, such as self-com-

[32] *Ibid.*, Proposition 27, Dem.

placency, pride, humility, penitence, dejection, self-glorifi-
cation, shame, and modesty, are conceived, in general, as
varieties of pleasure and pain. Humility, for example, is
pain accompanied by the idea of our weakness.[33] By com-
bining the proposition that the contemplation of our weakness is painful with the proposition that the contemplation
of ourselves in our active powers is a pleasure, Spinoza
concludes that men are naturally envious, that is, they rejoice over the weaknesses of their equals and sorrow over
their virtues. This, however, is quite consistent with the
veneration of superiors, for " no one envies the virtue of
one who is not his equal." [34] Pride and humility, again, are
contrasted not so much as emotions, for they frequently
coexist, but in their effects; and humility and dejection —
abjectio, " the thinking too meanly of ourselves by reason
of displeasure " — are rare, for human nature, in itself
considered, strives against them with all its might.

Among the passions, finally, we have a large group defined as varieties of desire: Spinoza mentions regret, emulation, gratitude, benevolence, anger, ferocity, fear, daring, cowardice, consternation, civility, ambition, luxury,
drunkenness, avarice, and lust. The list includes states of
varied psychological character, and the definitions are
here, as elsewhere, arbitrary. Anger, for example, is defined as the desire to do ill to the hated object. It is easy to
see that, just as inclination and aversion were defined without any explicit reference to their conative tendencies, so
anger might equally well have been defined as, e.g., pain
excited by the contemplation of an injury, had Spinoza's
mind but apperceived it so. Of course what psychology re-

---

[33] *Ibid.,* Proposition 55, *Scholium.* The futility of such an abstract
definition becomes apparent when we apply it to the case, say, of a man
pinned down beneath the wreck in a railway accident and conscious at
once of his pain and of his helplessness.

[34] *Ibid.,* Proposition 55, Cor. II.

quires is not formal definitions of this sort, but the analysis and genetic interpretation of the states themselves as they arise and pass in human experience.

The above classifications are not formally made by Spinoza, but correspond in general to the order of treatment in the summary of results which follows the fifty-nine propositions of Book III. The list does not profess to be complete, but it suffices, Spinoza says, for the uses of life to have a general knowledge of the passions, and his aim has been to give this knowledge by showing that they all spring from the threefold root of desire, pleasure, and pain. It has already been remarked that the " affects " have to do not only with the mind's passions, which are said to consist in confused ideas and which are ascribed to man as acted upon and limited in power, but also with the mind's actions, which consist in adequate ideas and express the mind's own intrinsic energy. These actions are all embraced, according to Spinoza, under *fortitudo,* the firm and steadfast courage of the mind acting from its own inner energy, and its two varieties, *animositas* and *generositas,* nobility of feeling in regard respectively to our own affairs and to those of others; [35] all are derived from combinations of pleasure and desire. They have, therefore, the character of affections, but they are not analyzed as such. They are treated rather as virtues with reference to other qualities, e.g., envy and disdain, which spring from the same root, namely, the mind's tendency to represent to itself only those things which affirm (*ponunt*) its power of acting.[36]

---

[35] *Ibid.,* Proposition 59, *Scholium.*

[36] *Ibid.,* Proposition 54. The demonstration of the fact of this tendency of the mind, asserted by the proposition, is characteristically artificial. It is as follows: " The *conatus,* or power of the mind, is the mind's very being. But evidently the mind's very being only affirms what the mind is and is capable of being, not what it neither is nor can be. Consequently it endeavors to represent to itself only what affirms or posits its own power of acting: q.e.d."

The crowning affection in Spinoza's system, the intellectual love of God, is similarly treated; that is to say, it is treated not as a specifically subjective state of feeling, but as identical with the blessedness of virtue, consisting in the conscious fact of free activity derived from intuitive insight into the identity of the individual with the necessary order of the universe.

Two other writers of the seventeenth century may be briefly mentioned in conclusion as adding somewhat to the impression made by these great systems of the state of the affective psychology of the time — Bossuet and Pascal. Jacques B. Bossuet (1627–1704) wrote at length on the feelings and passions in his treatise, *De la connoissance de Dieu et de soi-même.*[37] His significance lies in his eclecticism. On the logical-formal side he follows in the main Aquinas, on the physiological, Descartes. His views are set forth with remarkable lucidity. He distinguishes between (sense) pleasure and pain, which, as localizable he classes with sensations, and joy and grief, which as unlocalizable he classes with the passions and refers to appetite. Pleasure is " an agreeable feeling which conforms to nature," pain, " a disagreeable feeling, contrary to nature," while passions are motions arising from our external or internal feelings (*sentiments*) and principally from pleasures and pain. More precisely a passion is " a movement of the soul which, touched by the pleasure or pain felt (*ressenti*) or imagined in an object, pursues it or withdraws from it." [38] The primary passions, as Aquinas taught, are eleven, all relative to the one fundamental passion of love. The Cartesian *admiratio* is excluded from the list on the ground that it is excited in us by a novel object before

[37] Published 1722 under the title, *Introduction à la philosophie* (*Œuvres*, V, 20–110).

[38] *Ibid.,* 25.

we either love or hate it.[39] The relation of soul and body is so established by divine ordinance that certain sensations or feelings (including imaginations) attach to certain movements of the body, and, conversely, that certain movements of the body follow the " intellectual " operations of the soul.[40] It is to the former aspect of the relation that we have chiefly to look in explaining emotion. Without attempting, with Descartes, to trace the process for the several emotions in detail, Bossuet succinctly sets forth the general conception of, first, the effect of the agitation in the brain on the animal spirits, then of these on the heart involving the whole series of vasomotor changes and their expression, finally of the accompanying discharge by the motor nerves to the muscles. He attributes the diversity of the excitement and agitation of the " spirits " to the diversity of the passions, but at the same time declares the agitation of the " spirits " to be a necessary consequence of the violent impression that certain objects make in the brain.[41] In the same connection he teaches that the passions, viewed in their bodily aspect, " appear to be nothing else than an extraordinary agitation of the spirits or of the blood on occasion of certain objects to be avoided or pursued." [42] These movements are all naturally adapted to the pursuit or avoidance of the object. This natural teleology extends even to the external signs, the appropriate means

[39] The criticism is worthless, of course, except on the assumption that love (of which hate is the negative) is essential to an emotion (the distinction between which and passion is not yet drawn in the modern way), but the language used is noteworthy: *elle ne fait en nous aucune émotion ni aucune passion par conséquent. Ibid.*, p. 26. *Emotion* here denotes, apparently, the agitation.

[40] *Ibid.*, c. III, 52–64.

[41] *Ibid.*, 50 f.

[42] *Ibid.*, 51. Cf. 65 where, speaking of the imaginations that arise in a state of, e.g., anger, Bossuet says, " It is not so much these thoughts which we should consider as the movements of the brain with which they are connected, since it is by the latter that the passages are opened, the spirits flow," etc.

designed by nature for expressing the emotion to others. Passion may be controlled by indirect methods, such as breathing, diet, religious meditation, but the greatest stress is laid by Bossuet on the direct action of voluntary attention, by which passion is capable of being both excited and allayed.[43]

Blaise Pascal (1623–1662) treats of the feelings only incidentally, except for a little tract on the passion of love.[44] This, probably a youthful composition, consists of a series of loosely connected aphorisms based on observation and, possibly, personal experience, and shows the broad and quick generalization, much of it true, much palpably false and exaggerated, which characterizes this sort of writing. But although not a psychological treatment of the subject, it, like other discussions of the theme from Plato down, includes under it a variety of psychologically distinguishable affections besides sexual love. It also contains a number of striking observations which show how greatly Pascal appreciated the place of passion in human life and the intimate connection of its emotional, intellectual, and practical manifestations. Great minds are marked by great passions. The passions, indeed, though occasioned by the body, are the mind's sentiments and thoughts; are, in fact, the mind itself and fill up its entire capacity.[45] Pure thought cannot be long maintained, it wearies and oppresses. Man craves excitement and action, relief from monotony. The two grand passions of mankind are love and ambition, and the most desirable life appears to be that which begins with the former and ends with the

[43] *Ibid.*, 68 f.

[44] It was first published by Cousin in 1843. The MS., not Pascal's, attributes it to the philosopher, and the authorship has never been seriously disputed. The work fills about ten pages in the English translation of O. W. Wight, *The Thoughts, Letters and Opuscules of Blaise Pascal*, 515–525.

[45] *Loc. cit.*

latter. Man is born for pleasure; in giving himself to pleasure, therefore, he follows reason. Again, love gives intellect and is sustained by intellect. The object of love is beauty, which is identified with the pleasing.[46] In proportion as we have more intellect, we find more original beauties; but this is not necessary in order to be in love, for when we love we find but one. But for the pleasure of love to be solid and permanent, it is sometimes necessary not to know that we love, for attachment to the same thoughts wearies the mind. Hence the demand for novelty, which is not, in itself, infidelity. One of the most striking of the aphorisms is that which declares that the passion cannot exist without excess; hence it is that we care not what the world says, for we know that our conduct ought not to be condemned, since it springs from reason. Let us not, says Pascal in another place, exclude reason from love. The poets were wrong in picturing Love as blind. " Reason " here is apparently identical with consciously natural and so self-justifying impulses, like the *raisons* in the oft-quoted saying of the *Thoughts: Le cœur a ses raisons que la raison ne connaît pas.*[47]

But the distinctive claim of Pascal to a place in the history of the psychology of feeling is found not in such vaguely suggestive and unanalyzed ideas as these, but rather in his subtle appreciation of the influence of habit on the mechanism of belief. The question is as to the truth or falsity of the articles of the Catholic faith. They can be neither proved nor disproved. Pascal tries to show that there are overwhelming practical reasons for laying stakes on their truth. If, nevertheless, the sceptic says that he can't believe, Pascal replies that he can: the way is, to stop arguing and cultivate the moral life; attend mass;

[46] *Ibid.,* 518 f.   [47] *Ibid.,* 236.

sprinkle holy water — act, in brief, as if you believed. Belief follows by virtue of the habit which is our nature operating on autosuggestion. We acquire the sentiments and beliefs which we imagine and express in our acts. Pascal made only a beginning in the analysis of the process, but he has struck out an original path along which psychologists have since traveled who have treated of the influence of association and habit on the formation of belief, sentiment, character, and conduct.[48]

[48] *Cf.* F. Pillon, " Sur l'imagination affective," *Rév. Phil.* LXIII (1907), 233.

CHAPTER VIII

AFFECTIVE PSYCHOLOGY IN THE EIGHTEENTH CENTURY: BRITISH MORALISTS AND ASSOCIATIONISTS

Like the discussions of the affective life in antiquity and the Middle Ages, the great systems of the passions in the seventeenth century arise in and are finally related to practical interests. Descartes and Malebranche study the passions with a view to their rational control; Hobbes and Spinoza examine them, the one in order to understand the forces to be taken account of in the complex machinery of society, the other to explain the process by which the individual escapes from bondage to external things and rises to freedom of action and spiritual peace in the intuition of his identity with the one infinite and eternal Substance. The treatment of affective phenomena in the eighteenth century is characterized in a marked degree by relation to similar practical interests. Pleasure and pain, the sentiments, emotions, and passions, are regarded pre-eminently as motives and springs of action, with reference to their bearing on virtue and vice, or at least on the happiness or the dignity of human life. This was especially the case among British writers, many of whom were professed moralists and all of whom were influenced by the ethical discussions for which the century is famous. The psychology of the affections is intimately bound up with controversies concerning egoism and altruism, hedonism and, in general, the ends and standards of conduct and the powers at man's disposal for his guidance; and it is usually connected also with more ultimate views relating to the order and government of the world. The aesthetic interest, too, plays a part; the earliest writers on the subject being especially struck by the analogy between beauty and virtue.[1]

The point of departure for a good deal of the discussion is Hobbes's conception of human nature as essentially self-seeking, a conception expressed with brutal cynicism by Bernhard de Mandeville (1670–1733) in the *Fable of the Bees* (1705), which represented man on his spiritual side as nothing but a compound of passions, and the moral virtues as " the political offspring which flattery begot upon pride."[2] The opponents of this view, seeking to vindicate the honor of virtue, were led perforce to consider the origin and bearing of the affectional impulses. The line of least resistance was to claim for the altruistic sentiments and impulses the same originality that belonged to the egoistic, and to combine this with the assertion of an innate moral sense, or other subjective criterion, which naturally secured for the former a superior moral value. This was the line taken by Shaftesbury, Hutcheson, Butler — substituting " conscience " for the " moral sense " of his predecessors — and also, in substance, at the turning point of the century, by the Scotch Intuitionists. The Associationists, on the other hand, whether agreeing or not with these writers as to the relative moral value of benevolence and self-interest, repudiate the theory of an innate moral sense as a relic of the doctrine of innate ideas demolished by Locke, and seek to establish a moral system on experiences developed by association. Adam Smith (1723–1790) forms in so far a connecting link, as he too rejects the doc-

---

[1] Shaftesbury introduces the aesthetic element into morality by making the moral guide a sense of the fitness of things. *Inquiry Concerning Virtue and Merit*, Book I, Part II, sec. iii. One of the earliest works on aesthetics in modern times was the *Inquiry into the Origin of our Ideas of Beauty and Virtue* by his follower, F. Hutcheson, published in 1725.

[2] *Fable of the Bees*, 37.

trine of a moral sense and finds the foundations of all our
sentiments in sympathy.[3]

The main psychological differences in this controversy
— we have only incidentally to take note of the ethical —
relate thus, broadly speaking, to the views taken of the
original constitution of human nature. Human nature itself
is regarded by all the writers of the period as having a constitution relatively fixed in character, equipped, whether
by nature or by Providence, with certain endowments, the
same everywhere and at all times. The only questions were
as to what these endowments were and how they were related, what was primary, what derived, and how the secondary formations might be brought about under the conditions of individual experience. The main scientific
advance, effected by associationism and the utilitarian
ethics making use of this principle, lay in the attempt to derive as much as possible by assuming as original as little as
possible. The idea of explaining any features of the phenomena by reference to racial development had still to
come.

A favorite theme with many writers was that of the natural teleology of the affections. The conception takes on
various forms, and, in the absence of evolutionary principles, the adaptation in question is wont to appear as a more
or less artificial contrivance. Thus the Third Earl of
Shaftesbury (1671–1713) compares the affections and
passions with the cords and strings of a musical instrument, which have a certain natural proportion. Hence
arises the inquiry into the " different tunings of the passions " whereby men become so (morally) different, and
the endeavor to show what combinations and degrees of
kindly public and of private self-related affections lead to

[3] *The Theory of Moral Sentiments,* Part II, sec. I, chap. V.

the individual's happiness, together with the manner in which the "unnatural affections," which are founded neither on public nor on private interest, lead to misery.[4] Francis Hutcheson (1694–1747) declares the passions to be "by nature balanced against each other, like the antagonistic muscles of the body," separately occasioning distortion and irregular motion, while jointly "they form a machine, most happily subservient to the necessities, convenience, and happiness of a rational system."[5] When Joseph Butler (1692–1752) says of sudden anger that it is not merely raised by, but is chiefly intended to prevent or remedy harm, as distinct from injury,[6] he is but illustrating his thesis that the passions and affections afford " as certain instances of final causes," that is, of intelligent creative design, " as any whatever."[7] Henry Home, Lord Kames (1696–1782), following Hutcheson and Butler, undertakes to show that the passions, however perverse, " are by nature modeled and tempered with perfect wisdom for the good of society as well as for private good."[8] Home extends this conception of designed adaptation to the involuntary expression of the emotions considered as natural signs. He finds in their general uniformity evidence of " the anxious care of Nature to discover man to each other," and comments at length on their utility in this respect. They produce in the spectator various emotions, all tending to wise and good ends. And that there might be no mistake in interpreting these signs, this art was not left to be learned by experience, but "man is provided by nature

[4] *Inquiry Concerning Virtue and Merit,* Book II, Part I, sec. iii. (*Characteristics of Men,* I, 291 f.)

[5] *An Essay on the Nature and Conduct of the Passions and Affections,* Sec. VI, 181; cf. W. R. Scott, *Francis Hutcheson,* 203.

[6] *Fifteen Sermons,* VIII, *Upon Resentment,* sec. 12.

[7] L. Stephen, *English Thought in the Eighteenth Century,* II, 49.

[8] *Elements of Criticism,* 182. (Chapter II, Part VII deals with " Final Causes of the more frequent Emotions and Passions.")

with a sense or faculty that lays open to him every passion by means of its external expressions." [9] The " common sense " thinkers of the Scotch School express similarly generous conceptions of man's natural endowments. The affections, malevolent as well as benevolent, are parts of our constitution, given to us by our Maker for good ends. Desires for power, esteem, and knowledge point to nature's purpose in fitting us for social life.[10] Even the desire for posthumous fame, which Adam Smith had resolved into an illusion of the imagination,[11] is regarded by Dugald Stewart (1753–1828) as plainly intended by nature to influence all men and as probably implanted by her in our constitution. This passion, according to Thomas Brown (1778–1820), gives evidence of the beneficence of a disposing Providence, which has not made general happiness to depend on the accidents of worldly fame.[12] The original principles of our nature are, no doubt, powerfully influenced by habit and association, but are not derived from them, as in the " plausible " but " factitious " systems of the Associationists.[13]

The method adopted for settling all disputes in this field was the appeal to introspection and to common observation of life. This to writers of the common-sense moralizing type appears relatively easy. " The parts and properties of

---

[9] *Ibid.*, 441. (Chapter XV deals with " External Signs of Emotions and Passions.")

[10] Thomas Reid, *Essays on the Active Powers of the Human Mind,* III (*Works,* II, 560–571).

[11] *The Theory of Moral Sentiments,* Part I, sec. I, chap. I, 4.

[12] D. Stewart, *The Active and Moral Powers of Man* (*Works,* VI, 146 f.). T. Brown, *Lectures on the Philosophy of the Human Mind,* LXX, 475.

[13] D. Stewart, *op. cit.,* 166. Regarding the relation of such teleology to the unhistorical attitude of the eighteenth century philosophers, who talked of abstract human nature, assumed to be the same in all times and places, cf. the remarks of L. Stephen, *English Thought in the Eighteenth Century,* II, 73 f.

the mind," writes Shaftesbury, " their mutual relation and dependency, the connection and frame of those passions which constitute the soul or temper, may be easily understood by anyone who thinks it worth his while to study this inward anatomy," our lamentable ignorance of this subject being due solely, he explains, to the fact that so few of us endeavor to become anatomists of this sort.[14] Hutcheson expresses the same opinion. " Nothing more is necessary," he says, " than a little attention to what passes in our own hearts, and consequently every man may come to certainty in these points without much art or knowledge of other matters." [15] The aim of the inquiry being practical, these writers disparage attempts, like those of Descartes, at explaining the physiological mechanism of the passions; Shaftesbury, for example, sharply contrasts the worthlessness of philosophy of this " super-speculative " sort with the knowledge gained by friendship and correspondence in the world, by which we learn how passion is increased or diminished " as it is fed by opinion and influenced by custom and practice." [16] Even the Associationists are at a loss when called upon to give an account of the connection of the emotion with the bodily mechanism. David Hartley (1705–1757) began bravely with a theory of " vibratiuncles," [17] of which he made no effective use and which he later abandoned; while Abraham Tucker (1705–1774), who significantly traces the origin of emotion to the child's efforts to get control of his motor mechanism and therewith to modifications in the circulation and in the movements of

[14] *Inquiry Concerning Virtue and Merit,* Book II, Part I, sec. II. (*Characteristics of Men,* I, 283 f.)

[15] *An Essay on the Nature and Conduct of the Passions and Affections,* Pref. v.

[16] *Advice to an Author,* Part III, sec. I. (*Characteristics of Men,* I, 190 ff.)

[17] *Observations on Man,* Part I, chap. I, sec. II.

the " animal spirits," gives over the description of these bodily changes to the painter, sculptor, and anatomist. He declares that their influence on " the mental organs " belongs to no professor whatever, " as lying beyond the reach of any science yet attained by human sagacity." [18] Among all the writers of the period no one has a clearer conception of scientific aim and method along purely psychological, that is, introspective lines, than Thomas Brown. His own practice, indeed, is far from perfect: the moral interest is ever uppermost. He cannot, for example, resist the temptation afforded by the analysis of moral regret and gladness arising from our own actions, to preach a sermon on the misery of vice and the happiness of virtue.[19] And his analysis is no doubt defective. But he goes far to formulate the true aim of the study when he defines his method of inquiry into the " internal affections " to be simply " to consider the circumstances in which they arise, and the circumstances which follow them, with the relations which they appear to us mutually to bear to our external feelings, and to each other." [20] Brown, while emphasizing the importance of analysis, also insists on the recognition of the complex whole; he is more keenly aware than most writers of the limits of analysis and of the infinite variety in the unity of a single emotion.

In the matter of terminology there is no little confusion. " Feeling " is used generally to denote any state of consciousness of which the mind is susceptible, whether regarded as content or as act, the implication being that consciousness is passively affected, that it does not produce its content spontaneously from itself.[21] Thomas Reid (1710–

---

[18] *The Light of Nature Pursued*, Part I, chap. XXI, sec. I.
[19] *Lectures on the Philosophy of the Human Mind*, LXX, 468.
[20] *Ibid.*, XXXII, 213.
[21] Thomas Brown treats of the " feelings " under the heads of (1) the

1796) remarks on the ambiguity of the term which denotes, according to him, either (1) perception of objects
by touch, or (2) sensation in which the feeling is identical
with its object. The latter term, however, is commonly
reserved for feelings derived from the external senses, bodily appetites, bodily pleasures and pains, while there are
other feelings of a nobler nature accompanying our affections.[22] Feelings of the latter sort are generally conceived as a kind of sensation and are commonly referred
by those writers who regard them as connatural, and not
derived by transference and association from pleasures
and pains, to an internal sense or senses.[23] Lord Kames
appears to approach the more modern usage when he defines feeling as " that internal act by which we are made
conscious of our pleasures and pains ";[24] but as he also
declares it to be the genus of which sensation is the species
and allows that the two terms may, in certain cases, be
used indiscriminately, it is evident that the general meaning of the term for him too is that of consciousness as passively affected. The term " affection " is pretty nearly, if
not quite, synonymous with " feeling " and is used interchangeably with sentiment, emotion, and passion. It is the
favorite term with Shaftesbury for any and all of these
phenomena. Hutcheson defines " affections or passions "

---

external susceptibilities, (2) the intellectual susceptibilities, (3) the susceptibilities of emotion. There is a noteworthy absence of any reference to
specific feelings of " will." *Ibid.*, XVII, 106 ff.

[22] *Essays on the Intellectual Powers of Man*, Essay I, chap. I (*Works*,
I, 230).

[23] The most lavish use of this conception is made by Hutcheson, who in
his *System of Moral Philosophy*, Book I, chap. II and in his *Philosophiae
moralis institutio compendiaria*, lib. I, chap. I, secs. 4–14, enumerates more
than a dozen " senses " besides the traditional bodily five. In his *Essay on
the Nature and Conduct of the Passions*, sec. 1, he groups them all under
five: the external senses, an internal sense (including pleasures of imagination, aesthetic pleasures, etc.), a public sense, a moral sense, and a
sense of honor. Cf. J. Martineau, *Types of Ethical Theory*, II, 535 f.

[24] Henry Home, *Elements of Criticism*, Appendix II, 509.

as " those modifications or actions of the mind consequent
on the apprehension of certain objects or events " conceived, in general, as good or evil.[25] This is the traditional
and most commonly followed usage. When a distinction is
drawn between the affections and the passions, it is usually
with reference to a difference in vivacity. The more violent
and turbulent emotions are called passions, the affections
are the gentler. " Passions," says Tucker, " are the fever
of the mind, affections are like the steady beating of the
pulse." [26] For Richard Price (1723–1791) the affections
are the desires founded in, and essential to the rational
nature; they become passions when strengthened by instincts, but seldom or never affections.[27] David Hume
(1711–1776) similarly speaks of a passion, as commonly
understood, as " a violent and sensible emotion of the
mind, when any good or evil is presented, or any object
which, by the original formation of our faculties, is fitted
to excite an appetite." He too connects the calm affections
with reason, but goes farther than Price, for he makes reason to consist in them.[28] Reid, on the other hand, classifies
the affections under " animal principles of action," apart
from reason, a classification for which he is sharply taken
to task by his disciple Stewart, who adopts in general his
conception of passion as an agitation of the mind, occasional and limited, like a storm or tempest.[29] Stewart uses
by preference the term " emotion," and this is done still
more decidedly by Thomas Brown who regards emotions
as forming truly " a separate class of the internal affections

[25] *An Essay on the Nature and Conduct of the Passions,* sec. 1.
[26] *Light of Nature Pursued,* Part I, chap. XXI, sec. 18.
[27] *A Review of the Principal Questions and Difficulties in Morals,* 117 f.
[28] *Treatise of Human Nature,* Book II, Part III, sec. VIII, 213 f.
[29] T. Reid, *Essays on the Active Powers of the Human Mind,* III, (*Works,* II, 560–571). D. Stewart, *Outlines of Moral Philosophy,* Part I', chap. I, sec. 4.

of the mind " and defines them as " vivid feelings, arising immediately from the consideration of objects . . . or from other prior emotions." [30] We here come upon a new distinction, that of emotion and passion. Hume had already made the distinction in noting as " a remarkable property of human nature " the fact that " any emotion which attends a passion is easily converted into it," although it may be originally not only different from the passion, but even contrary to it. [31] But what precisely the distinction is, is not quite clear. The probable interpretation is perhaps suggested by Lord Kames: emotion and passion, according to him, are each a mental motion or agitation, but the latter always includes in addition a consequent desire aroused by and related to an object, whereas emotion may be unaccompanied by desire, is a passive feeling, and cannot properly be said to have an object. He is perplexed, however, by the feelings excited in us by signal exhibitions of virtue, whereby we are disposed to qualities of a similar character. A feeling of this sort cannot, he says, be called an emotion, because it arouses desire; nor, again, a passion, because it has no object. But he finally calls it an emotion, " the sympathetic emotion of virtue." With desire and relation to an object as the distinguishing marks of a passion, we escape the difficulty of a classification based on a mere difference of degree: we can now have refined as well as gross passions. But it is a little startling in this connection to find the pain of the gout mentioned as a passion co-ordinate with grief, the reason, no doubt, being that it too is accompanied by the desire of relief. [32] Brown makes emotions a separate class of the internal affections, namely " vivid feelings arising immediately from the considera-

[30] *Lectures on the Philosophy of the Human Mind*, XVI, 102 f.
[31] *Treatise of Human Nature*, Book II, Part III, sec. IV, 198.
[32] H. Home, *Elements of Criticism*, Chap. II, Parts I–II.

tion of objects . . . or from prior emotions; " passions, he holds, are not a distinct class of emotions, but merely names for our desires when very vivid or very permanent.[33] The alternative of permanence is certainly an advance. The term " sentiment " is less used by British writers than the other terms here mentioned and is rarely defined. Lord Kames defines it vaguely as a " thought prompted by a passion "; his chapter on the sentiments is devoted to descriptions of emotional states culled from polite literature.[34]

The most notable progress in scientific method in the treatment of the affective life was made by the Association-ists. As already indicated, their main object was, on the one hand, to refute those theories of ethics which regarded the altruistic sentiments as ultimate and which appealed to " conscience " or the " moral sense " as to an oracle; and, on the other hand, to furnish a basis for morality by an analysis and construction which reduced moral princi-ples to and derived them from simple elements combined by association in the experience of the individual. The ele-ments of the construction were derived from John L. Locke (1632–1704). In his *Essay Concerning Humane Understanding* Locke had treated of " Modes of Pleasure and Pain." [35] These he explained, were " simple ideas " re-ceived both from sensation and from reflection, and to them good and evil are relative: good being that which is apt, directly or indirectly, to cause, increase, or preserve pleasure or to avert or diminish pain, and evil being the

[33] *Lectures on the Philosophy of the Human Mind*, XVI, 102; LXV, 437.

[34] H. Home, *op. cit.*, chap. 16.

[35] Book II, chap. XX. It is of doubtful propriety to classify Locke's theory among the " intellectualistic " doctrines of the feelings, as Wundt does, *Grundzüge der physiologischen Psychologie*, II, 363. He certainly calls them " ideas," and does not distinguish them as a specific kind of mental content; but his use of the term " idea " is notoriously ambiguous.

contrary. The passions hinge on pleasure and pain and the good and evil causing them. The bodily changes which accompany the passions, not being always sensible, make no necessary part of their idea. This observation, however, is incidental. Locke's chief aim is to show that our " ideas of the passions " are got from sensation and reflection. This deduction is rather assumed than demonstrated, and the whole treatment is confessedly incomplete. Nevertheless, Locke's common-sense views of the relation of good and pleasure and his plausible derivation of the complex emotions from a basis of simple pleasures and pains were of paramount importance in the development of ethical and psychological theories throughout the century. The first definitely to grasp and in a thoroughgoing fashion to apply the principle of association to the mental life was David Hartley whose theory was set forth in a Latin essay, *Conjecturae quaedam de sensu, motu, et idearum generatione* in 1731 [36] and eighteen years later elaborated in a *magnum opus*, the *Observations on Man*. The principle, to be sure, seems to have been, as it were, floating in the air. Similar views were expressed at about the same time in an anonymous tract, *An Enquiry into the Origin of Human Appetites and Affections, Showing how Each Arises from Association*,[37] while in France the theories of Condillac and especially those of C. Bonnet often show a remarkable coincidence with those of the " father of association." [38] Hartley himself acknowledges indebtedness to J. B. Gay in his *Essay on the Fundamental Principles of Virtue and Morality*, which, by asserting " the possibility of deducing

[36] Reprinted in S. Parr's *Metaphysical Tracts by English Philosophers of the Eighteenth Century*, 98 f.

[37] This was written, as the title further states, " for the use of young gentlemen at the universities." It defends a utilitarian hedonism. It was published in 1747 and is also reprinted in Parr, *op. cit.*, 60 f.

[38] Cf. *Encyclopedia Britannica*, 9th ed. article: " Hartley."

all our intellectual pleasures and pains from association," [39] led him to examine into the power of association,
its causes and consequences generally; while to Locke he
ascribes the foundations of the theory and to Newton the
suggestion of that conception of vibrations which he regarded as its physiological basis. It was his merit, however, to have been the first to conceive of association as
a principle universal in the mental world analogous to
that of gravitation in the physical world, nor is it his
least credit that he formulated his principle in terms
more in harmony with recent views than some later for-
mulations: the only association recognized being that of
contiguity.

The sensations from which every form of mental life is
ultimately derived are conceived by Hartley as due to
vibrations of the particles in the medullary substance of
the nerves, whence they are communicated to the brain by
the " ether," or " a most subtle kind of spirit." This theory, it may be observed, marks a transition from the older
to the newer physiology, for the " ether," the conception
of which was borrowed from Newton, was supposed to
permeate the solid matter of the nervous system and no
longer, as in the ancient doctrine of " animal spirits," to
fill merely the ventricles or to be transmitted through tubes
in the nerves.[40] When the sensory vibrations subside, they
leave their trace in the brain in a tendency to fainter vibrations, " vibratiuncles," to which " ideas " of sensation
correspond. These vibratiuncles, like Hobbes's " decaying

[39] Preface, *Observations on Man.*

[40] It is interesting to see the old doctrine still persisting in the middle
of the eighteenth century. The author of the anonymous tract, *An Enquiry,*
etc., tells us (Parr, *op. cit.,* 60), that the generality of physicians and anatomists hold that the nerves are tubular, but that others regard them as made
up of filaments without cavities; that the transmission is too rapid for the
safety of the nerves to suppose the mechanism of transmission to be assumed. The author does not commit himself to either side of the controversy.

sense," are the source of memory and imagination and, through contiguous and successive association, of all the higher forms of mind. Such are the principles of Hartley's theory.[41]

Pleasure and pain are the primary " accidents " of sensation. Finding that one may give place to the other by increase or diminution, Hartley concludes that they are fundamentally identical. " Pain," he says, " is only pleasure increased, so to say, beyond a certain limit." This is explained by the theory of vibrations. Generally speaking, pleasure is connected with moderate normal, pain with immoderate abnormal vibrations.[42] Mental pleasures and pains are derived from sensory pleasures and pains by association. The sensory experiences, namely, leave traces, " a disposition in the nervous system to run into miniature vibrations of the same kind," and these latter are excited by the recurrence of circumstances associated with the original experiences. Gradually these miniature pleasures and pains are transferred to the words and other symbols of the objects and circumstances. Then, as a great variety of such miniatures are transferred upon each word, and as words affect each other by association, a compound vibration may be excited, " formed from a variety of miniatures." Accordingly, compound or mental affections " will arise from simple bodily ones by means of words, symbols, and associated circumstances." Hartley makes skilful use of these principles in explaining the connection of mental pleasures and pains with specific classes of sensory affection. The greater part of our intellectual pains, he holds, are deducible from the physical pains of " feeling," i.e., touch, whereas touch has but a small share, as compared

[41] *Observations on Man,* Part I, chap. I, sec. II, Prop. IX.
[42] *Conjecturae quaedam de sensu, motu et idearum generatione,* Proposition 6.

with taste, in the formation of our intellectual pleasures. A great part, indeed, of our intellectual pleasures are said to be deducible ultimately from taste, which, moreover, in a peculiar way, is the source of our social pleasures: food being habitually enjoyed in company. But each sense contributes in varying degrees and under varying circumstances to the production of both pleasures and pains of the " intellectual " order, residual vibrations on the physical side and contiguous associations of diverse sorts on the mental, being the principles obtaining throughout.[43]

The same principles apply to "passions or affections," which are nothing but aggregates of simple ideas, or traces of sensible pleasures and pains, which by their number and reciprocal influence make up for the faintness and transitory nature of each taken singly. Hartley groups all pleasures and pains under seven heads: sensation, imagination, ambition, self-interest, sympathy, theopathy, and the moral sense, and his view is that, with sensation as the common foundation, each kind contributes to generate the succeeding and to remodel the preceding, " till at last, by the numerous reciprocal influences of all these upon each other, the passions arrive at that degree of complexness which is observed in fact and which makes them so difficult to be analyzed." [44] In this scheme the " moral sense " is made the last term of the deduction, at the opposite extreme from Shaftesbury and Hutcheson. The most general classes of affections are love and hatred, the one including all pleasurable, the other all painful affections. When these attain a certain degree, they incite to action and are then known respectively as desire and aversion, which are, therefore, only love and hatred in action. " A desire or

---

[43] *Theory of the Human Mind,* chap. II.

[44] *Observations on Man,* Part I, chap. III, sec. III, Proposition LXXXIX.

aversion sufficiently strong to produce an action that is not automatic primarily or secondarily " constitutes will; the action which follows being in this, as in all other cases of desire and aversion, wholly " the result of associated powers and circumstances." Hope and fear, fluctuating with circumstances and the state of the body, attend on desire and aversion, and joy and grief arise when they are at an end. Then, when joy and grief are at an end, " there generally remains a pleasing or displeasing recollection or resentment," which recurs with the idea of the object or its associates. There is thus a natural history of the passions. Formed of a complexity of associated ideas, the number and mutual influence of which account for their intensity, the " general passions of human nature " are ten in number: five " grateful " or pleasant, — love, desire, hope, joy, pleasing recollection — and five " ungrateful," or unpleasant, — hatred, aversion, fear, grief, displeasing recollection. These follow one another in a natural order of succession and the members of each group enhance one another. Violent passions are due to unnatural associations brought about by increase of the vibrations attending the principal ideas. They disorder the understanding and also affect the self " with the peculiar interesting concern supposed to flow from personal identity." They are a temporary and even, when habitual, a permanent madness.[45]

Materialistic as are the foundations of the system, the consequences of which were developed later by Joseph Priestley (1733–1804) and Erasmus Darwin (1731–1802), the applications which Hartley himself made of his principles are singularly orthodox. Temperamentally an optimist, he seeks to show that the tendency of the associated pleasures and pains in human nature is to beget universal

[45] *Loc. cit.*

happiness; he even maintains " that all individuals are always and actually infinitely happy." [46] He defends the traditional morality, asserts the existence and authority of a moral sense and of pure benevolence, the origin of which is ascribed to the sentiments arising from social intercourse and their associated pleasures, and holds that the moral sense " carries us perpetually to the pure love of God, as our highest and ultimate perfection," a love which " affords a pleasure which is superior in kind and degree to all the rest of which our natures are capable." [47] The main point for us to note, however, is that of all these sentiments he attempts a scientific derivation and that in this attempt he is largely successful. He was, of course, by no means the first to apply to the affective life a principle as old in its recognition as Plato and Aristotle; yet, as Leslie Stephen justly observes, " no one had explained the power of association with regard to the emotions with so much ingenuity and, as association is doubtless a true cause, Hartley had really the merit of improving our conception of the mode in which the moral sentiments are generated in the individual." [48] Stephen's criticism that his weakness for ethics lies in his individualistic method applies with equal force to his psychology.

Allied to Hartley in his use of association, but less rigorous in method, Abraham Tucker, the industrious author of *The Light of Nature Pursued*,[49] sought also to develop a system of ethics on the psychological foundations laid down by Locke. This system, more succinctly formulated

[46] *Ibid.*, Part II, chap. I, Proposition IV.
[47] *Ibid.*, Part I, chap. IV, sec. 6; Part II, chap. III, Proposition LXXI.
[48] *English Thought in the Eighteenth Century*, II, 70.
[49] Tucker was a rich amiable country gentleman who spent his summers on his estate and his winters in London. He composed his book, somewhat prolix but containing much that is of interest and value, leisurely during the last twenty years of his life.

later by Paley, was individualistically hedonistic, a development of the ideas sketched by Gay. The vivifying ingredient of all our actions is the idea of satisfaction or pleasure. The ultimate end of action is happiness, " a man's own happiness." [50] The practice of benevolence arises from the consideration that it conduces to this end. Feelings of pleasantness and unpleasantness are kinds of sensations, or perceptions, and apparently belong to the " capacity " of the Understanding rather than to the " power " of Will with a more immediate source in " some particular organ or fibre . . . that affects us with satisfaction or uneasiness." [51] By these we are respectively attracted and repelled, always according to the present occasion. They are, however, not separate motives to action, as Locke conceived, since diminution or avoidance of uneasiness is an approach to satisfaction. Pain and pleasure are both positive and distinct experiences; pleasure is not mere absence of pain; and pleasures differ in degree if not in kind.[52] The original source of pleasure is sensation, external or internal, including those arising " from the free circulation of the blood and humors in health and (probably) from the easy flow of spirits along the mental organs," i.e., the brain, when anything engages our attention. Tucker thinks — and the suggestion is in the direction of the more modern " peripheral " theory and away from Hartley's " vibratiuncle " doctrine — that perhaps " all the pleasures of imagination and reflection which we feel in seasons of joy, or hope, or desire, or other agreeable situations of mind " may consist in these internal sensations.

[50] *Light of Nature Pursued,* Part I, chap. XXV, 365.
[51] *Ibid.,* chap. I, 32–41 ; chap. XVII, 219.
[52] Tucker is not a learned author. The doctrine that pleasure is mere absence of pain he ascribes to " Hieronymus," while he attributes to Epicurus the absurdly incongruous teaching that all pleasures are equal in degree and differ only in kind. *Ibid.,* chap. VI, 79.

But besides these pleasures of internal sense, Tucker recognizes others which come " when reflection· has learnt its play " such as the pleasures of reading, conversation, amusements, and worldly success. These are not innate, but are derived by processes of association and translation.[53]

We thus have named the great principles by which Tucker seeks to explain the major part of our affective experiences, including the emotions, so far as they are not originally interwoven in our constitution. By " translation " he means the transference of a pleasure or displeasure from one object to another through association, e.g., from the end to the means, as in the case of the miser. The term introduces nothing new in principle, nothing not included by Hartley under " association," but it enabled Tucker to fix attention on the development of motives as distinct from the associations out of which new motives grew. Another great principle which he regards as contributory to the translation of motive into act, is sympathy. In a short chapter of two and a half pages,[54] he remarks on the extent, occasions, advantages, and disadvantages of this sentiment, the origin of which he refers, in many cases, to conscious or unconscious imitation. But he does not go beneath the surface of the subject; he contributes nothing to the analysis or deduction either of imitation or of the sympathetic resonance.

We have already mentioned Tucker's theory of " passion " as originating in the child's efforts to control movement; it remains to add that, on the inner side, it arises in a felt obstruction to the movement seeking the satisfaction of desire, which he held, with Locke, to be an element in all our passions. The passions, in fact, are only so many dif-

---

[53] *Ibid.*, chap. XXII, sec. 1, 256.   [54] *Ibid.*, chap. XIX.

ferent forms of desire.[55] In the working out of the idea that passion is connected with checked movement, an idea which applies to all the passions the principle which St. Thomas asserted as distinctive for the " irascible," the theory itself meets with a difficulty in hope, " where no endeavors of our own appear necessary," so that the author is not quite sure whether so gentle a thing ought to be reckoned among the passions at all.[56] Love and hatred, again, he declared to be not so much passions in themselves as aptitudes for being excited to passions by objects. The feeling which Tucker here shows for psychological differences in affective states commonly grouped together, he is unable to carry out on any principle, and so, like so many others, he contents himself with discoursing with some fullness on certain phenomena called " passions " that appear to him important, and dismissing many more as modifications of those described. Of those which he describes more particularly, his theory of grief is characteristic and his theory of mirth shows him at his best. The difficulty which grief offers to a hedonistic deduction is that it keeps the mind intent on a troublesome idea which one would think it would endeavor most strenuously to throw off. Tucker meets this difficulty by a double hypothesis of utility, first, that grief originally arose from the same conditions that are operative in want, where an evil is kept before the mind that the ideas of removing it may be the more readily suggested; secondly, that expressions of grief excite sympathy in our fellows and so call forth help and relief. Then ensues

[55] *Ibid.*, chap. XXI, sec. 2. Aversion, flight, or avoidance is regarded by Tucker as the negative phase of desire, not as its opposite. We always seek satisfaction.

[56] Contrast the account given of joy, *ibid.*, sec. 4, which is produced when the mind is put upon " stretching her mental optics " to get a stronger view of the pleasing object, and a full flow of animal spirits heightens and prolongs the delightful sensations : all this being done with some " considerable degree of exertion."

the potent operation of " translation." " The mind having
found the contemplation of evil and the increasing of her
sensibility of its pressure expedient, desire, as is usual in the
like cases, becomes translated to the means, and her view
terminates upon afflicting herself as much as possible, without prospect of any further end to be attained thereby." [57]
The theory of mirth, frequently expressing itself in
laughter, resumes in its own language both ancient and
modern doctrines of its general conditions and anticipates,
as regards " wit," the Kantian doctrine of the comic.
Tucker rejects the view that it arises from contempt by
observing that contempt and laughter do not always go together and by a cogent appeal to the mirthful laughter of
children. It is occasioned rather " by a sudden influx of
spirits generally, if not always, turned from some other
channel," and laughter, when not produced mechanically,
is excited by three concurrent causes, to wit: (1) a stretch
of attention loosened at once, (2) the suddenness of the
relaxation, and (3) the want of employment by the mind
of the spirits so discharged, which then play upon the risi-
bilities. This last condition explains why we are not excited
to laughter by any and every joyful, but unexpected, idea.
Wit consists in allusion, and " the most diverting humor is
that which raises your expectation of something very serious, and then, upon breaking the jest, cuts in short with
an issue very different from what you expected." [58]

The two principles chiefly employed to combat the theory of an innate moral sense we have found to be association and sympathy, the latter subordinated to the former in
Hartley, the two relatively co-ordinate in Tucker. Both of
them had been disparaged by Hutcheson, who regarded
association as purely incidental and sympathy as a dis-

[57] *Ibid.*, sec. 8.   [58] *Ibid.*, sec. 15.

guised form of selfishness. On the other hand Adam Smith (1723–1790) pursuing the same psychological method, ex-- alts sympathy to the rank of a supreme principle, finding in it the original source of our sense of propriety, of approval and disapproval, of merit and demerit, and of duty. He seeks to show that while the appearance of utility confers on actions, as on works of art, a certain beauty, the moral sentiments are not derived from its perception, but rather themselves tend to work out the general happiness conformably to the designs of Providence.[59] This theory is subtly elaborated; but we can deal here only with its foundation. According to Smith, then, sympathy, which exists in some form in all men, however selfish, arises in individual experience by imaginatively conceiving in ourselves the feeling of another in a given situation, and " it is the impressions of our own senses only, not those of his, which our imaginations copy." [60] This serves to excite in us some degree of the same emotion. How this emotion, which is ours, comes to be felt as his, Smith does not explain. Nor does he distinguish between a reflective and an instinctive reproduction of another's feeling, nor has he any conception of an hereditary transmission of instincts incorporated in the structure and dispositions of a nervous system slowly developed and embodying the results of the past experiences of the race. His illustrations of the theory are first drawn from cases of what appear to be instinctive emotional reactions, apart from reflective imagination, and, so far as they are thus regarded, the instinct is for him simply a *datum*. We " naturally," he says, draw back our own leg or arm when we see a blow aimed at another's; the mob watching a dancer on the slack-rope " naturally "

---

[59] *Theory of the Moral Sentiments,* sec. I, chap. I.
[60] *Ibid.,* chap. I, 3.

writhe and twist and balance their bodies as they see him do; and so of innumerable other cases. Sensitive persons looking on sores or ulcers feel an itching sensation in the corresponding part of their own bodies. In other cases the process described by Smith seems to be more reflective, for although a fellow feeling may in some cases be aroused from the mere view of another's emotion, i.e., of its expression, that, of itself, may excite in us a very different feeling; the furious behavior of an angry man, for instance, is more likely to exasperate us against himself than against his enemies, until we know the occasion of his anger. " Sympathy, therefore, does not arise so much from the view of the passion as from that of the situation which excites it," and, accordingly, it is possible to feel for another, e.g., a sick child, an insane person, or the dead, a passion of which he is himself incapable.[61] Smith discourses of the pleasure attending the mutual exercise of this instinct, a pleasure which indicates the trend to happiness of the moral sentiments which grow out of it. The only point, however, which we are concerned to note is that he bases his doctrine on what are for him clear observations of human nature. He takes the pleasure of sympathy and the pain at its absence as settled facts and criticizes the only attempts known to him to explain them, namely, the theory of self-love and the theory of enhancement of feeling; the one on the altogether insufficient ground that they spring up too rapidly for the intervention of interested considerations, the other on the assumption, to the theory in question of doubtful relevancy, that while sympathy enlivens joy, it alleviates grief. That explanatory principles should be found in biological evolution never occurs to him.

This common defect of writers of the eighteenth century

[61] *Ibid.*, chap. I, 7.

attaches also to the most elaborate and ingenious attempt made by any writer of the century to treat of "the passions," on sensationalistic and associational principles, that, namely, of David Hume (1711–1776). Hume devotes the whole of the second book of his *Treatise on Human Nature* (1739) to this subject, and there is a corresponding "Dissertation on the Passions," containing the same argument in condensed form, in the *Essays* (1748).[62] It furnishes the connecting link between his general theory of knowledge and his theory of morals; but while this ethical bearing determines, as in other writers of the period, to a large extent the choice of topics and methods of treatment, it is not made particularly prominent in the course of the discussion, which has its own independent psychological value and interest. Hume distinguishes two sorts of "impressions": original, of sensation, and secondary, of reflection. To the former belong bodily pains and pleasures together with all ordinary sensations. The latter are derived from the former, either directly or by interposition of their ideas; they include "the passions and other emotions," some calm, as the sense of beauty, some violent — and these are passions in the more proper sense — such as love and hate, joy and grief, pride and humility. The more important division is into direct and indirect passions. The direct passions are derived immediately from good and evil, that is, pleasure or pain, and include desire, aversion, grief, joy, hope, fear, despair, and security; the indirect are derived by "conjunction of other qualities," and include pride, humility, ambition, vanity, love, hatred, envy, pity, malice, generosity, and their dependents. Both kinds are "founded on pleasure and pain"; all that is requisite to

---

[62] *Essays, Moral, Political and Literary*, Vol. II, 139–166. Cf. also the first of the essays treating "Of the Delicacy of Taste and Passion."

produce an affection of any kind is to present some good or evil,[63] the mind tending to unite itself with the one and avoid the other by an original instinct. When we knowingly give rise to a movement of any sort, the internal impression is termed will; volition, therefore, aiming to obtain pleasure or avoid pain, is reckoned with the direct passions.[64] Good and evil, certain or probable, produce respectively joy and grief; uncertain, they give rise to fear or hope, according to the degrees of uncertainty on the one side or the other. But " besides good and evil, or in other words pain and pleasure, the direct passions frequently arise from a natural impulse or instinct, which is perfectly unaccountable." To impulses of this class Hume reckons " desire of punishment to our enemies and of happiness to our friends "; also " hunger, lust, and a few other bodily appetites." In these cases the relation of impulse and pleasure is reversed; these passions — meaning, apparently, the felt internal pressure of the instinct — produce good and evil, and do not, like the other affections, proceed from them.[65] It is quite in Hume's manner to refer to a " natural instinct " what he is unable to explain by association. He argues quite plausibly for the original reference of pride and humility to self, which by a peculiar use of terms he calls their " object," on the principle that " unless nature had given some original properties to the mind, it could never have any secondary ones." [66] But he applies the principle also to cases which, from his own point of view, seem by no means so simple, and which he elsewhere in a manner tries to explain. It is thus he treats of the connection of love and benevolence, or desire for the object's happiness, and,

[63] *Treatise of Human Nature*, Book II, Part III, sec. IX, 214.
[64] *Ibid.*, Part III, sec. I, 181.
[65] *Ibid.*, sec. IX, 214 f.
[66] *Ibid.*, Part I, sec. III, 80.

conversely, of hatred and anger, or the impulse to effect his misery. After rejecting the hypothesis that the conjoined tendencies are really one, since, among other reasons, there is no inconsistency in connecting love with desire of misery, or hate with desire of happiness, he falls back on the assumption that the actual conjunction is " an arbitrary and original instinct," a mysterious union effected by nature in the original constitution of the mind. Yet a little later he appears to explain the conjunction of love and benevolence from the coincidence of the pleasure of benevolence with the pleasure derived by sympathy and from the pleasure of the person loved, and pain from his pain, " from which correspondence of impressions," he says, " there arises a subsequent desire of his pleasure and aversion to his pain." [67]

Turning now to the indirect passions, we come to the most important part of Hume's " system." The fundamental passions are pride and humility and love and hate, and they are accounted for by associations based on two " established " properties of the passions: (1) their object is self, (2) their sensation, or feeling, is either pleasant or painful; and on two " supposed " properties, inductively observed, of their causes; (1) their relation to self; (2) their tendency to produce a pain or pleasure independent of the passion. Comparing the two sets of properties, " the true system," he writes, " breaks in upon me with an irresistible evidence. That cause which excites the passion is related to the object which nature has attributed to the passion; the sensation which the cause separately produces is related to the sensation of the passion. From this *double relation of impressions and ideas* the passion is derived.

[67] *Ibid.,* Part II, sec. VI, 154; Cf. sec. IX. On the apparent inconsistency and its bearing on the ethical theory, cf. T. H. Green, *Introduction to Hume,* sec. 41 f.

The one idea is easily converted into its correlative, and the one impression into that which resembles and corresponds to it. With how much greater facility must this transition be made, when their movements mutually assist each other, and the mind receives a double impulse from the relations both of its impressions and ideas? " [68] We owe the passions, then, at least the indirect passions, to the combined influence of the association of impressions and ideas and of the directions or impulses furthered by the association. [69]

The doctrine thus abstractly stated will be made clearer by the illustration which Hume uses, namely, the pride a man feels in the possession of a beautiful house. The cause of this passion, as Hume describes it, is the quality of beauty in the house, which, as its " subject " is related to the " object," the self, as his property. The operating " ideas," then, are those of (a) the beautiful house, and (b) the self owning the house, the former associated with the latter, or, as Hume also says, " converted into " it, by the principle of causality, a man's property being something which " produces effects on him and he on it." In other cases the association might be through resemblance or contiguity. The operating " impressions " are the " sensations " (c) of the pleasure excited independently of the passion by the quality of beauty, and (d) of the resembling pleasure of pride. [70] The two pleasures mutually confirm one another. This gives us the " double relation," on the one hand, of (a) and (b), a relation of ideas, and on the

---

[68] *Ibid.,* Part I, sec. V, 85.

[69] The dual causation is brought out especially forcibly in Hume's " Dissertation on the Passions," sec. II.

[70] Hume notes as a " remarkable difference " between impressions and ideas that while the latter are associated by resemblance, contiguity, or causality, the former are associated only by resemblance, a peculiarity which strikes the reader as the more remarkable, if, as Hume holds, ideas and impressions differ intrinsically only in vividness, *Treatise of Human Nature,* Part I, sec. IV, 82.

other of (c) and (d), a relation of impressions. The general system thus outlined is subject to various limitations, as, e.g., in pride and humility, that the relation to ourselves of the things producing pain or pleasure must be close, peculiar, or only shared by a few, and easily discernible; it is also limited by the inconstancy of the cause, the brevity of its connection with ourselves and the influence of custom.[71] The important conditions are facility of transition between the ideas and congruence of the related impressions. If we substitute " uneasiness " for " pleasure " in the above account of pride, we get humility, the cause of which is related to self, the quality independently disagreeable and the passion itself disagreeable also. The associations between the ideas and the impressions constitute the passion and define its direction. What holds of pride and humility holds *mutatis mutandis* of love and hate, except that here we have to make the more important substitution of the idea of another for the idea of self. If an object has no relation to an idea of self or other person or if, having this relation, it is unattended by any impression of pleasure or pain, it arouses no emotion. Nor will it be a steady and durable cause of a passion, however pleasant or painful, without the transition of ideas which relate it to persons. On the other hand, whatever has this double relation must necessarily excite the passions: a particular passion, according to the idea of the object — self or another — and the pleasant or uneasy impression.[72]

The above principles are used by Hume to explain not only the fundamental passions of pride and humility, love and hate, but " a transition of passions " of every kind, for often one passion gives rise to or combines with another. The number of ideas involved may be of any degree

[71] *Ibid.*, Part I, sec. V, 87.   [72] *Ibid.*, Part II, sec. II, 126.

of complexity. In love and hatred, for instance, we have not only a relation of the idea of a thing or quality to another, but also often the idea of the relation of the other person to ourselves. The movement of transition is not infrequently based on sympathy, which is itself, as Hume describes it, due wholly to association. He derives it from the " idea " of another's affection suggested by its expressions and converted into an " impression " by " the idea, or rather impression, of ourselves," which imparts something of its own vividness to ideas brought into relation with it. This relation is established by contiguity and resemblance, the contiguity of men in society and the many resemblances they bear to one another, amidst all their variety, both in body and in mind.[73] Why the expressions of feeling in another should arouse the " idea " or " copy " of it in ourselves, the theory does not explain, and we are tempted to ask whether Hume, with his tendency to refer to " natural instinct " what he cannot explain by association, would have adopted the naïve view that we are originally endowed with a capacity for interpreting emotional signs. Nor does it explain how, after the " idea " is excited and raised to the intensity of an " impression," even assuming that the " idea of ourselves " is capable of effecting the transformation, it should be felt not simply as ours, but as another's. For, surely, sympathy is a feeling both with and for another; but there is nothing in Hume's derivation of it to suggest that it is anything more than a feeling in one resembling that in another.[74] Nevertheless the reader cannot fail to be struck by the simple ingenuity of an explanation which evidently contains a large measure of truth and whose most obvious defect, apart from the faulty

[73] *Ibid.*, Part I, sec. XI, 111–114.
[74] Cf. T. H. Green's criticism, *Introduction to Hume,* sec. 40.

underlying "atomism" of the whole psychology, is the absence of a phylogenetic point of view. This ingenuity, this subtlety in the application of his principles, adapting them to special cases, qualifying and supplementing them here and there with considerations drawn from the circumstances of their operation, is a constant source of fascination and surprise in Hume's discussion. Sometimes it is not sympathy, but comparison, acting in a manner the opposite of sympathy, which determines the transition. Thus " when our fancy considers directly the sentiments of others, and enters deep into them, it makes us sensible of all the passions it surveys, but in a particular manner of grief or sorrow. On the contrary, when we compare the sentiments of others to our own, we feel a sensation directly the opposite to the original one, viz., a joy for the grief of others, and a grief for their joy." [75] This is one of the main principles operating in malice and envy. The contemplation of another's pleasure " naturally " gives us pleasure, that of another's pain, pain: this was involved in the derivation of sympathy; but for this very reason, Hume holds, the opposite effect is produced when we compare these feelings in him with our own. Yet these opposite effects are not always produced, and when this is the case the result is explained by some countervailing principle. For example, a man, " indulged in pleasure " learns of a friend's affliction. On the principle of comparison the " reflected uneasiness " from his friend would only enliven his own pleasure. But it does not do this. Why? Because, says Hume, the grief is here supposed to be the predominant passion, and " every addition falls to that side and is swallowed up in it without operating in the least on the contrary affection," the rule being that the predominant factor in a compound defines

[75] *Treatise of Human Nature*, Part II, sec. IX, 165.

the hedonic character of the whole.[76] Hume is thus never at a loss to meet refractory cases. He finds for example an apparent contradiction to " my system " in the mixture of benevolence with compassion and of anger with malice, " for as pity is an uneasiness and malice a joy arising from the misery of others, pity should naturally, as in all other cases, produce hatred and malice, love," [77] that is, according to the " system," the " impression " of pleasure or pain should associate to itself a resembling pleasure or pain, and not, as is apparently here the case, a passion of opposite quality. He solves the difficulty by interpreting the principle of a double relation of impressions and ideas as including not only relations of resembling impressions of pleasure and pain, but also similarity or coincidence of " impulse." In the case in question the impulse of benevolence coincides with that of pity, the impulse of anger with that of malice. When a conflict arises between " dissimilarity of sensations " and " similarity of directions," the result depends on which preponderates. In the present instance we have to take account of the influence of sympathy, the " secondary sensation " derived from the imagination of weal or woe in another. If the impression so derived is weak, the uneasiness of the feeling, says Hume, induces hatred; if strong, it redoubles the tendency of the passions. The general conclusion is that benevolence " arises from a great degree of misery, or any degree strongly sympathized with "; and conversely of hatred or contempt.[78]

---

[76] *Ibid.*, sec. VIII, 162.

[77] *Ibid.*, sec. IX, 166.

[78] *Ibid.*, 171. There would be no difficulty if we could accept literally and as complete Hume's definition of pity as " desire of happiness to another and aversion to his misery," which is also his definition, in the same content, of benevolence: the two names would then signify the same thing. The difficulty arises from observing the dissimilarity of the sentimental im-

The principle of relative strength in the ingredients of an association here invoked serves also to elucidate many other cases. Respect, for instance, is a passion, according to Hume, compounded of love and humility. Why it is not always excited by an object of worth belonging to another he explains by supposing that the object may be one peculiarly fitted to excite love, but imperfectly fitted to excite pride, and that, accordingly, the degree of humility aroused by comparison may be so small as to be scarcely felt, or, indeed, imperceptible.[79] In other cases stress is laid on the subtle influences of the imagination. This explains, for instance, why, in general, we are less affected by remote objects than by those near at hand: contiguous objects, by reason of their relation to ourselves, approach the force and vivacity of an impression, whereas remote objects, by virtue of the interruption in the manner of conceiving them, " appear in a weaker or more imperfect light " and hence the respective objects exert a proportionate effect on the will and passions. The same principle explains why distance in space has less influence than in time, there being, according to Hume, in the latter case a greater interruption in the thought. It explains too, assuming a tendency to move in the order of time, that is, from present to future, why the same distance in the future has a superior effect above that in the past. But there are certain phenomena which seem to show the opposite effects. Thus, as Hume puts the matter, esteem and admiration for an object are

---

pressions, the pleasure and pain, in the two passions. It is noteworthy that while, with that looseness of expression which attaches to his literary style, he seems in the course of the discussion to shift the question, he does not here, as in the case of the connection of love and benevolence, fall back on the easy hypothesis of a " natural instinct."

[79] *Ibid.*, sec. X, 175. " No quality in another gives rise to humility by comparison, unless it would have produced pride by being placed in ourselves ; and *vice versa.*"

increased (1) by a very great distance, (2) more by distance in time than in space, and (3) more by distance in
past time than in the future. The first of these phenomena
is explained by supposing that the soul is enlarged and
delighted by the contemplation of a vast expanse of space
or a vast extent of time, and that the feelings thus excited
are transferred to the associated object; the second, by assuming that when opposition and difficulty are not enough
to discourage, they invigorate the soul and enhance its
sense of the object. Transition in time, it is noted, is more
difficult than in space; and similarly of the third, the increased difficulty of moving over the past makes the object
appear more impressive.[80]

It is perhaps the very skill displayed in the application
of his principles which creates at times the impression in
Hume of a deduction as " logical " and scholastic as anything we find in Spinoza. Occasionally he supports a de-
fensible thesis by very questionable arguments, as where
he denies that the object of love and hatred is the cause on
the ground that they have the same object in common, and
that, therefore, their sensations being contrary, they must
destroy one another and so prevent the passions from ever
making their appearance. Obviously the common object
here is only the same in the generic sense, namely, some
other person, and there are plenty of differences in persons. Nor is Hume always consistent. His "system " of
the indirect passions requires a " double relation of impressions and ideas " for their production; yet in the very context in which he is expounding it with special reference to
pride, he makes the emotion depend on the direct excitement of a mental organ naturally disposed to its production, the important idea of the self, which the theory

<hr />

[80] *Ibid.*, Part III, secs. VII and VIII.

assumes as a condition, being here regarded as a consequence.[81] In spite, nevertheless, of obvious shortcomings, Hume's must be reckoned as the most original and brilliant attempt to work out in detail a system of the passions by the unsupplemented methods of eighteenth century associationist psychology. His is the classical exposition of the subject from the associationist point of view, with little regard for physiology, only here and there a suggestion of the comparative method [82] and with no concept at all of the light which the biological generalizations of the century following had to throw upon some of its more obscure problems. His successors in the nineteenth century may improve in details, but they add nothing in principle, except as they are influenced by ideas of biological development; while they all fall short by comparison in acumen, geniality, and charm of style.

[81] " We must suppose that nature has given to the organs of the human mind a certain disposition fitted to produce a peculiar impression or emotion which we call *pride*. To this emotion she has assigned a certain idea, *viz.*, that of *self*, which it never fails to produce. . . . The organs are so disposed as to produce the passion ; and the passion, after its production, naturally produces a certain idea." *Ibid.*, Part I, sec. V, 85 f. The inconsistency is pointed out by T. H. Green, *Introduction to Hume*, sec. 39, who observes, with critical remarks on the consequences, that the process is assimilated by Hume himself to the physiological process by which we get a special sensation.

[82] Cf. *Ibid.*, Part II, sec. XII on the love and hatred of animals.

CHAPTER IX

AFFECTIVE PSYCHOLOGY IN THE EIGHTEENTH CENTURY: FRENCH AND GERMAN

The genius of the affective life in the eighteenth century was the French philosopher Rousseau (1712–1778). No writer of the century exerted so powerful an influence in bringing about the recognition of feeling, in the broad sense of the term, as over against the exaggerated claims of the intellect, in the guidance and inspiration of life, and in the settlement of the problems most deeply affecting it. This influence contributed in no slight degree to the further recognition of the place of feeling in the content of the mental life, such as we find, for example, among German writers at the end of this and the beginning of the following century, when for the first time in the history of psychology, feeling is assigned a co-ordinate position with intellect and will. But Rousseau himself contributes practically nothing directly to the psychology of the subject. He had, indeed, a remarkable talent for literary description and this, together with the frankness of his disclosure of his own emotional personality, makes his writings a veritable treasure-trove for the modern psychologist, but the bent of his own genius and the peculiarities of his aims prevented Rousseau himself from making any systematic psychological elaboration of his material. He was more the prophet and apologist of the feelings than their scientific analyst, the apologist in particular of the *sentiment intérieur* as an authoritative guide in morals and religion. His pre-eminence lay in the creation of a vivid impression of the importance of feeling in molding opinion and instigating action, and this not only in fact, but of right, with a corresponding depreciation of the intellect as subject to all manner of sophistication.[1] In this regard he selected certain feelings as "natural" in opposition to others conceived as "factitious," this being the final word in establishing their authority. Like all his contemporaries he thought of the natural as the primitive, given endowment. The discovery of these "natural" feelings, blended as they now so often are with their opposites, is left to a delicate tact acquired by knowledge of the world.[2] This tact would seem to be itself a kind of feeling. At any rate the "feeling" to which Rousseau appeals as the final arbiter and the thing of ultimate value in human nature is found, on inspection, to be of complex psychological character. It always, indeed, denotes something inwardly and individually subjective, but it includes, according to the occasion of its use and the exigencies of the controversy in hand, such diverse psychological functions as desire and sentiment, unbridled emotion, aspiration, appreciation of values, self-consciousness, the immediacy of experience, and the intuition of theoretical principles. Rousseau fails to recognize the differences.[3] The great fact for him is that feeling is fundamental and of supreme value.[4]

[1] Thus of Mme. de Warrens he says that her faults were due to her errors, not to her passions; that her heart guided her right, but that she listened to her reason, which guided her wrong, *Confessions*, Book V (*Œuvres*, I, 341). Montaigne seems to have thought similarly of himself, for he writes: "I find my concupiscence less debauched than my reason," *Essays*, II, xi.

[2] "One must know how to analyze properly the human heart in order to disentangle the true feelings of nature. A delicacy of tact is necessary, which can only be acquired by intimacy with the great world," *Confessions*, Book XI (*Œuvres*, II, 490).

[3] Cf. A. C. Armstrong, "The Idea of Feeling in Rousseau's Religious Philosophy." *Arch. f. Gesch. d. Phil.*, XXIV, 242–260.

[4] *Exister pour nous, c'est sentir* (for us to live is to feel), *Émile*, (*Œuvres*, IV, 326). In a note he observes that in certain regards ideas and

Rousseau, the sentimentalist, furnishes in his own person a conspicuous illustration of the restless fluctuations of the life of feeling. This was connected with his neurotic temperament. His distinction between " natural " and " factitious " feelings was meant to call attention to still another factor in producing changes of feeling, namely, a social. The corruption of human nature was due, according to him, in large measure to a perverted civilization. Under his influence the ideal of the " natural " was found in the noble savage. It is interesting to observe that the writer, François René de Chateaubriand (1768–1848), who drew the romantic picture of this ideal in *Atala* was also the author of an impressive literary portrayal of the changes of feeling brought about by advancing civilization. Chateaubriand's main purpose is to extol the social influence of Christianity. He derives his material in part from a comparison of modern with ancient poetry and romance.[5]

There is little of moment to record in the affective psychology proper of eighteenth century French writers that we do not find among their English contemporaries. The prevailing type of reflection was sensationalistic, and this was largely influenced by Locke. The views of human nature taken by writers of this tendency were not essentially different from those derived by English authors from the teachings of Locke and Hobbes. The combination of a physiological treatment of the affections with this sensationalism may probably be connected with the native tradition established by Descartes. But however influenced, the views were expressed with characteristic vigor and independence.

feelings are the same: if, namely, attention is directed to the object and only secondarily, by reflection, on ourselves, it is an idea; conversely it is a feeling. Both likeness and distinction are too vague for criticism.

[5] *Génie du christianisme*, Books II, III (*Œuvres*, II, 208 f.).

The protagonist of French sensationalism, Étienne Bonnot de Condillac (1715–1780), after endowing his hypothetical statue with the sense of smell, conceives of pleasure and pain as arising from the agreeableness and disagreeableness respectively of the odors experienced. What makes them agreeable or disagreeable he does not seek to explain, nor does he make clear the distinction between the agreeable and disagreeable and the pleasure and pain qualities, the derived or secondary sensations. Thus derived, however, they — pleasure and pain — become, through memory and association, the sole motives of action. Almost, if not quite, as primitive as pleasure and pain is surprise or astonishment; this is due to the instantaneous transition from one sensation to another. Pleasures may be divided into bodily and mental, but both kinds are essentially the same. Pleasures vary in intensity, rise and fall, and, if the intensity is increased beyond a certain point, pass over into pain. There is no experience of indifference; what is supposedly such is a judgment of the experience in retrospect. Emotion arises from the vivacity of a sensation causing a diffusion of the excitement over the whole body. Comparison of present pain with past pleasure is the occasion of the feeling of need and desire for its satisfaction. Exclusive or dominant desire is passion. Love and hate, hope and fear, arise from desire for pleasure and aversion to pain. The liveliest passions arise from the conflict between hope and fear, by which desire is inflamed and augmented.[6]

The general principles of these deductions are common to all the writers of this sensationalistic tendency, however different the details or varying the emphasis. In the reaction from the traditional rationalism and conventional

---

[6] *Traité des sensations,* chaps. I–III (*Œuvres,* III, 70 f.).

morality, the passions are extolled as the great impelling forces of human nature. Strong passions, thinks C. A. Helvétius (1715–1771), characterize strong men: when we cease to be impassioned, we grow stupid. According to this author the two forces which move the soul are strong passions and *ennui*. Under certain circumstances, the pain of *ennui* may become the soul mover. The passions are all rooted in physical sensibility, all spring from self-love, from desire of pleasure and aversion to pain. The only " natural " passions are those directly based on the physical appetites; the rest are " artificial," modifications due to social influences. Thus Helvétius seeks to show how even those passions which, like avarice, ambition, pride, and friendship, seem farthest removed from sensuous feeling, have their origin in and are relative to sensible pleasure and exhibit the transformation, under social influences, of the conceptions of good and evil, which, denoting in the first instance sensible pleasure and physical pain, are gradually extended to include everything that can procure or increase the one or can avoid or diminish the other. Temperament and the physical constitution have little influence on the passions, which are rather the effect of instruction.[7] Delisle de Sales (1743–1816) expresses similar views.[8] According to him there are but two primitive passions, love and ambition, the one inspiring to physical, the

[7] *De l'Esprit*, Disc. III (*Œuvres*, I, 265 f.); *De l'homme*, chap. I (*Œuvres*, II, 202 f.), is a pedagogical application of the principles set forth in the former. The author acknowledges his obligations to Locke — " *Dans le sentier du vrai il marcha devant nous*," (he preceded us in the path of truth), *Épitre sur l'orgueil* (*Œuvres*, III). A. Keim, *Helvétius, sa vie et son œuvre*, 277, speaks of Helvétius' analyses of the passions as *d'une rare vigueur satirique, d'une ironie magistrale* (of unusual satirical force, of outstanding irony). His greater forerunner along this path was, of course, Hobbes.

[8] *De la philosophie de la nature*, Book I, Part II, chap. 12 (*Œuvres*, IV, 100–172), where the passions are briefly treated.

other to intellectual pleasures. Both spring from self-love, which is the common root of all the passions.[9] The origin of some of them, from this point of view, the author traces. He too lays stress on the influence of social factors. The mechanism of the passions is treated in a single page; they are referred, in general terms, to the violent excitement of the sensitive and intellectual " fibres." Other writers of a materialistic tendency incline to emphasize the influence of the stomach.[10]

Julien Offray de Lamettrie (1709–1751), a physician and an exponent of materialism, is remembered as one who defended the development of a physiological explanation of mental life in contrast to Descartes' dualism. With regard to feelings, Lamettrie claimed that the material body has three attributes: extension, the ability to move (*la force motrice*), and the capacity to feel (*sentir*). The term feeling in this case, however, is used in a general sense to mean consciousness. He speaks of *l'âme sensitive* as giving rise to two additional faculties: one, of a mechanical nature, which furnishes sensation, memory, imagination, and ultimately the passions, while the other faculty depends upon the organic dispositions of the body, giving rise to inclinations, appetites, attention (*pénétration*), instinct, and thought (*conception* or *compréhension*). The passions are habitual modifications of animal spirits which furnish

---

[9] For saying this Pope is lauded as one who by a stroke of genius put into a word what Locke had taken twenty pages to show. *Ibid.*, art. III.

[10] Cf. J. le R d'Alembert, who recommends careful abstinence from anything that might injuriously affect a part so important for the state of the soul, especially in times of restlessness, grief, and violent passion, *Essai sur les éléments de philosophie*, sec. 8. He refers the opinion that the seat of the soul was the stomach to Parmenides; J. O. de Lamettrie, *Man or Machine*, 13, refers it to J. B. van Helmont. M. de Montaigne, *Apologie sur Raymund de Sabunde*, (*Essais*, II, chap. 12), refers it to Epicurus, but the passage cited (Lucretius, *De natura rerum*, III, 142), speaks of the chest. It was Bacon's view. Cf. W. Wundt, *Physiologische Psychologie*, VI, 132.

almost continually to the soul agreeable or disagreeable
sensations. These in turn inspire the soul with desire or
aversion towards outside objects. From thence spring the
passions: love, hatred, fear, boldness, pity, ferocity, anger,
and gentleness, all related to desires and wishes. Love and
hatred, however, are the two passions from which the
others are derived. The above passions he also refers to as
affections, retaining the term *passions* especially for those
feelings during which our equilibrium is upset and we no
longer are influenced by the laws of reason. Passions vary
according to the age of the body, as is apparent when those
of youth are contrasted with those of old age. The affections he differentiates into those which are controlled by
will and those which are involuntary, being produced by
minute movements of heart, lungs, and pulse. He describes
the inclinations as natural preferences which are developed towards certain particular objects. Appetites are more
fundamental. They depend upon organs which make us
like what is good for us and dislike what is bad for us. Instincts, in turn, are mechanical dispositions which direct
man's actions so that he may preserve his life without
learning to do so. Lamettrie, however, does not relate these
instincts to the affections or passions.[11]

In another direction Pierre Louis Moreau de Maupertuis
(1698–1759) fairly represents the eclectic moralizing
treatment of affective phenomena. He advocates hedonism,
but holds that neither the body alone, nor the soul alone,
is the instrument of pleasure. His definition of pleasure is
one that in substance has been frequently repeated,
namely, " every perception which the soul would rather
experience than not experience," and a like definition
mutatis mutandis is given of pain. All pleasures and pains,

---

[11] *Traité de l'âme,* I, 83–145.

thus, belong to the soul. They are divided into bodily and mental merely for convenience. The sensationalists are right in regarding the pleasures of avarice and of ambition for power as only bodily pleasures in prospect, and conversely of the pains arising from loss of wealth or of power. But there are certain pleasures peculiar to the soul. These are reduced to two kinds, one experienced in the practice of justice, the other in the vision of truth. A comparison of these with bodily pleasures in respect to durability, extent, and effect shows their superiority.[12]

While much of the French writing on the affective life is at this time more literary than scientific and much that passed for scientific did little more than express the philosophical prejudices or rapid, more or less acute and often openly cynical observations of experienced men of the world, the work of Charles Bonnet (1720–1793), the Swiss naturalist, stands out, along with that of Condillac, as perhaps the most conspicuous attempt at a systematic scientific psychology made by any French writer of the century. His *Essai analytique sur les facultés de l'âme*, published in 1759, five years after the anonymously published *Essai de psychologie*, which it expanded, criticized, and corrected, can be read today with more sympathy by a psychologist who espouses the principle of a thoroughgoing correlation between neural and psychic activity, while at the same time maintaining the irreducible empirical dualism, than almost any other work produced prior to the rise of what, with a presumption born of ignorance, is called the " new " psychology.[13]

Bonnet, jealously defending his originality, is yet ob-

---

[12] *Essai de philosophie morale*, chap. I (*Œuvres*, I, 193 ff.).

[13] Besides the works mentioned, Bonnet also wrote an essay entitled, *Hypothèse sur l'âme des bêtes et leur industrie* and included an " Essai d'application des principes psychologiques de l'auteur " in his most famous philosophical treatise, *Palingénésie philosophique*, 1769, in which he advo-

viously influenced by writers of various schools, between whom he seeks to maintain a balance. He thus combines, not without inconsistency, the sensualism of Locke with the intellectualism of Leibnitz, the spiritualism of Descartes with the materialistic determinism of Lamettrie. His principles of psychology have the closest kinship with those of his English contemporary, Hartley, but were probably derived independently. He deduces the content of consciousness in its whole extent from observation and elaboration of particular sensible experiences, which, like Hartley, he connects with specific energies of vibrations of the nerve fibres. The action of the fibres leaves traces in the brain as dispositions to particular forms of movement and these are connected together by laws of association, which are the counterpart of the laws of the association of ideas. Bonnet carries the principle of association farther than any other French writer. More definitely than Hartley, whose attention is mainly directed to the action of the single fibres, he avails himself of the hypothesis of their intercorrelations. He distinguishes, moreover, between the " sensible " and the " intellectual " fibres, the latter, though of essentially the same nature as the former, being assumed as the basis of abstraction and the higher mental processes. Back of all this mechanism, there lies for him, as for Descartes, a substantial immaterial soul acted on by the material environment by a sort of *influxus physicus* — theoretically, the mode is more " occasionalistic " — and reacting in definite ways according to its own intrinsic nature, though, as its contents are mechanically determined, its " activity " would appear reduced to little more than that of a passive spectator.

-----

cates a " preformation " theory of evolution, and speculates at large on the nature and development of souls.

Bonnet's doctrine of the feelings is briefly as follows: [14] we distinguish in a sensation between that which characterizes or indicates the presence of an object and that which denotes the way the soul is affected, its transition to a state better or worse, which so determines it to act. This latter moment is feeling and accompanies in a greater or less degree all sensations.[15] Bonnet, however, is prevented by an imperfectly developed terminology from maintaining this distinction and speaks in the sequel of feelings more as independent sensations than as accompaniments or aspects of sensations; he distinctly asserts that they can be remembered,[16] but, in spite of this, he never suggests their association or transference.[17] The two main species of feeling are pleasure and pain, which, in agreement with the utility doctrine current at the time, are assumed to be directly or indirectly connected with the weal or woe of the individual. The degrees of feeling form a single scale, like that of temperature; the very same fibres can yield pleasure or pain according to the intensity of the stimulus. The fact that the same sensation can be agreeable to one person and disagreeable to another depends on the temperament, the greater or less adaptability to excitement, of the fibres.[18] To the same cause is due the wide range of individual dispositions. Bonnet lays great stress on the law of relativity in the affective life, on the importance of novelty, with its feeling of surprise, and of change as a condition of pleasure, holding that a persistent stimulus has very much the same

[14] For an excellent account of Bonnet's psychology, see Max Offner, "Die Psychologie Charles Bonnet's" in *Schriften der Gesellschaft für psychologische Forschung*, 1893, V, 553–722.

[15] *Essai analytique sur les facultés de l'âme*, sec. 116; cf. 83, 118, 195.

[16] *Ibid.*, secs. 413, 546, 547.

[17] A strong point, in M. Offner's opinion (*op. cit.*, 660) in favor of his independence of Hartley.

[18] *Essai analytique sur les facultés de l'âme*, secs. 120, 121, 386.

effect, as regards its demands on the nervous energy, as one that is too strong.[19] He describes, but hardly attempts to explain, the phenomenon of fatigue.[20]

At first dividing feelings into the three classes of bodily, mental, and mixed,[21] he afterwards used the more serviceable distinction of absolute and relative.[22] An absolute feeling is one arising from a certain excitement of the sense fibres, a relative feeling is one that arises from a conscious comparison. The latter is composite, including both the absolute feelings of the components and the feeling due to their relations. This forms the basis for a theory of harmony and disharmony and hence of beauty and ugliness. Harmony consists in a definite sequence or connection of movements in different fibres such that their action together gives pleasure, though each singly might be indifferent or even painful. This fact of pleasure from the harmonious action of related elements is to be simply accepted as belonging to our natural constitution.[23] It is because of the pleasure thus aroused that anything is called beautiful. Because of this relation to harmonious organic action, the beautiful is also the useful.[24] Beauty connects itself with the pleasure of activity, which is greatest when unity is combined with variety in the greatest economy of effort.[25]

---

[19] *Ibid.*, sec. 121.
[20] Cf. Offner, *op. cit.*, 663.
[21] *Essai de psychologie,* chap. 65, 213 f. Ordinarily only the first two were recognized. To the third class Bonnet ascribed those due to the imagination.
[22] *Essai analytique sur les facultés de l'âme,* sec. 350.
[23] *Ibid.*, secs. 369, 370, 373, 374, 400, 659.
[24] *Ibid.*, sec. 374.
[25] *Ibid.*, secs. 380–386. The theory that all activity is, as such, pleasant was held by two writers cited by Sir W. Hamilton, *Lectures on Metaphysics and Logic,* II, 465: J. B. Du Bos, *Réflexions critiques sur la poésie,* I, i, secs. 1, 2; and L. J. Pouilly, *Théorie des sentiments agréables,* chaps. 1–5. M. Mendelssohn, who at first criticized Du Bos's statement that even an unpleasant idea might be agreeable if gratifying the mind's primary want of occupation, later admitted its truth, *Rhapsodie* (*Philosophische Schriften,* II, 17). The question is connected with the experience of *ennui,* which Con-

This view, which appears as an intellectual commonplace in a number of writers, is given by Bonnet an organic basis. What is said of harmony and the beautiful hold *mutatis mutandis* of disharmony and the ugly.

The influence of Bonnet was considerable not only in France, but also in Italy and Holland, and especially in Germany, where the " fibre " psychology, as it was called, had many adherents; and those who accepted the general principles followed Bonnet in the main in his doctrine of the affections. This was particularly the case with C. F. von Irwing in the psychological part of his *Erfahrungen und Untersuchungen über die Menschen,* and even J. G. Sulzer seems influenced by him in his treatment of the sense feelings, while J. N. Tetens expressly relates his own doctrine to Bonnet's. Similar influences appear in J. Lossius, M. Hissmann, and others. To the critics the " fibre " psychology seemed more illustrative of ingenuity than illuminating.[26]

The German affective psychology of the eighteenth century, including the early years of the nineteenth, shows solid achievements. It is characterized by comprehensiveness of aim, shows much patient analysis, and wins in the end the clear recognition that feeling, which medieval writers had connected closely with desire and many modern writers since Descartes still more closely with cognition, is as distinct and unique an aspect of mental life as knowing or striving. This achievement has for its historical background and presupposition the doctrine of mental

---

dillac, *Traité des sensations,* 1, 2, sec. 26, referred to comparison with earlier happier conditions ; Bonnet, to poverty of relations or duration of experience affording no sufficient excitement to the activity of comparison, *loc. cit.*

[26] On Bonnet's influence in general, see Offner, *op. cit.,* 716 ff. ; for his influence in particular on German affective psychology, see Johannes Speck, " Bonnet's Einwirkung auf die deutsche Psychologie, IV," *Arch. f. Gesch. d. Phil.* XI, 1897, 187 ff.

" faculties." The whole movement is predominantly under the influence of Leibnitz, as that of the English and French psychology was predominantly under the influence of Locke.

Gottfried Wilhelm von Leibnitz (1646–1716) who has comparatively little to say about feeling,[27] contains, indeed, the germs of the later doctrine of feeling as a distinct faculty. But as he recognizes only the faculties of understanding and will and lays special stress on the fundamentally perceptive force of the monads, the appetitive being essentially for the enlargement of perception, his influence was in the main favorable to the " intellectualistic " interpretation. This was both a ban and a stimulus to much of the psychological thinking of Germany in the eighteenth century and, after numerous efforts at revolt, it was finally broken by the general acceptance of the tripartite division of the mental faculties established by Mendelssohn, Tetens, and Kant. For Leibnitz, feelings (*sentiments*) are sensations, obscure perceptions, or ideas. Pleasure and pain are sensations respectively of perfection and imperfection, whether in ourselves or in another.[28] They accompany and are never found apart from ideas. But again, they are related to will as motives to action and have a teleological character. All activity of the soul is pleasant; the feeling of beauty lies midway between sensuous desire and rational volition.[29] Besides these general and somewhat confused indications of doctrine, Leibnitz has something to

[27] For a complete account of his doctrine on the subject, see C. Albrich, " Leibnitz's Lehre vom Gefühl," *Arch. f. d. ges. Psych.*, XVI (1910), 1 ff.

[28] *Nouveaux essais sur l'entendement humain,* chap. XXI, sec. 41, (*Opera* II, 261 f.).

[29] On the contradictory tendencies in Leibnitz's doctrine, see J. Orth, *Gefühl und Bewusstseinslage,* 6 f. Orth's sketch in this connection of the history of the term " feeling " among the German writers of the eighteen century is a contribution to which the present writer is largely indebted for the account which follows.

say in detail about various kinds of feelings, sensible and intellectual, about the laws of feeling, e.g., its dependence on the intensity and duration of the ideas to which it is attached, and about emotion. He several times refers to his definition of love — " pleasure from another's happiness " — as one fitted to put an end to controversy.[30]

Christian Wolff (1679–1754), through whom the ideas of Leibnitz were principally conveyed to the generation following, defines pleasure and pain respectively as intuitive cognitions of real or fancied perfection and imperfection.[31] It is a bodily imperfection, for example, the dissolution of organic continuity, which is the cause of the pain of a cut finger. The intuitive perception of the state of body or soul in the experience of pleasure and pain is always confused, even when attention is directed to the analysis of its cause.[32] The " intellectualism " of this Leibnitzo-Wolffian position must not be exaggerated or misconstrued. By " intuitive cognition " or " perception " probably nothing more was meant than immediate, unreflective awareness. The doctrine seems to be that in pleasure and pain we are directly aware of our state of well- or ill-being, of our or another's perfection or imperfection, or what appears such to the feeling. The teleological implications of the experiences are emphasized together with the unclear immediacy of the awareness. Nor can the doctrine be easily impugned unless we are prepared to distinguish between the feeling and awareness of the feeling or to deny its teleological character. The difficulty arises in part from the undeveloped terminology. As " ideas " denoted for Locke

<hr />

[30] *Die philosophischen Schriften von G. W. Leibnitz*, I, 73. Cf. L. Couturat, *La logique de Leibnitz*, 567.

[31] *Psychologia empirica*, secs. 511, 518; cf. his *Vernünftige Gedanken*, secs. 404, 417.

[32] *Psychologia empirica*, sec. 536. For a criticism of this position, see M. Mendelssohn, *Briefe* (*Philosophische Schriften*, I, 152).

all that is presented to a conscious mind, so all "awarenesses " for the Leibnitzians were designated as " perceptions " or " cognitions," between which the only psychological distinctions discovered by them were those of
clearness and obscurity. These were interpreted by the law
of continuity as a scale of degrees by virtue of which even
the conscious might pass gradually into the unconscious,
and *vice versa*. There was a dim apprehension that the various contents of these awarenesses differed in character
and function, but what these differences were could not be
adequately expressed. The " intellectualism " of the doctrine lay in the assumption that they were all relative to the
development of clear and adequate ideas.[33]

While only two mental faculties, cognition and appetition, or understanding and will, were recognized, opinion
was divided as, with which of the two, affective phenomena
should be more particularly grouped. Johann Augustus
Eberhard (1739–1809) and, at first, Dietrich Tiedemann
(1748–1803) made cognition primary.[34] According to the
former, emotions and passions belong to the "inner
sense "; they are species of sensations and, like all sensations, exhibit the mind as passive. According to the latter,
however, passions, at least, play the more active role of an
habitual striving after sensations and ideas.[35] Tiedemann
in this same work does not treat specifically of pleasure
and pain, but only of agreeable (*angenehm*) and disagreeable (*unangenehm*) sensations. Why some sensations are
agreeable and others disagreeable, he finds inexplicable; it
belongs to the mysterious constitution of things. Similarly

---

[33] The imperfection of the terminology is seen, e.g., in Wolff's definition
of *Fühlen* as touch (*Vernünftige Gedanken*, 221), and in his distinguishing
and then immediately identifying *Unlust* and *Schmerz*, (*Ibid.*, 260).

[34] J. A. Eberhard, *Allgemeine Theorie des Denkens und Empfindens*, 33 f.
D. Tiedemann, *Untersuchungen über die Menschen*, I, Vor., xxiii.

[35] *Ibid.*, I, Vor., xxviii.

of individual differences; they cannot be accounted for on the theory of the forgotten associations of childhood, as Charles Perrault (1628–1703) supposed.[36] " Feeling " (*Gefühl*) denotes for Tiedemann, as for Wolff, the sense of touch. Later he gave up the idea of a single *Grundkraft*, adopted the tripartite division of the mental faculties and referred experiences of agreeableness and disagreeableness and of emotion to a special " feeling " faculty and the passions to a conative.[37] He also discovered that the distinction between the pleasant and the unpleasant rested on definite grounds, the primary grounds being, as he states them, three, — (*a*) power and weakness, (*b*) easy and difficult exercise of the faculties, and (*c*) association.[38]

Christian August Crusius (1715–1775) on the other hand, attaches feeling to will, a term which, as he uses it, embraces a diversity of powers, including impulse and desire. Pleasure and pain, the agreeable and the disagreeable, satisfaction and dissatisfaction, arise from the fulfillment or thwarting of volition. This is a fact of experience. We may conclude that when anything is found to be pleasant or unpleasant there was a desire precedent, although we might not have been conscious of it.[39] F. V. Reinhard (1753–1812) may be classed with Crusius as emphasizing the primacy of will, though later, like Tiedemann, he adopted the doctrine of three mental faculties.[40]

A position of considerable importance in the movement

---

[36] *Traité des sensations*, Part II.
[37] *Handbuch der Psychologie*, 181.
[38] *Ibid.*, 151.
[39] *Anweisung vernünftig zu Leben*, 25–27. Crusius seems not to use the terms *Lust* and *Unlust*, which do not occur in the rather full index to this short little volume of nearly 900 pages, but, like Tiedemann, *angenehm* and *unangenehm* and their congeners.
[40] Cf. M. Dessoir, *Geschichte der neueren deutschen Psychologie*, 181, 183 ff.

which led to this doctrine must be ascribed to J. G. Sulzer (1720–1779), who assumed one ultimate *Grundkraft* manifested in two principal distinct faculties, the *Vorstellungsvermögen* and the *Empfindungsvermögen*. These he defined respectively as " the faculty of presenting something, or of cognizing the nature of things," and " the faculty of feeling (*empfinden*) or of being pleasantly or unpleasantly affected." [41] In thus distinguishing processes relative to the cognition of objects and those which characterize the state of the subject, Sulzer recognizes affective phenomena as *sui generis* [42] and, as conation cannot be identified with either process, implies a trinal division of the faculties. But his terminology is defective; an *Empfindung* is still a *Vorstellung*, though distinguished from the perceived object. [43] Pleasant and unpleasant feelings are connected, the one sort with ease and rapidity, the other with hindrance in conative tendency. [44] What especially determines them is the furthering or inhibiting of the flow of ideas. [45] K. F. Hungar (1761–1804) criticized Sulzer's division of the faculties, the one fundamental faculty being, according to him, animal feeling (*animalisches Empfinden*). This he defined as anticipatory feeling of the relation of demand to supply of vital energy. If this feeling is one of the customary relation, it is satisfaction; if restraint or excess, it is dissatisfaction or pain. [46] The influence of Wolff, combined

---

[41] " *auf eine angenehme oder unangenehme Art gerührt zu werden.*" *Vermischte philosophische Schriften*, 225.

[42] See A. Palme, *J. G. Sulzer's Psychologie und die Anfänge der Dreivermögenslehre*, 29 ff.

[43] *Op. cit.*, 229.

[44] " *Ohne Begierde kann es in der Welt keinen wirklichen Grad des Vernügens geben*"; *Vermischte philosophischen Schriften*, I, 13. Cf. C. A. Crusius, *loc. cit.*

[45] *Ibid.*, I, 20.

[46] " *Empfinden ist das Vorgefühl der Ubung oder Einschränkung oder Überspannung meiner wesentlichen Kräfte. Das Vorgefühl der ersteren ist Vergnügen und das letztere nach Verhältnis bald Missvergnügen, bald Schmerz.*" Quoted by Orth, *op. cit.*, 17. Cf. M. Dessoir, *op. cit.*, 200.

with the tendency to connect feeling with action, is clearly seen in J. J. H. Feder (1740–1821), who subordinates will to understanding in the operation of the soul's one fundamental intelligence and makes the affective opposites to consist in the feelings of power and of limitation; this being, in dynamic terms, the same thing, practically, as the consciousness of perfection and imperfection.[47] M. Hissmann (1752–1784), a pupil of Feder, illustrates the arbitrariness of an effort to escape from the prevalent confusion in the terminology. He distinguishes sensations (*Sensationen*) and feelings (*Empfindungen*, Fr. *sentiments*) by reference to their supposed organs. Sensations, namely, he defines as "pleasant, unpleasant, or indifferent impressions of external objects on our *coarser* senses," feeling as "the reception of pleasant and unpleasant impressions obtained by the two *finer* senses, the eye and the ear." The pleasant and unpleasant modifications of the "inner sense" he calls *innere Empfindungen*, reserving the term *innere Gefühle* for those modifications of it which are indifferent.[48] Such artificial distinctions only added to the confusion.

The first to advance definitely the doctrine of a tripartite division of the mental faculties, with a distinct faculty of feeling, seems to have been Moses Mendelssohn (1729–1786), who in 1766 published his *Bemerkungen über die Erkenntnis-, Empfindungs- und Begehrungsvermögen*. In his earlier *Briefe über die Empfindungen* (1755), in which the current views of affective experience were discussed in the form of letters supposed to pass between two young men, one English, the other German, he had already remarked on the opposition of feeling and thought,[49] but

---

[47] J. Orth, *op. cit.*, 17 ; M. Dessoir, *op. cit.*, 252 f.
[48] M. Hissmann, *Geschichte der Lehre von den Associationen der Ideen*, 95 n. In his *Psychologische Versuche*, 98, he discourses further on the distinction between *innere Empfindungen* and *innere Gefühle*.
[49] "*Wir fühlen nicht mehr sobald wir denken*" (*Philosophische Schrif-*

there is no suggestion for him in this of a departure from the traditional doctrine of the faculties. In the *Bemerkungen,* however, the *Empfindungsvermögen* is regarded as a distinct power intermediate between the cognitive and the conative; it is defined as the faculty by virtue of which we feel (*empfinden*) pleased or displeased and approve or disapprove. It includes, apparently, what still later in the *Morgenstunden* (1785) Mendelssohn called the *Billigungsvermögen,* a faculty identical, to all appearances, with the *vis aestimativa* of medieval writers and which, if it contains desire at all, contains it only in the germ. Pleasure and displeasure are quite distinct from desire and aversion, quite other than conations. The view put forth with approval in the *Briefe über die Empfundungen* that these affective qualities belong to the consciousness of perfection and imperfection in the object, is afterwards retracted, or at least qualified, as contrary to experience; Mendelssohn, however, continues to hold that they mark the consciousness of perfection and imperfection, if not in the object, then in ourselves.[50]

Mendelssohn was a popular writer and exerted a wide

---

ten, I, 9). This perhaps is not to be taken absolutely. The statement occurs in a passage in which Mendelssohn is speaking of the intellectual control of passion, much after the fashion of Descartes.

[50] The first to give a real explanation of pleasure, according to *Briefe* (*Philosophische Schriften,* I, 145), citing De Maupertuis as authority, was Descartes, who held that it arises from the perception that an object is perfect in its kind. In the Introduction to the *Rhapsodie, oder Zusätze zu den Briefen über die Empfindungen* (*Philosophische Schriften,* II, 10), Mendelssohn remarks that this is not always the case. Among other illustrations he refers to the pleasure in tragedy. He traces this to a pleasure in perfection, however, that is not in the object, but in ourselves, in our apprehension or knowledge. The general conclusion is that what is evil or defective excites a mixed feeling compounded of displeasure in the object and satisfaction in its presentation. Even this does not hold if the object touches us too nearly for us to make the distinction; physical pain, for example, is never pleasant, since we are unable to separate the object from our presentation of it. The passage is a striking illustration of the effort to recognize empirical facts and at the same time uphold the essentials of a rationalistic teleology.

influence; among others whom his doctrine of feeling influenced was Kant. But a writer of far greater intrinsic importance than Mendelssohn, one far more original and
psychologically profound, was the author of the *Philosophische Versuche über die menschliche Natur und ihre
Entwickelung,* Johann Nicolas Tetens (1736–1807). This
path-breaking work was published in two volumes in 1777.
Tetens goes to work deliberately and cautiously. It takes
him nearly six hundred pages of analysis to prepare for the
conclusion that the human faculty of cognition requires
for its working only the three faculties of feeling (*Gefühl*),
presentation, and thought. This being premised, he has
only to include the last two under the common term, the
understanding, and we arrive at the threefold division of
all the mental powers as feeling, understanding, and the
Thätigkeitskraft, or will.[51] This division he finds convenient for his purpose, but he will not ascribe to it more
reality than comes to it from observation. Ultimately the
soul is for him a simple unity with but a single *Grundkraft*
expressing itself in different modes.

The term "feeling" (*Gefühl*) in the above division is
explained as including (1) the susceptibility to modifications, and (2) the "bare feeling" (*das blosse Gefühl*) of
the changes. This "feeling," for which the term *Empfindung* is also used, is inexplicable. But it has three characteristics. First, its object is always present;[52] secondly,
it has degrees — in a complex object the whole may be
felt distinctly, while the elements can only be felt obscurely; thirdly, what is felt is always a passive modifica-

---

[51] *Philosophische Versuche,* I, 590, 625.
[52] By the "object" Tetens means what is felt. He does not distinguish
between object and content. The mark of immediacy is intended to distinguish feeling from memory, anticipation, and presentation, the objects of
which are respectively past, future, and present, in all three temporal dimensions.

tion of the soul.[53] A complete classification of *Empfindungen* is perhaps impossible. We can, nevertheless, distinguish among the things felt: (1) the absolute objects and changes of things in or outside us; (2) the objective connections and relations of these things; (3) the subjective connections and relations of objects in our present state; (4) their influence on our self-active power. The first two include both inner and outer feelings (sensations, *Empfindungen*), the third and fourth only inner. To the third belong, among others, the feelings of the good, the beautiful, and the true; to the fourth, the feelings of interest, importance, force, life, etc.[54] In spite of the recognition which this classification makes of feelings of relation, as well of outer relations as of inner, Tetens insists that the immediate object of feeling is always an absolute; in all so-called feelings of relation we find on closer scrutiny a feeling of the absolute quite distinct from a cognition of the relations of two objects, for example, as like or different.[55] Again, the act of feeling is always simple; all manifoldness belongs to the object.[56]

It seems evident from all this that by *Gefühl* or *Empfindung* Tetens understands the immediacy of experience as

[53] *Ibid.*, I, 170 ff. The third characteristic is regarded by Tetens as one to be specially noted. We can "feel" ideas, pleasures, emotions, etc., but not the activity of the soul as such. "It is never the activity itself, never the conation (*Bestreben*) itself which we immediately feel; it is an after-effect of something which is not produced at the moment by our self-active power, but which has already been produced, when it is an object of feeling" (*Ibid.*, 174). And again, "When an activity is felt" — the remark applies, e.g., to the activity of thinking — "at this moment it is a passive change which is felt. Its efficient *actus* is interrupted" (*Ibid.*, 178).

[54] *Ibid.*, 190.

[55] Tetens gives the following illustration: "I see that the tower is farther away than the house, that a bit of water is nearer than the wood beyond. Now whether this is a thought or a feeling, neither arises without these arising, as I turn my eyes from the one to the other, a change takes place in me different in degree, rank, or other qualities from what takes place in a different case, which change is felt as something present and absolute, or can be so felt." (*Ibid.*, 199 f.)   [56] *Ibid.*, 255.

the primary reaction of the soul to impressions of every sort.[57] The contents of experience have their distinctive qualities, which are inexplicably given, found, ultimate, and absolute. Of these contents we may have varying degrees of awareness; many of them are very obscure. We must distinguish the capacity for this primary and immediate mode of experience from the more active functions of presentation, thought, and conation, though the latter are in part conditioned by it and in part serve to generate feelings in it. As immediacy of experience, feeling would seem to be coextensive with the whole of the mental life viewed in one of its aspects. Tetens, however, does not explicitly teach this, but the term as he uses it is clearly very broad; it includes all sensations and is by no means limited to the affective phenomena of pleasure and displeasure. As we have seen, the feelings, although distinguished from the understanding, are yet grouped, in the first instance with the processes of cognition. But affective phenomena in the narrower sense are also included, for among the various relations felt are the relations of felt objects to the state of the soul at the time and to its faculties and powers. These feelings, whether arising from physical impressions or from ideas, are " affecting sensations " (*affizirende Empfindungen*). They cause agreeable or disagreeable, pleasant or unpleasant *Empfindnisse*.[58] The affective qualities, it should be noted, are not qualities of the

[57] He himself speaks of it as a " reaction "; it resembles, he says, the reaction of bodies, with the qualification, however, that the latter implies the acting of one body on another, and we are not in a position to assert a similar relation in souls (*ibid.*, 171; cf. 258 ff.). Here he contends that it is fittingly regarded as a reaction of the soul, not of the brain, even though we suppose that there is always — which is not proved — a modification of the brain accompanying it.

[58] Tetens is at a loss for a German word to express the affective character of these experiences, but suggests (*ibid.*, 185 n.) as perhaps not unsuitable *gemüthlich*, a word, he says, taken over by Klopstock from the *Herrnhüter*.

objects; the harmony is not pleasant, but the effect of the harmony — the feeling in the soul. And they are not separable from the feelings to which they are attached except by abstraction; they are attributes of feeling not superadded feelings. [59] To make the point clearer, Tetens mentions a distinction that had already been drawn by some between *Empfindung* and *Gefühl*. According to this, the total impression has two sides, or aspects, the *Empfindung* of a thing and the *Gefühl* of a change in ourselves. The affective qualities would belong to the latter. Though mentioning this terminology, Tetens nevertheless concludes to abide by his own and call the whole felt change an *Empfindung*.[60] No word has yet been coined to denote the affective aspect of experience as such, and the *Gefühl* of the tripartite division of the mental faculties in Tetens must not be interpreted in this sense. The actual state of the nomenclature at the time when Tetens wrote is expressed in his own statements as follows: " *Gefühl* and *Fühlen* have acquired a range about as extended as *Empfindung* and *Empfinden*. Yet we can detect a difference. *Fühlen* refers more to the *actus* of *Empfinden* than to its object and *Gefühle,* as over against *Empfindungen,* are those states in which merely a change in us and on us is felt, without our recognizing the object through this impression. Again, in the *Empfinden* of a thing, we comprehend at the same time *that* we perceive and distinguish; *Gefühl* is broader and includes the obscurest feeling, where the act of feeling recognizes no distinctions in the felt. The weakest and

[59] In this connection Tetens takes occasion to criticize, along with the *Zufriedenheitsfibren* of Search, the hypothetical constructions of the fibre psychology represented by Bonnet ; *ibid., 211.*

[60] According to the former representation the *Empfindnisse* are what they are so far as they are *Gefühle,* not *Empfindungen ;* from this it follows, observes Tetens, that in early life the soul is affected with pure *Gefühle,* since it has not yet learned to relate its inner states to objects ; *ibid.,* 216 f.

obscurest *Fühlen,* however, is called by many an obscure *Empfinden.*" [61]

The advance — to call it such — to a distinctive use of the term *Gefühl* for experiences of pleasure and displeasure is made by Immanuel Kant (1724–1804). Already in 1763 he had acknowledged the distinction between the faculty of cognition and feeling as the faculty of sensing the good.[62] In the *Critique of Pure Reason* (1781) he excludes feeling altogether from the sphere of cognition; judgments of pleasure and pain do not belong to transcendental philosophy, but to practical.[63] In the Introduction to the *Critique of Practical Reason* (1788) he speaks cautiously of the relation of pleasure to conation, and, since to make the latter depend on the former would lead to an empiristic ethics, which he wishes to avoid, defines both in such a way as not to prejudge this relation.[64] He does not here expressly distinguish a special faculty of feeling. But already, shortly before the publication of this work, he had announced to Reinhold the view that the mind's faculties are three — faculty of knowing, feeling of pleasantness and unpleasantness, faculty of appetition. The *Critique of Pure Reason* had to do with the first, that of the *Practical Reason* with the third; he is now engaged on a work having to do with the second. In the Introduction to the work referred to, the *Critique of Judgment* (1790), the distinction is formally proclaimed with a sharpness that leaves nothing to be desired; the three faculties are irreducible, they cannot be derived from a common root.[65] This division gives

[61] *Ibid.,* 167, quoted by Scheidler, article *Gefühl* in Ersch und Gruber *Allgemeine Encyklopädie,* cf. *ibid.,* 215.
[62] *Werke,* ed. Rosenkranz, I, 109.
[63] *Kritik der reinen Vernunft* (*Schriften,* ed. Kirchmann, III, 520).
[64] Vor., viii.
[65] *Kritik der praktischen Vernunft* (*Schriften,* ed. Kirchmann, X, 488), Letter of Dec. 28, 1787. *Kritik des Urtheilskraft, Einl.* III, 13.

the framework for the *Anthropology* (1798), which contains Kant's most important observations in the field of empirical psychology.

The doctrine of the threefold division of the mental powers found wide acceptance (Tiedemann, Reinhold, Hoffbauer), though the opinion that the various powers were rooted in and relative to a common *Grundkraft,* in particular the cognitive, still found advocates and the terminology expressing affective states still remained unsettled. A. Platner (1744–1818), for example, considered all mental phenomena as either ideas or the effects of ideas; pleasantness and unpleasantness belong to sensation; *Gefühl* denotes a kind of judgment, *urtheilen* or *beurtheilen*.[66] As late as 1812 J. G. F. Maass treated the *Gefühlsvermögen* as a branch of the presentative faculty; feelings, according to him, being a " special class of sensations," namely, subjective sensations having reference to the state of the subject.[67]

The conception of the nature of pleasurable and disagreeable experiences, whether regarded as belonging to a separate faculty or not, varies among the German writers of this period between the view that it is consciousness of a perfection or of an imperfection, either in the object or in the subject, and the view that it expresses a favorable or unfavorable relation to the vital powers. This last was the view of Kant, who defined pleasure (*Vergnügen*) as the feeling of the furtherance and pain as the feeling of the hindrance of life.[68] A peculiarly interesting and precise for-

---

[66] Evidently a *vis aestimativa*. A. Platner, *Philosophische Aphorismen,* II, 647.

[67] *Versuch über die Gefühle,* II, Introduction.

[68] *Anthropologie,* sec. 58. Cf. this with the definition of *Lust* in the Introduction to the *Kritik der praktischen Vernunft*: " Pleasure is the representation of the agreement of the object or the action with the subjective conditions of life," where the emphasis on " subjective " distinguishes

mulation of this view is made by L. H. Jakob (1759–1827).
If the organic forces, he says, are acting in suitable harmony, so that they are just sufficient for their end, there
arises an indifferent feeling of being alive (*ein gleich-
gültiges Lebensgefühl*) which is, as it were, the basis of all
other feelings and ideas and the accompaniment of all other
psychical activities. If the forces acting are raised to a
higher level and set in a gentle and adapted play, there is
pleasure; if they are checked and disturbed in their actions
and life is interrupted, there is displeasure. If the organic
forces are so disturbed as to be no longer instrumental to
life, feeling disappears altogether either temporarily or
permanently, either in a part of the body or in the whole,
and in the last case the man is dead.[69] Here the doctrine is
expressed in organic terms. Crusius and Sulzer express
it in psychological terms of tendency or appetition: what
satisfies the tendency is pleasant, what thwarts it is unpleasant.[70] This also includes the furtherance or hindrance
of ideas. The two doctrines, the one relating to the consciousness of perfection, the other to the play of the vital
or psychic powers, are combined by J. C. Hoffbauer (1766–
1827) who says that pleasure in a thing is the greater, the
greater the perfection discovered in the object and the
greater and freer the work of the mind; and conversely of
displeasure.[71] He defines feelings as "states of the soul

---

the doctrine from the common form of the biological theory. In the
Anthropologie, under the rubric of sense-pleasure, from the conception of
life as a constant play of antagonism between the furthering and the hinder-
ing conditions, Kant draws the conclusion that every pleasure must be preceded by pain, a revival of the almost forgotten view of Plato, little in harmony with the generally optimistic temper of the age.

[69] *Grundriss der Erfahrungs-Seelenlehre,* sec. 125, 528.

[70] C. A. Crusius, *Anweisung vernünftig zu Leben,* sec. 24; J. G. Sulzer,
Vermischte philosophische Schriften, I, 20.

[71] *Naturlehre der Seele,* 255. Cf. K. H. Haydenreich, "everything is
pleasant that satisfies the impulse to life and to ideas." *Aufsätze in Cäsars
Denkwündigkeiten,* 161.

which we strive either to retain or to get rid of." [72] The state of indifference is probably never natural, but only one which our states of pleasure and displeasure tend to approach.

Immanuel Kant at last presented his theories regarding the feelings as such in his *Anthropologie* which appeared in 1798. After explaining pleasure and pain, he distinguishes emotions (*Affekte*) from passions (*Leidenschaften*). He describes an emotion as a feeling (*Gefühl*) of pleasantness or unpleasantness (*Lust, Unlust*) under existing conditions which do not allow the subject to deliberate as to whether to reject the object or to give in to it. On the other hand the passion is an inclination (*Neigung*) which can hardly or not at all be overmastered by the subject's reason. [73] Kant's belief that the dominant and determining element in an emotion is a feeling of pleasantness or unpleasantness is in so far traditional. [74] His characterization of both emotions and passions as irrational is also in accord with theories of long standing. In fact he goes so far as to declare that being subject to the emotions and passions is a disease of the mind (*Krankheit des Gemüts*) since the dominance of both inhibits reason. [75] Both need the services of a psychiatrist (*Seelenarzt*) for their cure, though he may treat them in different ways.

In this respect Kant shows emotions and passions to be similar but he distinguishes them from each other by their differences in duration. Such differences are apparent in his

---

[72] *Ibid.*, 24, 240.

[73] *Anthropologie*, sec. 71.

[74] This tradition may be traced back to Aristotle who describes emotions (πάθη) as states accompanied by pleasure or pain. *Ethica Nicomachea*, II, 5; *Ethica Eudemia*, II, 2; and *Magna moralia*, I, 7, 8.

[75] *Anthropologie, loc. cit.* Such a point of view was held by the Stoics, notably by Zeno, in the fifth century B.C. (J. Stobaeus, *Eclogae*, II, 7, 1 and 2).

definition of passions as inclinations (*Neigungen*) which he describes as habitual sensory desires.[76] Emotions are turbulent but temporary. He further emphasizes this difference by describing an emotion as a flood of water breaking through a dam, while a passion resembles a stream that is continually deepening its bed. An emotion acts as a shock, but a passion is more like consumption or gradual emaciation. The experience of an emotion is similar to that of drunkenness, from which one may readily recover, while a passion is more like illness following the taking of poison.[77] This characteristic of duration he applies to emotions alone, dividing them into the sthenic and asthenic emotions, being influenced avowedly by Brown.[78] The sthenic emotions are produced by an exciting cause that soon exhausts them, while asthenic emotions are caused by a vital force which tends to prolong them. These two types of emotion act as symptoms indicating the degree of mental illness that the subject is experiencing.

The passions Kant divides into the innate and the acquired. The two innate passions are the inclination for liberty, a love of life, and that for sex. They are ardent, being accompanied by emotions. The former preserves the individual, the latter the race. The acquired passions are ambition, domination, and avarice. These are cooler pas-

---

[76] *Anthropologie*, secs. 77, 78. W. F. Volkmann, *Lehrbuch der Psychologie*, II, 508 holds that Kant was the first to carry through this stricter distinction between *Affekt* and *Leidenschaft*. A. Koch, *Psychologie Descartes'*, 191 f. holds that Descartes' theory is essentially the same as this one of Kant. R. Descartes, *Les passions de l'âme*, I, 27–29 explains how in a strong emotional disturbance the emotion is not only expressed but it may be strengthened and prolonged by the continued motion of the spirits. H. Home, *Elements of Criticism*, 41, makes much the same distinction. He gives desire as the distinguishing characteristic of a passion and as every passion ceases upon attaining its ultimate end, some passions may persist throughout life. *Ibid.*, 122 ff.

[77] *Anthropologie*, sec. 72.

[78] *Ibid.*, sec. 74. Cf. Thomas Brown, *Lectures on the Philosophy of the Human Mind*, 340, 437.

sions, being under the sway of a determination to gain certain ends.[79]

In spite of the fact that Kant has described the emotions as maladies, he shows that they have certain hygienic values. Laughing has a salutary effect on the diaphragm as well as upon digestion. Similarly weeping brings relief in the event of grief.[80] We also find him acknowledging that passions may become reconciled with reason. The passion of hatred in its development becomes reflective.[81] The duration of the passion continues until its end is satisfied. When interruptions and obstacles occur to prevent the attainment of the end, emotions become passions, as in the case of love or of the desire to do good! [82]

J. G. F. Maass published in addition to his *Versuch über die Gefühle* a two volume work on the passions, *Versuch über die Leidenschaften,* in 1805. In this study he takes exception to several of Kant's statements in the *Anthropologie*. He considers the emotion (*Affekt*), not a feeling, but an inner perception strong enough to noticeably affect the inner sense.[83] Since Maass defines feelings (*Gefühle*) as inner sensations (*subjective Empfindungen*) he must assume a close connection between emotions and feeling. Moreover he grants that emotions may be pleasant (*angenehm*), unpleasant (*unangenehm*) or of mixed feelings.[84] Maass also differs from Kant in refusing to admit that

---

[79] *Ibid.,* secs. 79 and 85.
[80] *Ibid.,* secs. 75, 77.
[81] *Ibid.,* secs. 72, 78. Cf. H. Home, *Elements of Criticism,* 46.
[82] *Ibid.,* sec. 79.
[83] *Versuch über die Leidenschaften,* sec. 6. In adopting this point of view Maass has shown that he prefers to adhere to the intellectualistic interpretation of feeling from which Mendelssohn, Tetens, and Kant freed themselves when they considered feeling independent of cognition. He reverts to such views as those held by Leibnitz, *Nouveaux essais,* II, chap. XXII, sec. 72, and Eberhard, *Allgemeine Theorie des Denkens und Empfindens,* 33 ff.
[84] *Versuch über die Leidenschaften,* secs. 6, 8.

inability to reason is an essential part of the emotion. He maintains that the inhibition of reflection is rather a result of the emotion. Strong perceptions and clear ideas characterize the emotion and these drive the subject to action without leaving time for suitable reflection. In other words the emotion draws attention to itself and as a result thought is overlooked. He does agree with Kant in considering the emotions pathological, but he does not agree that all emotions are of this kind. Some are contemplative, ruled by ideas (*Vorstellungen*), such as the passive enjoyment of beauty. But if there is eagerness in the emotion and it is ruled by desire or contempt for the object, then the emotion becomes pathological.[85]

With regard to the passions (*Leidenschaften*), Maass and Kant are more in agreement. Maass describes the passion as a desire (*Begehren*) so strong that it dominates reason. It must be a sensory desire so that it *can* dominate reason. The passion forces the subject to act involuntarily. In so far passion is unnatural. It is blind and allows us to see but one side of a question. It turns attention to itself, its goal, and all related ideas, setting all forces to act to achieve its end. Reason must therefore become impassioned (*leidentlich*) in order to strive against it. He differs from Kant in not considering a passion a mere tendency (*Neigung*) but rather an actual desire, which does not become a habit since it already has the strength of a habit in order to have dominated reason. As in the case of the emotions, passions too are pathological and may be pleasant, unpleasant, or of mixed feelings.[86]

Maass' treatment of the passions is comprehensive and detailed. In classifying them he divides them into subjective and objective passions. The three subjective passions

[85] *Ibid.*, sec. 6.   [86] *Ibid.*, secs. 7–9, 16; *Abt.* XIV

are the desire for pleasure (*Lustsuch*), the shrinking from unpleasantness (*Unlustscheu*) and the horror of emptiness (*Leerheitsscheu*). The objective passions are (1) related to the subject, such as self-seeking, pride and a desire for freedom; (2) related to another person, such as love or hate, a thirst for honor and a desire to command; and (3) related to things, such as the enjoyment of the sensual, loathing, and the desire for possessing.[87] Another classification of the passions is into the psychological, the aesthetic, and the practical. The aesthetic passions are accompanied by an expression of the emotions.[88] Still another division of the passions Maass describes as hot and cold passions. The former are accompanied by emotions while the latter are not, although he adds that all passions have some emotion in them.[89] To complete his study of the passions, Maass describes how they are related to the body, to sensations, imagination, will, moods, capacities, the understanding, education, and to other passions. In turn he describes how each of these influences the passions. His conclusions are that certain passions should be modified and he offers practical rules for doing the same. However, he does not believe that they should be eliminated, as it is against the nature of man to abhor emptiness!

To conclude, during the eighteenth century the study of the feelings follows a system used for centuries, hallowed by tradition. The study is still made by philosophers and the subject matter is treated largely from a logical viewpoint. The psychological aspects of feeling, due to a more conscientious use of introspection, have more frequently been singled out and emphasized. The added knowledge of the nervous system has challenged the theories of dualism and parallelism. But the interest in the feelings has re-

---

[87] *Ibid.*, II, sec. 113.　　[88] *Ibid.*, I, sec. 8.　　[89] *Ibid.*, II, sec. 114.

mained keenly alive and a desire to consider them for their own sake foreshadows the coming outgrowth of psychology from philosophy. The nineteenth century, with its contributions from biology and with its laboratory methods of controlling conditions for studying the feelings, remains to bring the results of research in this field into a scientific setting severed from philosophical and practical relationships.

CHAPTER X

AFFECTIVE PSYCHOLOGY IN THE NINETEENTH CENTURY

The most striking division in theories of feeling and emotion during the nineteenth century is that between peripheral and central theories. The former, growing out of the sensationism of the empiricists and of Condillac, involve from the very beginning some degree of emphasis upon physiological organs: they are *peripheral psychophysiological theories*. The central theories are an issue from the school of Leibnitz and Wolff. During the first half of the nineteenth century — as indeed during the eighteenth — sensation alone was generally related to physiological organs and processes. The division between sensation and higher mental processes was a division between physiological and mental functions. Thus during this period central theories of feeling and emotion are *central psychomental theories* which seek to explain in terms of mental entities. After 1850, however, the hypothesis of a non-physiological mind or soul becomes extremely difficult to hold. Phrenology, though derided, has done its work. The central theories of feeling and emotion become *central psychophysiological theories*.

All of these theories have in general one feature in common: phenomenalism. Whether peripheral or central, they are theories of conscious feeling and emotion. Towards the end of the century, however, there appear a few positivistic heretics who dare to question the phenomenal dogma. The most striking feature of their theories, and historically the most important, is insistence that consciousness is of secondary rank, that it is an epiphenomenon. These theories can also be classified as peripheral or central. In order to bring out their basic feature, however, we have grouped them together at the end of the chapter under the heading *epiphenomenal theories*.

PERIPHERAL PSYCHOPHYSIOLOGICAL THEORIES

The difference between psychomental and psychophysiological theories is at first largely a matter of emphasis. Condillac, the great French sensationist, was both a psychophysiologist and a faculty psychologist. He held to the doctrine of " occasionalism," which made body the occasional but not real cause of conscious events. By and large, it is not until the end of the century that we find pure psychophysiological theories.

French Ideologists. Peculiarly enough, the first important peripheral psychophysiological theory of the nineteenth century is also one of the most pure in the sense in which this word has just been used. It is the theory of Cabanis [1] (1757–1808), a physician but also a legislator and philosopher, a member of the section on " analysis of sensations and ideas " of the newly formed Academy of Moral and Political Science. Cabanis is indeed an " Ideologist " [2] a follower of Condillac, but one influenced by the materialism so prevalent in France during the late eighteenth century. He accepts Condillac's sensationism, but without its soul and its occasionalism. The phenomenal world is related in a simple, direct fashion to the physio-

---

[1] F. J. G. Cabanis, *Rapports du physique et du moral de l'homme*, Paris, 1799–1802.

[2] Another leading ideologist was Destutt de Tracy. Cf. A. L. C. comte Destutt de Tracy, *Élements d'idéologie, première partie, idéologie proprement dite*, Paris, 1801.

logical organism: " In order to get a just idea of the operations resulting in thought, one must consider the brain as
a particular organ destined specifically to produce it; as are
the stomach and intestines to produce digestion." The consequence is a psychophysiological system with practically
no admixture of mental forces. The functions of the brain,
Cabanis points out, are essentially determined by peripheral excitation of nerves. It follows that consciousness is
essentially the outcome of such excitations. These excitations are of two main types, those due to external objects
— sensations — and those due to internal conditions —
visceral movements and what not. The sensationism of
Condillac, he feels, was correct in principle, but erred in
overlooking internal excitations. " Ideas and moral determinations do not depend alone upon what one calls sensations, i.e., distinct impressions received by the organs of
sense, properly so called, but rather the impressions resulting from the functions of several internal organs contribute
thereto more or less, and, in certain cases, seem to produce
them by themselves." To prove his point, Cabanis invokes
the mental effects of various visceral diseases. These he
summarizes with the statement: " Thus, cheerful or som-
bre ideas, kindly or harmful sentiments, are due in these
cases directly to the manner in which certain abdominal
viscera perform their respective functions: i.e., to the manner in which they receive impressions: for we have seen
that the first always depend on the second, and that every
movement presupposes an impression producing it."

The stage is set, obviously, for a theory of emotions, akin
to that of James, in which emotion is essentially the awareness of bodily changes. The theory, however, does not
materialize. Titchener, in citing Cabanis as a precursor of
James, admits that it is difficult to prove the point by spe-

cific quotation.[3] Indeed, we might add, specific quotation can disprove the point. In a healthy man, Cabanis notes, a good meal is followed by active digestion. " Let this man receive bad news, or let sad and troublesome emotions arise in his soul: at once his stomach and his intestines cease to act upon the food which they contain:" This suggests Pavlov, but not James.

With respect to the theory of pleasantness and unpleasantness Cabanis is extremely — unusually — explicit. Pleasantness, he believes, is the consequence of the relaxation of the peripheral endings of nerves, which facilitates their function; unpleasantness follows their constriction, attended by interference with their functions. This relaxation or constriction he thinks is a reflex: " the nerves exercise on themselves a true reaction for feeling as they exercise another on the muscular parts for movement." Such reflexes always involve nerve centers. They may involve only peripheral nerve centers, and thus be limited, or involve higher centers and be quite general Here again is a general relation to James' views, but only a very general one. The notion of a preliminary reflex response is indeed present, but this reflex represents in the main an effect of a sense organ upon itself, an idea foreign to James, and indeed, to modern views of emotion.

Cabanis obviously made emotions events in the cerebrospinal system. Bichat [4] (1771–1802), a contemporary of Cabanis, likewise a physician-psychologist, made them visceral events. Here arises divergence in the physiological theory which will make itself felt throughout the nineteenth century. Bichat drew a sharp distinction between animal life and organic life corresponding roughly to the

[3] E. B. Titchener, *Amer. J. Psychol.* XXV (1914), 426–447.
[4] M. F. X. Bichat, *Recherches physiologiques sur la vie et la mort,* 3rd ed., Paris, 1805.

modern distinction between cerebro-spinal functions and autonomic functions. The effect of emotions, he pointed out, was to produce changes in organic life. Again, the latter changes affect the emotions. Hence, " organic life is the point of termination, and the center from which start the emotions." Thus emotions are a function of the organs of the organic life, not of the brain. True, emotions influence external movements, but this is an indirect effect, produced by special neural connections or by some " sympathetic " influence on the brain.

Early in the nineteenth century there started in France a strong reaction against the monistic psychophysiology of Cabanis. Eclecticism and Spiritualism became the leading doctrines, and remained so for over fifty years. Comte, the great positivist, was never recognized officially in France. He was never able to secure a position in the French educational system. He was obliged, in the latter part of his life, to accept moneys from his admirers in England. Not until the time of Ribot, well after the middle of the century, did the psychophysiological point of view regain a position of importance in the psychology of France.

Associationists. The theories of Cabanis and Bichat are fragmentary. They figure rather incidentally in works which have no pretension to being systematic treatises. For a detailed and well-balanced peripheral theory we have to wait until the *Analysis of the Human Mind,* by James Mill [5] (1773–1836). For James Mill all conscious content is essentially sensory. He distinguishes three fundamental classes of phenomena: sensations, ideas, and trains of ideas. But ideas are copies of sensations. Many sensations are indifferent. Some, however, are pleasant; others, un-

[5] James Mill, *Analysis of the Phenomena of the Human Mind,* London, 1829.

pleasant. "The difference is that which is felt. A man knows it; and this is the whole account of the phenomenon." With pleasant and unpleasant sensations — and their copies, ideas — as a basis, Mill proceeds to elaborate a theory of emotion and motivation. Desire and aversion are simply ideas of pleasant or unpleasant sensations. Emotions — affections, in Mill's language — are complex ideas of the cause of a pleasant or unpleasant sensation plus its effect. They differ according to the temporal reference and the *certainty* of the pleasant or unpleasant sensation. Below is a schema indicating the emotions corresponding to the various forms of temporal reference, and of likelihood:

Pleasant sensation
- as past — sympathy
- as future
  - as certain — joy
  - as uncertain — hope

Unpleasant sensation
- as past — antipathy
- as future
  - as certain — sorrow
  - as uncertain — fear

In the special case where the cause is an action of the individual and the effect a future pleasure, called a motive, the complex idea tends to lead to action. If in such a case the idea of the action of the individual arouses the idea of its feeling (we should now say its kinesthetic image), action ensues. Such a train of associations is called a volition. Here we have a full-fledged hedonism.

Mill's psychophysiology is rudimentary. He asserts that sensations are related to sense organs. Of the details of the relation he has no more to say than that " the nerves appear to be necessary to sensation, though it is by no means ascertained in what way they become necessary." Indeed, he heads the first chapter of the *Analysis* with a quotation from Locke professing disregard for " speculations " concerning physiological correlates. Not until Bain [6] (1818–1903) do we find a peripheral psychophysiological theory which is at once physiologically sophisticated, as was that of Cabanis, and systematically developed, as was that of Mill.

Bain's doctrine of feeling and emotion is based upon a particular view of common sensibility (coenesthesis, *Gemeingefühl*). Common sensibility included pain, and pain in the nineteenth century was not generally distinguished from unpleasantness. Thus the theory of common sensibility of a physiologist was at least part of a theory of feeling. The physiologist, however, interested in organic structures rather than conscious phenomena, did not bother to generalize his theory to make it a theory of feeling. This task had to wait upon the physiologically inclined psychologist. Around the middle of the century a prevalent view of common sensibility made it dependent upon special forms of excitation, especially very intense excitation of any sensory nerve, although it was admitted that there were certain nerves which mediated no qualities other than common sensibility. It is this physiological point of view which forms the basis of Bain's theory of feeling and emotion. Following a usage common among associationists, Bain uses the term feeling to cover any content of consciousness. Feelings divide into primary ones — sensations — and secondary ones — emotions. Primary feelings have three characters: quality (by which Bain means affective

[6] A. Bain, *The Emotions and the Will*, London, 1859; 3rd ed., London, 1888.

value), degree (intensive and extensive), and special character (what is now called quality). Thus, for Bain, feelings in the modern sense of the word are attributes of sensations. So far, this is merely a sensationistic theory. What develops it into a peripheral physiological theory is the further relation of the affective attribute to peripheral physiological processes. Bain holds that in a general way pleasant feelings are those related to the natural stimulation of the various sense organs, unpleasant ones to excessive or inappropriate stimulation.

Turning to the manifestations — the expressive concomitants — of feelings, Bain states that they are vigorous with pleasant feelings, weak with unpleasant. This is the basis of his theory of motivation, which is an out-and-out hedonism. The concomitance of pleasant states with energetic responses brings about the concomitance of the former with movements appropriate to maintain them. This, in turn, results in an association such that pleasant states call forth movements appropriate to maintain them.

Bain's views of feeling, then, involve a peripheral physiological theory of their origin and a hedonic theory of their effects. He combines both under a single general principle which he calls the Law of Self-Conservation: "States of pleasure are concomitant with an increase, and states of pain with an abatement, of some, or all, of the vital functions."

As to emotions, they are for Bain compounds of primary feelings. His treatment of them is largely the application of his theory of feelings to specific complex situations. In so doing, he stresses relation to bodily expression rather than to stimulation because the latter relation often is obscure. Bain's treatment of emotions, however, is not wholly a matter of derivation. He introduces as an important concept that of harmony and disharmony. Harmony of constituent feelings yields pleasure, disharmony, pain. This is especially important in connection with the aesthetic emotions. Like Herbart, Bain tries to save the unity of his theory of feeling by extending it to cover this new case. He supposes that in harmony the nervous currents are mutually supporting, in conflict there is opposition and loss of power. This extension comes close to being an admission of the central theory of feeling. It goes to prove that the distinction between peripheral and central physiological theories is more one of emphasis than of fact — a point to which we shall return later.[7]

The peripheral physiological theory had developed by considering sensory pain as the prototype of unpleasantness. The more the mechanism of pain was investigated, the more difficulty arose for the theory. Bain we have just seen was forced to a supplementary quasi-central hypothesis in connection with the harmony of feelings. Herbert Spencer [8] (1820–1903) was forced to go even further in the direction of central contamination. Spencer uses the term feeling in the same general sense as Bain. All conscious stuff is feeling (besides this stuff, however, there is another constituent of consciousness, namely relations between feelings, but for our purposes this may be disregarded). Feelings subdivide as indicated in the diagram below. The subdivision on the left is according to what now would be called sensational or imaginal nature. The subdivision on the right is according to region of stimulation.

    [7] For a view similar to that of Bain, cf. G. H. Lewes, *Problems of Life and Mind,* 3rd ser., I and II, London and Boston, 1879–1880. Lewes emphasized the role of systemic sensations in emotion.
    [8] Herbert Spencer, *The Principles of Psychology,* London, 1855; Westminster ed., 3 vols., London and New York, 1901,

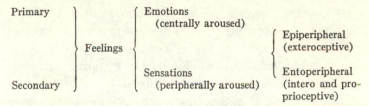

Primary		Emotions (centrally aroused)	
	Feelings		Epiperipheral (exteroceptive)
Secondary		Sensations (peripherally aroused)	Entoperipheral (intero and proprioceptive)

All feelings have a hedonic characteristic. Division of them into pleasant and unpleasant traverses all other lines of demarcation. What this division corresponds to neurally is not specified. Provided that activity is neither constant nor involuntary, pleasantness accompanies medium activities, when these activities are liable to be in excess or defect; it accompanies maximal activities, when there is no liability to excess or defect. Obviously, unpleasantness accompanies excessive or deficient activity.

So far we have a straightforward peripheral theory. At the end of the chapter on pleasure and pain, however, is this remarkable statement: " While Pleasures and Pains are partly constituted of those local and conspicuous elements of feeling directly aroused by special stimuli, they are largely, if not mainly, composed of secondary elements of feeling aroused indirectly by different stimulation of the nervous system." What Spencer has in mind is what may be termed moods, mental depression, and elation. In the chapter dealing with emotions we find the details of this central supplementation to his peripheral theory. Elation involves a high pressure throughout the nervous system, depression a low pressure. But how does difference in nervous pressure determine difference in feeling? Pains, being more intense than pleasures, are more closely associated with each other. Pleasures, however, are more numerous than pains, and are more variously linked with other elements of the mind. What, now, happens when the general pressure in the nervous system changes? " When this pressure is high, the less permeable lines of discharge, answering to the feebler associations among our pleasurable feelings, are filled by the escaping currents; and the aggregate of faintly-aroused ideas of pleasure grows in extent as well as in strength. As the pressure augments, this diffused consciousness of pleasure bears an increasing ratio to the diffused consciousness of pain — so producing in its ascending degrees a sense of satisfaction, of happiness, of joy for which no reason can be given. Contrariwise, a failing genesis of nervous fluid being followed by cessation of the efflux along the least permeable lines of discharge, and presently by its cessation along lines next to these in their small permeability, it inevitably happens that as the pressure goes on diminishing, the aggregate of faintly-aroused pleasurable feelings bears a decreasing ratio to the aggregate of faintly-aroused painful feelings. And when the pressure has fallen so low that currents pass only along very permeable lines, it results that the diffused consciousness, or vague background to our definite perceptions and ideas, comes to be composed mainly of the aggregate of faintly-aroused painful feelings — so producing gloom, and groundless fear, and despair."

As to emotion, Spencer holds an avowedly central theory, although it can be considered peripheral in the sense that the seat of the conscious emotion is the medulla oblongata (the seat of all feelings, for Spencer, both sensory and imaginal). Emotion is a complex of feelings aroused according to a special form of association, mainly phylogenetic. In fear, for instance, the nervous plexuses involved by the sight of an enemy become associated in the race — also to some extent in the individual's life — with those involved by the experience of battle. This association is via the cerebrum, which for Spencer is essentially a means for one part of the medulla to excite another — hence the view that emotions are centrally aroused feelings. Thus " The immediate perception, with the crowd of ideas resulting from preceding similar perceptions, arouses not only ideas of particular pains that have before followed such perceptions in the life of the individual; but through the inherited organization it arouses an indefinable sense of ill — a cloud of dim feelings of suffering that cannot be reduced to form because they have not been personally experienced — the emotion of *fear*."

What, now, is the relation of feeling and emotion to response? Here we come to Spencer's greatest contribution to the theory of feeling and emotion. Consciousness, for him, is the subjective aspect of what objectively is a nervous disturbance leading to nervous discharge. This objective aspect of consciousness has on the body a *general effect*, conduction along lines of least resistance to both viscera and peripheral musculature, and a *special effect*, due to the bodily change corresponding to any particular consciousness. Thus in studying the expression of feelings and emotions (what Spencer calls the language of emotions) two types of effects must be recognized, those of *diffused discharge* and those of *restricted discharge*. The latter he further divides into undirected (without motive) and directed.

A first law of diffused discharge is that *the amount of bodily movement is proportional to the intensity of the feeling or emotion*. An illustration is the loud cries of strong suffering. This law, however, is limited in its operation by an almost opposite one, namely that of *inhibition by the vagus*. Very intense feelings discharge over the vagus, and thus stop the blood supply, with consequent decrease of nervous discharge and of movement. An example is the prostration of grief. A third law of diffuse discharge is that *it affects muscles in the inverse order of their sizes and the weights of the parts to which they are attached.* An illustration is the expressiveness of the human face and extremities, where the muscles are small, for slight emotions. As excitement grows, movement spreads to bodily parts involving larger muscles, e.g., the central portions of the limbs. As to restricted discharge, it follows the law of serviceable associated habits (also stated by Darwin) largely of phylogenetic origin. When motivated, it further involves vicarious expression of inhibited actions (e.g., twitching of fingers when maintaining a " poker " face).

From the point of view of the theory of emotions this treatment of their bodily expressions is of the utmost importance. In the first place, it opens the way, for psychophysiologists with peripheral leanings, to a theory of the James type. For Spencer, an advocate of the two-aspect view of the mind-body relation, the bodily changes are essentially of reflex nature. Furthermore, a considerable part of emotions must be the awareness of them. Eliminate the perception of the exciting cause and its associated imagery from the emotion, and emotion is the awareness of bodily response. In the second place, even more important, we have here a potential behaviorism. Of this we shall say more in a moment. First, a few words on the position of Spencer with respect to psychological hedonism.

Bain was a hedonist. Spencer " commends " Bain's works to readers desiring detailed information on psychophysiological correlations. Does this mean that Spencer, too, is a hedonist? Yes and no. He does not deny hedonism — indeed, he accepts it in a general way. Pleasure is " a feeling which we seek to bring into consciousness and retain there," pain " a feeling which we seek to get out of consciousness and to keep out." It is undeniable that every animal habitually persists in each act which gives pleasure so long as it does so, and desists from each act which gives pain, although in the human race foresight introduces complications. But pleasures go in general with beneficial stimulation, pain with harmful stimulation, thus " it is manifest that in proportion as this guidance approaches completeness, the life will be long; . . . whence it follows that, as . . . the longer-lived individuals of any species will more frequently produce progeny than the shorter-lived, the descendants of the one must tend to replace those of the other — a process which . . . cannot but work towards maintenance and improvement of the guidance." Spencer is a hedonist then? No. When it comes to his doctrine of the will, the hedonism seems to evaporate. Why this anomaly? The truth is that psychological hedonism, for Spencer, is not a genuinely psychological doctrine. Psychology, for him, is the correlation between external (environmental) sequences of events and internal (intraorganic) sequences. The internal are of two kinds, objective (physiological) and subjective (conscious). The intercorrelations of these two kinds, however, constituting aesthophysiology, are not strictly speaking of the domain of psychology. As hedonism is obviously an aestho-physiological doctrine, it is little emphasized by Spencer.

We now return to a point made briefly above. The notion of psychology as a correlation between processes in the organism and processes in the environment, when coupled with a two-aspect monism, is a potential behaviorism. If physiological processes and conscious ones are but two aspects of internal processes, then a complete psychology may be written without reference to consciousness, for a complete psychology is simply a complete account of the correlations between environment and either (not both) aspects of internal changes. For the first eleven pages of the chapter in which he defines psychology, Spencer proceeds directly towards behaviorism, or at least towards an epiphenomenalism giving to consciousness but secondary importance. Then there is a sudden shift. It is as though he had lost courage. The characteristic of psychology which distinguishes it from all other science is, we learn, that it deals with consciousness. It is this sudden break with Comte which leaves Spencer in the classical tradition of the nineteenth century, the tradition emphasizing consciousness. It is the fact that this break is sudden — the fact that so much of Spencer is positivistic in the sense of Comte — that makes him a precursor of epiphenomenalists and behaviorists alike.

Darwin. Spencer was in many matters a follower of Darwin [9] (1809–1882); not, however, with respect to feelings and emotions. Darwin's classical work, *The Expression of Emotions in Man and Animals,* did not appear until the autumn of 1872.* The chapter of Spencer's *Principles of Psychology* entitled " The Language of Emotions," in which he propounds the laws of expression described above, was published as an installment in June, 1872. Darwin thought it worth while, after mentioning Spencer's contributions on the expression of emotion, to defend himself against the charge of " trespassing on Mr. Spencer's domain."

Darwin's book is the most important work on emotion of the nineteenth century. The expression of the emotions had

---

[9] Charles Darwin, *The Expression of the Emotions in Man and Animals,* 1872.

* Certainly not before August 22, 1872, when Darwin finished the last revision, and probably not until early November. Cf. F. Darwin, *The Life and Letters of Charles Darwin,* Vol. III, 171, London, 1887. [From this point on author's editorial comments are designated by an asterisk.]

been dealt with by many earlier investigators in addition to Spencer. As early as 1816, Bell [10] had written a monograph on this subject. Around 1860, in France, Duchenne (de Boulogne) [11] had experimented on the production of expressive movements by means of electrical stimulation. A little later, Piderit,[12] in Germany, had attempted a thorough analysis of emotional expressions.[13] Darwin's book, however, brought the results of all of these investigations together, generalized the universe of discourse to include both man and other animals, drew on an extraordinarily rich fund of concrete exemplifications, particularly in the case of animals, and organized the whole material under three simple general principles. Furthermore, the book was written delightfully, profusely illustrated, and was by the great Darwin. It could not but achieve prominence in its field.

As far as theoretical contribution is concerned, however, Darwin's book is not outstanding. The field is rigidly limited to the expression of emotions — there is no treatment of emotion in general. Furthermore, within the limited field, the three principles of expression which constitute Darwin's main theoretical contribution overlap markedly the laws propounded by Spencer. The principles are: (1) *The principle of serviceable associated habits:* "Certain complex actions are of direct or indirect service under certain states of mind, in order to relieve or gratify certain sensations, desires, etc.; and whenever the same state of mind is induced, however feebly, there is a ten-

---

[10] Sir Charles Bell, *Anatomy and Physiology of Expression, as Connected with the Fine Arts,* London, 1816; 7th ed., London, 1877.

[11] G. B. Duchenne (de Boulogne), *Mécanisme de la physiognomie humaine,* Paris, 1862; 2nd ed., Paris, 1876.

[12] T. Piderit, *Mimik und Physiognomik,* 1867; 2nd ed., Detmold, 1886.

[13] For a good review of the literature on facial expression, cf. A. Jeness, *Psychol. Bull.,* XXIX (1932), 325–350.

dency through the force of habit and association for the same movements to be performed, though they may not then be of the least use." (2) *The principle of antithesis:* "Certain states of the mind lead to certain habitual actions, which are of service, as under our first principle. Now when a directly opposite state of mind is induced, there is a strong and involuntary tendency to the performance of movements of a directly opposite nature, though these are of no use; and such movements are in some cases highly expressive." (3) *The principle of the direct action of the nervous system:* "When the sensorium is strongly excited, nerve force is generated in excess, and is transmitted in certain definite directions, depending on the connection of the nerve cells, and partly on habit: or the supply of nerve force may, as it appears, be interrupted. Effects are thus produced which we recognize as expressive."

Although Darwin's principles overlap Spencer's laws, there is, with respect to emphasis, considerable difference between the two men. In dealing with the expression of emotions Spencer lays major emphasis upon physiological mechanisms. Darwin admits inheritance of habits, and thus is able to admit as reflex many responses which come under his principle of serviceable associated habits. But these responses are always for him *habits* become reflexes, not *reflexes* originating from habits. He is concerned with genetic origin, not physiological mechanism, and this origin involves a considerable participation of consciousness. In the field of emotional expression Darwin is far less a forerunner of modern behavioral and physiological theories than is Spencer.

Allen. In discussing the relation of Spencer and Darwin to objective psychology we are getting ahead of our material. We are still concerned with the development of the peripheral psychophysiological theory. It was pointed out above that Spencer offered an example of the contamination of peripheral theories by supplementation with central mechanisms. Another example of such contamination is the theory of Grant Allen,[14] (1848–1899) important because through emphasis upon nutritional changes it is the precursor of the well-known central theories of Marshall and Lehmann.

Basically, Allen's theory is peripheral: " Pain is the subjective concomitant of destructive action or insufficient nutrition in any sentient tissue. Pleasure is the subjective concomitant of the normal amount of function in any such tissue." That the term " sentient " here excludes a central type of theory is made plain in regard to pleasure in general and in regard to " acute " pain. For instance, a more detailed statement concerning pleasure reads: " Pleasure is the concomitant of the healthy action of any or all of the organs or members supplied with afferent cerebro-spinal nerves, to an extent not exceeding the ordinary powers of reparation possessed by the system." In regard to " massive " pain, Allen is somewhat ambiguous.

This theory applies to the sensuous type of feeling. Although it is the most important type, for Allen, it is not the only type. In addition, there are intellectual feelings. For these Allen holds a central psychophysiological theory. They are the concomitants of normal or excessive function of the higher, co-ordinating, structures of the nervous system.[15]

James. Another, and even greater, difficulty for the peripheral psychophysiological theory arose from the

[14] Grant Allen, *Physiological Aesthetics,* London, 1877.
[15] For a view like Allen's cf. J. M. Baldwin, *Handbook of Psychology, Feeling and Will,* New York, 1891.

increase of knowledge concerning the mechanism of pain. Bain had based his theory of feeling — and consequently his theory of emotion — upon the physiological doctrine which made common sensibility depend upon a special form of excitation of *any* nerve. Pain (not distinguished from displeasure) and pleasure were characteristics of *any* sensory feeling. Spencer had followed suit. But even as Bain was developing his view of feeling and emotion, the doctrine of common sensibility underlying it was becoming suspect to many physiologists. Magendie, earlier in the century, had shown that injury to the retina or to the olfactory and auditory nerves did not produce pain. In consequence, Johannes Müller advanced the view that common sensibility depends not upon *any* type of sensory nerve, but upon a special modality — the somesthetic modality in modern terms. Weber, in his classical treatment of touch and common sensibility in 1846 finds a preponderance of evidence in favor of Müller's view.[16]

But how develop a peripheral theory of feeling on the basis of this new view? Objects of touch and internal stimuli are not the only ones to yield affective impressions. If feeling is essentially a matter of somesthesia, how explain the pleasantness of colors, the emotions aroused by music? This difficulty threatened for a time the very existence of the peripheral physiological theory. Attempts were made to avoid it by invoking association — Stumpf followed this procedure — but agreement of different individuals in matters of preference was hard to conciliate with the arbitrariness of association. If the peripheral theory was to be retained without flouting the facts of physiology,

---

[16] E. H. Weber, *Tastsinn und Gemeingefühl*, 1846; Hering's ed., Leipzig, 1905.

some natural bridge was necessary between sense organs such as the eye and the ear and the somesthetic sense organs.

This bridge was provided by the so-called expressive responses. As I have pointed out, the nineteenth century witnessed a growing tendency to emphasize the expression of emotion. This tendency culminated in 1872 with the publication of Spencer's chapter on the "Language of Emotions" and of Darwin's *Expression of the Emotions in Man and Animals*. Here we find not only considerable emphasis upon expressive responses, but also the view that these responses are largely reflex in nature rather than consequences of conscious emotion. Obviously, such expressions must stimulate the somesthetic end organs.

The honor of saving the peripheral physiological theory from complete extinction belongs to William James (1842–1910).[17] In 1884, in an article in the periodical *Mind*, James propounded a theory in which the activity of a single class of sense organs — the somesthetic ones — is induced by bodily responses, themselves brought about by stimulation of any sense organ whatever. James applied this theory to emotions alone, thus breaking not only with the tradition that emotion is a special case of feeling (in the narrow sense of pleasantness and unpleasantness), but also with the more general tradition that feeling and emotion are closely related.

The best known formulation of James' theory is not that of 1884, but a later one in a chapter of his *Principles of Psychology*, published in 1890. Its essence is clear in the following excerpts:

" Our natural way of thinking about these coarser emo-

[17] W. James, " What is an Emotion ? " *Mind,* IX (1884), 188–205 ; *Principles of Psychology,* New York, 1890, Vol. II, chap. 25 ; " The Physical Basis of Emotion," *Psychol. Rev.,* I (1894), 516–529.

tions is that the mental perception of some fact excites the mental affection called the emotion, and that this latter state of mind gives rise to the bodily expression. My theory, on the contrary, is that *the bodily changes follow directly the* perception *of the exciting fact, and that our feeling of the same changes as they occur* is *the emotion.*

"An object falls on a sense organ, affects a cortical part, and is perceived; or else the latter, excited inwardly, gives rise to an idea of the same object. Quick as a flash, the reflex currents pass down through their preordained channels, alter the condition of muscle, skin, and viscus; and these alterations, perceived, like the original object, in as many portions of the cortex, combine with it in consciousness and transform it from an object-simply-apprehended into an object-emotionally-felt."

"Common sense says, we lose our fortune, are sorry and weep; we meet a bear, are frightened and run; we are insulted by a rival, are angry and strike. The hypothesis here to be defended says that this order of sequence is incorrect, that the one mental state is not immediately induced by the other, that the bodily manifestations must first be interposed between, and that the more rational statement is that we feel sorry because we cry, angry because we strike, or tremble, because we are sorry, angry, or fearful, as the case may be."

Other important features of the theory are as follows: (1) The bodily changes "are so definitely numerous and subtle that the entire organism may be called a sounding board." (2) "Every one of the bodily changes, whatsoever it be, is *felt*, acutely or obscurely, the moment it occurs." (3) There are no special brain centers for emotion. (4) Objects exciting instincts also excite emotions, but emotions fall short of instincts — are "instinctive duds," as

Revault d'Allonnes later termed them. Some objects, however, excite emotions and not instincts.

In a subsequent formulation published in the *Psychological Review* for 1894, James somewhat modified his theory by adding that the perception which initiates the emotion is affective in nature and involves not an isolated object but a total situation.

It is habitual to link James' name with that C. Lange,[18] (1834–1900) who published a theory of emotions in Danish early in 1885. Indeed, it is habitual to speak of a James-Lange theory. Superficially, the theories are very much alike. Lange agrees that when a man speaks of his fear he refers to a perception of bodily responses. Where James, however, concludes that emotion is the awareness of bodily response, Lange concludes that emotion is the bodily response itself. The sensation of fear or anger — the emotion for James — is for Lange something which thwarts sensible discussion and lies without science. This difference in point of view turns out to be of marked historical importance. We shall postpone the treatment of Lange's theory until the section on epiphenomenal theories.

The originality of James' theory has been denied by Titchener.[19] There is no discovery, it is true, that has not definite roots in the past. But the roots of James' theory are nothing more than roots. The closest parallel is to be found in a work of the philosopher, F. A. Lange [20] — not the physiologist C. Lange of James-Lange fame — published around 1874. Discussing the problem of self-consciousness, he wrote: " It has always seemed to me that the

[18] C. Lange, *Über Gemütsbewegungen,* translated from Danish, 1885, by H. Kurella, Leipzig, 1887.
[19] See above, page 279.
[20] F. A. Lange, *Geschichte des Materialismus,* 2nd ed., Iserlohn, 1873–1875.

true circle of the nervous activity which plays such a large part in all sensation, has to date been considered hardly at all. With every intense excitation of the activity of the brain a stream of positive or negative effects runs through the whole body by means of the vegetative and motor nerves, and only in that we receive then reactions through sensitive nerves from the changes thus accomplished in our organism do we ' sense ' our own emotions (*Gemütsbewegungen*)." This is indeed the general mechanism adopted by James, but the theory is not developed any further — it remains a vague guess. Again, certain doctrines expounded in detail by physiologists have resembled the doctrine of James — but no more than resembled it. Beau [21] is sometimes cited in this connection. He did indeed stress a process of " nervous reflexion " in accounting for the different latent periods of touch and pain. Pain, he believed, came from a reflexion of the touch impulses back along the touch nerves to the periphery and then up again — still along the touch nerves — to the brain. But this reflexion within the afferent nerves is something quite different from James' motor-sensory mechanism.

James, as we have seen, did not extend his theory of emotions to include pleasantness and unpleasantness. This was donè almost at once, however, by Münsterberg [22] (1863–1916) as a further step in the development of his own motor theory. Experiments had satisfied him that pleasantness goes with a tendency to muscular extension, unpleasantness with a tendency to flexion. Following the pattern of thought which James used for emotion, Münsterberg holds " that extension and flexion are not caused by pleas-

---

[21] J. H. S. Beau, " Recherches cliniques sur l'anesthésie," etc., *Archives générales de médecine*, 4th ser., XXVI (1848), 22.

[22] H. Münsterberg, *Beiträge zur experimentellen Psychologie*, Freiburg, 1892, 216.

antness and unpleasantness, but on the contrary the reflexly aroused extensions and flexions are the conditions of those conscious processes, which we call pleasantness and unpleasantness. Flexion and extension cannot take place in our bodies without arousing by centripetal action qualitatively definite elementary conscious contents. Upon the addition of these contents to external sensation depends that which we are accustomed to call the feeling-tone of sensation."

CENTRAL PSYCHOMENTAL THEORIES

We have followed one of the main currents of theory — the peripheral one — through the entire nineteenth century. We now turn to the other main current, the one relating feeling and emotion to central processes. Whereas peripheral theories were from the very outset psychophysiological, central theories, until around 1850 — with the striking exception of the phrenological one, to be discussed later — were psychomental, i.e., formulated their explanations in terms of mental entities. The classical mental entities were faculties. They were not, however, the only ones. Reaction against faculty psychology led to Herbart's conception of the mind as a system of interacting ideas, and to Schopenhauer's voluntarism, in which mind, like everything else in the universe, is considered to be basically volitional.

Faculty Theories. Although faculty psychology was on the wane at the beginning of the nineteenth century, it was still fairly widespread. In Germany, the tradition of Leibnitz and Wolff persisted in the works of Beneke, an opponent of " old-fashioned " faculty psychology, but one who wished to replace it merely by a new faculty psychology more consonant with empiricism. The same tradition manifested itself in the philosophy of common sense of the Scottish School, particularly in that of its last great representative, Hamilton.

F. E. Beneke [23] (1798–1854), claiming to be even more empirical than Locke, rejects the notion of innate powers or faculties. He accepts, however, the notion of faculties built up by experience, and makes them the basic concepts of his psychological system. These faculties are dynamic, they are " strivings," in the sense that they strive to be completed (*ausgefüllt*) by stimuli. Upon the form of this completion depends pleasure and displeasure. Pleasure goes with the adequate or superabundant completion of a faculty, provided that the stimulus be not excessive. Displeasure goes with insufficiency of stimulation. If the stimulus increases gradually until it becomes excessive, the result is satiation and fatigue. If the stimulus is excessive from the very outset, the result is pain. Clearly, in this doctrine there is regard to the need of a certain balance between faculty and stimulus in order to have pleasure — excessive stimulation is painful — but the main emphasis is on *abundance*. The pleasant stimulus is the one which completes the faculty fully or even " superabundantly." This point is important, for it yields a differentiation between the views of Beneke and Hamilton which is of great importance in the subsequent development of affective theory.

Beneke has relatively little to say about emotions. They are essentially combinations and interactions of elementary faculties (or strivings) whose degree of completion or lack of completion is very marked. His most interesting contribution is the conception that unpleasant emotions in-

[23] F. E. Beneke, *Lehrbuch der Psychologie als Naturwissenschaft*, 1833; 3rd ed., Berlin, 1861.

volve conflict of faculties (or strivings) with consequent unpleasantness and pain.

Hamilton [24] (1788–1856), whose erudition was colossal, especially in respect to continental philosophers, adopts Kant's tripartite division of the mind into cognition, feeling, and conation. Feeling, however, is not strictly co-ordinate with cognition and conation. It is the passive side of a power, a capacity, whereas the latter are active features, faculties. Human energy, Hamilton conceives to be divided into various powers. Each power is both the faculty of a specific energy, and a capacity of an appropriate pleasure or pain, as the concomitant of that energy. What is it, now, which determines whether the capacity of feeling involved in a given power shall yield pleasure or pain? The perfection of the energy. " The more perfect, the more pleasurable the energy; the more imperfect, the more painful." But what determines perfection in this context? Perfection of an energy is determined on the one hand by relation to its power, on the other by relation to its object. " By relation to its power: An energy is perfect, when it is tantamount to the full complement of free or spontaneous energy which the power is capable of exerting. . . . By relation to the object about which it is conversant, an energy is perfect, when this object is of such a character as to afford to its power the condition requisite to let it spring to full spontaneous activity." In brief, " Pleasure is a reflex of the spontaneous and unimpeded exertion of a power, of whose energy we are conscious. Pain, a reflex of the overstrained or repressed exertion of such a power." Here we have a doctrine in which pleasure goes essentially with *balance*, as contrasted with the *abundance* stressed by Beneke.

For Hamilton, feeling is the fundamental category of

[24] Sir William Hamilton, *Lectures on Metaphysics and Logic,* edited by H. L. Mansel and J. Veitch, 4 vols., Edinburgh and London, 1859–1860.

affective psychology. What are now termed emotions, e.g., joy or fear, are essentially special cases of feeling. Classified according to their causes, feelings subdivide into sensations (closely related to the body) and sentiments (accompanying higher powers). The latter class includes what are now termed emotions — sorrow, repose, anxiety, joy, etc. Thus for Hamilton, emotions are the conscious concomitants of conation.[25]

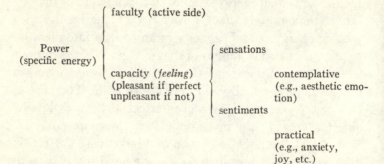

SCHEMA OF HAMILTON'S VIEWS ON FEELING AND EMOTIONS

The doctrines of Hamilton and Beneke have had an enormous influence on the theory of feeling and emotion in the nineteenth century. They are at the basis of almost all central psychophysiological theories. Indeed, these theories start as translations of the faculty doctrine into psychophysiological language. Dumont, one of the early advocates of a central psychophysiological theory, explicitly agrees that he is merely advocating a psychophysiological version of Hamilton. But more. The doctrines of Hamilton and Beneke retain much of their individuality throughout their subsequent development. Hamilton's emphasis upon

[25] In France this type of view is to be found in the school of Royer-Collard, who was an early disciple of Reid. Hamilton's theory is accepted by F. Bouiller, *Du plaisir et de la douleur*, Paris, 1865.

balance characterizes one main trend in central psycho-physiological theories, a trend which may be said to culminate in the theory of Lehmann. Beneke's emphasis upon abundance is equally characteristic of the other main trend, which culminates in the theory of Marshall.

I have stressed the influence of Hamilton and Beneke upon psychophysiological theories because such theories are dominant during the second half of the century. This influence also shows itself in the works of the " Act school," a minority group which may be considered as the purest development from faculty psychology because of its retention of the psychomental point of view.

Aristotle had provided a convenient distinction between an entity in the potential state and the same entity in the actual state. This distinction proved a godsend to those educated to stress a soul and its faculties, yet anxious to conform to the empirical trend of the times. They could admit the hypothetical — even dubious — nature of the soul as a potential entity, yet study it in its actual state by identifying mental processes with mental acts. An outstanding example of this procedure is the psychology of Franz Brentano [26] (1838–1917). Unfortunately Brentano's published works deal almost wholly with the basic principles of his system, not with its details. Thus his theory of feeling and emotion is given only in the sketchiest form. Psychology is for Brentano not the science of consciousness, but the science of what he calls psychical phenomena. These are acts, as distinct from the contents of consciousness which Brentano calls physical phenomena. Psychical phenomena subdivide, for Brentano, into three main groups, namely cognition, judgment, and the phenomena of love and hate. The latter include feelings, emotions, and

[26] F. Brentano, *Psychologie vom empirischen Standpunkt*, Leipzig, 1874.

volitions. Feelings, emotions, and volitions involve the same relation to objects, namely acceptance or rejection with respect to value. They differ in the nature of the objects accepted or rejected.

The greatest contribution of the Act school to affective psychology is in the work of Theodore Lipps [27] (1851–1914). For Lipps, psychology is the science not of consciousness in general, but of "individual consciousness." A consciousness is individual only in so far as it is considered the consciousness of some (real, not phenomenal) self or mind. Thus psychology becomes the science of the mind and of mental phenomena. It is true that the mind of the psychologist and the brain of the physiologist may ultimately refer to the same thing. As concepts, however, they are quite different, the one being described in terms of consciousness, the other in mechanistic terms.

Lipps' basic views on feeling and emotion are little different from those of Hamilton. Feelings are conscious activities which accompany apperception of an object. Pleasure is the symptom of congruence of the attention to and apperception of an object with the tendencies to such activities in the mind. The degree of pleasure is proportional to the amount of energy required and ready to be expended. Unpleasantness is the symptom of opposition between a requirement for attention or apperception and the readiness of the soul to satisfy this requirement. It increases with the increase of the requirement and with the lack of readiness to satisfy it. In a word, natural mental activity is pleasant, forced activity is unpleasant. Emotions are violent psychic activities monopolizing attention or apperception and thus involving marked dissociation. The ex-

[27] T. Lipps, *Leitfaden der Psychologie*, Leipzig, 1903.

pression of emotions is a consequence of them, not a part of them.[28]

The novelty of Lipps' affective views lies in the degree to which they stress the concept of empathy (*Einfühlung*). Empathy is essentially self-objectivation, " the objectivation of myself in an object distinguished from myself." This concept plays an enormous part throughout Lipps' psychology. Thus the basis of psychophysical parallelism is for him the fact that we instinctively project our consciousness into the physical movements of others, which we know to be related to brain processes. Empathy is involved in three main ways in Lipps' psychology of feeling and emotion. In the first place, all feelings referred to objects — e.g., the pleasantness of a color — are projected, for basically feelings are self-feelings: " In the feeling of pleasure I feel myself, namely in a pleasant mood, satisfied, pleased." In the second place, aesthetic feelings involve not only this general form of empathy, but a special form which Lipps calls " aesthetic empathy." In aesthetic enjoyment the object being enjoyed, the source of the enjoyment, is itself partly made up of projections of the self. In the case of a form, " I feel myself into the form, and *therefore* am pleased with the object." Aesthetic pleasure is " pleasure in the object, but not in the object as such, but only so far as I have felt myself into it." In the third place, empathy is at the basis of sympathetic feelings and emotions. When I see a man as angry, the anger is obviously projected by me into the object. But this projected anger tends in turn to arouse non-projected anger in me. " I become angry with the angry one." Such is the origin of sympathetic emotions.

[28] A similar view was taught in England by Ward. Cf. J. Ward, *Encyclopaedia Britannica*, 9th ed., 1886, article " Psychology."

Intellectual Theories. In eighteenth-century psychology there were two kinds of mental energy. One was explicitly recognized. It was the kind involved in powers such as reflexion. Emphasis upon this yielded faculty psychologies. The other was merely implicit. It was the energy back of the principle of association. It is by rendering explicit and by emphasizing this second kind of energy that Herbart [29] (1776–1841) developed his dynamic psychology, in which the basic feature is the energetic interaction of ideas.

For Herbart, feelings are essentially measures of the harmony or disharmony among ideas. Suppose that an act of perception a arouses the idea α, united with a into a complex $a + \alpha$. Suppose further that when α comes forward, it meets in consciousness an idea β, opposed to it. " Then α will be, at the same time, driven forward and held back. In this situation, it is the source of an unpleasant feeling which may give rise to desire, viz., for the object represented by α provided the opposition offered by β is weaker than the force which α brings with it." Suppose now that an act of perception a' calls forth an idea α', and that its progress into consciousness is favored by the presence in consciousness of an idea consonant with it. " This favoring is part of the process which takes place in consciousness, but in no way is it anything represented or conceived. Hence it can only be called a feeling — without a doubt a feeling of pleasure."

But what of so-called sensory feelings, which seem to adhere closely to the sensory material — the fragrance of the rose, for instance? They do not seem to be contingent on the mechanics of ideas. This problem, which always faces affective theories disregarding peripheral processes is solved

[29] J. F. Herbart, *Lehrbuch zur Psychologie,* Königsberg und Leipzig, 1816.

by Herbart in a manner typical for all such theories, namely by an extension of his general principle. Herbart admits that the agreeableness of colors, odors, etc., and also the aesthetic value of objects, is not dependent upon the facilitation of their perception by other ideas. Instead of such an external facilitation, he invokes an internal facilitation. The perception is to be considered as truly complex, no matter how simple it may appear. Being complex, its parts may be related to each other more or less harmoniously. Agreeableness and beauty are proportional to such harmony.

Motivation, for Herbart, is closely related to feeling. In general, the one is not the cause of the other, but rather both are dependent upon the interaction of ideas. If a concept α is driven forward in the face of opposition from a concept β, there occurs a desire for the object represented by α. In the preceding paragraph we saw that such interaction would likewise produce an unpleasant feeling. There is one exception to the lack of causal relation between feeling and desire, namely in the case of agreeable feelings (so-called sense feelings). Here Herbart makes desire the consequence of the feeling. Such desires, however, he believes to be few.

What, now, is the relation of desire to action? Herbart is an interactionist. He holds that causal relations hold between certain ideas and certain actions — particularly between the kinesthesis of movement and the corresponding real movement. Through association the ideas representing the consequences of the movements become linked with the kinesthesis, and thus give rise to the real movement. But desire of a consequence, as we saw above, is for him the supremacy of its idea in the face of opposition. This idea will arouse the kinesthesis to which it is linked, which in turn will cause the movement necessary to realize the consequence.

Emotions, finally, are distinguished by Herbart from feelings. They are conditions in which ideas are markedly out of equilibrium. When this departure from equilibrium involves an excess of ideas in consciousness, the emotion is an expansive one (*entbindend*). When ideas are abnormally few, the emotion is a narrowing one (*beschränkend*). Thus emotion, like desire, is related to feeling. Feeling, however, is in no wise basic; rather, all three states are co-ordinate manifestations of the same basic events, namely the dynamic interplay of ideas.

Herbart's system of psychology was carried on for many decades by a host of disciples.[30] Most of them, however, were educators whose main interest lay not in developing the system itself, but in its educational implications. Among psychologists and physiologists Herbart's influence was relatively weak. He had drawn a sharp line between physiology and psychology, and maintained that physiologists should not trespass upon the psychological domain. Physiologists took him at his word with respect to his own system of psychology. Physiologically inclined psychologists followed suit. Thus the intellectualistic theory of emotions and feelings, although it enjoyed a long life, was never an important factor in the history of psychology.

Volitional Theory. Herbart's mechanics of ideas was an intellectual alternative to the soul of faculty psychology. A voluntaristic alternative is proposed in the truly remarkable system of Schopenhauer [31] (1788–1860). For Scho-

---

[30] The best known followers of Herbart were Nahlowsky and Volkmann. Cf. J. W. Nahlowsky, *Das Gefühlsleben,* 1862; 2nd ed., Leipzig, 1884; W. F. Volkmann, Ritter von Volkmar, *Lehrbuch der Psychologie,* 3rd ed., Vol. II, Cothen, 1875.
[31] A. Schopenhauer, *Die Welt als Wille und Vorstellung,* Leipzig, 1819.

penhauer the basic factor in the universe is the will, a sort of *élan vital* of which the conscious will of the individual is but one manifestation. The so-called physical world — really a world of ideas — is nothing but the objectivation of the will, i.e., the will become idea.

Feelings — as also emotions — are particular states of the will manifesting themselves in particular forms of bodily objectivation — just as the individual's will as a whole manifests itself objectively as the whole body. Thus Schopenhauer holds the elements of a psychophysiological theory, but a psychophysiological theory with reverse emphasis, one that explains the physical by the mental. Pain and lust (*Wollust*) are the "forced, instantaneous willing or not willing of the impression which the body suffers." Pleasant and unpleasant sensations are lesser degrees of pain and lust. Emotions are violent movements of the will manifesting themselves objectively as bodily upsets.

An implication of the fundamental goalless nature of the will is that there is no such thing as true satisfaction. Only in its momentary objectification as cognition does the will have a motive and a goal. Thus motives and goals are mere appearances. When mankind reaches these apparent goals, there results not satisfaction, but boredom. Joy is not in *achievement,* for there is really no such thing, but in *achieving*. It is the rapid alternation from apparent wish to apparent satisfaction and on to a new apparent wish which constitutes joy. Slow alternation of this sort constitutes suffering.

Even the joy of achieving, however, is essentially negative. Pain, alone, is positive. Man does not note the smooth progress of the will, but only its thwarting. "Just as we do not feel the health of our whole body, but only the little place where our shoe presses; so do we not think of our affairs as a whole, which are going perfectly well, but of some unimportant detail, which bothers us."

Man is worse off than animals in respect of suffering. With greater cognitive power goes greater susceptibility to pain. It is indeed upon thwarting of the will that pain depends, but this thwarting must be accompanied by cognition. Using the simile of a stringed instrument: "The will is the string, its crossing or thwarting, the string's vibration, cognition the resonating box, pain is the tone."

In a very few cases, however, cognition is the instrument not of enslavement to suffering, but of liberation. Here we come to Schopenhauer's celebrated doctrine of aesthetic and philosophic contemplation. Such contemplation is the cognition, in objects, of the platonic ideas of which they are the momentary manifestation, the pure essences untrammeled by time or place or cause. In it the subject becomes free from the will; it is a pure intelligence without intentions or purposes. Thus the subject escapes the very possibility of suffering, for suffering and sorrow are the work of the will alone. In aesthetic contemplation, then, we have the intellect negating its very basis, namely the will. "The intellect, which originated merely as a tool of the will, and so remains in almost all men, whose lives are given up to using the intellect for gain — this intellect is used *abusively* in all free arts and sciences: and from such use come the progress and honor of the human race."

It is in the form given it by Schopenhauer that the mental point of view has shown the greatest vitality. *The Philosophy of the Unconscious* of E. von Hartmann provided a bridge, if one will, between Schopenhauer and modern psychology.[32] But the bridge was really unnecessary. Scho-

___

[32] E. von Hartmann, *Philosophie des Unbewussten,* Berlin, 1868.

penhauer's own way of thinking, without any changes or developments, was eminently suitable for the problems confronting the psychologists of human nature in the twentieth century. Explanation is not in phenomenal terms, but in terms of an unconscious back of and more basic than the phenomena. This unconscious is genuinely dynamic. Physiology is not denied, it is simply given second place as a form of explanation. Little wonder that Schopenhauer's will should survive unaltered in the philosophy of Bergson, his theory of feeling in the psychology of McDougall, and his whole system, to a large extent, in the systems not only of Bergson and McDougall, but of the whole psychoanalytic school.

CENTRAL PSYCHOPHYSIOLOGICAL THEORIES

At the beginning of the nineteenth century a current physiological view relegated the seat of the emotions to the viscera. Bichat, whom we have already discussed, exemplifies this view. Before central psychophysiological theories of feeling and emotion could freely develop it was necessary that this general conception be removed. The distinction of doing so falls in the main to the phrenologist, Gall [33] (1758–1828) and to the great physiologist, Flourens.[34] We shall discuss Gall's doctrine in the next paragraph. Suffice here to quote Flourens: " To get an idea of the degree of ignorance prevalent before Gall concerning the anatomy, and, even more particularly, concerning the physiology of the brain, one has only to read Bichat. . . . If I were to classify the services rendered to us by Gall, I should say that the first was to bring back the *moral quali-*

[33] F. J. Gall, *On the Functions of the Brain and of Each of its Parts,* translated from the French, 1822–1826, by W. Lewis, Boston, 1835.
[34] P. Flourens, *De la vie et de l'intelligence,* 2nd ed., Paris, 1859.

ties to the brain, where were already known to reside the intellectual faculties." * Flourens' contribution to the problem of feeling and emotion is twofold. On the one hand he argues from his remarkable experiments on ablation of nervous structures that Bichat's notion of the visceral localization is wrong. For him, "the unique seat of the passions is the brain," but they have no special centers in the brain. His second contribution is to argue from his experiments that the whole doctrine of sensationism is wrong: "A philosophy has said: to think is to sense. . . . To sense is not even to perceive. The brain alone perceives. Sensibility is in the nerves and the spinal cord, where intelligence is not, and intelligence is in the brain, where sensing is not." After Flourens, the door is open wide to central psychophysiological theories of feeling and emotion.

Special Organ Theories. Gall's phrenology not merely opened the way to central psychophysiological theories of feeling and emotion; he further formulated a specific form of this theory, namely that relating the affective life to special central organs. In the form given it by Spurzheim,[35] Gall's pupil and collaborator, phrenology distinguished thirty-five faculties, each related to a specific cerebral organ. Over half these faculties — twenty-one, to be exact — were "affective faculties," as opposed to intellectual ones. These affective faculties, divided into propensities and sentiments, correspond in many cases to what might nowadays be termed emotive traits: e.g., combativeness, hope, mirthfulness. Thus, through the medium of these faculties, emotions were related to the activity of specific regions of the

---

* Flourens continues: "And the second, to bring back insanity to this same organ, where one also knew was the seat of reason." Flourens has in mind here the astonishing views of the great psychiatrists Pinel and Esquirol on the seat of mania (largely the stomach).

[35] G. Spurzheim, *Outlines of Phrenology*, Boston, 1832.

brain. The organ of mirthfulness, for instance, lay " at the anterior, superior, and lateral part of the forehead."

The " special organ " theories were extremely slow to develop. Indeed, they may be said to have lain dormant for nearly a whole century. In spite of its success in lay circles, the detailed doctrine of phrenology was rejected by later men of science. Much research on brain localizations done during the nineteenth century was to prove of great importance to the theory of feeling and emotion after 1900. Until then, however, it lay pretty well divorced from affective theory. Bechterew's [36] (1857–1927) experiments, for instance, provide the material necessary for a " thalamic " theory of emotion like that of Cannon, but Bechterew himself does not propose such a theory. His conclusion merely constitutes a thalamic theory of *emotional expression*. During the nineteenth century central psychophysiological theories of feeling and emotion are concerned more with the nature of the central physiological process than with its locus.

Abundance Theories. The central theories relating feeling and emotion to physiological processes rather than to organs begin as faculty theories modified to fit the new emphasis on the physiological organism, as opposed to the soul or mind. Lotze [37] (1817–1881), the first to present an explicit statement of such a theory, definitely straddles the fence between faculty psychology and psychophysiology. By training he was both a philosopher and a physician. He received his doctorates in both fields within a few weeks' interval. This training manifests itself in a psychology which retains the conception of a soul, and to some extent

[36] W. Bechterew, *Archiv f. Pathol., Anat., und Physiol.*, 110 (1887), 102–154, 322–365.
[37] R. H. Lotze, *Medizinische Psychologie*, Leipzig, 1852.

the conception of faculties, yet considers consciousness to have a physiological basis. The latter is considered not the direct condition of the conscious event but the condition of the reaction of the soul which in turn produces the conscious event.

It was pointed out earlier that the emphasis of Beneke on abundance and of Hamilton on balance both persist in the central psychophysiological theories and characterize their two main trends. Lotze is on the side of abundance, although his theory also emphasizes balance. Indeed, he characterizes feeling as " the measure of the local and momentary consonance between the effect of a stimulus and the conditions of vital activity." In his detailed hypothesis concerning this relationship, however, it is apparent that balance per se is not the condition of pleasure. He holds that (1) when excitation is of normal degree, and induces a change in the nerves from which they can recover by normal metabolism, the result is indifference; (2) when excitation exceeds the normal and causes an unusually large change in the nerves, the result is pleasantness; (3) when excitation exceeds the normal and causes an unusually large change in the nerves without adequately increasing their power of recovery, the result is unpleasantness, and the degree of unpleasantness increases with the disproportion between change caused by excitation and power of recovery.

Emotions, Lotze believes, are states in which feelings are prominent and which involve a stoppage in the train of ideas. They involve to some extent specific bodily effects, although this specificity is overlaid by habit, imitation, and symbolism. When maximally intense, the specificity of bodily effect tends to disappear. In regard to the effects of intensity, Lotze cites approvingly the view of the physiologist Harless, that the more intense the emotion, the further down the spinal cord reaches its effect. The bodily effects of the weakest emotions are confined to the eye muscles. The strongest emotions involve the entire bodily musculature.

The " abundance " type of theory received considerable impetus from the writings of Leon Dumont, [38] whose main work was early translated into German. Dumont considers himself to be a follower of Hamilton. Intensity of stimulation, however, given a secondary place by Hamilton, is assigned a leading role by Dumont, just as it had been by Beneke. Pleasantness goes with an increase of the energy of the organism due to stimulation, pain with a decrease of this energy. While Lotze's theory was a mere amplification of faculty psychology, Dumont's is, as he himself admits, a mere translation of faculty psychology into psychophysiological language. The trend initiated by Lotze does not achieve physiological sophistication until the appearance of Meynert's theory relating feeling to the blood supply of nervous tissues. This theory was first presented before a congress of natural scientists in Salzburg in 1880. The date is important. It is four years before James' theory, five before Lange's.

Meynert [39] (1833–1892), a psychiatrist, develops his view of feeling by correlating unpleasantness with defense mechanisms, pleasantness with mechanisms of aggression. His starting point is a consideration of the physiological processes involved in a defense reaction to pain. Pain impulses are conducted through the gray matter of the cord, where they encounter inhibitions. Thus, to be effective,

[38] L. Dumont, *Théorie scientifique de la sensibilité,* Paris, 1875.
[39] T. Meynert, *Sammlung von popular-wissenschaftlichen Vorträgen,* Vienna and Leipzig, 1892, 43–67.

they require strong stimulation. If this condition is satisfied, there results (because of diffuse conduction in gray matter) an overflow of nervous energy giving rise to defense movements, but also — and this is more important — to *vaso-constriction*. This, in turn, results in *difficulty of breathing (Atemnot)* for the cells. It is the *chemical processes* occasioned by this difficulty of breathing which are the essential correlates of unpleasantness.*

Let us now turn to aggressive reactions, with which pleasantness correlates. Their essential feature is origin from weak stimulation, not adequate to force a path through the gray substance of the cord, and thus not producing vaso-constriction and difficulty of breathing for the cells. In consequence they involve chemical processes corresponding to *increased metabolism,* the essential correlate of pleasantness.

This view, based as it is on involvement or lack of involvement of the gray parts of the spinal cord, applies only to " sensory " feelings. Meynert promptly extends it to the " higher " feelings by a rather astonishing presupposition. He holds that the cortical cells involved in these " higher " processes have two functions, associative conduction and regulation of the local blood supply, and further that if they employ their energy for one function they cannot employ it for the other. From this it follows most beautifully that free activity of thought is accompanied by vaso-dilation and thus by pleasantness, impeded thinking by constriction and unpleasantness.

As to the emotions, Meynert has little to say about them, except that their most constant characteristic is predomi-

* Meynert is not wholly clear as to whether it is " difficulty of breathing " or the resulting chemical processes which underlie unpleasantness. A similar ambiguity occurs in his treatment of pleasantness.

nance of vaso-dilation in sthenic emotions, of vaso-constriction in asthenic ones, corresponding (via arterial changes in the brain) in the first case to a pleasant mood, in the second to an unpleasant mood.

Although Meynert presented a very sophisticated version of Lotze's " abundance " theory, he received relatively little attention from psychologists. The development from Lotze's view which achieved the greatest prominence in the nineteenth century is the theory advocated in Marshall's *Pain, Pleasure and Aesthetics* in 1894.

Marshall [40] (1852–1927) holds that pleasures and pains are essentially attributes, like intensity, which may appear with any conscious content. All pleasures, he believes, are connected either with active functioning or cessation of activities (relief), all pains with either excess of functioning or failure to function. These observations lead him to the hypothesis that: " Pleasure and pain are primitive qualities of psychic states which are determined by the relation between activity and capacity in the organs, the activities of which are concomitants of the psychoses involved. Pleasure is experienced whenever the physical activity coincident with the psychical state to which the pleasure is attached involves the use of surplus stored force — the resolution of surplus potential into actual energy; or, in other words, whenever the energy involved in the reaction to a stimulus is greater in amount than the energy which the stimulus habitually calls forth. Pain is experienced whenever the physical action which determines the content is so related to the supply of nutriment to its organ that the energy involved in the reaction to the stimulus is less in amount than the energy which the stimulus habitually calls forth."

[40] H. R. Marshall, *Pain, Pleasure and Aesthetics*, London, 1894.

What are the organs whose activities are concomitants of psychic states? Waste of a muscle, he tells us, may be the condition of pain — and to this extent his theory is peripheral. On the other hand, the very phrase " concomitant of psychic processes " suggests emphasis on the central portions of the nervous system. The truth is that Marshall's psychophysiology is too vague to allow his theory to be classified definitely as central or peripheral. All that can be said is that on the whole it tends to be central.

Equilibrium Theories. The second main form of the central psychophysiological theory, that following Hamilton rather than Beneke and emphasizing balance rather than abundance, appears in 1873 in a minor work of Fechner on evolution [41] (1801–1887). Feelings, for Fechner, are forms of common sensibility which correspond to modifications of our bodies. The nature of these modifications is deduced by Fechner from a general principle which he believes to hold throughout the universe — in the inorganic realm as well as the organic — namely the principle of stability. This principle states essentially that in any independent material system there is progress from lesser stability to greater stability and ultimately to a condition of more or less complete stability. Parallel to this physical tendency is the psychical tendency towards a satisfactory state. Thus pleasantness may be thought of as the correlate of the approximation and divergence of psychophysical movements to stability. More specifically, a psychophysical movement exceeding the threshold of consciousness will be pleasant according to the degree to which it approaches complete stability beyond a certain minimal approximation; it will be unpleasant according to the degree to which it diverges

[41] G. T. Fechner, *Einige Ideen zur Schöpfungs- und Entwickelungsgeschichte der Organismen,* Leipzig, 1873 ; *Vorschule der Aesthetik,* Leipzig, 1876.

from stability beyond a certain minimal divergence; it will be indifferent when it falls between minimal approximation and minimal divergence.

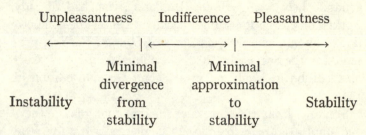

| Unpleasantness | Indifference | Pleasantness |

Minimal divergence from stability / Minimal approximation to stability

Instability — Stability

Fechner's main contribution to the psychology of feeling is not his psychophysiological theory. He himself considers it to be little more than a guess. His real contribution is in the formulation of a truly empirical system of aesthetics. He contrasts two forms of aesthetics, the philosophical — " aesthetics from above " — and the empirical — " aesthetics from below." The former must be left to the future. He himself is concerned only with the latter. Towards such an " aesthetics from below " he contributes in the first place three experimental methods which are still basic in the psychology of feeling. In the second place he presents in his *Vorschule der Aesthetik* a thorough systematization of the empirical knowledge of his time — including a mass of experimental data gathered by means of his own methods. The result is a group of laws and principles many of which retain their validity to the present day.

The line of thought followed by Fechner, namely that of relating pleasure to a condition of physiological equilibrium, appears in the writings of several important psychologists of the 70's and 80's.[42] It reaches its culmina-

---

[42] The notion of equilibrium as the basis of pleasure is emphasized by A. Horwicz, *Psychologische Analysen*, II, 2, Magdeburg, 1878; L. Stephen,

tion in the well-known theory of Alfred Lehmann [43]
(1858–   ). In 1887 the Royal Danish Scientific Society offered a prize for a monograph on the nature, laws, and
general theory of feeling. Lehmann, who had already
worked on aesthetic feelings, decided to enter the competi-
tion. The outcome was his *Laws of Human Feeling*, presented to the Society in 1888 and published in a first German edition in 1892 and in a second German edition in
1914.

Starting from the general principle that pleasantness
and unpleasantness are closely connected with the weal
and woe of the organism, Lehmann suggests that the
physiological correlate of hedonic tone is the degree to
which assimilation counteracts dissimilation during the
activity of any group of central neurones. If assimilation
(A) entirely counteracts dissimilation (D), i.e., if
$A/D = 1$, then the concomitant experience will be pleasant. If not, i.e., if $A/D < 1$, then the experience will be unpleasant. The degree of pleasantness, he further believes
to increase with the absolute value of D, while the degree
of unpleasantness increases both with the absolute value
of D and with the decrease of the value of the proportion
A/D.

A moment's thought will show that this view implies in
general a form of hedonism. If in the case of unpleasant
activity $D > A$, then the activity will soon come to a stop
due to exhaustion. Pleasant activity on the other hand,

The Science of Ethics, London, 1882; J. R. L. Delbœuf, *Éléments de psycho-
physique,* Liége, 1883 (with an interesting mathematical formulation); G.
Cesca, "Die Lehre von der Natur der Gefühle," *Vierteljahrsschrift für
wissensch. Philosophie,* X (1886), 137–165. (This article involves a good
historical discussion.)

[43] A. Lehmann, *Die Hauptgesetze des menschlichen Gefühlslebens,* translated from the Danish by F. Bendixen, Leipzig, 1892; 2nd, thoroughly revised ed., Leipzig, 1914.

where $D = A$, can persist. Lehmann develops this hedonism in considerable detail. Volition is for him controlled by attention, attention by feeling. Instincts involve inherited psychophysiological dispositions, but they are initiated by an unpleasant feeling and result in its removal. Even reflexes are hedonistically adaptive in that they yield avoidance of stimuli which, if felt, would be unpleasant and maintenance of stimulation which, if felt, would not be unpleasant.

An emotion, for Lehmann, is essentially a state of feeling, accompanied by a noticeable change of the self. Major emotions involve the central self. The sympathetic emotions and the aesthetic emotions only involve peripheral portions of the self. Continuation of a change in the self without the state of feeling originally accompanying it is a mood. The self, for Lehmann, is a complex product of past experience which may involve sensory components (somesthesia) but also complicated intellectual factors (knowledge of personal worth). Thus it is essentially dependent upon central physiological processes. As to the expressions of emotion Lehmann deals separately with the internal ones and external ones. The former he considers to be merely special cases of the general adjustment of the organism to internal and external conditions. Thus changes of breathing are related to changes in metabolic rate. When, as in excited emotions or marked unpleasantness, (but also in unemotional work), there is marked dissimilation, there results an increase in the production of carbon dioxide. If this increase is great enough, it leads to increase in the volume of air breathed. Again, vasomotor phenomena are essentially phenomena of general adaptation. Blood accumulates in the viscera at the expense of the periphery in the case of unpleasant feelings — but also in the case of mental work. In both cases this is a protection against external stimuli by decrease of sensitivity. The external expressions of emotion Lehmann considers to be largely reflexes. He brings his whole doctrine of emotion together in the following formula: " Emotion is a complex phenomenon, which begins as follows: an outer or inner stimulus causes a central condition which sets itself up in consciousness as an alteration of the self and under normal circumstances sets loose mimic reflexes and organic alterations of various kinds. With the strength of the bodily symptoms there increases in general the intimatenesses of the emotion, the involving of the subject; if the bodily symptoms fail to appear, then the condition has the character of imagined feeling."

Irradiation Theory. The theories considered above represent the main lines of development of the central psychophysiological viewpoint, but not the only ones. Studies of the expression of feelings and emotions — especially the classical work of Darwin — had emphasized the spread of nervous excitation manifested in these responses. Beaunis,[44] in his well-known monograph on internal sensation (1889) expressed the view that such irradiation was the essential feature of nervous excitation association with pain. Wundt [45] (1832–1920) went further and suggested the hypothesis that all of feeling is correlated with such irradiation.

It is not this feature of Wundt's theory, however, which is the most striking. Most psychologists had considered feeling to be qualitatively unidimensional — to be essen-

[44] H. Beaunis, *Les sensations internes,* Paris, 1889.

[45] W. Wundt, *Grundriss der Psychologie,* 14th ed., Stuttgart, 1920; *Grundzüge der physiologischen Psychologie,* 5th ed., Leipzig, 1902. An excellent exposition and critical discussion of Wundt's theory will be found in E. B. Titchener, *Lectures on the Elementary Psychology of Feeling and Attention,* New York, 1908, 125–168.

tially a matter of pleasantness or unpleasantness. Thus it was a radical departure from tradition, and one that excited much comment when Wundt in 1896 proposed his so-called tridimensional theory of feeling. Consciousness, for Wundt, involved two kinds of psychical elements, sensations and feelings. The latter, distinguished from the former by their subjectivity, are almost infinite in variety. From the qualitative point of view they cannot be arranged into an unidimensional system, but only into a three-dimensional one. The three necessary dimensions are pleasantness-unpleasantness, excitement-depression, and tension-relaxation. To these conscious dimensions of feeling correspond specific bodily changes. They are indicated in the figure below (P represents pleasantness, U unpleasantness, etc.).

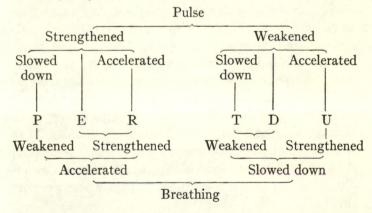

What, now, is the interrelationship between the feelings and the organism? Wundt conceives of the bodily changes as due largely to changes in inhibitory innervation originating in the brain, possibly in the frontal area. These changes in motor innervation, in turn, are ascribed to spreading of stimulation from sensory centers to motor ones. It is this latter spreading which, Wundt suggests, may be the physiological counterpart of simple feeling.

Emotion, for Wundt, is a derivative of feeling. It is a series of feelings united into an interconnected process and having as a rule a more intense effect on the subject than a single feeling. This subjective intensification is paralleled by an intensification of bodily concomitants. Not only are the bodily changes associated with simple feelings more marked, but there always occur besides certain changes in the external muscles — first, movements in the mimetic muscles, then movements of the arms and of the whole body (pantomimetic movements), finally, in extreme emotions, motor inco-ordinations. These expressive movements fall into three classes: purely intensive symptoms (e.g., strengthening of movements), corresponding to the intensity of the psychical elements; qualitative expressions (e.g., "bitter mouth"), corresponding to the quality of the feelings; and expressions of ideas (e.g., pointing to the object of the emotion), corresponding to the ideational content of the emotion. Expressive movements, however, are ambiguous symptoms of emotions: "The physical concomitants stand in no constant relation to the psychical quality of the emotion." This is so even in the case of internal bodily changes, where summation is apt to break up the correlation which one would expect because of the definite correlates of the constituent feelings when occurring singly.

As regards the quality of their constituent feelings, the emotions recognized in common speech usually represent a specific region on one particular dimension, but variable regions on the other dimensions. Thus joy is a pleasurable emotion which may be either exciting or depressing. Sorrow is an unpleasant emotion which may vary likewise in respect to excitement-depression. Expectation involves tension and either excitement or depression. The excitement-depression dimension is apparently always a variable. Emotions may also be classified according to the intensity of their feelings and according to their general form. These kinds of classification are secondary. The former is particularly ambiguous, for it does not correspond to the degree of concomitant bodily change.

Emotions may simply fade out, or they may be brought to a sudden end by abrupt change of ideational and affective content. Such abrupt termination of emotion is a volitional act. The emotion plus the volitional act constitute a volitional process. The prototype of the volitional process may be defined as an emotion which closes with a particular kind of pantomimetic act, namely one which results in an external change removing the emotion. The earliest volitional processes involve " unpleasurable feelings which arouse external movements which in turn produce contrasted pleasurable feelings." Seizing of food to remove hunger is an example. Motives involve both ideas and feelings. The role of the former, however, is secondary; it is only to arouse feelings. The feelings are the important factors in volitional processes. " All feelings, even those of relatively indifferent character, contain in some degree an effort towards or away from some end." Here, as in so many other systems of the nineteenth century, motivation is essentially hedonistic.

Learning Theory. Another line of development of central physiological theories is one where feelings are related to learning. In 1889–90, and again, in more detailed form, in 1893, B. I. Gilman [46] proposed the hypothesis that pleasantness and unpleasantness correlate with increase

---

[46] B. I. Gilman, *Amer. J. Psychol.,* VI (1893), 1–60.

and decrease of habit traces: " any presentation correlated with a bodily process that tends to fix a habit (increase a trace) is pleasurable; while any presentation correlated with a bodily process that tends to loosen a habit (decrease a trace) is painful." The latter case is exemplified in the occurrence of any process α-followed-by-other-than-β in a body where the trace α-followed-by-β exists. This theory has apparently received very little attention, although it involves a most interesting reversal of psychological hedonism as usually understood, in which it is not pleasure which determines behavior but behavior which determines pleasure. It is, however, basically identical with one of the most widely known theories of the twentieth century, that of L. T. Troland.

EPIPHENOMENAL THEORIES

All of the theories discussed so far have one characteristic in common, namely emphasis upon consciousness. This is indeed a general characteristic of nineteenth century psychology. Here and there, however, we have noted signs of impending revolt. Spencer, for instance, following Comte's positivism, at first defines psychology in a way wholly compatible with behaviorism — although a few pages later he feels forced to reinstate consciousness in its usual position of primacy. By about 1875 the opposition becomes fairly well defined. A number of prominent psychologists adopt the basic tenet that consciousness is a mere *epiphenomenon,* a sort of luxury superadded to the causal universe. It is with the theories of feeling and emotion of these dissenters that we shall be concerned in the present section.

James' theory of emotion is potentially an epiphenomenal theory, in that it makes of conscious emotion not a determinant of bodily action, but a mere index of it. This feature was little stressed by James. It was markedly stressed, however, by C. Lange [47] (1834–1900), a professor of pathological anatomy at Copenhagen, who proposed a theory in 1885 otherwise similar to that of James. Lange starts out by insisting that in the study of emotion bodily events alone, not sensations, constitute a scientific subject matter. But as the emotions have usually been dealt with subjectively, one has to start from a subjective definition and progress to the true subject matter by asking the usual question concerning bodily concomitants. Following this procedure, Lange finds that the essential bodily features for seven of the more important emotions are:

Disappointment: weakening of voluntary innervation.
Sorrow: weakening of voluntary innervation, vasoconstriction.
Fear: weakening of voluntary innervation, vasoconstriction, spasms of organic muscles.
Perplexity: weakening of voluntary innervation, inco-ordination.
Tension: increase of voluntary innervation, spasms of organic muscles.
Joy: increase of voluntary innervation, vasodilation.
Anger: increase of voluntary innervation, vasodilation, inco-ordination.

Are the various forms of bodily manifestation equally fundamental? He believes not. He thinks it likely that the primary manifestation, the one which in turn brings about the others, is change of vasotonus.

In any emotion, then, Lange points out, " we have as definite and palpable factors: (1) a cause, a sense impression, which usually operates through a recollection or an associated idea, and following this, (2) an effect, namely

[47] See above, page 297.

the vasomotor changes, caused by them in the bodily and mental functions." There arises the problem whether between these two terms there is a purely conscious emotion, or whether there is nothing between the terms. Lange answers that the purely conscious emotion which the layman believes to exist is nothing more than an hypothesis. This hypothesis he considers to be unverifiable (presumably because of its subjective nature) and unnecessary. But what of the person who says he feels conscious emotion? This, says Lange, may be considered merely the perception of his bodily changes. For "conscious emotion," then, Lange adopts essentially the view of James. He does not, however, consider "conscious emotion" to be a subject matter for science.* Scientifically, an emotion is simply a particular form of vasomotor response. "The truly scientific task in this field, is this, to establish the emotional reactions of the vasomotor system to influences of various types."

Lange's epiphenomenalism might have turned out to represent merely the reaction of a medical man to psychology rather than the symptom of a definite trend among psychologists. This, however, was not the case. Epiphenomenalism is the chief characteristic of French scientific psychology around the close of the century.

Ribot [48] (1839–1916), the Wundt of French psychology, started out as a philosopher. He was a pupil of Caro and Lachelier. Early in his career he turned away from the spiritualistic psychology then prevalent in France towards the physiological psychologies of England and Germany. Furthermore, during an interruption of thirteen years in

---

* "*Was sich, wie Farbenwahrnehmungen oder die Empfindung von Schreck oder Zorn, aller Diskussion entzieht, liegt damit ausserhalb des Gebiets der Wissenschaft.*"

[48] Th. Ribot, *Psychologie des sentiments*, Paris, 1897. Ribot's view of the mind-body problem is to be found in his book *Les maladies de la personalité*, Paris, 1885, 1–19.

his teaching career, he devoted himself assiduously to the study of neurology and psychiatry under such men as Magnan and Charcot. Thus when around 1895 he turned to the problems of affective life, he did so with the background and interests of a physiologist and clinician rather than of a psychologist in the classical sense.

Ribot is primarily a disciple of Spencer. He also shows, however, the direct influence of Auguste Comte, the great French positivist. Comte had proposed a wholly objective psychology. " The positivistic theory of affective and intellectual functions is thus irrevocably conceived as dealing henceforth with the study, both experimental and rational, of the various phenomena of internal sensibility manifested by the cerebral ganglia devoid of any immediate external organs, which constitutes nothing more than a simple general prolongation of animal physiology proper, thus extended to its ultimate fundamental attributes." [49] Spencer, so much a disciple of Comte in other respects, refused to follow him in disregarding consciousness. Ribot does not follow Comte all the way in this respect, but he goes much further than did Spencer. Like Spencer, he holds a two-aspect view of the body-mind relationship. Consciousness is merely another aspect of physiological processes. But nervous activity is far more extensive than consciousness. Only some of the nervous processes involve the conscious aspect. Consciousness in these cases is " something superadded," something which " completes " nervous processes but does not constitute them. " All manifestations of psychic life, sensations, desires, emotions, volitions, recollections, reasonings, inventions, etc., may be in turn conscious and unconscious." This implies that

[49] A. Comte, *Cours de philosophie positive*, Paris, 1830–1842; 5th ed., Vol. III, Paris, 1893.

" in any psychic event the fundamental and active element is the nervous process, that the other is but a concomitant." Ribot insists that " when a physiological state has become a conscious state, it has acquired thereby a special character, namely a definite relationship to antecedent states and to subsequent states. It becomes susceptible of recall, i.e., of being recognized as having occupied a definite position between other states of consciousness." Otherwise, however, he agrees with the metaphors that " consciousness is as a beam of light which escapes from a steam engine and illuminates it, but without having the slightest influence on its operation; it has no more effect than the shadow which accompanies the steps of a traveler."

Ribot's basic position with respect to feelings and emotions is well expressed in the first chapter of his *Psychology of Emotions,* published in 1895. The states vaguely known to us as " sentiments," " emotions," "passions," he insists, offer a double aspect, objective-motor phenomena, and subjective. Feelings and emotions are not psychical entities but psychophysiological ones. The most important aspect is the objective one. Pain and pleasure, as conscious states, are not fundamental elements of the affective life; " they are only marks, the foundation is elsewhere. What would be said of a doctor who confused the symptom with the disease? " An emotion always involves " a particular state of consciousness, particular modifications of the functions of organic life, movements, or tendencies to movement, arrest or tendencies to the arrest of particular movements."

The epiphenomenal view of feelings and emotions is given even greater definiteness in the works of Ribot's follower, Hartenberg [50] (1871–   ). In 1899, Hartenberg published an article on fear and the mechanism of emotion

[50] P. Hartenberg, *Revue philosophique,* XLVIII (1899), 113.

in general. Two years later appeared his book on timidity. One year after that he contributed a monograph on the anxiety neurosis. All are interesting. As we are concerned, however, with the general theory of feelings and emotions, not with specific discussions of them, we shall limit ourselves to a discussion of Hartenberg's general views on emotion.

For Hartenberg, James' theory is correct. It is not, however, a theory of emotion, but a theory of the *consciousness* of emotion. The emotion, for Hartenberg, involves four successive steps: arousal of a cortical motor pattern, somatic response, consequent afferent excitation, and a fourth step consisting from the physiological point of view in cortical nervous processes, from the psychological point of view in " the epiphenomenon of consciousness." To make this latter alone the emotion is to lose sight of the obvious unity of the entire reaction.

Ribot and Hartenberg follow James and Lange. Aside from stressing epiphenomenalism, they hold peripheral psychophysiological theories. The same epiphenomenal point of view has been developed in connection with a central theory of feeling and emotion by Paulhan [51] (1856–   ), a contemporary of Ribot and second only to the latter in general influence on modern French psychology. Paulhan's views on the mind-body relation are essentially the same as Ribot's. In an introductory chapter of his *Laws of Feeling,* he points out that man is " an ensemble of organs united and harmonized by one of those organs, the nervous system." The actions of the nervous system are all essentially of the reflex type. There are indeed two types of physiological processes, purely physiological ones

[51] F. Paulhan, *The Laws of Feeling,* translated from the French by C. K. Ogden, London and New York, 1930.

not accompanied by consciousness, and psychological ones which are accompanied by consciousness. " The difference between the two processes is due, not to the fact that one is accompanied by consciousness, but to the physiological differences which distinguish them, consciousness being merely a sign of those differences." " If we imagine all the physiological conditions of the conscious act to be present, we can very well conceive that consciousness may be suppressed without loss for the external manifestations of personality." Consciousness has a part, however, in psychology. Fundamentally, psychology studies the " physiological or psychophysiological process, beginning with a sensation and ending with an action. But it is precisely this phase of the process which is most difficult of access for physiological observations, and frequently it can only be suspected or guessed at by inference; it also happens to be that part which is frequently accompanied by consciousness. We at once see, therefore, the utility of these phenomena to us, for they are parallel to the processes which we are investigating, and can inform us as to their direction, their intensity, their associations, etc. Every psychological study is a physiological study, and we study the brain by studying the facts of consciousness, exactly as we inform ourselves as to a man's intelligence by listening to his words, which are its observable signs."

What, now, from this distinctly objective point of view are feeling and emotion? Both have certain basic characteristics in common. Both are expressions " of a more or less profound disturbance of the organism, due to the fact that a relatively considerable quantity of nervous energy is released without being able to be used in a systematic manner. An arrest of the tendencies aroused and a number of physical or psychical phenomena of various kinds are then produced. At the same time, one or several or all of the following phenomena always appear: persistence of tendencies, relative lack of co-ordination and sudden appearance of the phenomena produced, and the tendency of the awakened impulse to monopolize the field of consciousness."

In spite of their common basic features, it is possible to divide affective phenomena into various fairly well defined groups. A first group, which includes passions, sentiments, affective impulses and affective signs, is characterized by the *persistence* and *considerable organization* of the tendencies which produce them and by the relative unimportance of external stimulus conditions. The members of the group differ chiefly in respect of degree, except that affective signs differ from the other members in that they do not tend directly to produce movements. A second group, consisting of *affective sensations,* is characterized by the relative simplicity of the tendencies which produce them and the great importance of external conditions. A third group, finally, consists of what Paulhan terms *emotions.* These emotions are essentially by-products of the other two groups. They involve on the one hand shocks — affective phenomena due to the sudden blocking of impulses — and on the other hand pleasure and pain, which depend upon the degree of systematization of the tendencies which produce them. "Pleasure is the result of a growing systematization; pain is the result of a decreasing systematization; both of course imply . . . that the systematization is imperfect."

Although France is the principal locus of the epiphenomenal point of view in the late nineteenth century, it is by no means the only one. James' theory, we have seen, was potentially epiphenomenal, though not actually so. This potentiality was made actual by John Dewey [52] (1859–   ), leader of the Chicago School, the " cradle " of Behaviorism. For Dewey, conscious emotion — the " feel " of emotion — is but a part of emotion. Besides this, the emotion is a practical attitude, a readiness to act in certain ways : " Anger means a readiness to explode in a sudden attack, not a mere state of feeling." The emotion further involves an object, a thing or event about which one is emotional. In brief, emotion is an attitude towards an object, involving secondarily a " feel " due to bodily changes.

What kind of attitude? The attitude is always, Dewey holds, the rearousal of a useful set of movements. But what of the random activity so striking in the major emotions? This Dewey considers to be the result of conflict of previously useful acts. It is here that Dewey makes his greatest contribution to affective psychology. Emphasis upon conflicts of reaction patterns is one of the main features of the modern theory of emotions and feelings.

CONCLUSION

The nineteenth century is essentially a century of psychophysiology. On the one hand consciousness is the focus of psychological interest. On the other hand physiology assumes an ever increasing importance as an explanatory basis. These facts are naturally reflected in theories of feeling and emotion. Mental theories, fairly numerous at the beginning of the century, rapidly go out of fashion. They are replaced by psychophysiological theories. At first these theories are peripheral ones, for physiology penetrates into

---

[52] J. Dewey, " The Theory of Emotion, I, Emotional Attitudes," *Psychol. Rev.*, I (1894), 553–569 ; " II, The Significance of Emotions," *ibid.*, 13–32.

psychology through the sense organs. Later, with increased knowledge of physiology, there develop central psychophysiological theories. The early peripheral theories fail to account for the variable relation between feelings or emotions and external stimulation. James' brilliant development of the peripheral theory escapes this difficulty, but fails to make room for the prevalent hedonism. Towards the end of the century, it is the central psychophysiological theories which are dominant.

Throughout this development the primacy of consciousness in psychology has remained practically unquestioned. The psychophysiological point of view, however, holds implicit within itself a threat to this primacy. If consciousness invariably correlates with physiological processes, the reverse is not true. Causal sequences in conscious terms are thus always at the mercy of physiological interference. Only at the physiological level can uniformity of antecedent and consequent be expected. Appreciation of this state of affairs leads towards the end of the century to epiphenomenal views in which the primacy of consciousness is denied. Such views make conscious states the lesser and especially the less important parts of feelings and emotions.

CHAPTER XI

Affective Psychology in the Twentieth Century

For the theory of feeling and emotion, as indeed for all psychological theory, the first third of the twentieth century is a period of rapid development and of change. At the beginning of the century the dominant type of theory is psychophysiological. From the very outset, however, this dominance is challenged. The trend against the primacy of consciousness, manifested in the nineteenth century by what I have termed epiphenomenal theories, becomes increasingly marked after 1900. At first it displays itself by an attempt to reject consciousness entirely, even as a basis of inference. The result is a number of *objective* theories of feeling and emotion, such as that of Watson. Gradually, however, it becomes apparent that the trouble with the older systems is not their acceptance of consciousness as a basis of inference, but their insistence upon raising consciousness — ephemeral, non-causal — to the rank of a fundamental scientific reality. Exactly the same criticism holds for objective systems such as behaviorism. In consequence the trend against the primacy of consciousness becomes a trend in favor of the primacy of the organism. It gives rise to what may be termed organic theories of feeling and emotion. These theories are of two types, depending upon the general realm of facts from which they originate. Among psychiatrists such theories tend to be stated in terms of mental forces such as instincts, repressions, etc.; they tend to be *dynamic organic* theories. Among neurologists and physiologists they tend to be *physiological organic* theories.

PSYCHOPHYSIOLOGICAL THEORIES

For the first decade of the twentieth century psychophysiology was definitely " elementaristic." A feature of the theories of feeling and emotion of this period was specification of the place of pleasantness and unpleasantness in an " elementary " psychological system. The obvious possibilities were: (1) that pleasantness and unpleasantness were sensations; (2) that they were attributes of sensations; (3) that they were special elements. Wrangling about these three possibilities almost monopolized theoretical discussion and formulation of experiments. Stumpf [1] was foremost in the argument that pleasantness and unpleasantness were special sensations; Ziehen [2] stood for the view that they were attributes of sensations; Titchener,[3] for the Wundtian view that they were special elements. Cornelius,[4] and somewhat later, Krueger,[5] representing the school of *Gestaltqualität,* advocated the view that they were " total qualities." With the advent of the Gestalt school and the appreciation that mental elements were artificial constructs, this issue lost importance. It became apparent that except for its implications with respect to the nature

---

[1] C. Stumpf, " Über Gefühlsempfindungen," *Bericht über den II Kongress für experimentelle Psychologie,* Leipzig, 1907, 209; " Über Gefühlsempfindungen," *Z. f. Psychol.,* XLIV (1907), 1 (this article is an expansion of the preceding one) ; cf. also *Z. f. Psychol.,* XXVIII (1917), 263. An excellent exposition and critical discussion of Stumpf's theory will be found in E. B. Titchener, *Lectures on the Elementary Psychology of Feeling and Attention,* New York, 1908, 81–121.

[2] T. Ziehen, *Leitfaden der physiologischen Psychologie,* 12th ed., Jena, 1924, 290–294 and 355–358.

[3] E. B. Titchener, *A Textbook of Psychology,* New York (1909), 1919, 225–236.

[4] H. Cornelius, *Psychologie als Erfahrungswissenschaft,* Leipzig, 1897.

[5] F. Krueger, " Das Wesen der Gefühle, Entwurf einer systematischen Theorie," *Arch. f. d. ges. Psychol.,* LXV (1928), 91–128; cf. also " The Essence of Feeling, Outline of a Systematic Theory," in *Feelings and Emotions, The Wittenberg Symposium,* Worcester, 1928, 58–86.

of underlying neural processes the position with respect to this issue was a matter of systematic bias — a matter of the way in which the psychologist chose to construct his mental elements. In the following discussion little emphasis will consequently be placed on this feature of theories of feeling and emotion. In particular, no further mention will be made of men who, like Krueger, have not even attempted a physiological development of their views.

Peripheral theory. The peripheral psychophysiological theory received support from a number of important twentieth-century psychologists. Influenced, however, by the discussion on the relation of feeling to conscious elements, most of them sought merely to relate feeling with some more or less sensory physiological process without attempting to deal with the problem of the arousal of this process. Titchener, as stated above, believed pleasantness and unpleasantness to be the qualities of special affective elements. These elements, he suggested, were probably related to the excitation of free nerve endings. How these might be excited remained in the dark. Emotion he considered to be a complex conscious process involving indeed organic sensations aroused reflexly as in the James theory, but distinguished especially by the presence of affective elements. As he did not subscribe, for the arousal of the latter, to a mechanism such as James', he could not agree that James' theory was anything more than a theory of organic sensations in emotion.

Warren [6] held a somewhat different position in a similarly uninformative way. Feelings, he thought, were complexes of specific sensations, namely " systemic " (organic or pain) sensations. These sensations involved not only their various special qualities, but also a common " feeling

[6] H. C. Warren, *Human Psychology,* Boston and New York, 1920, 279.

tone." When they combined into feelings, the special qualities faded away leaving as a prominent feature only pleasantness and unpleasantness. Emotions were combinations
of feelings and motor sensations. As with Titchener, one
might expect of Warren marked approval of James' theory — for James, emotions were likewise combinations of
organic and motor sensations. But no, Warren disowns
James for insisting too much on motor sensations. As to
what alternative mechanism arouses the systemic sensations, Warren leaves us as much in the dark as does Titchener.

Even Nafe,[7] who has recently contributed important
experimental evidence bearing upon the relation of feelings
to sensory processes, does no more than touch upon the way
in which these processes may be aroused. His view is that
" Pleasantness, as a physiological experience, consists of a
pattern of discrete, bright points of experience in the general nature of a thrill but usually much less intensive.
Unpleasantness is similar but characteristically duller,
heavier, more of the pressure type of experience, and is
localized towards the abdomen or the lower part of the
body." As to the arousal of the bright and dull patterns,
Nafe merely states that they are reflex. It should be added,
however, that Nafe has never claimed that his view is a
complete theory of feeling. His treatment of the problem
occurs incidentally in works dealing with the general topic
of somesthetic sensitivity.

There are fortunately a few exceptions to the trend towards one-sided theorizing which has just been described.

[7] J. P. Nafe, " An Experimental Study of the Affective Qualities," *Amer.
J. Psychol.*, XXXV (1924), 507 ; " The Psychology of Felt Experience,"
Amer. J. Psychol., XXXIX, 1927, 387 ; " The Sense of Feeling," in *The
Foundations of Experimental Psychology*, Worcester, 1929, 411 ; " The
Pressure, Pain, and Temperature Senses," in *Handbook of General Experi-
mental Psychology*, Worcester, 1934, 1076.

Lagerborg,[8] in 1905, propounded in some detail a theory in which feeling is related to nutritional processes controlled reflexly in accordance with James' view. E. J. Kempf,[9] in a monograph dealing primarily with motivation, relates feeling and emotion to proprioceptive stimulation. He lays especial emphasis upon the peripheral nature of his theory: in a section headed " Peripheral Origin of the Emotions " he provides a remarkably good defense of the general principle of James' theory against the objections raised by the experiments of Sherrington and Cannon. The most noteworthy exception, however, to the trend toward narrowness of the peripheral point of view is the theory of F. H. Allport.[10] This theory, likewise patterned after that of James, covers both feelings and emotions. Basing his view largely upon the experimental work of W. B. Cannon, though rejecting much of the latter's interpretation, Allport holds that " The cranio-sacral division of the autonomic, supplemented under certain conditions by the cerebro-spinal system, innervates those responses whose return afferent impulses are associated with the conscious quality of pleasantness. The sympathetic division produces visceral responses which are represented in consciousness as unpleasantness." As for emotion, it is a complex of feeling and of a specific quality peculiar to each emotion. This specific quality, like feeling, is an awareness of bodily changes, but of changes of a different type: " The differentiating factor arises from the stimulation of the proprioceptors in the muscles, tendons, and joints of the somatic part of the organism . . . afferent impulses from these somatic patterns of response add to the autonomic core of sensitivity the

[8] R. Lagerborg, *Das Gefühlsproblem*, Leipzig, 1905.

[9] E. J. Kempf, *The Autonomic Functions and the Personality*, Nervous and Mental Diseases, Monograph Series, No. 28, New York and Washington, 1921.

[10] F. H. Allport, *Social Psychology*, Cambridge, Mass., 1924, 84–98.

characteristic sensory complexes by which one emotion is distinguished from another of the same affective class." Allport's specification of the mode of arousal of sensory processes enables him to connect his theory with the problem of motivation instead of leaving it hanging in the air like the theories of his predecessors. On the one hand, he is able to outline the arousal of emotions in terms of innate and conditioned responses; on the other, to describe the consequences of emotions in terms of the energizing effects of visceral responses. The result is that in spite of his definition of emotion in purely conscious terms Allport provides a picture of organic functions entirely comparable to those with which we shall deal later under the name *organic theories.*[11]

Central Theories. The compartmentalism of the peripheral theories — except for that of Allport — is not shared by the central physiological theories. As has been pointed out, the former need a bridge such as that provided by James, in order to connect with external stimulation and with behavior. Central theories, on the other hand, relate feelings and emotions to processes at the very junction between all afferent and efferent impulses. Thus proponents of such theories cannot escape dealing to some extent with general problems of motivation. The converse, however, is true only with marked qualifications. Psychologists interested in motivation are, indeed, drawn to central psychophysiological theories, *provided* that they are concerned with conscious feeling and emotion. But most of them are not. Thus we find relatively few central psychophysiological theories in the twentieth century, not because such theories are out of line with the development of modern em-

[11] For a somewhat different application of James' theory to the problem of feeling, cf. J. G. Beebe-Center, *Pleasantness and Unpleasantness,* New York, 1932, 410–417.

phasis upon motivation, but because they constitute an early stage of this development, since exceeded.[12]

The late nineteenth century had provided a number of different and definite central psychophysiological theories, that of Lehmann's being a good example. In the early twentieth century there was a tendency for adherents of the central point of view to agree with one of these theories rather than to formulate a new one. Not until the work of Troland [13] is there any real development of the central psychophysiological theory. Troland, like Lehmann, starts from the close connection of pleasantness and unpleasantness with biological advantage and disadvantage. Unlike the former, however, he considers the physiological processes underlying hedonic tone to be not mere correlates of biological welfare, but determinants of this welfare through their influence upon learning. In this respect he follows Gilman's " learning " theory. According to Troland, " The affective intensity of any individual consciousness is proportional to the average rate of change of conductance in the synapses, the activities of which are responsible for that consciousness." This proposition may be expressed mathematically. If affective intensity be represented by a (plus values being pleasant and minus values unpleasant), and average conductance of the synapses by c, one can write

$$a = k \frac{dc}{dt}$$

k being a constant, dc/dt being the expression for the rate of change of c with respect to t. Change in the conductance

[12] Max Meyer provides a good instance. In 1908 he published an interesting central psychophysiological theory of feeling. By 1911, however, he had gone behavioristic. M. Meyer, " The Nervous Correlates of Pleasantness and Unpleasantness," *Psychol. Rev.*, XV, 1908, 201–216, 292–322.

[13] L. T. Troland, " A System for Explaining Affective Phenomena," *J. of Abnorm. Psychol.*, XIV, 1920, 376–387; *The Mystery of Mind*, New

of synapses, the activities of which underlie consciousness at any given moment, is determined by two factors: (1) by two opposed types of sensory processes, namely beniception and nociception, the former increasing conductance, the latter decreasing it; (2) by exercise (increasing conductance) and disuse (decreasing conductance). Such change definitely alters the neural responses of the organism to stimulation, increase or decrease in the conductance of synapses evidently making the paths involving these synapses more liable or less liable to subsequent nervous conduction. Thus the neural correlates of pleasantness and unpleasantness may be considered to influence learning by "stamping in" and "stamping out" neural patterns.

As to emotion, Troland defines it in terms of changes in conductance due to the first of the factors mentioned above, namely beniception and nociception. These changes in conductance, which may be either primary or conditioned, he terms *retroflexes*. "An emotion is constituted by the series of psychical wants which ensue upon the excitation of a retroflex, under the condition that successful responses to such excitation are not fully prepared in advance." This series of psychical events includes typically: (1) a sensation or perception involving marked pleasantness or unpleasantness, i.e., physiologically, giving rise to marked retroflex action, either positive or negative. The feeling (and the retroflex action) may be primary, or conditioned. (2) Imagery of a *desideratum*, e.g., in the case of fear, imagery of escape. (3) Imagery of *means* to achieve the desideratum, e.g., in fear, of kinesthesis of running. This imagery, if in the focus of attention, is accompanied by an

York, 1926, 131–145; *The Fundamentals of Human Motivation*, New York, 1928, 284–300; *The Principles of Psychophysiology*, New York, 1932, Vol. III, 223–388.

appropriate motor response. Imagery of one means after another alternates, until appearance of an adequate one. Adequate imagery of means, accompanied as it is by behavior yielding the desideratum, e.g., in fear, escape, removes the original occasion of the emotion and thus brings it to its close.

Troland speaks of his system of motivation as a " hedonism of the past." It is obvious that the system involves a definite correlation between action and past pleasantness and unpleasantness, but it is also true that the system operates quite independently of these feelings. The causal links are all of them organic events: nervous excitations, synaptic conductances, muscular and glandular responses. It is only because of Troland's " conscious " bias that the non-causal relation of synaptic conductance to feelings is stressed and made to appear systematically paramount. Remove the effects of this bias, and Troland's system becomes a theory of functions of the organism in which the role of consciousness is merely that of an avenue of cognitive approach. In this respect Troland's theory constitutes a transition from psychophysiological theories to organic theories.

Another well-developed central psychophysiological theory is that of W. M. Marston.[14] Both feeling and emotion, for Marston, are objectively a particular kind of energy generated at the synapses of motor integration centers in the brain. Following the experimental findings of Cannon and Bard, Marston ascribes to these centers a position in or near the hypothalamus. The energy in question, which Marston calls *motor psychonic energy,* is based upon the

---

[14] W. M. Marston, " A Theory of Emotions and Affection Based upon Systolic Blood Pressure Studies," *Amer. J. Psychol.,* XXXV, 1924, 469; with C. D. King and E. H. Marston, *Integrative Psychology,* New York, 1931.

interaction of two classes of impulses, *tonic* ones (self-regulatory impulses from the muscles and glands) and *phasic* ones (impulses originating from environmental influences). Feeling depends upon the nature of this interaction. Pleasantness has as objective counterpart psychonic energy based upon alliance of tonic and phasic impulses; unpleasantness, psychonic energy based upon conflict of such impulses. " Both sensory and mental processes may be either pleasant or unpleasant. Thus when a group of impulses representing a sensation crosses through the correlation centers and produces a slight effect of alliance with the motor self-impulses upon entering the motor system, this sensation will be subjectively called a pleasant one, and vice versa. The same situation will hold for thought processes, such as percepts, concepts, introspections, etc.; these impulses, too, may achieve subsequent low-order integrations with the constant motor impulses, and thus be experienced as pleasant or unpleasant."

The interaction at the basis of psychonic energy may be of two types. It may be such that there is no perceptible alteration in the volume of the tonic impulses. In this case we have simply feelings. On the other hand, the interaction may be such that there is an alteration in the volume of the tonic impulses. In this case we have emotion. Interaction with change of volume of tonic impulses — emotional interaction — occurs when the phasic impulses are either markedly stronger or markedly weaker than the tonic impulses representing the motor condition of the organism. Stronger phasic impulses cause decrease of tonic impulses, weaker ones increase. As such interaction may also involve alliance or conflict, we have four possible primary types of interaction which correspond, according to Marston, to four primary emotions. These are indicated in the table following.

TABLE OF PRIMARY PHASIC-TONIC INTERACTION-TYPES AND
CORRESPONDING PRIMARY EMOTIONS,
ACCORDING TO MARSTON

General relation of the two impulses	Relative strength of the two impulses	Change in tonic impulses	Name of Emotion
Alliance	Phasic stronger	Decrease	Compliance
Alliance	Phasic weaker	Increase	Dominance
Conflict	Phasic stronger	Decrease	Submission
Conflict	Phasic weaker	Increase	Inducement

Each primary emotion, furthermore, may be either active or passive, depending on whether the interaction is such as to achieve an outlet to the musculature or not. Marston believes that all emotions are either active or passive forms of these primary emotions, or combinations of them. Desire, for instance, is a compound of active dominance and passive compliance. Thus, for Marston, all emotions can be reduced objectively to energy changes in motor centers based on the interaction of phasic and tonic impulses.

OBJECTIVE THEORIES

The nineteenth century, we have seen, witnessed a marked trend towards the objective in psychology. Indeed, towards its close, men like Ribot and some of his pupils were emphasizing objective factors more than subjective ones on the ground that consciousness was nothing but an epiphenomenon in an otherwise causally related universe. From such a position it was not a great step to the view that a truly scientific psychology must exclude introspective data altogether. This step was taken in the first decade of the twentieth century by two relatively independent groups, the *Reflexologists* and the *Behaviorists*.

In 1904, Bechterew,[15] a clinical and experimental neurologist, published an article entitled " Objective Psychology and its Subject Matter " in which he defended the thesis that introspective psychology must be supplemented by the objective study of psychic (conditioned) reflexes in order to yield a complete science. In 1913, was published in German his *Objective Psychology* in which he states the same view, but further implies that objective psychology is the only scientifically valid psychology. In 1923, finally, in the preface to the second edition of his *General Principles of Human Reflexology* he explicitly gives to objective psychology the leading — almost exclusive — role in psychology: "The study of subjective or conscious processes, which we discover in ourselves by introspection or self-observation, and with which ' subjective ' psychology, with experiments which merely aid introspection, has been occupied, can nowise be regarded as a branch of natural science, for in any science the method of investigation is primary, and the method of natural science has hitherto been strictly objective, and will remain so. . . . If we look into the future, we must see that ' subjective ' psychology will be merely a supplementary science conforming its aims to the data of the objective science of reflexology and only thus will subjective analysis (in the sense of verbal account) render services to the scientific investigation of human personality." In a nutshell: objective psychology is the only scientific psychology. As to consciousness, Bechterew does not deny it, but simply disregards it. We shall see that this is the exact position of the other leading objective psychologist of the twentieth century, J. B. Watson.

[15] W. Bechterew, *Objective Psychologie,* Leipzig and Berlin, 1913; " Emotions as Somato-Mimetic Reflexes," in *Feelings and Emotions, The Wittenberg Symposium,* Worcester, 1928; *General Principles of Human Reflexology,* New York, 1932.

What is Bechterew's position on feelings and emotions? It is given definite formulation in his paper "Emotions as Somato-mimetic Reflexes," read at the Wittenberg Symposium on Feelings and Emotions. As indicated by the title, Bechterew considers emotions to be *somato-mimetic reflexes* involving (1) changes in the viscera, (2) mimic movements, and (3) changes in reproductive-associative reflexes (e.g., change in speed of word associations). Of these three classes, the somatic (visceral) changes seem to be the more important, because they can be the causes of the others. As to feelings, he considers these to be changes in somato-mimetic tonus rather than specific reflexes. Somato-mimetic reflexes may be innate or acquired. The innate ones involve primarily fear, anger, love, satisfaction and dissatisfaction. The acquired ones are developed by conditioning, and involve specific cortical centers.

J. B. Watson,[16] the behaviorist *par excellence,* holds a theory of feeling and emotion similar to that of Bechterew. As early as 1914, in order to demonstrate the competence of behaviorism to cover the whole field of psychology, he outlined a view of affection which made it a form of instinctive behavior. This view, he points out, is a behavioristic transposition of the doctrine that affection is a special form of sensation. It further includes, we might add, the reflex mechanism proposed by James for emotion. Indeed, it is really a behavioral statement of Allport's theory. Stimuli calling out either overt or delayed responses arouse concomitantly afferent impulses from the reproductive organs and related erogenous zones. These impulses are of two fundamental kinds. One is connected with tumescence, rhythmical contraction of muscles and increase in the quan-

---

[16] J. B. Watson, *Behavior, an Introduction to Comparative Psychology,* New York, 1914; *Psychology from the Standpoint of a Behaviorist,* Philadelphia and London, 1919; *Behaviorism,* 1924; revised ed., New York, 1930.

tity of secretions. These impulses, if functioning alone, would lead to expansive and seeking movements and ultimately to the act of reproduction. It is these impulses, which, Watson states, "in current psychological terminology" are the bodily substrata of the emotion of pleasantness. The other kind of impulses is connected with shrinkage of the sex organs, relaxation of other muscular tissue, and inhibition of secretion. These latter impulses would, if functioning alone, give rise to movements of avoidance. It is they which constitute the so-called bodily substrata of unpleasantness. One or the other of these two kinds of impulses is probably aroused to some degree by any object whatever, largely due to the mechanism of habit.

What, now, of emotions? In fully developed form " an emotion is an hereditary 'pattern-reaction' involving profound changes of the bodily mechanism as a whole, but particularly of the visceral and glandular systems." This form, however, is rare, especially in adults. Usually, in emotion, " there can be noted only a reinforcement of inhibition of the habit and instinctive (exaggerated and depressed reflexes, for example) activities taking place at the moment." Watson believes that this is due to " the partial inhibition of the more external features of the primitive pattern types of emotion. . . . The implicit, namely glandular and smooth muscle side of the pattern remains. The emotionally exciting object releases important internal secretions which, without initiating new (part) reactions, reinforce or inhibit those actually in progress." Usually certain auxiliary or additional part reactions appear, such as we see in whistling while at work, etc. " When emotional expression is blocked in any one region, outlet seems to take place somewhere else." These vicarious expressions may range all the way from simple tightening of the grasp to complicated neurotic behavior. Although emotion is thus as a rule essentially excitatory, in its most extreme forms it becomes inhibitory: " the final stage in any great emotion would seem to be paralysis or the ' death feint.' "

There are, Watson believes, three emotional reactions belonging to the original and fundamental nature of man: fear, rage, and love. For each of these he specifies, in infants, the nature of the response and the stimulation which calls them forth. Rage, for instance, involves crying, screaming, holding of the breath, and slashing movements of the arms and legs. It is occasioned by hampering of movements. In adults, these basic emotional reactions rarely appear. Instead, there occur emotions of the consolidated type, or emotional attitudes, which are combinations of emotion, instinct, and habit. As in the case of feeling, conditioning plays a very important role in the emotions of adults. " It seems safe to say that when an emotionally exciting object stimulates the subject simultaneously with one not emotionally exciting, the latter may in time (often after one such joint stimulation) arouse the same emotional excitation as the former. It is probable that conditioned reflexes of the second, third, and succeeding orders are also continually arising."

The reader may wonder why, with Watson, feeling is not, as with Bechterew, a special form of emotion—particularly since feeling involves visceral response (tumescence, etc.). The answer is that feeling involves primarily organized behavior (seeking, avoidance) while emotion is primarily a visceral matter. The former type of reaction Watson terms instinctive, agreeing withal that the distinction between emotion and instinct is far from definite.

In his text of 1919, Watson questioned the notion of the utility of all emotions. This critical attitude is even more marked in his more recent *Behaviorism*. Here the feature of emotion which is most stressed is its biological inadequacy — indeed, it is this feature which Watson uses to define the class of emotional reactions. Emotional reactions are those which diverge from a norm which the scientist would wish to set. Such divergence takes the form of superfluous reaction (e.g., crying), impeded reactions (e.g., paralysis), reactions not sanctioned by society (e.g., stealing, murder), reactions belonging properly to other stimuli (e.g., homosexual relations). A very interesting feature of this change in Watson's emphasis is that it tends to make emotion a particular kind of *stimulus response correlation* rather than a particular kind of response. Inadequacy of response is obviously inadequacy relative to a particular stimulus. To blush when asked a question is an inadequate response; when subjected to cold, it is not. This tendency is common to much modern work on emotion.

DYNAMIC ORGANIC THEORIES

The psychophysiological theories involve emphasis upon consciousness; the objective theories upon behavior. What we term *organic theories* involve emphasis upon the real, permanent organism. Clearly, a psychophysical relation such as that between brilliance and intensity of stimulus is a characterization of the organism. The organism is such that this particular relationship holds. To the man brought up in the tradition of a science of consciousness, this circumstance merely offers a means of explanation for the facts of consciousness. To the man brought up in a biological tradition, it offers a means of studying the organism by psychological techniques. The same can be said of behavioral correlations. They, too, can be considered either as fundamental behavioral facts to be explained by hypotheses about the organism, or as symbols of basic organic functions. It may seem that the parallel is misleading, that behavioral facts *are* facts about the organism without any further interpretation. A little thought, however, will show that a correlation between voltage across a grid and the number of times a rat crosses the grid per unit time is far from being a direct description of processes in the rat. It is really a correlation between one external force producing a hypothetical excitation in the rat and another external force produced by hypothetical muscular contractions in the rat.

RAT
(ORGANISM)
Stimulus→ Excitation→ Central→ Contractions→ Behavior
| process

But to return to our main point. Facts of consciousness and facts of behavior, to one interested in the organism, are indices of processes within the organism. Furthermore, they are the main indices of such general processes as learning, fatigue. It is not surprising, therefore, to find a number of psychologists, particularly ones with medical-physiological training, considering conscious and behavioral facts as nothing more than indices — and thus not inconsistent with each other — of that which really seems to them important, namely processes in the organism.

A first group of such men is one where psychiatric training predominates. The men in it are concerned especially with fathoming the mechanisms of the organism which comes to them as a " mental " patient and in thus achieving a method of cure for this patient. The symptoms which it presents are behavioral and conscious peculiarities almost impossible to interpret in neural terms, but fairly easy to interpret in terms of common-sense mental forces such as wishes, repressions, and the like. In consequence, these men develop a conception of the organism as endowed with such common-sense forces rather than as a purely physico-chemical system. Their theories of feeling and emotion are *dynamic-organic* theories.

The best known of these scientists is undoubtedly Freud.[17] His theory of feeling illustrates admirably his emphasis upon fundamental biological functions rather than upon consciousness or behavior. The discussion centers upon the role of pleasure and pain in motivation, not upon their physiological basis. " It seems as if our entire psychological activity were directed towards gaining pleasurable stimulations, towards avoiding painful ones, that it is regulated automatically by the pleasure principle." This hedonism, however, operates according to two very different principles. One, the more primitive, called by Freud the *pleasure principle*, involves a wholly specious form of satisfaction. The organism, whose psychical equilibrium is disturbed by a need, hallucinates the desired object. Freud believes this to occur extensively in children. He points out that it is also a frequent occurrence in normal dreaming. Such an organism further disregards unpleasant stimulation. This is illustrated by repression. It is only when the pleasure principle has failed to yield satisfaction that the second fundamental principle comes into play, the *reality principle*. This principle is essentially a realistic pleasure principle. It continues to strive for pleasure, but does so by

[17] Sigmund Freud, *Beyond the Pleasure Principle*, New York, 1924; *A General Introduction to Psychoanalysis*, New York, 1920, especially pp. 340–355; *New Introductory Lectures on Psycho-Analysis*, New York, 1933, especially pp. 113–152. Cf. also E. Jones, *Papers on Psychoanalysis*, New York, 1913, 10–34; W. Stekel, *Conditions of Nervous Anxiety*, London and New York, 1923; O. Fenichel, *Outline of Clinical Psychoanalysis*, New York, 1934, 46–69.

a different method. Instead of hallucinating desired ends, it represents reality and seeks pleasure within its limits. One of its features is to give up present insecure pleasure for later more secure pleasure. Freud characterizes it as a utilitarianism, adding, however, that it is one based ultimately on hedonism. He further states that its advantage over the pleasure principle is well expressed by Bernard Shaw in the words: " To be able to choose the line of greatest advantage instead of yielding in the direction of the least resistance."

The part which these two principles play in the ontogeny of the organism is sketched as follows by Freud. At first, it is the pleasure principle which holds full sway. Gradually, the reality principle obtains the upper hand. A part of the organism's activity, however, continues to obey the pleasure principle, namely *phantasy*. Furthermore, the sexual instincts lag behind the *ego instincts* in their conversion to the reality principle. There results a close relation between the sexual instincts and phantasy — where repression is all-powerful — and between ego instincts and perception. Another consequence is that the realm of sexuality provides a weak point in mental organization. Delay in conformance of the sexual instincts to the reality principle constitutes a marked part of disposition to become neurotic.

Freud is not, however, an out-and-out hedonist. To the pleasure principle and reality principle he added in 1922 a third basic principle of motivation, the *repetition compulsion*. In traumatic neuroses — e.g., war neuroses — he pointed out, the patient's dreams of the traumatic situation cannot possibly be considered as pleasurable wish fulfillments. They are reinstatements of situations involving only pain. To explain these reinstatements, and also many other occurrences such as the repetitive play of children,

Freud posits the fundamental principle of repetition compulsion, which he believes to antedate even the pleasure principle in time of appearance. All instincts, he believes, are essentially manifestations of the repetition compulsion, they are tendencies towards the reinstatement of earlier conditions. Indeed, they hark back to the original inorganic condition, so that paradoxically, " the goal of all life is death."

Only in seeking to give his doctrine of motivation a more general biological formulation does Freud bring up the question of the basis of pleasure and pain. Pleasurable excitation, he believes, " *in some way* involves lessening, lowering, or obliterating the amount of stimuli present in the psychic apparatus. This amount, on the other hand, is increased by pain. Since such processes of pleasure are concerned with the destinies of quantities of psychic excitation or energy, we call considerations of this sort *economic*. It thus appears that we can describe the tasks and performances of the psychic apparatus in different and more generalized terms than by the emphasis of the pursuit of pleasure. We may say that the psychic apparatus serves the purpose of mastering and bringing to rest the mass of stimuli and the stimulating forces which approach it." This basic biological notion, furthermore, is adequate to account for the repetition compulsion. It is essentially an attempt to restore control of a mass of stimuli originally too powerful for the organism to handle. This is achieved by allowing the organism to develop further with each repetition its basic defense to the mass of stimuli — a sort of psychic antibody.

With respect to emotion we again find Freud emphasizing general biological functions: " What psychology has to say about emotions — the James-Lange theory, for instance — is absolutely incomprehensible for us psychoanalysts." " An emotion, in the first place, includes indefinite motor innervations or discharges; secondly, definite sensations which, moreover, are of two kinds, the perception of motor activities that have already taken place, and the direct sensations of pleasure and pain, which give the effect of what we call its feeling tone. But I do not think that the true nature of the emotion has been fathomed by these enumerations. We have gained deeper insight into some emotions and realize that the thread which binds together such a complex as we have described is the repetition of a certain insignificant experience. This experience might be an early impression of a very general sort, which belongs to the antecedent history of the species rather than to that of the individual. To be more clear; the emotional condition has a structure similar to that of an hysterical attack; it is the upshot of a reminiscence. The hysteric attack, then, is comparable to a newly formed individual emotion, the normal emotion to an hysteria which has become a universal heritage."

Freud's views of emotion have been developed in detail only in the case of anxiety. He distinguishes three main types of anxiety, i.e., *objective anxiety, neurotic anxiety,* and *moral anxiety (guilt)*. These represent acknowledgments of weakness by the ego in the face of demands made by the three main entities with which the ego has to deal. Objective anxiety results from weakness towards *reality;* neurotic anxiety from weakness towards the *id* (essentially the passions); moral anxiety from weakness towards the *super-ego* (essentially conscience). As will be apparent from the more detailed description below, it is objective anxiety which is fundamental. Neurotic and moral anxiety are derivatives of it.

The basis of objective anxiety is for Freud always a

traumatic factor, a situation characterized by sheer *magnitude of excitation,* " in which the efforts of the pleasure principle come to nothing " and which " evokes in mental experience a condition of tense excitation which is felt as pain and which cannot be mastered by discharge." Objective anxiety may be primary or secondary (our terms, not Freud's). In primary objective anxiety it is the *occurrence* of the traumatic factor which generates the anxiety. Chronologically birth is the first traumatic factor. Others occur subsequently whenever the ego comes into contact with excessive libidinal demands, or when there is somatic injury of the sexual function. The resulting anxiety, however, is always patterned after that of the birth trauma.

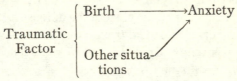

Traumatic Factor
- Birth ———————→Anxiety
- Other situations

PRIMARY OBJECTIVE ANXIETY

In secondary objective anxiety, it is not the occurrence of a traumatic factor which generates anxiety, but the *likelihood of its recurrence.*

Likelihood
of
Recurrence ———————→Anxiety
of
Traumatic Factor

SECONDARY OBJECTIVE ANXIETY

The second main type of anxiety, neurotic anxiety, is reducible to objective anxiety. Here the individual is unconsciously afraid of his own libido, but this fear in turn rests upon fear of objective consequences, upon fear of a traumatic factor. This traumatic factor in men is *castration,* in women *withdrawal of care by the parents.*

Excessive	Likelihood of	
Instinctual———→	Recurrence of ———→	Anxiety
Demand	Traumatic Factor	

NEUROTIC ANXIETY

An important feature of neurotic anxiety is the way in which anxiety and neurotic symptoms are interchangeable. An agoraphobiac may begin his illness with an attack of anxiety in the street. He then develops a symptom, street-phobia. This is a defense against the likelihood of recurrence of the traumatic factor. Similarly, if one prevents an obsessive from carrying out, say, his washing ceremonial, he has an attack of anxiety. Here the defense against likelihood of recurrence of the traumatic factor — whatever it may be — is removed; likelihood of recurrence again exists: there results neurotic anxiety.

The motivational importance of anxiety for Freud is manifested in its relationship to repression. In anxiety-hysteria, Freud used to consider the repression as primary, anxiety as a consequence due to transformation of repressed libido. More recently, however, his view has become the reverse. It is anxiety which brings about the repression. The process may be illustrated as follows: a boy represses desire for his mother and develops anxiety. What really happens is not a mere transformation, but the following more complicated sequence: desire for mother — fear of punishment (e.g., castration) — repression of love — anxiety. The process of repression itself Freud pictures as similar to normal thinking, but unconscious. The ego, aware that an instinctual impulse would lead to danger, and unable to assimilate the impulse into itself, proceeds to anticipate the satisfaction of the impulse, and thus enables it to reproduce in thought the dreaded danger situation. Thereupon the pleasure-pain principle automatically represses the dangerous impulse.

The third form of anxiety, moral anxiety or guilt, is likewise based upon objective anxiety. In the development of the child the super-ego is essentially the successor to parental authority. Thus guilt-anxiety due to the super-ego is the successor to objective anxiety — to fears of the loss of love of the parents and of punishment. Freud does not feel able, however, to give a more detailed account of this rapprochement.

There are several striking features in this treatment of emotion. Conscious emotion is but a symptom of the operation of fundamental biological processes, and it is these fundamental processes, not the conscious emotion, which are the main subjects of investigation. Freud's lecture on " Anxiety and Instinctual Life " gives but a few words to the description of conscious anxiety. Emphasis is entirely on the traumatic factor, its mode of occurrence, its motivational influence. The terminology is indeed largely introspective, but this is simply because Freud defines his motivational concepts in introspective terms. Indeed, Freud's dynamic account of fundamental biological processes in the organism lends itself astonishingly well to translation into ordinary physiological terminology: very briefly, anxiety is a reflex (birth trauma) to a class of stimuli (other traumatic factors), subject to conditioning (secondary objective anxiety, neurotic, and moral anxiety), and involving certain inhibitions (repression). There need be no opposition, then, between such an account of emotion as Freud's and the other type of organic view, namely the physiological.

We have just pointed out that Freud's theory, though little concerned with consciousness, is nevertheless introspective in the sense that its motivational concepts are defined in terms of consciousness. The behavioristic counterpart of Freud's theory is that of Pierre Janet.[18] Like Freud, Janet is concerned primarily with dynamic processes in the organism. Instead of defining these concepts introspectively, however, Janet defines them behaviorally. Whereas Freud's unconscious is full of ideas and wishes, Janet's is full of tendencies to movement.

Feeling (*sentiment*), for Janet, covers not only pleasantness and unpleasantness, but all the moderate emotions. Indeed, pleasantness is for him a moderate emotion in that it is quite distinct from sensory pleasure (with which he is not concerned) and quite similar to joy; unpleasantness likewise, in that it is distinct from sensory pain (also disregarded by Janet) and identical with suffering. Feeling, Janet holds, is essentially a mode or form of response. He conceives of the individual as involving a large number of *tendencies to actions* (essentially reflexes, but without the implication of physical specificity of stimulus, neural path, and response). These tendencies to action vary at any moment in *degree of activation:* the lowest degree of activation is mere latency. Next comes " erection," involving merely implicit action. Next comes automatism, where the action is overt, but where it is isolated and fails to arouse other tendencies. Finally comes overt integrated action. It is the degree of activation of the tendencies at any given moment which determines the feelings. The primary action — " what the person is doing " — is as it were colored by

---

[18] P. Janet, *De l'angoisse à l'extase,* Vol. II, Paris, 1928. (Vol. I is primarily a case history). For a brief statement, cf. " La tension psychologique et ses oscillations," in *Nouveau traité de psychologie,* edited by G. Dumas, Vol. IV, Paris, 1934, 386–411.

the pattern of activations of the moment. When the primary action tendency alone is activated, when there is no coloration in the sense above, there results a feeling of emptiness (*sentiment du vide*), of unreality. When secondary tendencies are activated at the same time as the primary one, and add their energy to it, there is a feeling of pressure (*sentiment de pression*), a feeling of being driven, which manifests itself in different ways according to the particular pattern of activation: *ardor* is a diffuse form of agitation; *passion* a specific form of agitation (one referring to a particular object); *worry* involves exaggeration of a particular type of conduct, namely cautious conduct; *boredom* involves exaggeration of another particular type of conduct, namely search for distraction.

Besides feelings due to particular patterns of activations of tendencies there are those due to the *psychological tension* of the individual, to his general mental level. High psychological tension involves both a high degree of activation and a high level of complexity of the tendencies activated. Low psychological tension involves but a moderate degree of activation of simple ("low") tendencies. It is marked oscillations of the psychological tension of the individual which give rise to morbid excitation (high tension) and depression (low tension). In the case of depression, resulting in impossibility of carrying out actions adequate for adaptation, there occur *psychological derivations,* i.e., the energy originally destined to the production of high-grade actions is expended in the production of quite uncalled-for low-grade actions.

As to emotions, they depend for Janet primarily upon a *drop* of psychological tension. They are characterized by inadequacy of action due to this drop. The inadequacy of action may be a direct consequence of the drop, or may be a consequence through psychological derivation, an overflow of energy not expended in adaptive thought into inferior mechanisms, producing the so-called expressions of emotion. Furthermore, as the emotion continues, there develops fatigue, which tends to reduce even more the psychological tension and thus to aggravate the emotional excitement.

The theories of Freud and Janet, we have pointed out, may be contrasted as introspective and behavioral forms of the dynamic organic theory. Intermediate between them in respect to this contrast is the theory of J. T. MacCurdy.[19] For MacCurdy, affect (emotional consciousness) is awareness of a *repressed* instinct at work. More specifically, he holds that in emotion the stimulus arouses not only conscious perceptions and overt behavior, but also unconscious processes, namely instinctively impelled ideas. These tend to become conscious, but, being inhibited, remain coconscious (i.e., unconscious, but active). They do reach consciousness, but only as affect, not in their original guise. They likewise reach motor manifestation, but only as emotional expression, not as instinctive responses. The subject, unaware of the co-conscious genesis of the affect and the emotional expression, considers them to be the products of his conscious state. Affect and emotional expression are to some extent alternatives — in any given case, the less the expression, the greater the affect. The theory holds, MacCurdy believes, even for so-called abnormal emotions. These are not really " abnormal emotions " but normal emotional responses to abnormal stimuli (ideas).

For all three of the men referred to above, emotion is in some sense abnormal. It has about it something of a trauma

[19] J. T. MacCurdy, *The Psychology of Emotion,* London and New York, 1925.

(Freud) or of inadequacy (Janet) or of repression (Mac-Curdy). Markedly opposed to this conception is that of McDougall [20] for whom emotion is essentially the aware-ness of instinct at work under perfectly normal conditions as well as under conditions of stress.* McDougall is a great admirer of Freud. " I believe," McDougall writes in the in-troduction of his *Abnormal Psychology,* " that Professor Freud has done more for the advancement of psychology than any student since Aristotle." Nevertheless his own theory of feeling and emotion — as indeed his whole psy-chology — is quite different from that of Freud. The main difference lies in McDougall's far greater emphasis upon purposive determination. The major factors of determina-tion in McDougall's theory are instincts. Feelings and emo-tions are little more than their by-products.

Let us first consider McDougall's doctrine of feeling. Freud's instincts are very unspecific, their end being largely determined by hedonic factors. McDougall's instincts — he distinguishes fourteen of them — are extremely specific, and thus the field of action of hedonic determination is far more restricted; indeed pleasure and displeasure affect mental life only in selecting the *means* to be employed in achieving instinctive ends. But further, McDougall's view of the basis of pleasure and displeasure makes them a sort of conscious luxury. Pleasure and displeasure do indeed sustain or deflect striving and strengthen or weaken the tendency to strive in the same way again. But pleasure and displeasure are themselves determined by successful or un-successful striving. Thus exactly the same system of mo-tivation could be achieved by merely relating success in

[20] W. McDougall, *Outline of Psychology,* New York, 1929.
* McDougall's theory is a much earlier one than MacCurdy's — chronological order has here been sacrificed to bring out McDougall's emphasis upon the normality of emotion.

striving to strengthening of striving and recurrence of similar means, failure to weakening of striving and resort to different means.

In regard to emotions, McDougall also minimizes the role in comparison to Freud. They too are in a sense epiphenomena. McDougall accepts James' theory as a part of the truth. Emotions do involve *awareness of bodily changes* — albeit this awareness may be imaginal. But emotions further involve a conative factor, an *immediate experience of striving*. " When we are afraid," writes McDougall, " we feel the impulse to retreat or escape from the object that frightens us; when we are angry, we feel the impulse to attack the object that angers us." Indeed, it is this latter factor which is primary. The various major emotions are essentially indicators of the working of different instinctive impulses, and the expressions of these emotions are mere adaptations of the body to the various modes of instinctive activity.

The dynamic organic theory of feeling and emotion is the product of the clinic rather than of the laboratory. Of late, however, it has benefited by a number of contributions from experimental psychologists. Particularly noteworthy is the work of Lewin and his followers and of A. K. Luria. Lewin [21] has been primarily concerned with laying a conceptual foundation akin to the system of Freud, but constructed in such a fashion as to be experimentally verifiable. His followers have been concerned with the experimental development of his basic views. Thus Dembo [22] has shown that anger may be described as a state of tension aroused by conflict, the tension leading to at-

[21] K. Lewin, *A Dynamic Theory of Personality,* New York and London, 1935.
[22] T. Dembo, " Der Ärger als dynamisches Problem," *Psychol. Forsch.,* XV (1931), 1–144.

tempts at vicarious relief and ultimately breaking through to the motor system in consequence of a sudden increase in its intensity. Luria [23] is less systematic and more behavioristic than Lewin. He lays a good deal of emphasis upon his " method of representative response " in which behavior is considered not for itself, but solely as a symptom of basic organic functions. Studying emotional disorganization by this method, Luria is led to insist upon the limitation of the disorganization to specific functional (as opposed to morphological) systems, the greater sensitiveness to disorganization of systems involving cortical control, the tendency to " short-circuit " responses involving a high level,[*] and the tendency for functional barriers to lose their effectiveness.

PHYSIOLOGICAL ORGANIC THEORIES

Another group of men emphasizing the organism rather than either consciousness or behavior is one where physiological training has been important. Here we find not only physiologists proper, such as Head and Cannon, but psychologists with much physiological training — Dumas, for instance. Their theories of feeling and emotion may be termed *physiological organic theories*.

Head. Head's [24] contribution to the theory of feeling is a by-product of his interest, as a practising neurologist, in the effects of brain lesions upon the general functions of the organism. In collaboration with Holmes, he made a very complete study of two groups of patients suffering from

[23] A. K. Luria, *The Nature of Human Conflicts*, New York, 1932.
[*] Luria calls this tendency the " law of the catalytic action of the stimulus."
[24] H. Head and G. Holmes, " Sensory Disturbances from Cerebral Lesions," *Brain*, XXXIV (1911), 102–254.

cerebral lesions. One group involved patients with lesions of the optic thalamus. The other involved patients with lesions of the cerebral cortex. Observations upon the latter group of patients showed marked blunting and sometimes complete abolition of recognition of posture and of passive movement, of two point discrimination, of localization, and of thermal discrimination. On the other hand, it was found — and this is the most interesting point to us — that " Stationary cortical lesions, however extensive, which cause no convulsions or other signs of irritation and shock, produce no effect on sensibility to pain. Destruction of the cortex alone does not disturb the threshold for the painful or uncomfortable aspects of sensations."

In striking contrast with these observations were those upon the patients suffering from thalamic lesions. Head and Holmes wrote: " The most remarkable feature in that group of thalamic cases with which we have dealt in this work is not loss of sensation, but an excessive response to affective stimuli. This positive effect, an actual overloading of sensation with feeling tone, was present in all our twenty-four cases of this class. . . . This excessive response may be accompanied by much or by little loss of sensation, but the extent of this loss bears no relation to the amount of the over-reaction to painful stimuli. It is only necessary that sufficient sensory impulses capable of exciting discomfort should still be able to reach consciousness. If this is possible, the affected half of the body will respond more profoundly than normal parts to all painful stimuli, in spite of the gross loss of sensation. . . . But the characteristic thalamic response does not consist in an excessive reaction to painful stimuli only. In suitable cases we have shown that the response to pleasurable stimuli, such as warmth, is also greater on the affected side. Moreover, the manifestations of general mental states of pleasure and discomfort may be more pronounced on the abnormal half of the body."

From the fact that cortical lesions alone do not " disturb the threshold for the painful or uncomfortable aspects of sensations," whereas thalamic lesions are associated with excessive hedonic reactions to stimuli applied to the affected side, even though the sensory threshold for these stimuli remains unchanged or is even increased, Head and Holmes concluded: (1) That lesions determining enhanced hedonic tone do so by impeding the inhibitory effect of the cortex upon thalamic activity, and (2) that the thalamus is the seat of the neural processes underlying hedonic consciousness. Concerning the neural paths which are known to run from the cortex to the thalamus, they wrote: " The only function which can be ascribed to these cortico-thalamic paths is that through them the cortex controls, in some way, the activity of the thalamus. If this view is correct, lesions which interrupt these paths, but leave intact the main substance of the optic thalamus must lead to a permanent overactivity of functions exercised by that organ. Any afferent impulses which are capable of exciting this part of the brain will act on an uncontrolled center and must, consequently, evoke excessive effect." Concerning the role of the optic thalamus, they wrote: " We believe that the essential organ of the optic thalamus is the center of consciousness for certain elements of sensation. It responds to all stimuli capable of evoking either pleasure or discomfort, or consciousness of a change in state. The feeling tone of somatic or visceral sensation is the product of thalamic activity, and the fact that a sensation is devoid of feeling tone shows that the impulses which underlie its production make no thalamic appeal."

Cannon. Head's contribution is to the theory of feeling what that of W. B. Cannon [25] is to the theory of emotion. The focus of Cannon's interest is well illustrated by the title of his celebrated book: *Bodily Changes in Pain, Hunger, Fear and Rage.* He concentrates on the *expression of emotions* and their *neural mechanisms,* not on conscious emotion. The latter is used merely to mark off certain bodily changes for the purpose of investigation. Chapter One points out that emotions are accompanied by bodily changes, and that these changes are worthy of study by the physiologist. Chapters Two to Seventeen describe such studies, very largely on animals, where there can be no question of observations of conscious emotion. In the first edition of the book it is not until the last chapter that we get back to conscious emotion with a critique of James' theory. In the second edition the critique is amplified and there is added Cannon's " thalamic " theory of conscious emotion. Otherwise, however, the second edition is like the first in dealing almost exclusively with bodily changes and neural mechanisms. Clearly, to consider Cannon's " thalamic " theory of the physiological correlate of conscious emotion as his whole theory of emotion would be like considering the exposed portion of an iceberg as the whole iceberg. Cannon has been concerned with certain emergency functions of the organism, of which conscious emotion is no more than one phase.

[25] W. B. Cannon, " The Interrelations of Emotions as Suggested by Recent Physiological Researches," *Amer. J. Psychol.,* XXV (1914), 256–282; *Bodily Changes in Pain, Hunger, Fear and Rage,* New York and London, 1915, 2nd, revised, ed., 1929; " The James-Lange Theory of Emotions: a Critical Examination and an Alternative Theory," *Amer. J. Psychol.,* XXXIX (1927), 106–124; " Again the James-Lange and the Thalamic Theories of Emotion," *Psychol. Rev.* XXXVIII (1931), 281–295 (Reply to criticisms in E. B. Newman, F. T. Perkins and R. H. Wheeler, " Cannon's Theory of Emotions, a Critique," *Psychol. Rev.,* XXXVII (1930), 305–326) ; " The Story of the Development of Our Ideas of Chemical Mediation of Nerve Impulses," *Amer. J. of the Medical Sciences,* CLXXXVIII (1934), 145.

The reaction system involved in the major emotions has for Cannon many characteristics in common with simple reflexes: the complex of bodily alterations constituting the expression of rage, for instance, appears shortly after birth. It is a prompt response to an appropriate stimulus. " It is a constant and uniform response — so much is this so, indeed, that there is no mistaking its character whether it be manifested by the diverse races of man or by the lower animals. It is like the reflexes also in being a permanent mode of reaction: throughout life, the characteristic display of the rage-response may be suddenly evoked in all its elaborateness. Further, it is a response to a fairly definite stimulus — an inner stimulus which arises when there is a hampering or checking of motion or an opposition to one or another primary impulse. Finally, the rage-response is like the simple reflexes in being useful."

It is a reaction system which involves not the cortex, but the diencephalon. Decorticated cats show upon recovery from anesthesia a group of remarkable activities such as are usually associated with emotional excitement — a sort of sham rage. P. Bard,[26] a collaborator of Cannon, found that this sham rage " regularly developed after removal of all parts of the brain cranial to the middle of the diencephalon and after removal of the dorsal part of the thalamus. It invariably failed to appear after sections which separated the ventral and most caudal fractions of the lower half of the diencephalon from the mid-brain." He concluded that " sham rage " was probably conditioned by neural mechanisms in the hypothalamus. These mechanisms, he further suggested, are probably normally under

[26] P. Bard, " A Diencephalic Mechanism for the Expression of Rage, with Special Reference to the Sympathetic Nervous System," *Amer. J. Physiol.*, LXXXIV (1928), 490–515; " Emotion, I: The Neuro-Humoral Basis of Emotional Reactions," in *Handbook of General Experimental Psychology*, Worcester, 1934, 264–311.

the inhibitory control of the cortex. Although evidence is not as definite in respect to other forms of emotional response, Bard thinks that it indicates for all emotional expressions, with the exception of those indicating pleasure, a localization of centers within the diencephalon. There is little doubt but that Cannon accepts Bard's conclusions.

It is with the visceral aspect of the emotional reaction that Cannon has been primarily concerned, although he recognizes that emotional expression involves both a visceral and skeletal part — indeed, that the visceral part is not even absolutely essential. The outstanding feature of visceral expression in the case of major emotions is for Cannon the excitation of the sympathetic division of the autonomic nervous system. This division is the antagonist of the cranial-sacral division in the sense that when identical viscera are innervated by both divisions the effect of the one is usually opposite to that of the other. Thus the heart is accelerated by excitation of the sympathetic fibres leading to it, slowed down by excitation of the cranial-sacral fibres. The antagonism of the two divisions is paralleled by the antagonism of the biological functions which they subserve, adjustment to conditions of stress (sympathetic) and adjustment to normal conditions (cranial-sacral). It is also paralleled by their role in emotion, major emotions involving the sympathetic, minor ones (e.g., the delight of eating), the cranial-sacral.

The sympathetic division of the autonomic system is characterized by diffuse conduction. Excitation of it results not in selective influence on specific viscera innervated by it, but in diffuse influence upon almost all. Thus in the major emotions there are not specific patterns of visceral changes corresponding to specific emotions, but rather a single pattern for all emotions. The more important of these changes are acceleration of the heart, constriction of the blood vessels, inhibition of stomach contractions, raising of the hair, increased liberation of sugar from the liver, enlargement of the pupil, and increased secretion of adrenin by the adrenal glands.

This latter bodily change has the peculiar capacity to reinforce and prolong the activity of the sympathetic division of the autonomic nervous system. " Adrenin . . . in extraordinarily minute amounts, affects the structure innervated by the sympathetic division of the autonomic system precisely as if they were receiving normal impulses. For example, when adrenin is injected into the blood, it will cause pupils to dilate, hairs to stand erect, blood vessels to be constricted, the activities of the alimentary canal to be inhibited, and sugar to be liberated from the liver. These effects are not produced by action of the substance on the central nervous system, but by direct action on the organ itself."

Adrenin is not the only secretory product of sympathetic stimulation to reinforce the effects of the latter. Smooth muscles, when stimulated sympathetically, discharge a substance into the blood stream, which can have effects similar to sympathetic impulses. Cannon has called this substance *sympathin*. There appear to be two distinct kinds of sympathin. Sympathin E (excitatory) is given off by smooth muscles excited to contract by sympathetic impulses. It affects in a like manner other organs which contract in response to sympathetic excitation. Sympathin I (inhibitory) is given off by muscles which are sympathetically relaxed. It so affects other organs which are sympathetically relaxed.

As has been indicated, Cannon holds that in the major emotions the bodily changes have high adaptive value. He writes: " Every one of the visceral changes that have been noted — the cessation of processes in the alimentary canal (thus freeing the energy supply for other parts); the shifting of blood from the abdominal organs to the organs immediately essential to muscular exertion; the increased vigor of the contraction of the heart; the discharge of extra blood corpuscles from the spleen; the deeper respiration; the dilation of the bronchioles; the quick abolition of muscular fatigue; the mobilizing of sugar in the circulation — these changes are directly serviceable in making the organism more effective in the violent display of energy which fear or rage or pain may involve."

What is the relation between the sympathetic expression of emotion described above and conscious emotion? It is here that Cannon propounds the " thalamic theory " which is so often considered his entire theory of emotions. The relation cannot, Cannon feels, be such as James' theory would require — conscious emotion cannot be the (sensory) awareness of the bodily changes. The changes occur too late, for one thing. For another, the sensitivity of the viscera is too slight. Instead, Cannon believes that conscious emotion is correlated with a specific activity of the thalamus. Emotion is awareness of thalamic excitation rather than of bodily changes. The thalamic excitation results on the one hand in conduction to the cortex with consequent consciousness of emotion; on the other hand in conduction to the viscera and periphery, with consequent bodily changes. This theory can be schematized as shown at top of the next page.

Cannon's theory of emotion is obviously not a complete theory. It passes rapidly over the minor emotions without making it clear whether they are to be dealt with in some special manner or whether they are to be considered as akin

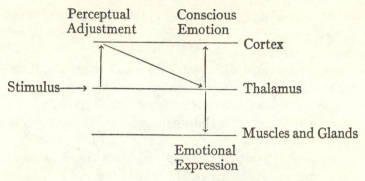

to the major emotions except for their relation to the parasympathetic rather than the sympathetic system. Furthermore, even with respect to the major emotions, Cannon deals very little with their manifestations in skeletal musculature. Strictly speaking, Cannon's theory is one of the visceral mechanism of the major emotions, no more. This is not meant to be a criticism. Cannon surely shares with Freud the distinction of having contributed more to our knowledge of emotions than anyone else in the twentieth century. It is meant only to point out that even the notable contribution of Cannon still leaves unfilled the need for a truly general physiological organic theory of emotion.

Dumas. The nearest approach to filling this need is provided by Georges Dumas.[27] He brings together not only the partial theories of Head, Cannon, and Darwin, but adds to these the serviceable part of the work of the psychophysiologist. Many a lacuna in the total picture, furthermore, is filled in by interpretations based upon his own experiments.

With respect to feeling, Dumas starts out by distinguishing pleasantness and unpleasantness (*agréable et désa-*

---

[27] G. Dumas, *La tristesse et la joie,* Paris, 1900; *Nouveau traité de psychologie,* edited by G. Dumas, Vol. II, Paris, 1932, Book III, 221–443; Vol. III, Paris, 1933, Book II, 41–292.

gréable) from pleasure and pain (*plaisir et douleur*). The former are not sensory, the latter are so, though not in an epicritic sense.

Of pleasantness and unpleasantness, Dumas feels, little can be said. All the attempts to discover their physiological concomitants have failed. His theory reduces really to the assertion that there is in the organism a special function related to preferential choice, distinct from the (sensory) mechanisms of pain and pleasure, and to the suggestion that the centers involved are in all likelihood thalamic.

Of pleasure and pain, on the other hand, especially of the latter, Dumas has much to say. Both are essentially forms of somesthetic sensitivity: " It is through organic sensibility that we enjoy, as it is through it that we suffer. There is only pain of the skin, of the membranes, of the coverings of organs, of the muscular-tendinous masses, etc.; there is not even pleasure, despite the affective complexity which distinguishes pleasure from pain, except in the domain of the stomach, of the buccal-pharyngeal region, of the sexual organs, of the muscular-tendinous masses, etc." As to the specific mechanisms, Dumas is particularly detailed in regard to pain. Following Pieron,[28] he combines the theories of both von Frey and Goldscheider. Pain may be either the primary consequence of excitation of a *special interoceptive* sensory system, or the consequence of *strong stimulation of any interoceptive* sensory system or of a particular exteroceptive system, namely that for prick. In all cases, it is mediated directly by the thalamus. The visceral expressions of weak pain are acceleratory (e.g., increased heart rate) via sympathetic dominance, except in the case of prolonged stimulation resulting in exhaus-

[28] H. Piéron, " La dynamogénie émotionelle," *J. de Psychol.*, XVII (1920), 937–945; *Le cerveau et la pensée*, Paris, 1923 (Eng. transl. by C. K. Ogden, London, 1927).

tion. The visceral expressions of very violent pain are inhibitory (e.g., decreased heart rate), via parasympathetic
dominance. As to the expression of pain in the striped
musculature, it involves primarily contractions which en-
able the organism to exert an effort. In the hands such contractions take the form of clenching of the fists. In the face
they take the form of the grimace of pain produced by opposition of antagonists. These contractions involving effort are, Dumas believes, true defense reactions. He cites
evidence that they raise the threshold both of pain and of
such expressions of pain as the enlargement of the pupil.

As to pleasure, Dumas believes that it involves a neural
mechanism much like that of pain, although ignorance prevents us from specifying it exactly. It is likewise largely interoceptive and mediated by the thalamus. One peculiarity,
however, distinguishes it from the mechanism of pain. It
is markedly dependent upon prior emotional conditions.
Thus there can be no lust during fear. This fact indicates,
Dumas believes, that the mechanism of pleasure is more
developed in an evolutionary sense. Dumas considers lust
(*volupté*) to be the prototype of pleasure, though there are
other forms, such as the pleasures of eating, drinking, and
tickling. Pleasure, like pain, has bodily expressions, acceleratory for weak pleasures, inhibitory for strong ones.
Its expression in the face is closely related to the smile, involving, as it does, a general lifting of the features. This
effect Dumas explains in terms of Spencer's principle of
least resistance: the smile is the " easiest reaction of the
face "; it involves synergic muscles, muscles which help
each other. It is thus the natural consequence of a moderate
excitation of the facial nerves.

It is with respect to emotion that Dumas most clearly
shows himself to be a biological psychologist, one con-

cerned with basic functions of the organism. Although Cannon deals with emotions as functions of the organism, he is wont to use the term emotion as equivalent to conscious emotion. Dumas not only deals with emotions as general organic functions but, following the example set by Ribot, formally defines them accordingly. They are " complex states, composed psychologically of tendencies which are excited, slowed down, impeded, enhanced, revolted, etc., sometimes complicated by impulsions, as in anger, anxiety, fear, always accompanied by organic modifications some of which seem to be localized, others diffuse, and by a corresponding conscious state which may, according to circumstances be pleasant, unpleasant, or mixed."

Dumas accepts Cannon's theory as a nucleus for his own theory of emotions. This is all the more a compliment to Cannon because Dumas introduced James' theory to French psychologists and long was one of its staunch advocates. Not only is the theory of Dumas, however, far larger in scope than Cannon's, but it involves certain definite qualifications of the latter theory.

In the first place, following Ribot, Dumas distinguishes *emotional shocks* from *emotions* proper, although he admits that the two can often be separated only by abstraction. The emotional shock is essentially a clash between the momentary trend of thought and action and some new and incongruent event. An example is the " shock " felt as one scans the list of death notices and suddenly finds the name of some friend whom one thought to be perfectly well. The emotion, on the other hand, is the consequence of such a clash. Dumas distinguishes three magnitudes of emotional shocks. *Minor shocks,* such as the reaction to the slamming of a door or to the firing of a gun, are essentially excitatory. They involve excitation of the sympathetic system strong enough to accelerate the bodily changes under the positive influence of this system, but not strong enough to inhibit processes under the positive dominance of the parasympathetic system — e.g., digestive secretions.[29] These minor shocks do not develop into emotions proper. They are essentially surprise reactions. *Medium shocks,* such as the reaction to the sudden appearance of a real danger, involve in the main the excitation of the sympathetic system to a sufficient degree to bring about not only its acceleratory effects, but also inhibitory ones, thus producing the picture of bodily changes so well demonstrated by Cannon. It is medium shocks which are the usual forerunners of the so-called *major* emotions — fear, anger, etc. Indeed, these shocks are so closely bound up with the consequent emotions that the two are not distinguished in usual parlance. *Major shocks,* finally, such as the reactions to a shell exploding among neighboring soldiers in a trench, involve either bodily responses of extreme excitation, markedly lacking in co-ordination, or, on the contrary, a state of bodily collapse. The former Dumas interprets as due largely to overflow of excitation of the sympathetic system; the latter, which occurs only under conditions of extreme stimulation, as a generalized inhibition. Like medium shocks, major ones are followed by emotions proper, the most frequent being fear, but the violence of the shock and the disorder of its manifestations frequently obscures the consequent emotion.

With respect to the conscious side of emotional shock, Dumas seems to accept a Jamesian view. " We have no need to say that the emotional shock, considered from the

---

[29] Cf. C. Kling, " The Role of the Parasympathetics in Emotion," *Psychol. Rev.*, XL (1933), 368–380.

conscious side, is but the grouping of the precise or confused sensations which correspond to the local or general
reactions which constitute physical manifestations; and
that it suffices, in order to make the synthesis of the psychical shock, to enumerate and put in order, among the
preceding reactions, those which are conscious." Should
we stress this passage, we would have to say that Dumas
represented a combination of the theories of James and
Cannon. I feel, however, that this is merely a remnant of
his earlier view, left by oversight in his newer work.

With respect to emotions proper — the phase of emotion
following the shock — Dumas accepts Cannon's general
view that the specific emotional quality is not awareness of
bodily movements but rather an awareness of neural activity in the region of the thalamus. This neural activity, he
agrees, results on the one hand in conduction of impulses
to the cortex, giving rise to the "*proprum quid*" of conscious emotion, and on the other hand in conduction of impulses to the viscera and skeletal muscles, giving rise to the
expression of emotions. In matters of detail, however,
Dumas frequently disagrees with Cannon. To begin with,
Dumas feels that the term emotion, as used by Cannon,
covers too limited a field. Besides the emotions recognized
by Cannon, which Dumas calls active emotions, he recognizes passive emotions, such as passive sorrow. The *active
emotions* are indeed characterized by marked sympathetic
excitation. The *passive emotions* may be characterized by
excitation which, because of its excessive character, produces inhibitory symptoms, but they may also involve lack
of excitation due to diminution of normal peripheral stimulation, or exhaustion due to excessive cerebral emotional
activity. Furthermore, Dumas believes that there are, besides these *major emotions,* certain *minor emotions* which

involve the mechanisms of feeling primarily, to which are added patterns of reaction in the smooth and striate musculature which do not have specific centers.

Even in the case of active emotions Dumas thinks that Cannon's description is somewhat schematic. Besides the *general mechanism* provoking qualitative changes in the diffuse activity of the sympathetic system there are a number of additional *specific mechanisms* whose nature is at present not fully understood. Many of these mechanisms, Dumas thinks, are manifestations of the *principle of overflow* — of " derivation," as he calls it — which goes back to Herbert Spencer. (This is reminiscent of Freud's view that in hysteria anxiety and overt symptoms are alternatives.) Laughter, he points out, consists essentially of clonic contractions of the expiratory muscles. What causes them? In the laughter of joy it is a sudden increase in excitation which thus overflows. In the laughter of humor it is excitation involved in such activities as attention which, upon sudden cessation of need for attention, overflows into the expiratory centers. The same mechanism, Dumas believes, is responsible for the laughter of tickle, the excitation originating in this case from masses of sense organs in the ligaments and tendons. Sobbing, for Dumas, is quite similar physiologically to laughter. Here also there are clonic expiratory contractions though also some inspiratory contractions. Both are induced by overflow of emotional excitement incapable of finding an outlet in movements of anger and violence (sobbing, Dumas points out, involves an element of resignation — inhibition). Weeping also is due to overflow of excitation devoid of a motor outlet. It differs from sobbing in that it is not as subject to voluntary inhibition. Thus as an alternative to emotional action the child both sobs and weeps, the adult only weeps. The mechanism of derivation is also at the basis of emotional sweating and blushing. Not all excitatory emotions involve these bodily changes. They occur only in certain fears, in embarrassment, and in shame, where motor inhibition is manifest.

As to the direction which overflow of excitation takes, it is determined very largely, Dumas thinks, by the principle of *ease of movement* (Spencer's third law of diffuse discharge): All other things being equal, the smaller muscles and those with the least load will react more readily. Another important principle applying to direction of overflow is that of *proximity to exciting centers*. Dumas cites evidence that sweating, blushing, and gooseflesh progress from the head and neck downward. This he explains in terms of the greater number of synapses in the sympathetic system as the innervated organs become more distinct from the centers in the region of the thalamus.

An important consequence of this amplification of Cannon's view is Dumas' conviction that different emotions do *not* have identical forms of expression, even visceral. " Each definite emotion, be it active or passive, involves a sort of physiological regimen, now stable, now unstable, now fleeting, now durable, but sufficiently specific to avoid its being mistaken for that of another emotion. If for each emotion one adds to circulatory differentiations those yielded by temperature, by dynamometric force, by respiratory and urinary eliminations, one obtains, it would seem, elements of differentiation adequate to individualize organically the active or passive forms of the emotions in question."

Special Problems. Contributions to the physiological organic theory are by no means limited to the work of Head, Cannon, and Dumas. These men, especially the last two, are merely the outstanding systematists in the field. Besides them, a large number of investigators have made valuable theoretical contributions with respect to special problems. Indeed, it is the quality and scope of this specialized theoretical literature which yields the greatest proof of the inherent soundness of the physiological organic point of view.

One special problem which has received considerable attention is that concerning the nature of the central conduction giving rise to emotional bodily responses. The older view assumed a sort of overflow. L. Lapicque [30] in 1911 applied his concept of chronaxy to the interpretation of this overflow. The sympathetic and cerebro-spinal systems, he points out, differ greatly in the order of their chronaxies (1/10 sec. and 1/1000 sec., respectively). Under normal conditions of excitation, difference of chronaxy prevents excitation of the one by the other — except by certain definite paths involving gradual changes of chronaxy. With high intensity and summation, however, interaction of the two systems occurs over paths not involving graduated changes in chronaxies — there is an " overflow " from the cerebro-spinal to the sympathetic systems. Piéron [31] also favors a view of this type, though he believes that " overflow " occurs only in animals having a well-developed nervous system, and then only in intense emotions. Interesting experimental developments of Lapicque's theory have been made by Bourguignon [32] and his followers. [33] More recently, the notion of " overflow " has been displaced by that of " decrease of cortical inhibition." This notion is

[30] L. Lapicque, " Essai d'une nouvelle théorie de l'émotion," *J. de Psychol.*, VIII (1911), 1–8.
[31] Cf. footnote 28.
[32] G. Bourguignon, *La chronaxie chez l'homme*, Paris, 1923.
[33] Cf. J. Mazurkiewicz, " Deux ordres d'émotivité au cycle de la vie humaine, définis par les résultats de recherches sur la chronaxie vestibulaire," *Arch. Internat. de Neurologie*, 27e série, 54e année (mars, 1935), iv–xiii.

present in the general theories of Head and Cannon, although not much stressed. It has been emphasized recently by Darrow,[34] who believes that in excited emotions there is removal of cortical inhibition of lower centers by conflict within the cortex.

Another problem to receive much attention is that of the neural motor mechanisms involved in emotional expression. A first feature of this problem concerns the role of learning in the formation of such mechanisms. The older view minimized this role.[35] Watson emphasized it. In recent literature, Landis [36] stands for a relatively large participation of learning, Bard,[37] for a relatively slight one. A second feature of this problem concerns the relative prominence of various responses in the emotional syndrome. The recent literature abounds in divergent estimates of various objective emotional indices.[38] At present the trend seems to favor circulatory changes.

A third problem, finally, has been discussed extensively among psychiatrists with a neurological bias, particularly in France. It is the problem of autonomic types. In 1910, H. Eppinger and L. Hess [39] correlated *vagotonia*, i.e., the hyperexcitability of the parasympathetic division of the autonomic nervous system, with certain neurotic pecu-

[34] C. W. Darrow, " Emotion as Functional Decortication : the Role of Conflict," *Psychol. Rev.*, XLII (1935), 566–578.

[35] Cf. G. W. Crile, *The Origin and Nature of the Emotions,* Philadelphia and London, 1915.

[36] C. Landis, " Emotion, II : The Expressions of Emotions," in *A Handbook of General Experimental Psychology,* Worcester, 1934, 312–351 ; *Emotion, in Psychology, A Factual Textbook,* by E. G. Boring, H. S. Langfeld, H. P. Weld *et al.,* New York, 1935, 397–419.

[37] P. Bard, " On Emotional Expression after Decortication, with Some Remarks on Certain Theoretical Views," *Psychol. Rev.,* XLI (1934), 309–329, 424–449.

[38] Cf. Landis, *op. cit.;* H. F. Dunbar, *Emotions and Bodily Changes,* New York, 1935.

[39] H. Eppinger and L. Hess, *Vagotonia, Nervous and Mental Disease Monographs, Ser.,* No. 20, New York and Washington, 1917 (original in German in 1910).

liarities. They further contrasted it with *sympathicotonia*. This line of thought has been developed along both clinical and physiological lines by H. Claude and D. Santenoise,[40] who have adduced evidence for the correlations between autonomic tonicity and mental disorders indicated in the following table. (The middle row of the table indicates the clinical indices of the various autonomic conditions which the authors consider the most reliable.) The detailed nature of these correlations suggests, according to Santenoise,[41] the hypothesis that "organic-vegetative disturbances may play a part in the genesis of certain psychopathic states." This hypothesis, in turn, has led him to physiological investigations seeking to define experimentally both the causes and the effects of autonomic hyper- and hypo- tonicity. A first step in this direction is his recent demonstration that the pancreas secretes a hormone necessary to the maintenance of the tonus of the vagus, and further, that pneumogastric excitation through thyroid secretion plays an important role in cellular metabolism.[42]

CONCLUSION

The trend displayed by the theory of feeling and emotion since the turn of the century is unmistakable. At the beginning, the psychophysiological point of view, inherited from the previous century, is still preponderant. Theory is essen-

[40] H. Claude, D. Santenoise and R. Targowla, " An Attempt at a Biologic Diagnosis of States of Excitement and Depression," *Arch. of Neurol. and Psychiatry*, XIII (1925), 729–742.

[41] D. Santenoise, " Système organo-végétatif et psychoses fonctionelles," *Encephale*, XXII (1927), 554–561 ; *Pneumogastrique et glandes endocrines*, Paris, 1927.

[42] Cf. also M. Laignel-Lavastine, *The Concentric Method in the Diagnosis of Psychoneurotics*, London and New York, 1931. For a good review of the whole problem, cf. A. Ferraro, " Importance of Vegetative Nervous System in Mental Disorders," *Psychiatric Quarterly*, III (1929), 330; for its early history cf. W. H. Veil, Vagotonie und Sympathikotonie, *Deutsche mediz. Wochenschrift*, L, 1 (1924), 511–513.

TABLE FROM CLAUDE, SANTENOISE AND TARGOWLA *

Schematic Presentation of Psychoses According to Neurovegetative Reactions

Vagotonia	Sympathicotonia	Neurotonia Vagotonia + Sympathicotonia	Normal Neurovegetative Reactions	Hyponeurotonia		
				Temporary	Modifiable	Irreducible
Oculocardiac reflex = + Solar reflex = 0 Sharp reactions to eserin and pilocarpin Tolerance to atropin Tolerance to glucose	Oculocardiac reflex = 0 Solar reflex = 0 Sharp reactions to suprarenal extract and atropin Weak tolerance to glucose	Oculocardiac reflex = + Solar reflex = +		Oculocardiac reflex = 0 Solar reflex = 0 or + Appear after a few days	Oculocardiac reflex = 0 Solar reflex = 0 Appear after use of certain pharmacodynamic agents	Oculocardiac reflex = 0 Solar reflex = 0 Nothing modifies this state
Manic-depressive { Mania, Depression	Emotionally unstable	Degenerates Outbursts of delirium	Various systematized delusional states	Intoxication psychoses		Prolonged asthenia
Mixed states	Mania with anger Affective melancholia Emotionally unstable with anxiety Emotive confusion	Obsessions Impulses Intermittent instinctive perversions Toxicomaniacs			Temporary asthenia	
Epilepsy { Convulsive attacks; Equivalents { Excitation, Depression }						Dementia praecox

* Cf. footnote 40.

tially the specification of a correlation between consciousness and the physiological organism. Reaction against this view, however, is already apparent at the close of the preceding century, with the stressing of the epiphenomenal nature of consciousness. By about 1910, behaviorism, which resolutely turns its back on consciousness, develops. The theory of feeling and emotion becomes a matter of correlating forms of behavior with processes within the organism. Behaviorism, however, is not the only development from epiphenomenalism. Parallel with behaviorism there develops what I have called the organic point of view, for which the locus of psychological theory is a real, permanent organism, whether mental, as for Freud and McDougall, or physical, as for Cannon and Dumas. The theory of feeling and emotion here becomes a matter of organic function, of correlation (and causation) *within* the organism, not between it and an external realm of consciousness or behavior. At the time of writing it seems that this third point of view is still growing rapidly, although behaviorism has long passed its zenith. *The* modern theory of feeling and emotion is the organic theory.

The trend is plain. Its interpretation is not. Many forces have obviously been at work. To try to specify the main ones is hazardous. We may venture, however, to present our own convictions. A scientific theory is a description of causal interrelations. Psychophysiological correlations are not causal. Thus in scientific theories, psychophysiological correlations are monstrosities. This does not mean that such correlations have no part in science. They are the instruments by which the psychologist may test his theories. They cannot, however, be a part of his theories. The same is true, I believe, of correlations between behavior and the organism. " Angry " behavior is just as much of an epiphe-

nomenon, of a non-causal entity, as " angry " consciousness, and thus belongs as little in a scientific theory. None
the less, its correlation with some organic event is an admirable instrument for the development of a scientific psychological theory. Theories such as those which we have
termed organic, on the other hand, consisting essentially
of relationships within a causal system, namely the real,
permanent organism, are obviously satisfactory from a scientific point of view. If these considerations are correct, the
trend in theories of feeling and emotion during the last
third of a century represents a distinct progress.[43]

[43] In connection with this general point of view cf. E. G. Boring, *The
Physical Dimensions of Consciousness*, New York and London, 1933.

BIBLIOGRAPHY

Petrus Abelardus, *Ethica, scito te ipsum,* III, in J. P. Migne, *Patrologiae cursus completus, series latina* (Paris, 1855), CLXXVIII, 636 f.

Aetius, *Opera* (translated by Cornarius, Basel, 1542), IV, 21, 4.

Albertus Magnus, *Ethica; Opera omnia* (ed. Borguet, Paris, 1890), VII, 260; III, 3, 2 f.; V, 3, 6, 61.

——, *Summae de creaturis,* Q. 66, 1; Q. 67, 1; *Opera omnia* (ed. Borguet, Paris, 1890), XXXV, 554, 557.

——, *Parva naturalia,* Tract. I and II; *Opera omnia* (ed. Borguet, Paris, 1890), IX, 1 f.

——, *Summa theologiae,* II, 5, Q. 25; *Opera omnia* (ed. Borguet, Paris, 1890), XXXII, 269 f.

C. Albrich, "Leibnitz's Lehre vom Gefühl," *Archiv für die gesamte Psychologie* (1910), XVI, 1 f.

Alcher of Clairvaux, *De spiritu et anima,* IV, XXI, XXVI, in J. P. Migne, *Patrologiae cursus completus, series latina* (Paris, 1887), XL, 781–798.

J. le R. d'Alembert, *Essai sur les éléments de philosophie,* sec. VIII (*Œuvres,* Paris, 1759), II, 68.

Alexander of Aphrodisias, *Commentaries in Aristotelis Topica* (ed. Aldus, Venice, 1495), II, 96, 181.

Alfred Anglicus, *De motu cordis* in C. S. Barach, " Excerpta e libro Alfredi Anglici de motu cordis," *Bibliotheca philosophorum mediae-aetatis* (Innsbruck, 1878).

Grant Allen, *Physiological Aesthetics* (London, 1877).

F. H. Allport, *Social Psychology* (Cambridge, Mass., 1924), 84–98.

Anaxagoras, *Pseudo-Aristotelis de plantis* in *Aristoteles, Opera* (ed. Bekker, Berlin, 1831), II, 815 a 15 ff.

Andronicus of Rhodes, περὶ πάθῶν, *On the Passions,* 1, 11 in J. v. Arnim, *Stoicorum veterum fragmenta* (Leipzig, 1903), III, 96 ff.

Anonymous. *An Enquiry into the Origin of Human Appetites and Affections, Showing how Each Arises from Association* in S. Parr, *Metaphysical Tracts by English Philosophers of the Eighteenth Century* (London, 1837), 98 f.

Antisthenes, *Fragments* in Diogenes Laertius, *Lives of Eminent Philosophers* (translated by C. D. Yonge, London, 1848), VI, 3; IX, 101.

Aristotle, *De anima*, I, 1, 10; II, 3, 11; III, 2, 7. *De generatione animalium*, II, 3. *De memoria*, I. *De motu animalium*, 10. *De partibus animalium*, I, 4; II, 4 f. *De plantis*. *Ethica Eudemia*, II, 2, 7. *Ethica Nicomachea*, I–IV, VII, VIII, X. *Magna moralia*, I, 7, 8; II, 7. *Metaphysica*, I, 3; XI, 7. *Physica*, VII, 3. *Physiognomica*. *Poetica*, 6 f. *Politica*, I, 2, 12; III, 15; V, 11; VIII, 5, 7. *Problemata*, IV; XI, 31, 32; XXVII, 9. *Rhetorica*, I, 11; II, 1–12. *Topica*, IV, 5. *Aristoteles, Opera* (ed. Bekker, Academica Regia Borussica, Berlin, 1831), I–III.

——, *Nicomachean Ethics* (translated by F. H. Peters, London, 1881), X, 4–7.

A. C. Armstrong, " The Idea of Feeling in Rousseau's Religious Philosophy," *Archiv für die Geschichte der Philosophie* (1911), XXIV, 242–260.

Aspasius, *Aristotelis ethica Nicomachea*, 44, 12 in G. Heylbut, *Commentaria in Aristotelem graeca* (Berlin, 1889), XIX, 1.

——, *De passionibus* in Albertus Magnus, *Ethica*, III, 3, 2 f.; *Opera omnia* (ed. Borguet, Paris, 1890), VII, 260.

Augustine, *Confessiones*, I, III, IV, X in J. P. Migne, *Patrologiae cursus completus, series latina* (Paris, 1845), XXXII, 63, 162, 233, 788, 802.

——, *De civitate Dei*, IX, XIV in J. P. Migne, *Patrologiae cursus completus, series latina* (Paris, 1845), XLI, 255, 259, 381, 408.

——, *De genesi ad literam*, 7, 18 in J. P. Migne, *Patrologiae cursus completus, series latina* (Paris, 1841), XXXIV, 219 f.

——, *De trinitate*, IX, 8; X, 12; XII in J. P. Migne, *Patrologiae cursus completus, series latina* (Paris, 1845), XLII, 967, 984, 997–1042.

——, *Enarratio in psalmum*, XXXV, 13, 14; LXXIX, 17; LXXXV, 14–20 in J. P. Migne, *Patrologiae cursus completus, series latina* (Paris, 1865), XXXVI, 351; XXXVII, 1026, 1892 f.

F. Bacon, *Advancement of Learning*, Book II; Book VII, 2 f. (ed. Spedding, Boston, 1872), III, 437 f.; V, 20 f.

——, *Novum Organum* (ed. Fowler, Cambridge, 1878).

R. Bacon, *Opus majus*, Part VII (ed. Bridges, Oxford, 1897), II, 223 f.

A. Bain, *The Emotions and the Will* (London, 1859).

J. M. Baldwin, *Handbook of Psychology, Feeling, and Will* (New York, 1891).

P. Bard, " A Diencephalic Mechanism for the Expression of Rage, with Special Reference to the Sympathetic Nervous System," *American Journal of Physiology* (1928), LXXXIV, 490–515.

——, " Emotion, I: The Neuro-Humoral Basis of Emotional Reactions," *Handbook of General Experimental Psychology* (Worcester, 1934), 264–311.

——, " On Emotional Expression after Decortication, with Some Remarks on Certain Theoretical Views," *Psychological Review* (1934), XLI, 309–329, 424–449.

Basil the Great, *Epistolae*, CCLXI in *The Nicene and Post-Nicene Fathers* (ed. Wace and Schaff, New York, 1895), 2nd ser., VIII, 299.

J. I. Beare, *Greek Theories of Elementary Cognition* (Oxford, 1906), 212.

J. H. S. Beau, " Recherches cliniques sur l'anesthésie," *Archives générales de médecine* (1848), XXVI, 22, 4th series.

H. Beaunis, *Les sensations internes* (Paris, 1889).

W. Bechterew, *Archiv für pathologische Anatomie und Physiologie* (1887), CX, 102–154, 322–365.

——, " Emotions as Somato-Mimetic Reflexes in Feelings and Emotions," *The Wittenberg Symposium* (Worcester, 1928), 270–284.

——, *General Principles of Human Reflexology* (New York, 1932).

——, *Objective Psychologie* (Leipzig and Berlin, 1913).

J. G. Beebe-Center, *Pleasantness and Unpleasantness* (New York, 1932), 410–417.

Sir Charles Bell, *Anatomy and Physiology of Expression, as Connected with the Fine Arts* (London, 1816).

F. E. Beneke, *Lehrbuch der Psychologie als Naturwissenschaft* (Berlin, 1861).

A. W. Benn, " Aristotle's Theory of Tragic Emotion," *Mind*, N.S. (1914), XXIII, 84–90.

J. Bernays, *Grundzüge der verlorenen Abhandlung des Aristoteles über die Wirkung der Tragödie* (Breslau, 1858).

M. F. X. Bichat, *Recherches physiologiques sur la vie et la mort* (Paris, 1805).

J. Bock, *On the Heart* (Rotterdam, 1648).

Boethius, *De consolatione philosophiae*, I, 7 in J. P. Migne, *Patro-*

logiae cursus completus, series latina (Paris, 1847), LXIII, 552, 585.

J. Bonaventura, *Sententiae*, I–IV; *Opera* (ed. Franciscan, 1895).

H. Bonitz, *Index Aristotelicus*, κίνησις, κινοῦν, πάθος, πάθημα in *Aristoteles, Opera* (ed. Bekker, Academica Regia Borussica, Berlin, 1870), V.

C. Bonnet, *Essai analytique sur les facultés de l'âme* (Geneva, 1759), secs. 83, 116–121, 195, 350, 386, 400, 413, 546–547, 659.

——, *Essai de psychologie*, chap. LXV (London, 1754), 211 f.

——, " Essai d'application des principes psychologiques de l'auteur," *Palingénésie philosophique* (Geneva, 1769).

E. G. Boring, H. S. Langfeld, H. P. Weld, *et al.*, *Emotion in Psychology, A Factual Textbook* (New York, 1935), 397–419.

J. B. Bossuet, *De la connaissance de Dieu et de soi-même; Œuvres* (Paris, 1846), V, 20–110.

F. Bouiller, *Du plaisir et de la douleur* (Paris, 1865).

G. Bourguignon, *La chronaxie chez l'homme* (Paris, 1923).

F. Brentano, *Psychologie vom empirischen Standpunkt* (Leipzig, 1903).

V. Brochard, " La morale d'Épicure," *L'Année philosophique* (1903), XIV, 8–12.

T. Brown, *Lectures on the Philosophy of the Human Mind*, XVI, XVII, XXXII, LXV, LXX (London, 1860), 102–106, 213, 340, 428–475.

J. Burnet, *Early Greek Philosophy* (London, 1892), 36, 140.

J. Butler, *Fifteen Sermons*, Sermon VIII, sec. 12; *Works* (ed. Gladstone, Oxford, 1897), II, 120.

F. J. G. Cabanis, *Rapports du physique et du moral de l'homme* (Paris, 1799).

W. B. Cannon, " Again the James-Lange and the Thalamic Theories of Emotion," *Psychological Review* (1931), XXXVIII, 281–295.

——, *Bodily Changes in Pain, Hunger, Fear, and Rage* (New York and London, 1915).

——, " The Interrelations of Emotions as Suggested by Recent Physiological Researches," *American Journal of Psychology* (1914), XXV, 256–282.

——, " The James-Lange Theory of Emotions: a Critical Examination and an Alternative Theory," *American Journal of Psychology* (1927), XXXIX, 106–124.

——, "The Story of the Development of our Ideas of Chemical Mediation of Nerve Impulses," *American Journal of the Medical Sciences* (1934), CLXXXVIII, 145.

H. Cardanus, *De subtilitate*, XIII, XIV, in Sir William Hamilton, *Metaphysic*, XLIII, 458 f.

O. Cassmann, *Psychologia anthropologica* (Hanover, 1594), Part I, chap. XV, 311, 406; Part II, 63–121.

G. Cesca, "Die Lehre von der Natur der Gefühle," *Vierteljahrsschrift für wissenschaftliche Philosophie* (1886), X, 137–165.

A. E. Chaignet, *Histoire de la psychologie des Grecs* (Paris, 1887), II, 140–149.

Chalcidius, *Timaeus Platonis* (ed. Meursius, Leyden, 1617).

F. R. Chateaubriand, *Le génie du christianisme,* Books II, III, especially chap. IX; *Œuvres* (Paris, 1802), II, 208, 234.

Chrysippus, *On the Passions*, IV, 6; V, 2 in C. Galen, *De Hippocratis et Platonis placitis, Opera omnia* (ed. Kühn, *Medicorum graecorum opera,* Leipzig, 1821), V, 181 f., 404, 438, 444.

——, *On the Passions*. J. v. Arnim, *Stoicorum veterum fragmenta* (Leipzig, 1903), III, 120–123.

M. T. Cicero, *Fragmenta Academicorum posteriorum*, I, 38; *Opera* (ed. Baiter and Kayser, Leipzig, 1863), VI, 77–82.

——, *De finibus bonorum et malorum*, I, 56; III, 16, 31; *Opera* (ed. Baiter and Kayser, Leipzig, 1863), VI, 103, 157 f., 163.

——, *De oratione,* 2; *Opera* (ed. Baiter and Kayser, Leipzig, 1863), II, 59 f.

——, *Tusculanae disputationes,* II, 7; III, 75; IV, 6–47; *Opera* (ed. Baiter and Kayser, Leipzig, 1863), VI, 287–349.

S. Claramontius, *De conjectandis cuiusque moribus et habitantibus animi affectibus* (Helmstadt, 1665), 165.

H. Claude, D. Santenoise, and R. Targowla, "An Attempt at a Biologic Diagnosis of States of Excitement and Depression," *Archives of Neurology and Psychiatry* (1925), XIII, 729–742.

Cleanthes, *On Pleasure* in Diogenes Laertius, *Works* (translated by C. D. Yonge, London, 1848), VII, 175.

Clement of Alexandria, *Stromateis* (ed. Potter, Oxford, 1715), II, 460.

A. Comte, *Cours de philosophie positive* (Paris, 1893), III.

E. B. de Condillac, *Traité des sensations,* I–III, *Œuvres* (Paris, 1798), III, 70 f.

Constantine of Carthage, *Opera Constantini* (Basel, 1536), IV, 8, pp. 90 f.

E. M. Cope, *Introduction to Aristotle's Rhetoric* (Cambridge, 1867), App. D. to Book I; 234 f.; II, I, 8n.

H. Cornelius, *Psychologie als Erfahrungswissenschaft* (Leipzig, 1897).

Costa-ben-Luca, *De differentia animi et spiritus* in C. S. Barach, *Excerpta e libro Costa-ben Lucae de differentia animi et spiritus* (translated by Johannes Hispalensis, *Bibliotheca philosophorum mediae-aetatis*, Innsbruck, 1878).

V. Cousin, " Un fragment inédit de Pascal: discours sur la passion de l'amour," *Révue de deux mondes* (Sept., 1843), 990–1007.

L. Couturat, *La logique de Leibnitz d'après des documents inédits* (Paris, 1901), 567.

G. W. Crile, *The Origin and Nature of the Emotions* (Philadelphia and London, 1915).

Hjalmar Crobus, " Zur Geschichte der Liebe als Krankheit," *Archiv für Kulturgeschichte* (1905), III, 66–86.

C. A. Crusius, *Anweisung vernünftig zu leben* (Leipzig, 1774), 24–27.

C. W. Darrow, " Emotion as Functional Decortication: the Role of Conflict," *Psychological Review* (1935), XLII, 566–578.

Charles Darwin, *The Expression of the Emotions in Man and Animals* (New York, 1890).

J. R. L. Delbœuf, *Éléments de psychophysie* (Liége, 1883).

Delisle de Sales, *De la philosophie de la nature*, Book I, Part II, chap. XII; *Œuvres* (Paris, 1804), IV, 100–172.

T. Dembo, " Der Ärger als dynamisches Problem," *Psychologische Forschung* (1931), XV, 1–144.

Democritus, *Fragmenta*, 6, 15, 17, 31, 105, 191, 235, 387, in H. Diels, *Die Fragmente der Vorsokratiker* (Berlin, 1903), I, 384–447, 470.

——, *Fragmenta* in H. Diels, *Doxographi graeci* (Berlin, 1879), 390–391.

——, *Fragmenta ethica*, 1, 17, 20, 31, 191, 235 in F. W. A. Mullach, *Fragmenta philosophorum graecorum* (Paris, 1860), I, 340 f., 348, 355.

——, in Theophrastus, *De sensu*, 58; *Opera* (ed. Schneider, Leipzig, 1818), I, 670.

—— in E. Zeller, *Die Philosophie der Griechen* (Tübingen, 1844), I, 809.

R. Descartes, *Epistolae* (Amsterdam, 1650), I, 6, 8, 11, 84.

——, *Les passions de l'âme; Œuvres* (ed. Cousin, Paris, 1825), I, 7–50; II, 51, 52, 68–70, 86, 93, 102–147; III, 211–212.

——, *Les lettres*, I, 8, 11, 84, *Œuvres* (ed. Cousin, Paris, 1825), IX, 242 f., 381, 413.

——, *Principia philosophiae* (Amsterdam, 1644), IV, 190.

——, *Tractatus de homine* (Amsterdam, 1677), I, 14, 56; IV, 56–61.

——, *Traité de l'homme; Œuvres* (ed. Cousin, Paris, 1824), IV, 335–428.

M. Dessoir, *Geschichte der neueren deutschen Psychologie* (Berlin, 1894), 181–185, 200, 252 f.

A. L. C. Destutt de Tracy, *Éléments d'idéologie, première partie, idéologie proprement dite* (Paris, 1801).

J. Dewey, " The Significance of Emotions," *Psychological Review* (1894), I, 13–32.

——, " The Theory of Emotion, Emotional Attitudes," *Psychological Review* (1894), I, 553–569.

F. Dieterici, *Die Philosophie der Araber im zehnten Jahrhundert* (Leipzig, 1871), VII, 14, 37.

Diogenes of Apollonia *Fragmenta* in Theophrastus, *De sensu*, 43; *Opera* (ed. Schneider, Leipzig, 1818), I, 664.

Diogenes Laertius, *Works* (translated by C. D. Yonge, London, 1848), II, 85–90; VI, 3; VII, 4, 110–178; IX, 8, 101; X, 28–175.

Dionysius Areopagita, *De divinis nominibus,* II, 9, in Thomas Aquinas, *Summa Theologica,* Q. XXII, A 3, prima secundae partis; *Opera* (Paris, 1871), II, 205.

Dionysius Heracleota, *On Pleasure* in Diogenes Laertius, *Works* (translated by C. D. Yonge, London, 1848), VII, 167.

B. Domanski, *Die Psychologie des Nemesius* in *Beiträge zur Geschichte der Philosophie des Mittelalters,* III (ed. Baumker und Hertling, Munster, 1893).

J. B. Du Bos, *Réflexions critiques sur la poésie et sur la peinture* (Paris, 1719), I, secs. 1, 2.

T. Duboscq, " Les émotions d'après St. Thomas," *Annales de philosophie chrétienne* (1915), N.S. XXXIV 15–25, 169–183.

G. B. Duchenne (de Boulogne), *Mécanisme de la physiognomie humaine* (Paris, 1862).

G. Dumas, *La tristesse et la joie* (Paris, 1900).

——, *Nouveau traité de psychologie* (ed. Dumas, Paris, 1933), II, Book 3, 221–443; III, Book 2, 41–292.

L. Dumont, *Théorie scientifique de la sensibilité* (Paris, 1875).

H. F. Dunbar, *Emotions and Bodily Changes* (New York, 1935).

J. Duns Scotus, *Quaestiones supra libros Aristotelis de anima*, sec. VIII, Dist. 2, *Opera* (ed. Vives, Paris, 1891), III, 693 f.

——, *Reportata Parisiensia*, III, d. 26, Scholia, *Opera* (ed. Wadding, Lyons, 1639), XI.

C. L. Duprat, " La psycho-physiologie des passions dans la philosophie ancienne," *Archiv für die Geschichte der Philosophie* (1905), XVIII, 395–412.

J. A. Eberhard, *Allgemeine Theorie des Denkens und Empfindens* (Berlin, 1786), 33 f.

Empedocles, *Fragmenta* in H. Ritter and L. Preller, *Historia Philosophiae Graeco-Romanae* (Gotha, 1888), III, 139.

Epicurus, *Opera* in Diogenes Laertius, *Works* (translated by C. D. Yonge, London, 1848), X, 28–175.

——, *Letters* in R. B. Hicks, *Stoic and Epicurean* (New York, 1910), 172, 275.

——, *Epicurea* (ed. Usener, Leipzig, 1887), 143.

Epiphanius, *Adversus haereses*, III, 2, 9 in J. P. Migne, *Patrologiae cursus completus, series graeca* (Paris, 1858), XXIII, 909, 975.

H. Eppinger, and L. Hess, " Vagotonia," *Nervous and Mental Disease Monographs Series* (New York and Washington, 1917), XX.

M. Equicola, *Libro di natura d'amore* (Venice, 1526), Books I–VI.

J. S. Ersch and J. G. Gruber, *Allgemeine Encyklopädie*, " Gefühl " (Leipzig, 1818).

Eusebius, *Praeparatio evangelica* (ed. Gaisford, Oxford, 1843), XIV, 18; XV, 20, 21.

B. Eustachius, *Opuscula anatomica* (Venice, 1564).

J. R. Fabri, *Cursus physicus* (Geneva, 1625).

G. T. Fechner, *Einige Ideen zur Schöpfungs- und Entwichelungsgeschichte der Organismen* (Leipzig, 1873).

——, *Vorschule der Aesthetik* (Leipzig, 1876).

J. G. H. Fedei, *Grundriss der philosophischen Wissenschaft* (Coburg, 1767).

O. Fenichel, *Outline of Clinical Psychoanalysis* (New York, 1934), 46–69.

A. Ferraro, " Importance of Vegetative Nervous System in Mental Disorders," *Psychiatric Quarterly* (1929), III, 330.

M. Ficino, *De voluptate;* 2. *Opera* (Paris, 1541), I, 1010–1036, 1039.

P. Flourens, *De la vie et de l'intelligence* (Paris, 1859).

L. De la Forge, *Traité de l'esprit de l'homme* (Paris, 1666).

Fracastorius Hieronymus, *De sympathia et antipathia rerum* (Venice, 1546), chap. 20.

S. Freud, *A General Introduction to Psychoanalysis* (New York, 1920), 340–355.

——, *Beyond the Pleasure Principle* (New York, 1924).

——, *New Introductory Lectures on Psychoanalysis* (New York, 1933), 113–152.

E. Friedrichs, *Platons Lehre von der Lust im Gorgias und Philebus* (Halle, 1890), I, D.

C. Galen, *De Hippocratis et Platonis Placitis*, II, 8; IV, 6, 7; V, 2. *Opera omnia* (ed. Kühn, *Medicorum graecorum opera*, Leipzig, 1821), V, 181, 273, 360, 404–444.

F. J. Gall, *On the Functions of the Brain and of Each of its Parts* (translated by W. Lewis, Boston, 1835).

J. Gardair, *Philosophie de St. Thomas, les passions et la volonté* (Paris, 1892), 60 f., 125 f.

J. B. Gay, *Essay on the Fundamental Principles of Virtue and Morality* in D. Hartley, *Observations on Man* (London, 1801), Preface.

Aulus Gellius, *Noctes Atticae* (ed. Lion, Göttingen, 1825), XIX, I, 592.

J. Gerson, *Mystica theologia*, 9, 13, 15, 21, *Opera.* (ed. du Pin, Antwerp, 1706).

——, *Mystica theologia*, 15 in A. Stöckl, *Geschichte der Philosophie des Mittelalters* (Mainz, 1864), II, 1090.

B. I. Gilman, " The Psychology of Pain and Pleasure," *American Journal of Psychology* (1893), VI, 1–60.

T. Gomperz, *Griechische Denker* (Leipzig, 1893), III, 336.

B. Gracian, *L'homme de cour* (Paris, 1685).

T. H. Green, *Introduction to Hume*, II, secs. 39–42, *Works* (London, 1885), I.

Gregory of Nyssa, *De anima et resurrectione,* 56, XXV, 115–180; and *de hominis opificio,* 12, 18, XXIV, 107, 125, in J. P. Migne, *Patrologiae cursus completus, series graeca* (Paris, 1859).

G. Grote, *Plato and Other Companions of Socrates* (London, 1867), II, 561, 569, 574.

Sir William Hamilton, *Lectures on Metaphysics and Logic* (ed. Mansel and Veitch, London, 1861), II, Lecture XLI–XLIII, 414–475.

P. Hartenberg, " La peur et le mécanisme des émotions," *Revue philosophique* (1899), XLVIII, 113–134.

D. Hartley, *Conjecturae quaedam de sensu, motus et idearum generatione,* Prop. 5 and 6 in S. Parr, *Metaphysical Tracts by English Philosophers of the Eighteenth Century* (London, 1837), 60 f.

" David Hartley," *Encyclopedia Britannica* (9th edition, 1875).

——, *Observations on Man* (London, 1801), Pref.; Part I, chap. I, sec. 2; chap. III, sec. 3, Prop. lxxxix; chap. IV, sec. 6; Part II, chap. I, Prop. iv; chap. III, sec. 7, Prop. lxxi.

——, *Theory of the Human Mind* (ed. Priestley, London, 1775), II, III.

E. von Hartmann, *Philosophie des Unbewussten* (Berlin, 1868).

W. Harvey, *Exercitatio anatomica de motu cordis et sanguinis* (Frankfort, 1628).

K. H. Haydenreich, *Aufsätze in Cäsars Denkwürdigkeiten* (Berlin, 1787), 161–164.

H. Head and G. Holmes, " Sensory Disturbances from Cerebral Lesions," *Brain* (1911), XXXIV, 102–254.

Hecato, *On the Passions* in Diogenes Laertius, *Works* (translated by C. D. Yonge, London, 1848), VII, 110.

C. A. Helvétius, *De l'esprit,* Disc. III, 5 f., *Œuvres* (Paris, 1818), I, 265 f.

——, *De l'homme, de ses facultés intellectuelles, et de son éducation;* I. *Œuvres* (Paris, 1818), II, 202 f.

——, *Épître sur l'orgueil; Œuvres* (Paris, 1818), III.

Henricus Gandovensis, *Quodlibeta theologica* (Venice, 1613), VIII, Q. 15; XI, Q. 8, 9; II, 36 f., 205–210.

Heraclitus, *Fragmente,* 77, 117, 118 in H. Diels, *Die Fragmente der Vorsokratiker* (Berlin, 1903), 58 f., 73, 78.

J. F. Herbart, *Lehrbuch zur Psychologie* (Königsberg and Leipzig, 1816).

Herillus, *Of the Passions* in Diogenes Laertius, *Works* (translated by C. D. Yonge, London, 1848), VII, 166.

R. D. Hicks, *Aristotle's De Anima* (Cambridge, 1908), lxxii.

——, *Stoic and Epicurean* (New York, 1910), 102 f., 172, 275.

——, " Stoics," *Encyclopedia Britannica* (9th edition, 1875).

Hippocrates, *Ancient Medicine* (*Genuine Works of Hippocrates* (ed. Adams, London, 1849), I, 171–174.

——, *De flatibus*, VI, 3; *Opera* (ed. Kühn, *Medicorum graecorum opera*, XXI, Leipzig, 1825), I, 569 f.

——, *De natura hominis; Opera* (ed. Kühn, *Medicorum graecorum opera*, XXI, Leipzig, 1825), I, 348–371.

——, *De salubri victus ratione; Opera* (ed. Kühn, *Medicorum graecorum opera*, XXI, Leipzig, 1825), I, 616–666.

——, *Œuvres complètes d'Hippocrate* (translated by E. Littré, Paris, 1839), I, 444.

——, *The Sacred Disease, Genuine Works of Hippocrates* (ed. Adams, London, 1849), II, 855, 856.

M. Hissmann, *Geschichte der Lehre von der Associationen der Ideen* (Göttingen, 1777), 95.

——, *Psychologische Versuche* (Göttingen, 1788), 98.

T. Hobbes, *De corpore politico*, II, 5; IV, 25; *Works* (ed. Molesworth, London, 1839), English Works, I, 389–409; Latin Works, I, 331–389.

——, *De homine*, sec. II, chaps. 11–13; *Works* (ed. Molesworth, London, 1839), Latin Works, II, 94–118.

——, *Human Nature*, chaps. 5–10; *Works* (ed. Molesworth, London, 1839), English Works, IV, 25–59.

——, *The Elements of Law, Natural and Politic,* Part I, chap. 9 (ed. Tönnies, London, 1889), 47, 182, 208 f.

——, *Leviathan*, Part I, chaps. 3–13; Part II, chaps. 17, 25, 31; *Works* (ed. Molesworth, London, 1839), English Works, III, 12–116, 153–352.

——, *Physics*, IV, 25, sec. 13; *Works* (ed. Molesworth, London, 1839), English Works, I, 409 f.

J. C. Hoffbauer, *Naturlehre der Seele* (Halle, 1796), 225, 240, 255.

H. Home, *Elements of Criticism,* chaps. II, XII–XVII (Edinburgh, 1785), 33–194, 366–509.

A. Horwicz, *Psychologische Analysen* (Magdeburg, 1878), II, 2.

Hugo of Saint Victor, *De sacramentis,* I, 7, 11 in J. P. Migne,

Patrologiae cursus completus, series latina (Paris, 1880), CLXXVI.

——, *De anima*, II in J. P. Migne, *Patrologiae cursus completus, series latina* (Paris, 1880), CLXXVI.

D. Hume, *Dissertation on the Passions; Essays Moral, Political, and Literary* (ed. Green and Gross, London, 1875), II, 139–166.

——, *Of the Delicacy of Taste and Passion; Essays Moral, Political, and Literary* (ed. Green and Gross, London, 1875), I.

——, *Treatise of Human Nature*, Book II (ed. Green and Gross, London, 1739), 75–228.

F. Hutcheson, *An Essay on the Nature and Conduct of the Passions and Affections*, Pref. v; secs. I–VI (London, 1728), 1–191.

——, *An Inquiry into the Original of our Ideas of Beauty and Virtue* (London, 1725), sec. VI.

——, *A System of Moral Philosophy* (Glasgow, 1755), Book I, chap. II.

——, *Philosophiae moralis institutio compendiaria* (Glasgow, 1755), Book I, chap. I, secs. 4–14.

D. Irons, " Descartes and Modern Theories of Emotion," *Philosophical Review* (1895), IV, 291–302.

C. F. von Irwing, *Erfahrung und Untersuchungen über den Menchen* (Berlin, 1777).

Isaac Stallensis, *De anima;* J. P. Migne, *Patrologiae cursus completus, series latina* (Paris, 1855), CXCIV, 1875–1890.

L. H. Jacob, *Grundriss der Erfahrungs-Seelenlehre* (Halle, 1800), sec. 125.

W. James, *Principles of Psychology* (New York, 1890), II, chap. XXV.

——, " The Physical Basis of Emotion," *Psychological Review* (1894), I, 516–529.

——, " What is an Emotion? " *Mind* (1884), IX, 188–205.

P. Janet, *De l'angoisse à l'extase* (Paris, 1928), II.

——, " La tension psychologique et ses oscillations," *Nouveau traité de psychologie* (ed. Dumas, Paris, 1934), IV, 386, 411.

A. Jenness, " The Recognition of Facial Expressions of Emotion," *Psychological Bulletin* (1932), XXIX, 325–350.

Jerome, *In Ezechielem*, I, 7; in J. P. Migne, *Patrologiae cursus completus, series latina* (Paris, 1884), XXV, 706 f.

H. H. Joachim, " The Platonic Distinction between ' True ' and

'False' Pleasures and Pains," *Philosophical Review* (1911), XX, 471–497.

John de Indagine, *Physiognomics;* in G. B. Porta, *De humana physiognomia* (Naples, 1598).

John of Damascus, *Expositio fidei orthodoxae,* II, 13–16 in J. P. Migne, *Patrologiae cursus completus, series graeca* (Paris, 1860), XLVII, 470–472.

——, *Institutio elementaris ad dogmata,* 9 in J. P. Migne, *Patrologiae cursus completus, series graeca* (Paris, 1860), XLVII, 825.

John of Salisbury, *Policraticus,* VIII, 5 in J. P. Migne, *Patrologiae cursus completus, series latina* (Paris, 1900), CXCIX, 720.

E. Jones, *Papers on Psychoanalysis* (New York, 1913), 10–34.

N. Jossius, *Tractatus novus, utilis, et iucundus, de voluptate et dolore, de risu et fletu, somno et vigilia* (Frankfurt, 1603), II, 16; IV, 39.

I. Kant, *Anthropologie in pragmatischer Hinsicht* (Leipzig, 1868), secs. 58, 71–79, 85.

——, *Briefe; Schriften* (Berlin, 1900), X, 488.

——, *Kritik der reinen Vernunft;* Introd., 18; *Schriften* (Berlin, 1900), III, 520.

——, *Kritik der praktischen Vernunft* (ed. Kirchmann, Berlin, 1869), 5, 8.

——, *Kritik der Urtheilskraft* (ed. Kirchmann, Berlin, 1869), III, 13.

——, *Des Daseins Gottes; Werke* (ed. Rosenkranz, Leipzig, 1838), I, 109.

A. Keim, *Helvétius, sa vie et son œuvre* (Paris, 1907), 277.

E. J. Kempf, "The Autonomic Functions and the Personality," *Nervous and Mental Diseases, Monograph Series* (New York and Washington, 1921), XXVIII.

C. Kling, "The Role of Parasympathetics in Emotion," *Psychological Review* (1933), XL, 368–380.

A. Koch, *Die Psychologie Descartes' systematisch und historisch-kritisch bearbeitet* (Munich, 1881), 128–224.

F. Krueger, "Das Wesen der Gefühle, Entwurf einer systematischen Theorie," *Archiv für die gesamte Psychologie* (1928), LXV, 91–128.

——, "The Essence of Feeling, Outline of a Systematic Theory,"

Feelings and Emotions, The Wittenberg Symposium (Worcester, 1928), 58–86.

M. C. de la Chambre, *Les caractères des passions* (Amsterdam, 1658), Pref., 1, 12 f., 33, 57, 131–134, 138–169; II, 394 f.; V, 54, 122, 128 f.

——, *L'art de connoistre les hommes* (Paris, 1660), 85.

——, *Le système de l'âme* (Paris, 1665), Pref., V, 361–418; VI, 497.

F. Lactantius, *De ira Dei*, 14, 4 f.; 15, 8–12 in J. P. Migne, *Patrologiae cursus completus, series latina* (Paris, 1844), VI, 96–123.

——, *Epitome divinarium institutionum*, 38, 8 in J. P. Migne, *Patrologiae cursus completus, series latina* (Paris, 1844), VI, 1024, 1045.

——, *Institutiones divinae*, III, 23, 9, 10; VI, 18, 22; 20, 2 in J. P. Migne, *Patrologiae cursus completus, series latina* (Paris, 1844), VI, 111, 698, 1013.

——, *Fragmenta* in F. S. Brandt and G. Laubmann, *Fragmenta in corpore scriptorum ecclesiasticorum latina* (Vienna, 1890), XXVII, 157.

A. Lafontaine, *Le plaisir d'après Platon et Aristote* (Paris, 1902), 50, 54.

R. Lagerborg, *Das Gefühlsproblem*, 38 (Leipzig, 1905), 131–136.

M. Laignel-Lavastine, *The Concentric Method in the Diagnosis of Psychoneurotics* (London and New York, 1931).

J. O. de Lamettrie, *Traité de l'âme* (Amsterdam, 1774), I, 83–145.

——, *Man or Machine* (London, 1750), 13.

C. Landis, "Emotion, II: The Expressions of Emotions," *A Handbook of General Experimental Psychology* (Worcester, 1934).

C. Lange, *Sindnsbewegelser*, 22; in R. Lagerborg, *Das Gefühlsproblem* (Leipzig, 1905), 38.

——, *Uber Gemütsbewegungen* (translated by H. Kurella, Leipzig, 1887).

F. A. Lange, *Geschichte des Materialismus* (Iserholm, 1873).

L. Lapicque, "Essai d'une nouvelle théorie de l'émotion," *Journal de psychologie* (1911), VIII, 1–8.

F. La Rochefoucauld, *Réflexions, sentences, et maximes morales* (Paris, 1665).

A. Laurentius, *De risu*, II; in N. Jossius, *Tractatus novus* (Frankfurt, 1603), 368 f.

A. Lehmann, *Die Hauptgesetze des menschlichen Gefühlsleben* (translated by F. Bendixen, Leipzig, 1892).

G. W. von Leibnitz, *Die philosophische Schriften* (ed. Kirchmann, Berlin, 1868), I, 73.

——, *Nouveaux essais sur l'entendement humain* (Paris, 1765), chap. XX, sec. 6; chap. XXI, sec. 41, 42, 72.

Léon l'Hébreu, *Dialoghi di'amore* (Venice, 1565).

Leonardo da Vinci, *Treatise on Painting* (London, 1877), 23.

G. E. Lessing, *Hamburgische Dramaturgie* (Hamburg, 1767), 75–78.

G. H. Lewes, *Problems of Life and Mind* (London and Boston, 1879), 3rd Series, I and II.

K. Lewin, *A Dynamic Theory of Personality* (New York and London, 1935).

T. Lipps, *Leitfaden der Psychologie* (Leipzig, 1903).

J. Lipsius, *Physiologiae Stoicorum*, III, Diss. VI, IX; *Opera omnia* (Wesel, 1675), IV.

J. Locke, *An Essay Concerning Human Understanding* (London, 1690), Book II, chap. XX.

R. H. Lotze, *Medizinische Psychologie* (Leipzig, 1852), sec. 13, 36, pp. 156, 234–281, 518.

Lucian, *Scholia ad Lucian; Luciana Samosatensis opera* (ed. Jacobitz, Leipzig, 1836), IV, 211.

C. T. Lucretius, *De rerum natura* (ed. Munroe, London, 1864), III, 142, 152–160, 288–306; IV, 859 f.

A. K. Luria, *The Nature of Human Conflicts* (New York, 1932).

J. G. E. Maass, *Versuch über die Gefühle, besonders die Affekte* (Halle, 1812), I, sec. 5, p. 13, Pref. to Vol. II.

——, *Versuch über die Leidenschaften, theoretisch und practisch* (Halle, 1805), XIV, secs. 6–10, 113–114.

J. T. MacCurdy, *The Psychology of Emotion* (London and New York, 1925).

N. Malebranche, *De la recherche de la vérité*, IV, V, *Œuvres* (ed. Simon, Paris, 1853), II, 340–520.

B. de Mandeville, *The Fable of the Bees* (London, 1723), 37.

F. Marbach, *Die Psychologie des Firmianus Lactantius* (Halle, 1889), 56–61.

H. R. Marshall, *Consciousness* (London, 1909), 250, 373–379.

——, *Pain, Pleasure, and Aesthetics* (London, 1894), 15–32.

M. W. Marston, " A Theory of Emotions and Affection based upon Systolic Blood Pressure Studies," *American Journal of Psychology* (1924), XXXV, 469.

——, King, C. D., Marston, E. H., *Integrative Psychology* (New York, 1931).

J. Martineau, *Types of Ethical Theory* (Oxford, 1889), I, 343–372; II, 535 f.

P. L. M. de Maupertuis, *Essai de philosophie morale; Œuvres* (Lyons, 1761), I, 193 f.

J. Mazurkiewicz, " Deux ordres d'émotivité au cycle de la vie humaine, définis par les résultats de recherches sur la chronaxie vestibulaire," *Archives internationales de neurologie* (March, 1935), iv–xiii.

W. McDougall, *Outline of Psychology* (New York, 1929).

P. Melanchthon, *Commentarius de anima* (Wittenberg, 1558).

M. Mendelssohn, *Bemerkungen über die Erkenntniss- Empfindungs- und Begehrungsvermögen* (Leipzig, 1766).

——, *Briefe über die Empfindungen; Philosophische Schriften* (Leipzig, 1777), I, 8–94, 115–145, 152.

——, *Rhapsodie oder Zusätze zu den Briefen über die Empfindungen; Philosophische Schriften* (Leipzig, 1777), II, Introd., 1–17.

——, *Morgenstunden oder Vorlesungen über das Dasein Gottes; Philosophische Schriften* (Leipzig, 1777), II, 294 f.

M. Meyer, " The Nervous Correlates of Pleasantness and Unpleasantness," *Psychological Review* (1908), XV, 201–216, 292–322.

T. Meynert, *Sammlung von popular-wissenschaftlichen Vorträgen* (Vienna and Leipzig, 1892), 43–67.

Richard of Middletown, *Super sententiis Petri Lombardi* (Brescia, 1591), III, 26–27.

J. Mill, *Analysis of the Phenomena of the Human Mind* (London, 1869), chap. XVI–XXII.

M. de Montaigne, *Essais* (Bordeaux, 1580), I, 4; II, 12; III, 5, 13.

——, *Essays; Works* (ed. Wight, New York, 1872), II, 11, 12.

J. P. Müller, *Handbuch der Physiologie des Menschen* (London, 1842), II, 543.

H. Münsterberg, *Beiträge zur experimentellen Psychologie* (Freiburg, 1892), 216.

J. P. Nafe, "An Experimental Study of the Affective Qualities," *American Journal of Psychology* (1924), XXXV, 507.

——, "The Pressure, Pain, and Temperature Senses," *Handbook of General Experimental Psychology* (Worcester, 1934), 1076.

——, "The Psychology of Felt Experience," *American Journal of Psychology* (1927), XXXIX, 387.

——, "The Sense of Feeling," *The Foundations of Experimental Psychology* (Worcester, 1929), 411.

J. W. Nahlowsky, *Das Gefühlsleben* (Leipzig, 1884).

Nemesius, *De natura hominis*, 16–21, 96; in J. P. Migne, *Patrologiae cursus completus, series graeca* (Paris, 1836), XL, 803–843.

E. B. Newman, F. T. Perkins, R. H. Wheeler, "Cannon's Theory of Emotion, a Critique," *Psychological Review* (1930), XXXVII, 305–326.

A. Niphus, *De pulchro et amore libri* (Lyons, 1641), *De pulchro*, chap. XXXI–LXVIII; *De amore*, chap. XVI–XCVI.

M. Offner, *Die Psychologie Charles Bonnets Schriften der Gesellschaft für psychologische Forschung* (Leipzig, 1893), V, 553–722.

J. Orth, *Gefühl und Bewusstseinslage* (Berlin, 1903), 6–18.

R. Pade, *Die Affektenlehre des Johannes Ludovicus Vives* (Münster, 1893), 42.

W. Paley, *Principles of Moral and Political Philosophy; Works* (London), I, 27.

A. Palme, *J. G. Sulzer's Psychologie und die Anfänge der Dreivermögenslehre* (Berlin, 1905), 1–62.

B. Pascal, *Discours sur les passions de l'amour* (ed. Cousin, Paris, 1842).

——, *Pensées* (ed. Fougère, Paris, 1645), I, 7; II, 3.

F. Paulhan, *The Laws of Feeling* (translated by C. K. Ogden, London and New York, 1930).

L. Peregrinus, *De noscendis et emendandis animi affectionibus* (Leipzig, 1714), I, 8, 9, 11, 16; II, 107–128.

C. Perrault, *Traité des sensations*, II; *Œuvres* (Paris, 1725).

Philodemus, περὶ ὀργῆς *De ira* (ed. Gomperz, Leipzig, 1864), 164–165.

T. Piderit, *Mimik und Physiognomik* (ed. Detmold, 1886).

H. Piéron, "La dynamogénie émotionelle," *Journal de psychologie* (1920), XVII, 937–945.

——, *Le cerveau et la pensée* (Paris, 1923).

F. Pillon, " Sur l'imagination affective," *Revue philosophique* (1907), LXIII, 233, 240 f.

A. Platner, *Philosophische Aphorismen* (Leipzig, 1893), Vol. I, Book I, Part I, sec. 29, p. 647.

Plato, Cratylus, 419 C; *Gorgias,* 477, 499; *Laws,* 673 A, 790 A; *Phaedo,* 60 B; *Phaedrus,* 258 E, 267 C; *Philebus,* 12–16, 25, 31–36, 39, 42–44, 48–54, 63, 64; *Protagoras,* 358; *Republic,* 462, 584, 606; *Symposium,* 201; *Timaeus,* 64–71, 77, 81, 86–88; in B. Jowett, *The Dialogues of Plato* (Oxford and New York, 1892).

P. Plessner, *Die Lehre von den Leidenschaften bei Descartes* (ed. Hesse and Becker, Leipzig, 1888), I, D.

Plotinus, *Enneades,* I, 4; III, 4–6; IV, 4, 19–21, 23, 28 (ed. Müller, Berlin, 1878), I, 24, 217–219, 223; II, 56–58, 65.

C. Plutarch, *De cohibenda ira,* 6, 10; *Moralia* (ed. Bernardakis, Leipzig, 1891), III, 185, 192.

——, *De virtute morali,* 4, 7; *Morals* (ed. Goodwin, Cambridge, 1874), III, 470, 478.

F. Pollock, *Spinoza, his Life and Philosophy* (London, 1899), 201.

G. B. Porta, *De humana physiognomia* (Naples, 1586), I, 18.

S. Portius, *De dolore liber* (Florence, 1551), 10.

F. Poschenrieder, *Die platonischen Dialoge in ihrem Verhältnisse zu den hippokratischen Schriften* (Landshut, 1882), 48.

Posidonius, in C. Galen, *De Hippocratis et Platonis placitis,* IV, 7, in *Medicorum graecorum opera* (ed. Kühn, Leipzig, 1821), V, 416.

L. J. Pouilly, *Théorie des sentiments agréables* (Paris, 1747), I–V.

R. Price, *A Review of the Principal Questions and Difficulties in Morals* (London, 1787), 117 f.

P. S. Régis, *Cours entier de philosophie ou système général selon les principes de Descartes* (Amsterdam, 1691), *Métaphysique,* I, *Physique,* VI.

T. Reid, *Essays on the Active Powers of the Human Mind,* III; *Works* (ed. Hamilton, Edinburgh, 1863), II, 543–571.

——, *Essays on the Intellectual Powers of Man,* I, II, VIII; *Works* (ed. Hamilton, Edinburgh, 1863), I, 229 f.

T. Ribot, *Les maladies de la personalité* (Paris, 1885), 1–19.

——, *Psychologie des sentiments* (Paris, 1897).

——, *La psychologie anglaise contemporaine* (Paris, 1881), 53 f.

Richard of St. Victor, *De praeparatione animi ad contemplationem,*
3, 7; in J. P. Migne, *Patrologiae cursus completus, series latina*
(Paris, 1880), CXCVI, 3, 6.

J. J. Rousseau, *Confessions,* V, XI; *Œuvres* (Paris, 1822), I, 341;
II, 490.

——, *Émile ou sur l'éducation; Œuvres* (Paris, 1788), Vol. II,
Book IV, pp. 138–141.

D. Santenoise, *Pneumogastrique et glandes endocrines* (Paris, 1927).

——, "Système organo-végétatif et psychoses fonctionelles," *Encephale* (1927), XX, 554–561.

J. C. Scaliger, *De subtilitate ad Cardanum* (Paris, 1557), 347–350,
391, 429.

K. H. Scheidler, "Gefühl," in J. S. Ersch and J. G. Gruber, *Allgemeine Encyklopädie* (Leipzig, 1818).

A. Schopenhauer, *Die Welt als Wille und Vorstellung* (Leipzig, 1819).

L. Schutz, "Spirits," *Thomas-Lexicon* (Paderborn, 1892).

W. R. Scott, *Francis Hutcheson* (Cambridge, 1900), 203.

L. A. Seneca, *Epistolae ad Lucilium,* 59, 2; *Opera* (ed. Ruhkopf,
Leipzig, 1800), II, 265 f.

——, *De ira,* I, 3, 4; II, 1, 3, 19; III, 2; *Opera* (ed. Ruhkopf, Leipzig, 1800), I, 6, 9, 40, 43, 63, 93.

Sextus Empiricus, *Adversus Mathematicos* (Antwerp, 1569), VII,
93, 199, 203; XI, 73.

——, *Sexti philosophi Pyrrhoneorum hypotyposeon* (Paris, 1562),
I, 215.

Third Earl of Shaftesbury, *Characteristics of Men, Manners, Opinions, Times* (ed. Robertson, London, 1900), I, 13–80, 117–121,
189–200.

——, *Inquiry Concerning Virtue and Merit,* I, II (ed. Robertson,
London, 1900), I, 252–314.

A. F. Shand, *The Foundations of Character* (London, 1914), 73.

P. Shorey, *The Unity of Plato's Thought* (Chicago, 1904), 46.

H. Siebeck, "Die Anfänge der neueren Psychologie in der Scholastik," *Zeitschrift für Philosophie und philosophische Kritik*
(1888–1890), XCIII–XCV, 189, 256 f.

——, *Geschichte der Psychologie* (Gotha, 1880), I, 94 f., 224–234,
328, 489, 504.

——, "Zur Psychologie der Scholastik," *Archiv für die Geschichte
der Philosophie* (1889), II, 189.

P. Siegert, *Die Psychologie des T. Flavius Alexandrinas* (Breslau, 1892), 45 f.

A. Smith, *The Theory of Moral Sentiments*, Part I, sec. I, chap. I; Part II, sec. I, chap. V (ed. Stewart, Bonn, 1853), 47, 257.

Socrates in Xenophon, *Memorabilia of Socrates* (translated by Dakyns, London, 1890), II, 1, 18–22; IV, 5, 9–11.

J. Speck, " Bonnets Einwirkung auf die deutsche Psychologie, IV," *Archiv für die Geschichte der Philosophie* (1898), XI, 187 f.

H. Spencer, *The Principles of Psychology* (ed. Westminster, London, and New York, 1901).

J. Sperling, *Anthropologia physica* (Wittenberg, 1656), 2.

Sphaerus, *Dialogues on Love* in Diogenes Laertius, *Works* (translated by Yonge, London, 1848), VII, 178.

B. de Spinoza, *Ethics*, Pref. and Pt. III; *Works* (ed. Elwes, London, 1883), II, 128 f.

G. Spurzheim, *Outlines of Phrenology* (Boston, 1832).

W. Steckel, *Conditions of Nervous Anxiety* (London and New York, 1923).

M. Steinitzer, *Die menschlichen und tierischen Gemütsbewegungen als Gegenstand der Wissenschaft* (Munich, 1889), 17–26, 53–60, 131–141, 174–175; 233 f.

L. Stephen, *History of English Thought in the Eighteenth Century* (London, 1876), I, 165; II, 49, 70, 73 f.

——, *The Science of Ethics* (London, 1882).

D. Stewart, *Outlines of Moral Philosophy*, Part II, chap. I; *Works* (ed. Hamilton, Edinburgh, 1854), VI, 16–32.

——, *The Philosophy of the Active and Moral Powers of Man; Works* (ed. Hamilton, Edinburgh, 1854), VI, 126–341; VII, 131, 339–348.

J. A. Stewart, *Notes on the Nicomachean Ethics* (Oxford, 1892), II, 218 f., 435.

J. Stobaeus, *Eclogae* (ed. Gaisford, Oxford, 1822), II, 7, 58, 88–93, 172.

——, *Eclogae*, II, 160–162 in A. E. Chaignet, *Histoire de la psychologie des Grecs* (Paris, 1887), II, 140–149.

A. Stöckl, *Geschichte der Philosophie des Mittelalters* (Mainz, 1864), I, 344; II, 1090 f.

C. Stumpf, " Über Gefühlsempfindungen," *Bericht über den II Kongress für experimentelle Psychologie* (Leipzig, 1907), 209.

——, "Uber Gefühlsempfindungen," *Zeitschrift für Psychologie* (1907), XLIV, 1.

——, "Apologie der Gefühlsempfindungen," *Zeitschrift für Psychologie* (1916), LXXV, 1–38.

F. Suarez, *De actionibus qui vocantur passiones*, I, secs. 1–3; II; V; XII, secs. 1, 2; *Opera* (ed. Vives, Paris, 1856), IV, 455, 457, 461, 479.

——, *De angelorum natura*, III, sec. 1; *Opera* (ed. Vives, Paris, 1856), II, 7.

——, *De appetitu sensitivo*, V, secs. 7–10; *Opera* (ed. Vives, Paris, 1856), III, 766 f.

——, *De oratione mentali*, VI, VII; *Opera* (ed. Vives, Paris, 1856), XIV, 139, 148.

J. G. Sulzer, *Untersuchungen über die Ursprung der angenehmen und unangenehmen Empfindungen* (Leipzig, 1751), 52.

——, *Vermischte philosophische Schriften* (Leipzig, 1778), I, 8, 13–20, 225, 229.

Synesius, *Oratio de regno*, 10, in J. P. Migne, *Patrologiae cursus completus, series graeca* (Paris, 1859), XXXV, 1218.

B. Telesius, *De rerum natura juxta propria principia* (Naples, 1586), V, 9; VII, 3, 4, 5; pp. 117, 277, 362 f.

Q. F. S. Tertullian, *De anima*, 12, 16, in J. P. Migne, *Patrologiae cursus completus, series latina* (Paris, 1879), II, 707, 714.

J. N. Tetens, *Philosophische Versuche über die menschliche Natur und ihre Entwickelung* (Leipzig, 1777), I, 167–185, 190–199, 211–217, 255–260, 590–625.

Themistius, *Aristotelis de anima*, 90 b, in *Paraphrases Aristotelis librorum quae supersunt* (ed. Spengel, Leipzig, 1866), II, 197, 24; III, 5.

Theodoretus, *De curandis graecorum affectionibus* in J. P. Migne, *Patrologiae cursus completus, series graeca* (Paris, 1857), LXXXIII, 844–951.

Theodoretus in H. Diehls, *Doxographi graeci* (Berlin, 1879), 391.

Theophrastus et Aristoteles, *Pseudo-Alexander Problemata* (Aldi, 1513), I; II, 26, 35, pp. 257–267.

Theophrastus, *De sensu*, 29, 43, 58; *Opera* (ed. Schneider, Leipzig, 1818), I, 658, 664, 670.

Thomas Aquinas, *Commentaries in Aristotelis De Amine* I, sec. 2, *Opera* (ed. Vives, Paris, 1889), XXIV, 6.

——, *Commentaries in Sententias Petri Lombardi,* IV, D. 49, Q. 3; *Opera* (ed. Vives, Paris, 1882), XI, 461.

——, *De veritate catholicae fidei,* Q. XXVI; *Opera* (ed. Vives, Paris, 1889), XV, 250.

——, *De motu cordis; Opera* (ed. Vives, Paris, 1871), Opusc., 35.

——, *Summa Theologica,* I–II, Q. XXII–XLVIII, LXXXII; *Opera* (ed. Vives, Paris, 1895), II, 205, 319, 516.

C. Thomasius, *Further Elucidation by Different Examples of the Recent Proposals for a New Science for Obtaining a Knowledge of Other Men's Minds* (Halle, 1692).

——, *New Discovery of a Well-Grounded and for the Community most Necessary Science of the Knowledge of the Secrets of the Heart of Other Men from Daily Conversation, even against their Will* (Halle, 1691).

——, *Von der Artzeney wider die unvernünftige Liebe* (Halle, 1696).

D. Tiedemann, *Handbuch der Psychologie* (Leipzig, 1804), 149–202.

——, *Untersuchungen über die Menschen,* I, Pref. xxiiii, xxviii (Leipzig, 1777), II, 344–360.

E. B. Titchener, " An Historical Note on the James-Lange Theory of Emotion," *American Journal of Psychology* (1914), XXV, 426–447.

——, *Lectures on the Elementary Psychology of Feeling and Attention* (New York, 1908), 81–121, 125–168.

——, *A Textbook of Psychology* (New York, 1919), 225–236.

L. T. Troland, " A System for Explaining Affective Phenomena," *Journal of Abnormal Psychology* (1920), XIV, 376–387.

——, *The Fundamentals of Human Motivation* (New York, 1928), 284–300.

——, *The Mystery of Mind* (New York, 1926), 131–145.

——, *The Principles of Psychophysiology* (New York, 1932), III, 223–388.

A. Tucker, *The Light of Nature Pursued,* chaps. I, VI, XVII, XIX, XXI, XXII, XXV (ed. Mildmay, Cambridge, 1831), I, 21, 32–41, 79, 219, 250–256, 365.

W. H. Veil, " Vagotonic und Sympathikotonic," *Deutsche medizinischen Wochenschrift* (1914), L, 511–513.

Vincentius Belvacensis, *Speculum naturale, Opera,* in *Histoire littéraire de France* (ed. Échard, Paris, 1719), XXVIII, 62–75.

C. Vittichius, *Anti-Spinoza* (Amsterdam, 1690).

J. L. Vives, *Ad sapientiam introductio* (Bruges, 1524), 118–121, 204–254.

——, *De anima et vita*, I–III; *Opera* (Basel, 1555), II, 497–593.

W. F. Volkmann, *Lehrbuch der Psychologie* (Halle, 1856), II, 508.

J. Ward, " Psychology," *Encyclopedia Britannica* (9th edition, 1886).

H. C. Warren, *Human Psychology* (Boston and New York, 1920), 279.

J. B. Watson, *Behavior, an Introduction to Comparative Psychology* (New York, 1914).

——, *Psychology from the Standpoint of a Behaviorist* (Philadelphia and London, 1919).

E. H. Weber, *Tastsinn und Gemeingefühl* (ed. Hering, Leipzig, 1905).

O. W. Wight, *The Thoughts, Letters and Opuscules of Blaise Pascal* (New York, 1861), 236, 515–522.

William of Conches, *Physica* in K. Werner, " Die Entwickelungsgang der mittelalterlichen Psychologie," *Philos. hist. Classe* (Vienna, 1876), XXV, 84 f.

C. Wolff, *Psychologia empirica* (Leipzig, 1732), secs. 511, 518, 536.

——, *Vernünftige Gedanken vom Gott, der Welt und der Seele* (Leipzig, 1747), secs. 404–417; pp. 221–260.

W. Wundt, *Grundriss der Psychologie* (Stuttgart, 1920).

——, *Grundzüge der physiologischen Psychologie* (Leipzig, 1902), II, 287–336, 363; III, 239; VI, 132.

Xenophon, *Memorabilia* of Socrates (translated by Dakyus, London, 1890), II, 1, 18–22; IV, 5, 9–11.

E. Zeller, *Die Philosophie der Griechen* (Tübingen, 1844), I, 809; II, 1, 4, 308, 353; III, 386; IV, 579 f.

Zeno, in Nemesius, *De natura hominis*, 96, in J. P. Migne, *Patrologiae cursus completus, series graeca* (Paris, 1836), XL, 843.

——, in Q. S. F. Tertullian, *De anima*, 14, in J. P. Migne, *Patrologiae cursus completus, series latina* (Paris, 1879), II, 709.

——, in J. Stobaeus, *Eclogae*, II, 7, 1, 2 (ed. Gaisford, Oxford, 1822).

T. Ziehen, *Leitfaden der physiologischen Psychologie* (Jena, 1924), 290–294, 355–358.

INDEX

A

Abelard, P., 103
Abundance theories, 313–318
Admiratio, as considered by:
  Bossuet, 205
  Descartes, 150–168, 200
  Malebranche, 173, 181
  Spinoza, 200
  Thomas Aquinas, 114
Aegidius Romanus, 101
Aesthetic feelings, as considered by:
  Aristotle, 37, 52
  Bain, 284
  Fechner, 319
  Hamilton, 302
  Herbart, 307
  Hutcheson, 211, 217
  Lehmann, 320–321
  Lipps, 305
  Maass, 274
  Moralists, the, 211
  Schopenhauer, 310
  Shaftesbury, 211
  Thomas Aquinas, 114
Aetius, 4, 55
Affections, the, as considered by:
  Albertus Magnus, 101, 102
  Allport, 341
  Aristotle, 26–47, 58
  Augustine, 96–99
  Bacon, F., 141–143
  Bonaventura, 100, 102
  Bonnet, 255
  Brown, 216–219
  Butler, 213
  Chrysippus, 68
  Comte, 329
  Cyrenaics, the, 10
  Descartes, 162–164, 210, 246
  Duns Scotus, 103
  Eberhard, 258
  Epicurus, 60–63

Feder, 261
Gerson, John, 101, 104
Greeks, 12, 86–87
Gregory of Nyssa, 95
Hartley, 222, 224
Head, 366
Hippocrates, 5
Hobbes, 183, 188, 210
Holmes, 366
Hume, 218, 234–238
Hutcheson, 217–218
James, 296
Jossius, 214
Kant, 268
Lactantius, 92
Lamettrie, 250
MacCurdy, 362
Malebranche, 172, 210
Mandeville, 211
Melanchthon, 125, 133
Mill, 281
Nemesius, 90–93
Pascal, 207
Paulhan, 333
Plato, 11, 18–26
Plotinus, 81–85
Price, 218
Reid, 217–218
Religions, 87
Renaissance, 119, 123, 135–136
Ribot, 330
Scotch School, 214
Seneca, 69
Shaftesbury, 212, 217
Spinoza, 195–210
Stoics, the, 59, 65–67, 73, 80
Sulzer, 260
Telesius, 125, 135
Tetens, 265
Theodoret, 93
Thomas Aquinas, 108–115
Tiedemann, 258

411